An introduction to cognitive psychology

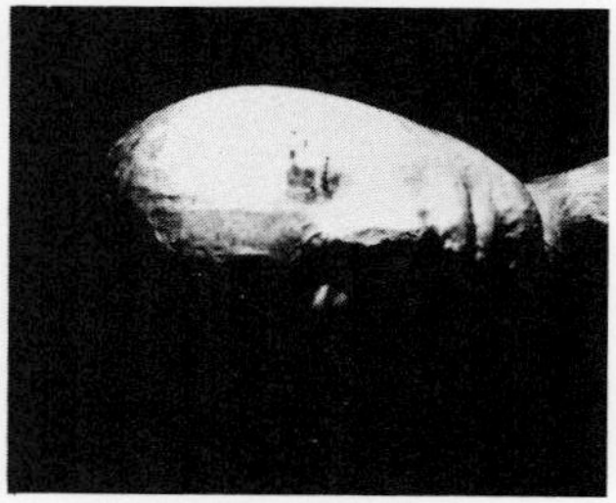

Core Books in Psychology Series
Edward L. Walker, Editor

Psychology: A Story of a Search
W. Lambert Gardiner, Sir George Williams University

The Uptight Society: A Book of Readings
Howard Gadlin, University of Massachusetts
Bertram E. Garskof, Federal City College

Human Socialization
Elton B. McNeil, The University of Michigan

Readings in Human Socialization
Elton B. McNeil, The University of Michigan

Comparative Animal Behavior
Richard A. Maier, Loyola University, Chicago
Barbara M. Maier

An Introduction to Cognitive Psychology
Melvin Manis, The University of Michigan

Experimental Contributions to Clinical Psychology
Erasmus L. Hoch, The University of Michigan

An introduction to cognitive psychology

Melvin Manis

The University of Michigan

Brooks/Cole Publishing Company,
A Division of Wadsworth Publishing Company, Inc.,
Belmont, California

ISBN 0-8185-0002-6

L. C. Cat. Card No.: 74-134763
Printed in the United States of America

1 2 3 4 5 6 7 8 9 10 — 75 74 73 72 71

This book is dedicated to my wife, Jean, and to our sons, Peter and David.

Preface

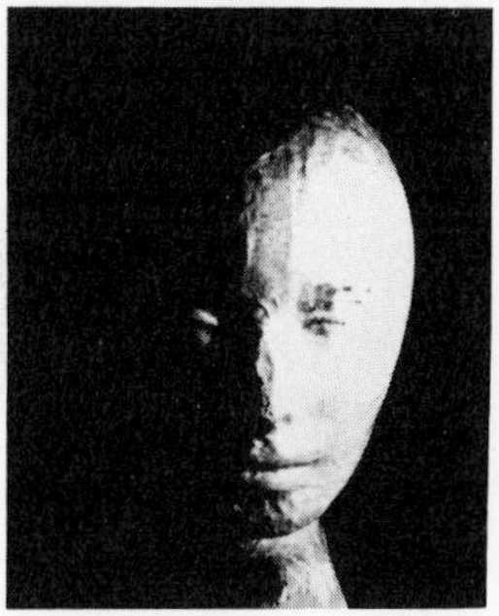

Psychological theorists have, in recent years, portrayed the human organism as a creature of increasing complexity and intelligence. In contrast to the psychoanalysts' emphasis on immature, irrational motives, and the S–R theorists' concern with simple habits, one hears more and more references to the individual's strategies, hypotheses, and intentions as determinants of his actions. Concepts of this type may be descriptively labeled as "cognitive," because they assign a prominent role to man's planful intellective processes in the guidance of his behavior. This book presents an overview of several research areas that fall within this cognitive tradition. The underlying principle of selection favored topics in which there exists a substantial and cumulative body of experimental literature. A variety of processes are thus considered, starting with classic topics like learning and memory, and continuing into such complex domains as conceptual behavior, language, problem solving, and cognitive dissonance.

As in many other areas of psychology, the cognitive domain seems, in large part, to consist of several well-mapped "islands of information" that are presently linked by a limited and inadequate system of theoretical bridges. This volume attempts, in the main, to sketch the main features of these islands, together with those few bridges that have been established to date.

I started this book in the fall of 1966, while I was a Fulbright lecturer at the University of Ghent. My main intent was to provide a broader and more intensive coverage of cognitive research and theory than was possible in the short paperback text that I had previously published (Manis, 1966). The present volume is based, in part, on that earlier work; however, in addition to the inevitable inclusion of more recent research, this book also contains several completely *new* sections, dealing, for example, with such topics as Piaget's theory of cognitive development, the computer simulation of human problem-solving, and theories of cognitive consistency.

While writing this book, I was primarily thinking of it as a text for use in advanced undergraduate courses. However, my experience with draft versions of the individual chapters suggests that it can be used effectively at the graduate level as well, if it is supplemented with reading assignments from more technical, specialized sources.

I would like to thank those graduate students and faculty members who read and commented on earlier versions of this book in seminars at the University of Michigan. In addition to these seminar participants, I am also indebted to several colleagues who read and criticized individual chapters; Frank Andrews, Robyn Dawes, John Hagen, Robert Lindsay, Ronald Tikofsky, and Robert Zajonc deserve special thanks for their efforts here. Edward L. Walker provided continuing support in his role as overall scientific advisor for the project, and Philip Cordova was a most helpful and patient copy editor.

I am indebted to Professor Leo Apostel for graciously providing clerical assistance when I started this book at the University of Ghent and to Alvin Zander and the staff at the Center for Research on Group Dynamics, who have provided me with comfortable office space and secretarial help during the past two years. Lastly, I am delighted to acknowledge the careful and most competent help of Mrs. Carrie Lewis and Mrs. Catherine Hoch, who typed the bulk of the manuscript and helped in assembling the figures and references.

Melvin Manis

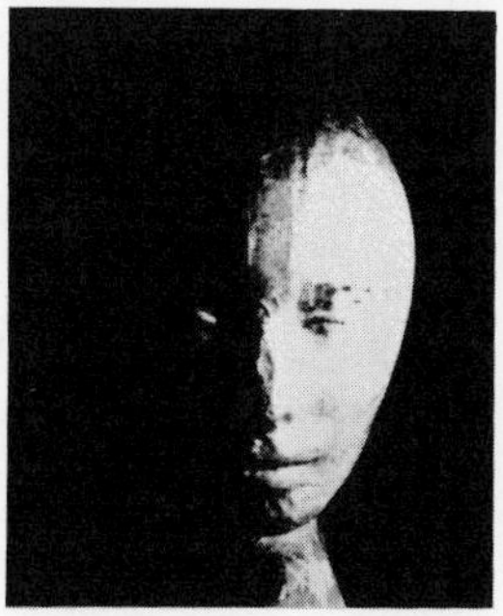

Contents

1 Basic processes

1 Learning and generalization

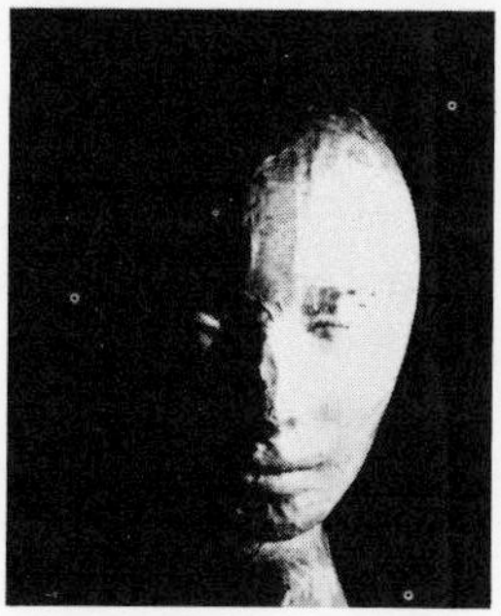

One of the most striking aspects of human behavior is its plasticity—man's almost infinite capacity to adapt his behavior to diverse conditions. In contrast to more primitive forms of life, man shows a startling variety of behaviors, depending largely upon the circumstances that surround him; he does not react in a stereotyped manner when faced with new problems, but is instead strikingly successful in his ability to alter his actions to meet the demands of his environment.

In trying to achieve a more adequate understanding of man's adaptability, psychologists have intensively studied the learning process. We should hasten to add that the term "learning," as it is used here, includes far more than the acquisition of knowledge that you may associate with formal education. Instead, it is typically defined as a relatively permanent behavioral change that results from practice. This definition does not differentiate between "intellectual" forms of learning, such as occur in the classroom, and the learning of such simple skills as the tying of one's shoelaces. While there are clearly important differences between the two cases, psychologists typically assume that similar processes are at work and strive, so far as is possible, to explain the more complex cases of learning in the same terms that are used in discussing more rudimentary instances. This stance is adopted in the interests of simplicity and generality.

Scientific theories are generally deemed successful if they use a limited number of simple but powerful generalizations to explain what have previously appeared to be baffling complex phenomena. Thus, we would ideally like to find a limited set of general propositions that would enable us to explain a wide variety of observed facts, just as the axioms of geometry may be used to deduce a variety of theorems. We will follow this approach as far as we can, both in explaining the learning process and in applying the principles of learning to account for more complex phenomena such as language and thinking. We should hasten to add, however, that since the higher mental processes cannot, at present, be adequately explained in terms of a few general propositions, we will continue to introduce new terms and concepts as they are needed.

The material that follows in this chapter will provide an introduction to learning concepts and phenomena that seem most applicable to an understanding of complex cognitive processes. A more complete treatment of this material may be found in Walker's *Conditioning and Instrumental Learning* (1966).

In the view of many learning theorists, learning occurs when the individual associates a new response with a given stimulus situation. For example, after a period of awkward trial and error, a child may learn that when given the stimulus "2 + 2," he should respond "4." By convention, the term "stimulus" is used in a very broad sense; the stimulus may be virtually any environmental element or setting that has a systematic effect upon behavior. Thus, the presence of his father (stimulus) will typically lead the little boy to use the word "Daddy" (response) more frequently than he does in situations where his father is not present. And, after learning has occurred, the stimulus "2 + 2" systematically elicits the response "4" from the child.

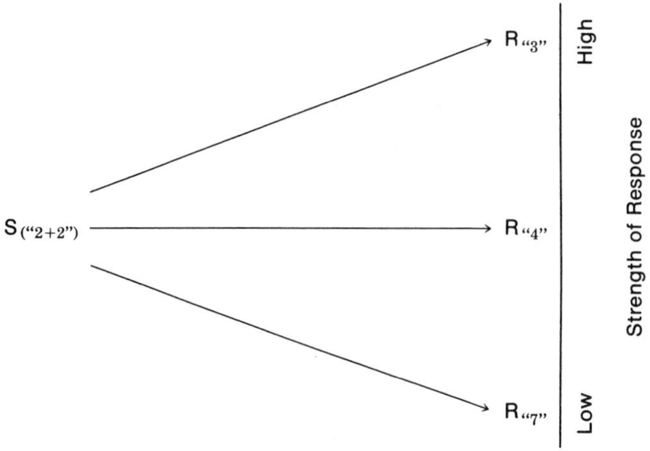

Figure 1

Hypothetical habit-family hierarchy in response to the stimulus "2 + 2."

A convenient way of representing the changes that take place during learning is the *habit-family hierarchy* diagrammed in Figure 1. This scheme is intended to convey the notion that the stimulus (S) of "2 + 2" tends to elicit a variety of responses (Rs), some more strongly than others. Thus, early in the learning of "2 + 2," the child's predominant response may be "3," which we have designated as $R_{\text{``3''}}$. As learning progresses, however, this response tends to become weaker (less probable), and the $R_{\text{``4''}}$ response, which was originally rather weak, gains in strength until it is the most likely response of all.

Reinforcement

We are now in a position to ask about the all-important factors that produce these changes in the habit-family hierarchy. In brief, under what conditions will the correct response, "4," rise to the top of the hierarchy? While psychologists do not unanimously agree in their answer to this question, it is clear that if the event (or events) that follows the individual's response is a positive experience (parental approval, for example), the response will typically gain in strength; that is, when the appropriate stimulus is subsequently presented, the rewarded response will appear with increasing speed. On the other hand, if a given response is followed by unpleasant events (disapproval), or if it has no discernible effect—either positive or negative—it will generally lose its strength and eventually disappear as a response to the stimulus. When a response is weakened because of its negative consequences, the change is the result of *punishment.* When a response is weakened because it has neither positive nor negative consequences, experimental *extinction* has occurred. Thus, if a child's parents refuse to respond to requests phrased in baby talk, this response pattern will soon lose its strength (that is, appear less and less frequently) and undergo extinction.

Summing up, then, the strengthening or weakening of a given stimulus-response association will partly depend on the effects that the response produces; more technically, these effects are referred to as *reinforcers.* A *positive reinforcer* is thus an effect (or outcome) that the individual seeks, and it serves to strengthen the association between the preceding response and the stimulus situation present when the response was performed. A *negative reinforcer,* on the other hand, refers to an effect (or outcome) that the individual would prefer to avoid, and it generally leads to a weakening of the response that has preceded it.

Does all learning depend upon the presence of reinforcers? Can a stimulus-response association be formed in the absence of a reinforcement? This issue has plagued learning theorists for several decades. In part, the answer depends upon the way in which we define reinforcement. For example, it is perfectly clear that learning can take place in situations where there is no external agent (for example, an experimenter or a teacher) to reinforce the learner. Thus, the student may read in an elementary psychology text that Wundt founded the first psychology laboratory in Leipzig; on the basis of his reading, the student may be quite capable of responding successfully when he is subsequently asked test questions concerning these aspects of psychology. To account for this apparent demonstration of learning without reinforcement, an advocate of the reinforcement concept might argue that in the past our student has been reinforced by his teachers for mastering his readings, and he thus automatically practices this skill when faced with new reading material. However, this argument is based on the questionable assumption that the learning of today's reading material is primarily based upon the reinforcements of yesterday's responses.

Some theorists have contended that the reinforcement principle is less fundamental to the learning process than our earlier discussion might imply. It has been suggested, for example, that reinforcements do not operate *automatically* to strengthen the responses that precede them, and cognitive theorists have long believed that reinforcements are mainly effective because of the information they provide; they inform the learner that his response was correct and thus encourage him to repeat the reinforced reaction on subsequent occasions. By contrast, a strong proponent of the reinforcement principle might contend that the reinforcement effect does not depend on the learner's "understanding" of the situation, but operates quite mechanically, regardless of the learner's cognitive insight. A more detailed discussion of this issue may be found on pp. 90–96.

The reinforcement principle has also been criticized by theorists who emphasize the role of *contiguity* in learning (see Guthrie, 1935). These investigators believe that associations are automatically formed between the individual's behavior and the situation in which it is enacted; through *contiguity,* stimuli and responses will presumably become associated even though there has been no reinforcement provided. There has been a lengthy history of experimentation devoted to the unraveling of this controversial issue (see Osgood, 1953).

It has proven to be a complex matter to assess the role of reinforcement as a determinant of learning, since reinforcements may plausibly occur in a variety of subtle ways; in some situations, there is often a possibility that even though reinforcements have not been explicitly provided, human subjects may reinforce themselves without the experimenter's intervention. In gaining information through reading, for example, there is always the possibility that the learner achieves some subjective satisfaction through the insights that are gained as he progresses through his text, or by asking himself questions and then checking the accuracy of his responses; if this is true (and the possibility cannot be easily ruled out), the learning that occurs in this setting might be attributed to the effects of self-administered reinforcement.

To overcome problems like this, many researchers have sought to evaluate the role of reinforcement in animal learning, where there seem to be fewer complications. In a famous experiment by Blodgett (1929), a group of hungry rats was permitted to explore a maze that did not have a food reward in the goal box. Another group of rats was placed in the maze when food was present in the goal box. While this second group readily learned the maze, showing a steady decrease in errors (that is, entries into blind alleys), the unrewarded group showed little improvement. After several days of unrewarded training, a food reward was finally introduced into the goal box for the group that had been exploring without reinforcement; for some of these rats the rewards were introduced on the third day of training, and for others on the seventh day. The results of this experiment are shown in Figure 2. Note that the introduc-

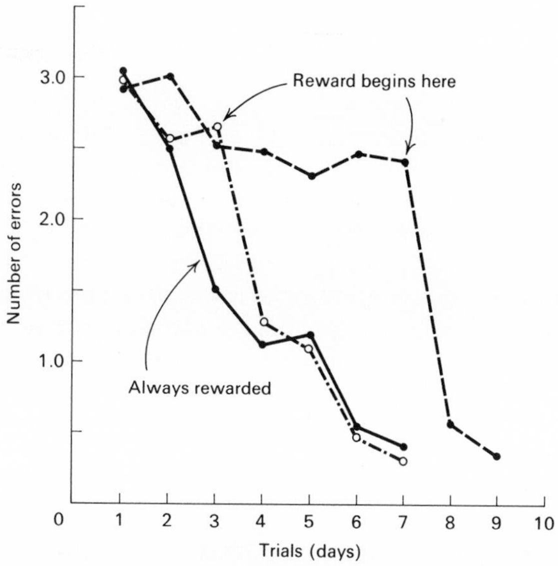

Figure 2

Example of latent learning. Following the delayed introduction of rewards, maze performance soon reaches level achieved by animals consistently rewarded throughout training trials. (Adapted from J. Deese, *The psychology of learning.* New York: McGraw-Hill Book Co., Inc., 1958. Data from Blodgett, 1929.)

tion of rewards resulted in a rapid decrease of errors, and that the animals receiving delayed rewards quickly attained the same performance level as the animals that had always been rewarded. This effect has been termed "latent learning"; it has been interpreted as an indication that the animals were learning about the maze during the unrewarded trials even though they continued to make many errors. Presumably, however, this learning remained "latent" and was not clearly apparent until the food rewards were later introduced.

Extrapolating from data of this sort (there have been numerous related experiments), many psychologists have concluded that learning may indeed take place even when there is no obvious reinforcement following the performance of a response. The Blodgett experiment leads to the further point that what has been learned may not be directly reflected in performance (that is, overt behavior); thus, even though Blodgett's unrewarded rats apparently learned a good deal about the structure of their maze, they did not reveal this knowledge (by avoiding the blind alleys) until the food rewards were introduced. This distinction between learning and performance holds true at the human level, too. For example, an individual's performance in a highly demanding athletic event may reflect not only his learned skill but also such variables as his level of motivation and the magnitude of the prize (if any) for which he is competing.

Intermittent reinforcement

Reinforcements often occur irregularly and do not invariably follow the performance of a correct response. Reinforcements that are presented intermittently may be programmed according to several different patterns. The experimenter may, for example, choose to reward every fourth response that fulfills his criterion of correctness (this is known as a *fixed-ratio* schedule); alternatively, he may arrange things so that the learner is "eligible" for a reinforcement every 4 or 5 minutes (*fixed interval*). B. F. Skinner and his associates have explored the behavioral consequences of various reinforcement schedules, and a detailed presentation of such research has been presented in a book by Ferster and Skinner (1957).

One of the best-known effects produced by intermittent reinforcement occurs when extinction procedures are introduced, by eliminating *all* rewards, regardless of the behavior that is enacted. Many studies have shown that intermittent reinforcement schedules typically lead to a rather slow extinction process, compared to the rate of extinction that follows continuous (100%) reinforcement. One of the more popular explanations for this effect is the so-called *discrimination hypothesis*, which is based on the assumption that the change from reinforcement to extinction is simple to detect when one has previously been reinforced for every correct response. By contrast, the change to extinction may be less discernible following intermittent reward, because the individual has had previous experience with non-reinforced trials that were subsequently followed by further reinforcements; he may thus interpret the extinction series as simply another "temporary dry spell" which must surely pass. Acting accordingly, he may continue to respond as before. Despite the plausibility of this account (see, in particular, Bridger and Mandel, 1965, which is discussed on pp. 95–96), the discrimination hypothesis is not fully consistent with the available data, as shown in a review by Lewis (1960).

Knowledge of results

In studies of human learning, it is often unnecessary to present the learner with any concrete reward; if there is motivation to improve, considerable learning may be achieved if we simply give the learner periodic feedback about how well he is doing. Psychologists refer to this as providing "knowledge of results." Thorndike (1932b) has shown that if a blindfolded person attempts to draw a 3-inch line, his performance will be rather poor and will not show improvement even though he is allowed to "practice." If, however, following each attempt, the experimenter measures the line that has been drawn and says "right" whenever the line deviates from the 3-inch standard by less than one eighth of an inch, and "wrong" on all other trials, the subject will show rapid improvement. Studies of this sort clearly indicate the importance of adequate knowledge of results in guiding learning. This principle proved particularly helpful in training gunners during the Second World War. When a gun has been fired, it is sometimes difficult to tell whether or not the target has been hit. The development of various training devices to give the gunner feedback about whether or not he had hit his target made it possible to improve greatly the effectiveness of gunnery-training programs.

Delay of feedback

Studies concerned with the effects of reinforcement upon animal behavior have uniformly shown that delay of reinforcement following a correct response slows learning and may indeed prevent it (Renner, 1964). Analogously, some psychologists feel that knowledge of results is most effective if it is presented immediately after the learner's response. However, the data are far from clear. It seems reasonable to assume that man's ability to speak to himself may enable him to bridge effectively the gap between his overt response and the eventual feedback or reinforcement. Unfortunately, this mechanism may be difficult to employ when the relevant stimuli and responses cannot readily be "stored" in verbal equivalents. For example, in teaching French we may ask for the English equivalent of the word *livre* and then wait, say, 15 seconds before telling our student whether his answer was right or wrong. This delay may have little impact upon learning speed, however, since the student can inwardly "rehearse" his answer until the feedback is given. In contrast, consider a time-estimation task, where the learner does not have a readily available linguistic means of storing and recalling the interval that he has just judged to be 33 seconds long. In such a situation we may indeed find that delayed feedback leads to impaired learning.

In discussing the effects of delayed rewards on learning, it is important to consider the individual's activities between the time of his response and the teacher's (or experimenter's) feedback. The available research suggests that delay of reward will be most detrimental to learning if, prior to the experimenter's feedback, the learner has engaged in additional activities similar to the behaviors he is learning. Thus, Ammons suggested (1956) that "Knowledge of performance serves as a reward, and what is rewarded is the ongoing behavior at the time of reward. When we delay knowledge we simply decrease the possibility that the behavior which we intend to reward is actually rewarded, and increase the possibility that some relatively irrelevant response is rewarded."[1] While this effect can be reduced if the learner is capable of symbolically reinstating his original response (the one being rewarded), it is likely that forgetting will impair covert reinstatement if—after each practice trial—our learner engages in other actions closely resembling the responses to be learned. For example, Lorge and Thorndike (1935) taught subjects to throw a ball at a target that was not visible to them. For single throws, performance was essentially unaffected by delayed knowledge of results. However, when the subjects were required to make a second throw before receiving feedback on their preceding attempt, performance was impaired.

Careful consideration of delayed reward (or feedback) suggests two different explanations for the observed impairment in performance. One of these, discussed above, is the notion that when the reward finally appears, it may strengthen the response just previously performed rather than the response actually instrumental in obtaining the reward. The second explanation focuses on the motivation of the learner. If the learner is forced to respond for long periods of time without knowing how he is doing, his motivation may flag and he may lose interest in the task.

[1] From Ammons, R. B. "Effects of Knowledge of Performance: A Survey and Tentative Theoretical Formulation." *J. Gen. Psych.*, 1956, **54**, 279–299. Quoted with permission of the publisher.

Learning through imitation and vicarious experience

Miller and Dollard (1941) suggested a learning theoretic rationale for imitation by theorizing that in many situations, the behavior of one person (the model) may serve as a cue which would guide the actions of another person (the observer), if *reinforcements were given to the observer whenever he imitated the model.* For example, consider a nine-year-old boy who has learned to greet his father at the front door when he hears the family car in the driveway; this action may be imitated by a younger brother, who has found that he, too, can gain reinforcement (candy or fatherly affection) simply by following the example of his older brother when he rushes to the door at the end of the work day.

Numerous experiments have followed this general pattern, studying the effects of variations in reinforcement upon the observer's imitative behavior. It has been clearly shown, for example, that if imitation is directly rewarded (that is, if the observer is reinforced whenever he imitates the model), imitation will occur with increasing frequency. By contrast, imitative behavior may be *decreased* in frequency if the observer is punished each time he starts to imitate or if he is verbally warned to avoid imitation of the model. These results closely parallel the effect that would be anticipated from a simple extrapolation of classic behavior principles; the only novel aspects of imitation, according to this account, are the utilization of an unusual *cue* (the model's behavior) and the fact that the response to be reinforced requires a "matching" performance on the observer's part.

Imitation studies have also dealt with more complex situations; perhaps most intriguing is the phenomenon of *vicarious reinforcement.* In vicarious-reinforcement studies, reinforcement is not provided to the imitator; instead, the imitator (or observer) is simply given an opportunity to view the consequences *to the model* that follow from the model's various acts. In a study by Bandura (1965), for example, three groups of children were shown a film in which a model enacted a variety of novel aggressive acts, some verbal and some physical. One group saw the model being rewarded generously for his aggressiveness; in a second group, the model was punished for his aggression; a third group was not shown *any* consequences resulting from the model's actions. Following these differing induction procedures, the children were placed in a test situation where the experimenters could observe and record each instance of imitative aggressiveness. The results are presented in Figure 3, which shows that there was relatively little imitation following vicarious punishment, as compared with the results obtained from subjects assigned to the vicarious-reward and the "no-consequence" conditions.

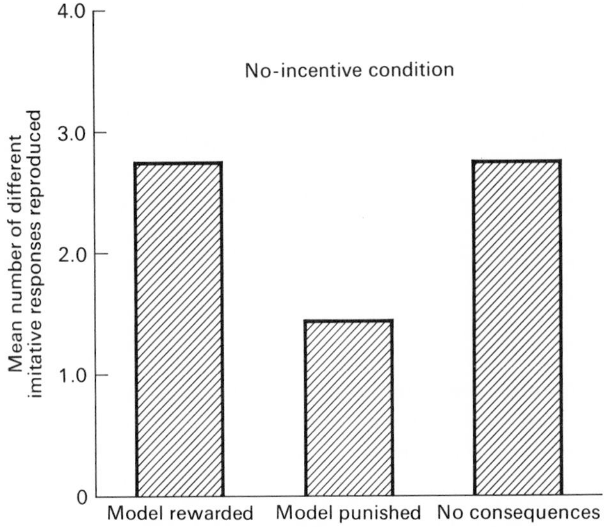

Figure 3

Mean number of different imitative responses reproduced by children on the basis of modeling experience in which model was rewarded, was punished, or suffered no consequences for its behavior. In a subsequent *positive incentive* condition (not shown), the children were offered highly attractive incentives for reproducing the model's actions. These incentives resulted in a substantial increase of imitation and eliminated the group differences shown in Figure 3.

Vicarious-reinforcement effects may work because of the observer's implicit assumption that he, too, may get rewarded (or punished) if he follows the example shown by the model. On the other hand, this explanation fails to show why the observer will *ever* imitate a model who has received punishment for his actions (as shown in Figure 3, there is some tendency for observers to imitate a model who has suffered punishment). Similarly, imitation has frequently been noted in situations where the model has not been reinforced in any observable way; thus, in the no-incentive condition of Bandura's study, imitation was just as common in the "no-consequence" group as it was among children who experienced vicarious reinforcement. Conceivably, the observer assumes that any consistent or strikingly novel pattern of behavior which is enacted without apparent reward is most probably accompanied (or followed) by some *unobvious* reinforcement, or else the model would have acted differently (Kelley, Thibaut, Radloff, and Mundy, 1962).

Another interpretation of the fact that observers often imitate an unreinforced model is based on the assumption that imitative acts have frequently received direct reinforcement in the past; as a consequence, most people have a learned tendency to imitate, even if the model's efforts appear to be fruitless. This analysis receives additional support from the finding that high-status models typically elicit more imitative behavior than do models of lower status, presumably because the imitation of high-status persons has more frequently led to direct reinforcement.

While there is ample evidence that imitative learning occurs with great frequency, there is as yet no fully satisfactory theory in this area. People do not always imitate, for example, even when they are exposed to high-status models; similarly, it is not clear why we imitate only certain aspects of the model's behavior and not others. Recent research on imitative behavior has been invaluable, however, in showing that *observational learning* (where the learner does not respond and does not receive reinforcement) is a real phenomenon which can be readily produced under controlled laboratory conditions. It has also been invaluable in showing how imitative behavior may facilitate the acquisition of novel behavior patterns (patterns that are unlikely to be produced "spontaneously" when the learner finds himself in an unfamiliar situation). Flanders (1968) provides an excellent review of the imitation literature.

Incidental (unintentional) learning

There is considerable evidence that human learning may occur even though the learner has not made a conscious effort to memorize or otherwise master the materials presented by the experimenter (Postman, 1964). This phenomenon, known as *incidental* learning, is typically studied by providing the experimental subjects with verbal materials which they must read, but without any expectation that they will later be tested for recall of this material. For example, in an experiment by Spear, Ekstrand, and Underwood (1964), subjects were initially presented with a series of word-pairs; their assigned task was to learn which word within each pair had been designated (arbitrarily) as *correct.* When this task had been mastered, the subjects were instructed to learn a list of paired associates; their task here was to learn the proper verbal response to several different stimulus words. The results showed that when the association to be learned consisted of words that had appeared *together* in the initial verbal discrimination task, learning was accomplished rather quickly—presumably because of the earlier contiguity of these elements. On the other hand, the learning of the paired associates was more difficult when the stimulus and response words had been presented *separately* in the discrimination series. Note that these results were obtained despite the absence of any deliberate intent to memorize the words that were presented together in the initial verbal discrimination task. While subjects normally show better performance when they have been *instructed* to learn something, as compared with the amount acquired under *incidental* learning conditions, this generalization does not always hold; the subject's intentions sometimes have virtually no impact on the amount that he learns (Mechanic, 1964).

Generalization: Going beyond what is given

Learning seems to be a relatively simple and straightforward process, so long as we limit our attention to the specific stimuli and responses directly involved in a given performance. For example, if a child has been consistently reinforced for cooperative behavior in stimulus situations involving other children, it hardly seems surprising that ultimately he will behave cooperatively. However, we should not be misled by the apparent simplicity of his performance, for it is probably accompanied by a variety of related sequences that have not been explicitly taught. For example, the child may exhibit a different form of cooperation when interacting with a new group of acquaintances. In the words of Jerome Bruner, people frequently tend to "go beyond what is given." The knowledge that the learner acquires is not limited to the particular stimuli and responses that may have been involved in his original learning experience.

In anticipation of the material to come, let us note that in "going beyond the given," two processes are involved. In the first process, stimulus generalization, a given response can often be elicited by stimuli not explicitly linked with it through direct training in the past. In the second process, response generalization, the learner may repeat previously rewarded behaviors in various ways, not restricting himself to the precise movements that have previously been successful.

Stimulus generalization

A response that has been associated with a given stimulus can usually be elicited by other stimuli, especially when these stimuli are reasonably similar to the stimulus involved in the original training. The fact that stimulus generalization occurs is often quite fortunate, for we are rarely exposed to precisely the same situation from one time to the next. Generalization permits us to show the steady effects of learning, despite the changing nature of the situations we encounter. The child who has learned to address his father as "Daddy" can respond quite adequately even though his father may look slightly different because he is wearing a new suit or a new tie. This type of generalization, which is based mainly upon the physical similarity of the relevant stimuli (father-in-a-blue-suit versus father-in-a-brown-suit), may be referred to as *primary* stimulus generalization.

A second form of stimulus generalization, which is particularly important for an understanding of complex human behavior, is *mediated* generalization. This term is reserved for cases in which stimulus generalization occurs despite an absence of physical similarity between the training stimulus (the stimulus involved in the initial learning) and other stimuli capable of eliciting the response. A child who has learned to answer the question "Who wrote the Declaration of Independence?" will probably be quite capable of responding correctly even if we alter the specific words in which this question is phrased. Moreover, if he can read, he will respond appropriately even when the question is presented in written rather than spoken form. In both of these cases, although we have modified the question (stimulus) so that its constituent physical properties have all been radically changed, our young learner may well respond quite correctly without further training. Mediated generalization is quite common; indeed, we would hardly consider that the child had successfully mastered the original question-answer sequence if he was unable to respond appropriately to a variety of wordings and methods of presentation.

The examples of generalization given above represent rather complex situations quite unlike the laboratory settings that most psychologists prefer to deal with. Let us turn, therefore, to a relatively straightforward procedure in which both primary and mediated stimulus generalization may be demonstrated in a simple laboratory experiment.

Consider a situation in which a series of words is repeatedly presented, one word at a time, on a screen. Assume that our subjects are instructed to press a response button as soon as each word appears. After our subjects have gone through this word list several times, we are ready to test for primary and mediated stimulus generalization. In this test we present our subjects with another series of words—some drawn from our original list and some not previously used in the experiment. The subjects are instructed to signal with the response button whenever they see a word drawn from the original word list.

Among the new items in our test list, we include some words that look like words from the original list. We may conclude that our subjects' behavior is the result of primary stimulus generalization if, for example, the word "joy" had been among the words initially presented and our subjects respond positively to words like "boy" or "toy" or "jot" (rather than to unrelated words like "bat" or "sun").

To test for mediated generalization, we would include in our test list several words that did not look or sound like those that had previously been shown but were nevertheless meaningfully related to those words, perhaps as synonyms. If (as above) the word "joy" had been among the original words, our subjects might, for example, show a strong tendency to respond when presented with the word "glee." If this were to occur regularly, we would conclude that our procedures had yielded evidence of secondary or mediated generalization.

While primary stimulus generalization seems readily understandable—partly because of simple perceptual errors—mediated generalization is somewhat more complex. In attempting to develop an explanation of this phenomenon, let us start with the fact that your body is quite richly endowed with proprioceptors, which are essentially receptors that "feed back" signals concerning your present posture and recent movements. In short, these receptors are stimulated by the reactions and the present state of your body rather than by the external stimuli that stimulate your eyes and your ears. When a soldier snaps to attention, his proprioceptors signal that his posture is erect and that his muscles are tensed. Similarly, when you react with fear following a narrowly averted automobile accident, your heart rate will usually be increased and you will doubtless be aware of this because of the sensitive feedback from your proprioceptors. Psychologists believe that this form of feedback is produced by virtually every response we make, although the resulting pattern of stimulation is usually not so dramatic or intense as that which accompanies fear.

Let us return now to our hypothetical experiment. Why do the words "joy" and "glee" elicit similar reactions? If your experimental subject was familiar with English, we would assume that presentation of the word "joy" automatically elicited a learned response, which some psychologists have referred to as a "meaning response." We shall elaborate this theory later on; for our present purposes it is sufficient to say that meaningful words produce responses in the listener or reader, even though these responses may often be impossible for an external observer to detect. These responses may, for example, consist of minimal changes in muscular tone, or in an altered pattern of neural firing. For the typical English-speaking adult in our experiment, we may therefore assume that the "meaning response" (r_m) to the word "joy" automatically produces a distinctive pattern of proprioceptive feedback or response-produced stimulus (s_m), as shown in Figure 4. If this analysis is correct, we can see that the effective stimulus for the button-pushing response in the initial phase of our

$$\text{JOY} \longrightarrow (r_{m_{joy}} \dashrightarrow s_{m_{joy}})$$

Figure 4

Meaning response (r_m) and its resultant pattern of proprioceptive feedback (s_m) following presentation of word "joy."

experiment may actually be the response-produced stimulus s_m, rather than the physical patterns of the letters "j-o-y" as they appear on the screen. This is shown in the sequence starting with "joy" in Figure 5. Now let us consider what will happen when a

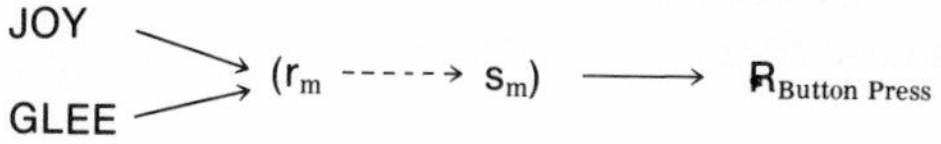

Figure 5

Mediated generalization based on similarity of meaning responses to words "joy" and "glee."

synonym for "joy"—"glee," for example—is presented during the test phase of the experiment. Since the two words have similar meanings, we assume that they elicit similar meaning responses in our subject and ultimately result in rather similar patterns of proprioceptive feedback. This is shown in Figure 5 by the arrows that converge on r_m, the meaning response common to both "joy" and "glee," and its associated feedback pattern, s_m. Note further that if stimulus s_m is, in fact, the effective stimulus for the button-pushing response, we would expect this behavior to be exhibited whenever the stimulus pattern s_m is present, whether this pattern results from a chain of events starting with the original training stimulus "joy" or is started by another word of similar meaning, such as "glee."

The importance of mediated generalization can be readily understood when we consider the variety of ways in which "the same" situation can occur. Think, for example, of the many ways in which a question may be phrased, or the many ways in which friendship can be expressed. The mechanism of mediated generalization permits us immediately to transfer well-practiced responses associated with one of these phrasings (or modes of expression) to others of equivalent meaning, without further training.

Response generalization

When a given response has been associated with some stimulus, there is often a tendency for that stimulus to elicit other related responses. For example, Underwood and Hughes (1950) presented a series of adjectives to a group of subjects and later asked them to recall as many words as they could. The errors in recollection were striking, for there was a strong tendency for subjects to respond with synonyms or words otherwise closely related to the adjectives on the original list. Such results suggest that learning often strengthens the association between a given stimulus and a cluster of related responses. *Primary response generalization* is based upon the physical similarity of the two responses (that is, they may employ the same muscle groups in a similar pattern of action); *acquired response generalization* occurs between response elements that differ in their physical characteristics. In the Underwood and Hughes experiment discussed above, the subjects' errors in recollection mainly involved words meaningfully related to the correct responses rather than words that looked or sounded like the correct answers.

Although the mechanisms underlying acquired response generalization are poorly understood at present, the importance of the phenomenon can hardly be overestimated. Consider a personality trait such as cooperativeness. Many parents would like their children to act cooperatively; however, they recognize that it is impossible to teach children *all* the different ways of being cooperative, because the children will encounter an infinite variety of situations. Under these conditions, child-training is often based on the assumption that reinforcement of a given instance of cooperativeness (for example, sharing one's toys) will strengthen the entire family (or cluster) of cooperative acts (for example, helping in community projects, working effectively with associates on a job, etc.).

There is, however, some disagreement among psychologists concerning response generalization. Some psychologists assert that learning strengthens *specific* responses, not response *clusters.* In a famous experiment conducted by Guthrie and Horton (1946), cats were placed in a glass box from which they could not escape unless they activated a release mechanism—a pole set on a rocking base. Motion pictures were taken of the cats' behavior, which showed a remarkable degree of stereotypy from one trial to the next. For example, one cat learned to activate the mechanism by brushing the right side of his body against the pole; this behavior remained remarkably stable throughout the experiment, even though the same results could have been achieved through a variety of responses. Despite this dramatic demonstration of response stereotyping, most psychologists believe that response generalization plays an important role in human and animal behavior, and several studies have now validated the phenomenon.

Figure 6 is designed to clarify the distinction between stimulus generalization and response generalization. As shown, stimulus generalization refers to the fact that several stimuli may be functionally equivalent; that is, a variety of related stimuli may all elicit a response originally linked to only one member of the stimulus set. In response generalization, on the other hand, a stimulus associatively linked with a given response acquires the capacity to elicit other related responses.

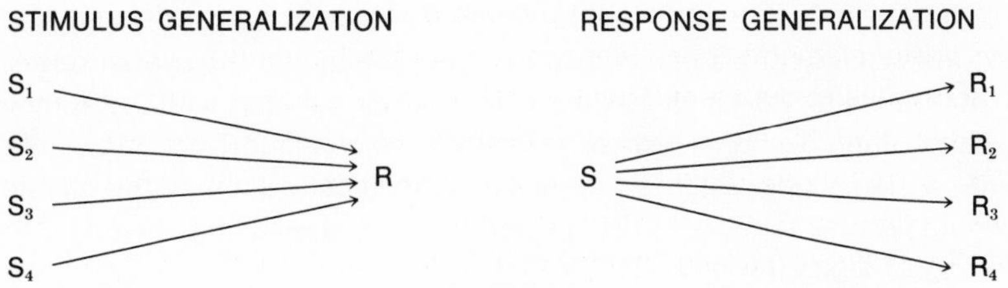

Figure 6

Diagrammatic representations of stimulus and response generalization.

The tendency to generalize from the explicitly "given" elements of a learning situation is an important and usually adaptive aspect of human behavior. In most situations it is primarily important that we correctly identify the category to which a stimulus belongs and that we select our response from an appropriate response cluster; the precise identification of a specific stimulus from among others in the same category, or the selection of a specific response from among a closely related set, is often unimportant. However, specificity is desirable in some circumstances, and in such cases it is necessary to overcome our generalizing tendencies. For example, a musician must learn to detect minor differences among musical notes (stimuli) on his score; moreover, while performing, he must learn to respond with the exact note called for rather than one that resembles it in some way. This type of learning requires extensive discrimination training based on the precise use of reinforcements. The learning situation must be constructed to ensure that reinforcements are provided only for proper stimulus-response sequences. Thus, reinforcement should be withheld when the desired response occurs at an inappropriate time (for example, in response to a stimulus that closely resembles the "proper" stimulus). Similarly, reinforcement must be withheld after a response that merely approximates the desired behavior. (See Walker's *Conditioning and Instrumental Learning,* 1966, for further details on discrimination training.)

Generalization and cognition

In many situations a given behavioral sequence can be performed either (a) by recalling the specific elements involved or (b) by remembering the elements because of their position within some more general cognitive structure. Suppose you were asked to remember the numbers 58121519222629. This is a long series, and you would doubtless have trouble recalling it all if you were to proceed digit by digit. However, the task becomes much simpler if you notice that the overall series can be broken into the units 5-8-12-15-19-22-26-29, in which we start with the number 5 and add 3, then 4, then 3, then 4, etc. Note that we have categorized many distinct elements into a single rule. Such a rule would dramatically simplify the memory task, for we would then be faced with the less arduous job of recalling one rule rather than a long string of digits (Katona, 1940).

Ideally, in mastering any new body of knowledge, it would be desirable if the material could be arranged according to general principles, without the need for extensive recall of details. A student's mastery of geometry, for example, should not reside in his ability to remember a series of specific proofs, but should instead consist of a few generalized skills concerning the manner in which proofs are demonstrated. If these general skills are properly learned and applied, they should enable the student to produce a variety of specific proofs even though the constituent details have not been memorized.

The merits of this general approach can be seen in any mathematical formula. Consider the formula for calculating the distance traveled by an automobile: $D = rt$, where D represents distance, r is the rate of travel, and t is the amount of time the car has been moving. This simple formula is a general statement conveying a great deal of specific information that would otherwise have to be either laboriously memorized or set down in a rather detailed and complicated table. Without the formula, we would be forced to remember an endless series of specifics if we wanted to know the distance traveled under a given set of circumstances. Thus, we would have to recall that at 45 miles an hour, a car will travel 90 miles in two hours; that at 50 miles an hour, it will travel 150 miles in three hours, and so on. It is clearly more efficient to forget the specifics and recall our general formula.

The mastery of a general formulation has another virtue: it enables us to deal successfully with new specific instances that we may not have previously encountered. Thus, the student will be capable of solving new "distance problems" not explicitly taught in class, for if he masters his general formula he is equipped to solve problems involving an endless variety of speeds and times.

Concreteness and abstraction

In our previous discussion we have contrasted two approaches to learning: (a) the specific approach, focusing primarily on all the detailed aspects of a given performance sequence, and (b) the general (or generic) approach, emphasizing the more inclusive categories within which a particular stimulus or response may be placed. The specific approach is often referred to as concrete, because it stresses the explicit details of the situation (the "givens" of an S-R sequence). The generic approach, in contrast, has often been termed abstract, because details of the situation are not emphasized and the individual seeks instead to abstract what he considers essential. Thus, in learning to solve a set of related algebra problems, he would largely ignore the particular wordings and quantities involved and retain instead the abstract association between the general class of problems and the appropriate mode of solution.

Unfortunately, at present only limited information is available concerning the factors that underlie development of the abstract approach. However, several studies have shown that people who have suffered brain injuries often show impaired abstracting ability. For example, they may find it difficult to note correctly the important general similarities between such discrete items as a car and a boat (both modes of transportation); instead, they may focus on unessential concrete details in terms of which the items being compared are identical (both cars and boats are made of metal).

This form of concreteness may also be revealed in nonverbal tests that require the subject to sort a variety of objects into groups whose members "belong together." Here the subject may be given such objects as a spoon, a knife, a candle, a hammer, some matches, a pipe, a ball, and so on. These objects can be grouped in many ways: by color, by the material from which they are constructed, by their uses, etc. After the subject has grouped the objects according to one system, he may then be asked to group them according to some other system. Typically, the brain-damaged person finds it more difficult to switch from one grouping to the next than does the normal person. It is as if the brain damage makes it more difficult for the individual to recognize that many abstract schemes may be employed in grouping the stimuli. Thus, if he finds color differences most striking and hence performs his initial grouping based on this principle, he may subsequently find it difficult to shift to another grouping (object uses, perhaps) that would require him to place objects of different colors into the same category. In this example, we may infer that the concrete color details have dominated our subject's sorting behavior and have prevented him from grouping the objects in other possible ways.

Some studies performed with these sorting techniques have suggested not only that abstract performance is impaired by brain damage but also that abstracting ability is deficient among schizophrenics and is typically quite limited in children. While some observers have suggested that the schizophrenic's concreteness represents a regression to the childish behavior of the youngster, this conclusion may be unwarranted, for the schizophrenic's performance often seems qualitatively unlike that of the child.

The concepts and experiments discussed in the preceding sections of this chapter have largely focused on theoretical issues. In recent years, however, there has been increased concern with the *application* of learning principles. The field of programmed learning provides the clearest example of this development.

Programmed learning: An application of learning principles

Perhaps the most widely publicized innovation in teaching technology within the past few decades has been the introduction of programmed learning techniques. Programmed learning procedures frequently involve the use of so-called teaching machines. As we shall see, however, the virtues of programmed instruction can often be realized without the utilization of any special gadgetry (see Table 1).

What do we mean by programmed learning? And how is it related to learning principles? The typical program consists of a carefully ordered series of questions presented one at a time. After writing out his answer to a question, the learner compares his response with the correct answer. If he is right, he goes on to the next question; if he is wrong, he can often arrange for the machine (or the program) to present the question again, when the entire set has been completed.

The main features of programmed instruction can often be realized without the aid of any "hardware." A good example of these features is shown in Table 1, which presents the beginning "frames" from a program designed to teach the basic operations associated with powers and logarithms. As shown in Table 1, the various questions of a program can appear in a simple workbook, with space left for the insertion of answers; the *correct* answers can be printed below each question, or in another section of the workbook (to minimize the temptation to cheat). In either case, the learner is instructed to answer each question in turn and to check the accuracy of each answer right after the question has been completed. In responding to the program shown in Table 1, the learner normally uses a blank sheet of paper to mask the correct answer to the frame that he is working on. After the answer has been entered in the space that is provided, the masking sheet is moved down the page until the correct answer is exposed. The learner thus gets immediate feedback as to the correctness of his answer.

*Table 1**

Powers and logarithms

1. In the equation $2 \times 3 = 6$, the number 6 is called the product of the factors 2 and 3. In the equation $2 \times 2 \times 2 = 8$, the number 2 appears ________ times as a factor.	
3	
2. The expression $2 \times 2 \times 2$ may be abbreviated as 2^3. In this abbreviated form, ________ represents the number of times that ________ appears as a factor.	
3 2	
3. In the abbreviated notation 2^3, 3 is called the *power* to which 2 is raised. In the expression 4^7, the number 4 is raised to the ________ power.	
seventh	
4. $10{,}000 = 10 \times 10 \times 10 \times 10 = 10^{—}$. In this abbreviated notation, the number 10 is raised to the ________ power.	
10^4 fourth	
5. Powers have important mathematical properties. $2^3 \times 2^5 = 2 \times 2 \times 2 \times 2 \times 2 \times 2 \times 2 \times 2 = 2^{—}$ $7^1 \times 7^3 \times 7^2 = 7 \times 7 \times 7 \times 7 \times 7 \times 7 = 7^{—}$ $23^7 \times 23^5 = 23^{—}$	
2^8 7^6 23^{12}	
6. The general product rule illustrated by these examples may be stated as follows: The power of a product equals the ________ of the powers of the separate factors.	
sum	

*From Lane, H., and Bem, D. *A laboratory manual for the control and analysis of behavior.* Belmont, Calif: Brooks/Cole Publishing Co., 1965.

While programmed instruction can often be adapted to a book-like format (see Table 1), mechanical presentation devices often provide certain advantages. For one thing, a machine can be constructed to control cheating. The learner may be *unable* to write in his response to a question once he has exposed the correct answer. Similarly, the machine may prevent the learner from advancing to the next question until he has attempted the one at hand (if he leaves an item blank and simply proceeds, this fact is automatically recorded, along with all other aspects of his performance). Another advantage of mechanical accessories is that they can often be used in presenting programmed materials to those who cannot read or write. Here, the lessons can be arranged so that the learner may simply push a button in an effort to match one of several answers (given in the form of pictures) with a question (also a picture). Finally, a mechanical gadget may have some motivational value, since levers and buttons may make the learning situation more interesting and attractive, especially to youngsters.

Regardless of the format used for display of the programmed material, several learning principles seem to be particularly pertinent. For one thing, the learner typically gets *immediate feedback* on the correctness of his responses. Immediate knowledge of results is rarely available in the typical classroom; and in the opinion of some critics, this not only reduces the effectiveness of the teacher's eventual feedback as a reinforcer but also lowers the student's incentive to learn.

A somewhat related feature of programmed instruction is the fact that the student must actively engage in the learning process; he cannot sit back passively, but must work steadily in order to complete his lessons. This ensures his participation and attention during the course of learning, although some studies (Goldstein and Gotkin, 1962; Alter and Silverman, 1962) show no difference in final performance between students who actively *write out* their answers and those who merely read the program.

A final principle incorporated in programmed instruction is *shaping,* or learning by *successive approximations.* By this we mean that a complex skill can often be taught if the component skills are taught gradually, in sequence, until the student's final performance can be emitted as a single act. For example, Skinner taught a pigeon to turn around in a clockwise circle by first reinforcing him for turning his head to the right; later reinforcements were delivered if the pigeon turned right and took one or two steps in that direction. By successively "demanding" additional components of the complete clockwise turn as conditions for the delivery of reinforcements, the experimenter can eventually induce the pigeon to perform this complicated maneuver in its entirety—a feat that would be rather unlikely to occur without preliminary shaping.

In a similar vein, the sequence of questions is of great importance in programmed instruction. By learning to respond appropriately to the early questions in the program, the student gradually acquires the capacity to answer the later, more difficult problems. There is, however, a difference from the concept of shaping as it applies in the laboratory. In the laboratory the final act includes, as components, the simpler skills that were strengthened early in the learning sequence; but in programmed instruction, the final performance (on the most difficult items, for example) rarely includes the responses that comprised the early steps. In any case, advocates of programmed instruction have been particularly emphatic about the importance of sequencing the lessons to be presented. Skinner, for example, recommends a program in which the successive steps are sufficiently small so that the learner rarely makes an error. The notion here is that through careful sequencing, the skills demanded at any given point in the learning process should have already been developed in the lessons that have gone before. In a sense, this emphasis on a logical sequence of questions as a means of teaching complex subject matter may be thought of as a modern version of the technique Socrates employed in his teachings. (See Cohen, 1962, for a comparison of programmed learning and Socratic questioning.)

Given this brief introduction, the reader may now wonder about the effectiveness of programmed learning. The effectiveness of a program depends upon how skillfully it is constructed; well-designed programs result from a very long and arduous process of pretesting and analytical thought. If most of the learners miss a given sequence of questions, the programmer knows that for some reason the students have not been adequately prepared for these materials, and that he must rework the lesson. In contrast, the classroom teacher may find it more difficult to determine just where a given presentation went astray.

A second consideration in evaluating programmed instruction is that it is most adaptable to subjects that readily lend themselves to a logical presentation; such subjects would include mathematics (especially geometry), physics, and the acquisition of certain simple skills such as may be called for in arithmetic or foreign languages. In contrast, subjects such as philosophy or history or American literature are more difficult to program effectively.

A final point is that programmed learning materials permit the learner to go as quickly or as slowly as he wishes, without worrying about the progress of his classmates. While this is generally advantageous, it is also true that in order to design any program, one must have some specific group of students in mind, in order to capitalize on their existing knowledge and general intellectual skills. This means, for example, that in a program designed for the average fifth-grader, the very gifted child, although he can work at his own rate, may find that the successive steps in the program are boringly small. He may be insulted at the very slow rate of coverage, even though leisurely presentation proves quite effective for the majority of his classmates.

With continued experience in this new field, we will doubtless develop a better understanding of the situations and populations for which programmed instruction is best suited.

Summary

1. Learning is defined as a relatively permanent behavioral change that results from practice. In its simplest form, learning is a process in which the individual associates a new response with a given stimulus; or it may consist of a strengthened association between a stimulus and a response.

2. The habit-family hierarchy is a convenient way to represent the changes that take place during learning. The basic notion here is that each stimulus tends to be associated with several alternative responses. As learning progresses, these responses are "reshuffled" so that a response that initially was only weakly associated with the stimulus may become strengthened until it dominates all the other alternatives. Similarly, a response that was initially the individual's dominant reaction to a given stimulus may become weaker.

3. When a response is followed by positive (or pleasurable) consequences, it is said to have been reinforced. Responses that are reinforced get stronger; that is, if a stimulus has led to a response which has in turn been reinforced, there will be an increased likelihood that when the stimulus is presented again, the reinforced response will be repeated. In contrast, a response followed by negative consequences (punishment) is generally weakened. Finally, a stimulus-response association that has become strong as a result of repeated reinforcement will get weaker if the reinforcement is subsequently withheld; this process is called experimental extinction.

4. Although learning may occur without obvious reinforcement, what has been learned may not be directly reflected in performance (what the individual actually does). The principle of reinforcement is thus primarily concerned with performance rather than learning.

5. Reinforcements often occur irregularly and need not follow the performance of every "correct" response. Intermittent reinforcement schedules typically lead to a rather slow extinction process, when compared to the rate of extinction that follows continuous (100%) reinforcement.

6. In human learning, considerable improvement may be achieved if the learner is given explicit feedback (knowledge of results) concerning how well he is doing;

without knowledge of results, the individual may show no improvement, even though he is given an opportunity to practice.

7. Some psychologists feel that knowledge of results is most effective if it is presented immediately after the learner's response; however, the evidence is not clear on this point. When delayed feedback does impair performance, two possible mechanisms may be at work: (a) When the feedback finally appears, it may affect the response just performed rather than the response for which the feedback was intended. (b) When people are forced to respond for long periods of time without being told how they are doing, they may lose interest in the task.

8. While there is general agreement concerning the effects of verbal rewards (such as "Good" or "That's right") on behavior, these data may be interpreted in two ways. Thorndike's Law of Effect emphasized the automatic strengthening of responses which occurs when they are followed by reinforcement; according to Thorndike, this strengthening occurs whether or not the learner has an appropriate "understanding" of the relationship between his behavior and the appearance of the reward. In contrast to this mechanistic view, some theorists have taken a cognitive position and have emphasized the information-giving aspects of reinforcement. That is, telling a person he is "right" affects his subsequent behavior by enhancing his understanding of what to do in this situation (the verbal reinforcement helps the learner to gain insight about the correct mode of behavior in that particular setting).

9. There is considerable evidence that people often learn by means of imitation. While there is as yet no fully satisfactory theory in this area, it is clear that learning may often occur in *observational situations*, where the learner neither responds nor receives reinforcements.

10. Learning often occurs even though the learner has not made a conscious effort to memorize or otherwise master the materials presented by the experimenter. This is known as *incidental* learning. Although learning is usually accomplished more effectively when there is an active intention to learn—as compared with the amount acquired under incidental learning conditions—this generalization does not always hold.

11. Upon learning a given stimulus-response sequence, the individual usually "goes beyond what is given"; that is, he may treat the specific stimulus and response elements of a single association as if they represented rather general categories. Two processes are involved here: stimulus generalization and response generalization.

12. In stimulus generalization, a response associated with a given stimulus through direct training may also be associatively linked with other stimuli as a further consequence of this training. Usually, this form of generalization is strongest when we consider stimuli closely related to one another. For example, a child who has learned to label a circular design (stimulus) as a "circle" (response) will also be likely to use this term in referring to "near-circular" shapes, such as the oval. In a case like this, where the generalization is based on physical similarity between the relevant stimuli, the process may be termed primary stimulus generalization. Mediated generalization

is based on the learned equivalence of stimulus elements that are physically unrelated.

13. In response generalization, learning generally strengthens a cluster of related responses rather than just one response. Here we may distinguish between (a) primary response generalization, where the responses are physically related in the sense that they involve similar muscle groups, and (b) acquired response generalization, which involves response elements that may differ in their physical characteristics.

14. By "going beyond what is given," the learner essentially emphasizes the general structure of the task he is learning, and he is somewhat less involved with recalling the specific elements that comprise the situation. This approach aids memory, for it is usually simpler to recall a general structure than it is to recall a series of isolated stimulus and response elements. Moreover, the general approach often enables the learner to deal successfully with specific instances not previously encountered.

15. People who have suffered brain damage often find it difficult to adopt the general (or abstract) approach. Instead, their cognitive processes may show a concrete emphasis upon specific details in problem solving, which may interfere with effective performance.

Supplementary reading

Walker, E. L. *Conditioning and instrumental learning*. Belmont, Calif.: Brooks/Cole Publishing Company, 1967.

2 Memory

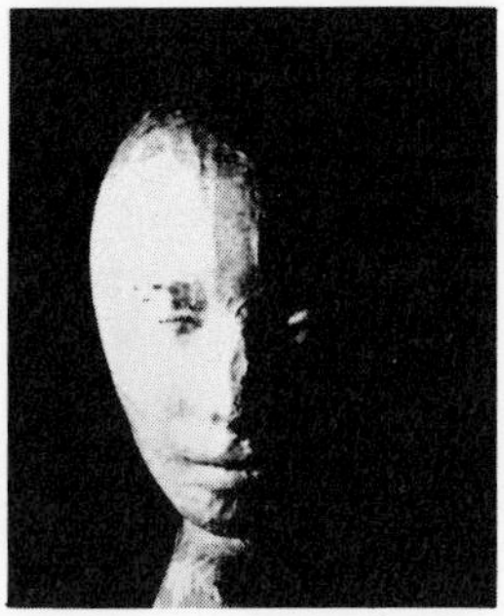

While learning permeates our everyday lives, we are all also quite familiar (sometimes unhappily) with the fact that many of the things we have learned are too quickly forgotten. Memory and forgetting are, of course, serious practical concerns of all of us, for the successful performance of many tasks depends upon how effectively we can recall and apply what we have learned in the past. The phenomena of memory are also important because of the theoretical implications they may have for an adequate understanding of human intellectual functioning.

In general, we say that *forgetting* has taken place when we observe that the passage of time is accompanied by a decrement in the performance of some learned activity. For example, although John Jones may have mastered the Gettysburg Address when he studied it as a grade school student, he may find that when he tries to recall it now, six years later, he can no longer recite it in its entirety. The difference between his earlier, perfect performance and his present, less-than-perfect performance is due to forgetting.

The scientific study of memory was inaugurated by Ebbinghaus in 1885, and his work is important for several reasons. First, it represents what is probably the earliest attempt to carry out quantitative, experimental research on one of the higher mental processes; before his time, objective research had been restricted to the study of sensation. Second, Ebbinghaus's work is important because he devised two techniques for the study of memory, both of which are still widely employed in experimental research. Ebbinghaus wanted to study the learning and retention of verbal materials that were independent of the learner's prior thought patterns. Starting with unfamiliar, seemingly unrelated elements, he hoped to explore the fundamental processes of memory within the relatively controlled conditions provided by his laboratory. In searching for verbal materials that were relatively "uncontaminated" by earlier association, he invented the nonsense syllable, which simply consists of a vowel surrounded by consonants, such as VEK or ZAT or CEV. As subsequent work (Glaze, 1928; Archer, 1960) has shown, such meaningless syllables do indeed have associations for most people. But such syllables have nevertheless remained in use, largely because they permit the study of memory in a setting where the materials are relatively unfamiliar and are but weakly embedded in the subject's cognitive and verbal habits.

In his studies of memory, Ebbinghaus also employed what has come to be known as the *method of savings*. In this method, memory is measured by having the subject relearn, to the point of complete mastery, the materials he is trying to remember. By comparing the speed required for complete relearning with the time required for initial mastery, the experimenter may devise a "saving score." For example, if a subject originally mastered a list of ten nonsense syllables after one minute of study, but required only 30 seconds to relearn it to perfection a month later, he would be given a saving score of 50%, which we would attribute to our subject's retention of the initially-learned materials.

The method of savings often reveals considerable retention in cases where the subject's inability to recall the original material may suggest that he remembers little, if anything. This is clearly illustrated in a study by Burt (1941) in which, for a period of time prior to his son's second birthday, he read the boy three passages in Greek from Sophocles' *Oedipus Tyrannus*; six years later, the boy learned these same passages plus several other selections from the same source. While it took 317 repetitions to master the old passages, the new selections required 435 repetitions. Since the old passages were learned in 73% of the time required for mastery of the new ones, we may conclude that the boy's retention of his early experience resulted in a savings of about 27% (even though it is certain that he could have recalled virtually none of this material had he simply attempted to recite the passages from memory, as required by the method of recall).

By studying his own retention for lists of nonsense syllables at varying time intervals after he had learned them, Ebbinghaus discovered what has come to be known as the "forgetting curve." His results have subsequently been replicated by other investigators and are graphically depicted in Figure 1. The figure shows that immediately after learning, we forget things rather rapidly, but that with the passage of time, the rate of forgetting becomes slower and slower. This change in the rate of

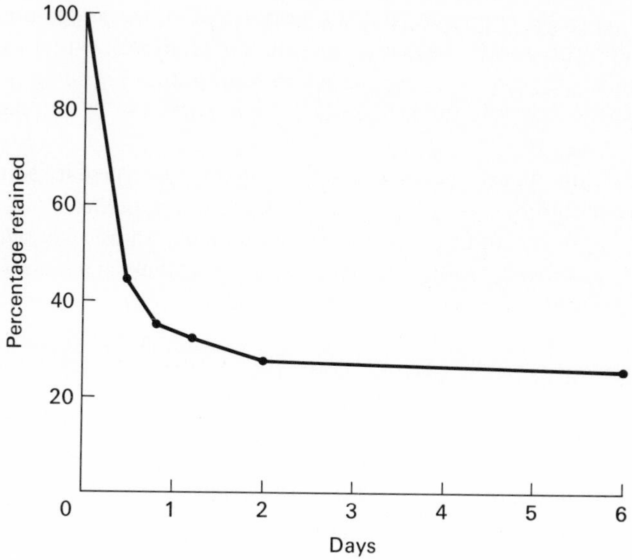

Figure 1

Ebbinghaus's retention for lists of nonsense syllables. (From *Experimental psychology* by Robert S. Woodworth. Copyright 1938 by Holt, Rinehart and Winston, Inc. Copyright © 1966 by Mrs. Greta Woodworth Herron, Svenson Woodworth, William Woodworth, and Virginia Woodworth. Reprinted by permission of Holt, Rinehart and Winston, Inc.)

forgetting is reflected in *Jost's Law,* which states that within a given time interval, we are more likely to forget memories of recent origin than those derived from long-past experience.

Forgetting and disuse

Many people think that forgetting results from the disuse of previously memorized material. They would explain John Jones' inaccurate recital of the Gettysburg Address by noting that he had not practiced this recitation for years and that, as a result, the constituent skills and associations had "weakened," something like an unused muscle.

In one sense, there is a certain naivety about the disuse theory, for even though the amount of material we forget tends to increase as time passes, time itself may not necessarily *cause* forgetting. We may profitably consider an analogy: children tend to grow with the passage of time, but does this mean that time causes growth? We might more plausibly conclude that the underlying biochemical and genetic processes that control growth have an opportunity to produce their effects as time passes. A similar argument may be applied to forgetting. Forgetting is caused by the events that occur after the initial learning experience, not by the passage of time.

For a long time, the disuse theory was widely rejected because it seemed too simple and failed to account for many important memory phenomena. More recently, however, it has enjoyed something of a revival, particularly among "duplexity" theorists (for example, Broadbent, 1958), who believe that two different memory systems affect our capacity for long-term and short-term retention.

Duplexity theorists typically assume that (a) recently-memorized materials will be forgotten (or decay) rather rapidly unless a person constantly practices them but that (b) older, better-consolidated memories may be maintained without the benefit of further practice or rehearsal. One example of short-term memory decay is the fact that people often find it difficult to remember a telephone number that they have just looked up in a directory, unless they repeat it to themselves before starting to dial; according to duplexity theory, a person's rehearsal of this newly-acquired material, before it has been consolidated in "long-term" storage, is presumed to retard the process of spontaneous decay. Other analyses of this phenomenon are possible, however. Repeated rehearsal may, for example, protect recent memories from *interference* (rather than spontaneous decay), which might otherwise be generated if we allowed our thought to turn to other matters. Melton (1963) presents an excellent discussion of some of the basic issues associated with the duplexity theory of memory.

Psychologists of the Gestalt school have traditionally favored a disuse principle to account for some of the phenomena of memory. They have long contended that the things we remember are stored in *memory traces* that presumably evolve into simpler structures with the passage of time. The Gestalt view is most applicable to perceptual memories, for it holds that modifications of the memory trace tend to reduce the imbalances and perceptual stresses that characterized the original stimulus. For example, according to what Gestalt theorists call the *law of closure,* one often sees incompleted familiar figures as if they were whole; an incompleted circle with a small gap in one side will thus generate perceptual "stresses" that will sometimes lead people to perceive this figure as if it were complete. When a figure of this sort is retained in memory, according to the Gestalt view, the memory trace will tend to change in the direction of completeness—even if the figure was accurately perceived at first. Consequently, if we conduct recall tests at varying intervals after the initial presentation of such a stimulus (by having people draw the original figure as they remember it), the gap in the circle should gradually shrink, until we reach a stage where the circle is remembered as having been whole rather than incomplete. Although there is good evidence that memory traces undergo systematic changes as time passes, the Gestalt emphasis on *perceptual* forces as active agents in memory distortion has not been verified (Holmes, 1968).[1]

Memory and response competition

One of the early and best-known experiments on memory (Jenkins and Dallenbach, 1924) clearly demonstrates the importance of the learner's activities after his initial exposure to the material he is attempting to retain. In this study, two students at Cornell University learned lists of nonsense syllables and were tested for retention two, four, or eight hours later. The experiment was designed so that the students sometimes slept during the time that elapsed between their original learning of the lists and the subsequent test for retention. At other times, they were awake during this period and went on with their normal daily activities. While there was a certain amount of forgetting under both conditions, the students forgot less material while they slept than they did during waking hours. (See Figure 2.)

Experiments of this sort suggest that the sheer passage of time is less important as a determinant of memory than are the learner's activities following the original learning experience. It is frequently the case, for instance, that the activities in which we engage, subsequent to learning, tend to interfere with or inhibit the recall of material memorized earlier. Psychologists speak of this phenomenon as *retroactive inhibition.*

A given activity will produce varying amounts of retroactive inhibition, depending upon the activity's particular relationship to the originally learned material. From the considerable research on this matter, one suggested conclusion is that, when tasks can be analyzed into stimulus-response sequences, retroactive inhibition is strikingly affected by the degree of similarity between the stimuli involved in the two tasks. On the one hand, it has been repeatedly shown that when the stimuli are relatively unchanged from one task to the next, but the required responses are different, a considerable amount of retroactive inhibition will be produced. On the other hand, better retention will result if the stimuli involved in the two tasks are quite different. Suppose you have been studying French vocabulary using a flash-card method in which you look at an English word (stimulus) and try to supply its French equivalent (response).

[1]See Walker and Weintraub, *Perception* (1966) for a fuller discussion of Gestalt theory.

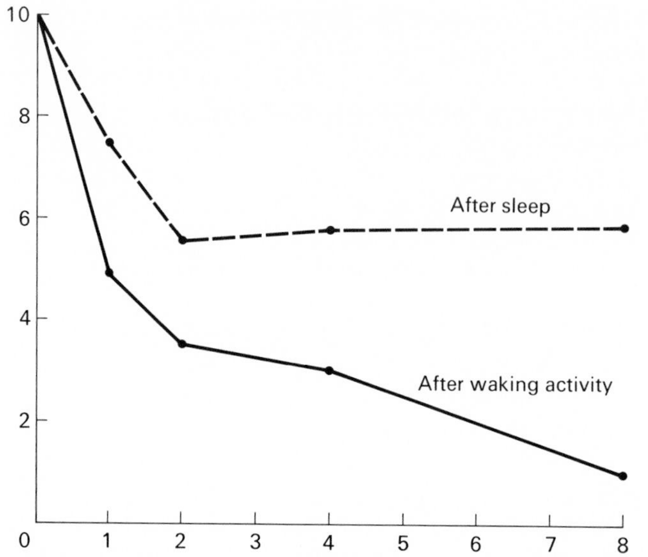

Figure 2

Effect on retention when sleep or waking activity follows initial learning. (Adapted from H. H. Kendler, *Basic psychology*. New York: Appleton-Century-Crofts, 1963. Data from Jenkins and Dallenbach, 1924.)

Your recall of this material will be inhibited if you next turn to the study of Russian (using the same study technique and the same group of vocabulary words), for in this case the same English words (stimuli) appear in both lessons, but you must learn two different responses to each—one French and one Russian. In contrast to the above sequence of study experiences, you would probably forget less of the French if you subsequently studied something unrelated to French, such as biological definitions. Figures 3 and 4 show how we may diagrammatically represent these two tasks in terms of their stimulus and response components.

Retroactive inhibition is primarily due to competition between responses. Thus, if a person studies Russian shortly after learning his French lesson, there may be two important consequences. First, the Russian words may compete with the French and produce an "unlearning" effect; that is, the Russian words may replace the French as learned responses to the various English stimulus words. Second, even if the French responses have not been forgotten, there is likely to be some confusion and competition between the French and Russian when we test the person for recall; he

INITIAL LEARNING	SUBSEQUENT LEARNING	RESULT INTERFERENCE AND FORGETTING
$S_{1_{English}}$ ⟶ $R_{1_{French}}$	$S_{1_{English}}$ ⟶ $R_{2_{Russian}}$	
door ⟶ porte	door ⟶ dvyer	door ⟶ porte door ⟶ dvyer
book ⟶ livre	book ⟶ knēga	book ⟶ livre book ⟶ knēga
red ⟶ rouge	red ⟶ krasne	red ⟶ rouge red ⟶ krasnē

Figure 3

A sequence that would produce marked retroactive inhibition due to similarity between stimuli in initial and subsequent learning tasks.

INITIAL LEARNING	SUBSEQUENT LEARNING	RESULT MINIMAL INTERFERENCE AND FORGETTING
$S_{1_{English}}$ ⟶ $R_{1_{French}}$	$S_{X_{Biol.\ Term}}$ ⟶ $R_{y_{definition}}$	
door ⟶ porte	dendrite ⟶	door ⟶ porte
book ⟶ livre	chromosome ⟶	book ⟶ livre
red ⟶ rouge	mitosis ⟶	red ⟶ rouge

Figure 4

Sequence that would produce minimal retroactive inhibition because of dissimilarity between initial and subsequent learning tasks. (Adapted from J. Deese, *Principles of psychology.* "Copyright © 1964 by Allyn and Bacon, Inc., Boston. Reprinted by permission."

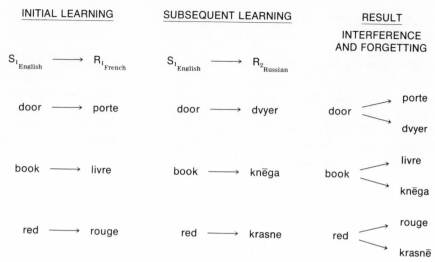

may mistakenly answer with a Russian word when he is being tested on his French lesson.

One of the best techniques for reducing retroactive inhibition is called *overlearning,* which involves the learner's continued practice at a given memory task even after he has reached a level of errorless performance. The available research thus suggests that if the student in our hypothetical French lesson had practiced his vocabulary lesson beyond the point of initial mastery, his retention of this material would have been much improved—despite the potentially disrupting effects of a subsequent study session involving Russian vocabulary.

In studying retroactive inhibition, we are concerned with the effects of subsequent activity on the retention of material learned in the past. *Proactive inhibition,* a related phenomenon, refers to the fact that some of the things learned in the past make it more difficult to remember things now being learned.

The importance of proactive inhibition was shown by Underwood (1957), who pointed out the dramatic contrast between the rapid decline in memory in Ebbinghaus's studies and the relatively slow rate of decline in more recent studies. Since Ebbinghaus always carried out his work on the learning and retention of nonsense syllables with a very experienced subject—namely, himself—his typically rapid rate of forgetting might have been due to confusion with other lists he had previously learned.

To clinch his argument, Underwood designed an experiment in which human subjects learned varying numbers of nonsense-syllable lists before being tested for retention of the last list they learned. His main purpose was to see if the amount recalled from this last list was affected by the number of lists that his subjects had learned in the past. His results showed clear evidence of proactive inhibition.

Underwood's results suggest that our ability to recall the things we have just learned may be drastically impaired if we have previously been forced to memorize large amounts of similar materials. While this conclusion clearly fits the data discussed above, we must be careful in applying this rule generally. For example, it seems most likely that a trained physician would be more successful in recalling the contents of an article dealing with tuberculosis than an engineer of equal intelligence, even though the physician would have read many more such articles in the past. How can this be reconciled with Underwood's findings? It seems most likely that Underwood's results are partly attributable to the fact that the successive materials learned in his studies were not organized in any meaningful way. Each list, for example, typically contained a set of unrelated words or nonsense syllables, and there was no logical relationship between one list and the next. In contrast, our hypothetical physician could probably fit the material on tuberculosis within the framework of other information he had acquired on this topic and hence could more easily recall it. The engineer's lack of a medical background might make it difficult for him to organize the material and relate it to other information with which he was familiar; he would thus have more difficulty recalling it than the doctor would.

Reconstruction versus reappearance

Many contemporary research studies and theories about memory assume that we are somehow able to store the events of the past so that they may be recovered when needed. This assumption is quite clear, for instance, in references to the so-called memory trace and in analyses of retroactive inhibition, where a newly learned response is sometimes said to have "replaced" an older, competing response, which may no longer be available. In such an approach, memory is conceived as a vast filing system in which we maintain the residues of prior experience; memories are assumed to lie dormant until they "reappear" (or are recalled) because of their association with *other* events (or eliciting stimuli, to use the behaviorist's terminology).

This approach to memory, which has been termed the "reappearance" hypothesis, has been severely challenged by theorists who favor a more *constructive* (or reconstructive) view of memory. Neisser (1967), for example, accepts the basic concept of memory storage but believes that effective remembering requires more than an efficient "filing system." He contends, instead, that acts of memory are in some ways similar to the achievements of the paleontologist, who may start with a few bone fragments and reconstruct the appearance of a long-gone dinosaur. In Neisser's view, memory follows a similar pattern in that we *reconstruct* that which we remember, starting from fragmentary elements that are recalled from prior cognitive acts.

An early version of the "reconstruction" viewpoint was presented by Bartlett in 1932. Bartlett denied the notion that we simply retain the things we wish to recall; he argued instead that, starting with some schematized dominant elements, we attempt to reconstruct (as best we can) that which has come before. Bartlett further contended that in these reconstructive attempts, there is an active effort to mold the material to the expectancies of the learner. In support of this hypothesis, he conducted several studies that used a repeated reproduction technique. Subjects in these experiments first read and then reread an American Indian folk tale. Fifteen minutes later they were asked to reproduce the story, and subsequent reproductions were obtained still later. Because of its origin in a foreign culture, the story had an unusual style and a supernatural content that contrasted with the stories most familiar to English-speaking peoples. The subjects' reproductions of the story included many alterations that generally served to make the tale more congruent with the subjects' cultural norms. For example, there was a tendency to add new material designed to make better sense out of elements that most of us would regard as being strange and unconnected. In general, what seemed to be remembered or preserved throughout each subject's several reproductions was a central meaningful "core." Using this basic core, people tended to reconstruct the "original story" by adding more detailed material, some of which was recalled and some invented. Thus, the individual's cultural expectancies, his personality, and his attitudes all contributed to what he "retained."

Unfortunately, the reconstruction hypothesis has not led to very much research—partly because suitable research methodologies have not been developed and partly because this theoretical approach has not been explicated in the concrete terms that are usually needed for the development of experimental research programs.

Forgetting and organization

While forgetting is a universal phenomenon, some matters are more readily forgotten than others. One important determinant of forgetting is the degree of organization within the content to be remembered; material that is well structured and tightly organized will generally be recalled far more successfully than material that is not.

For example, in an experiment by Miller and Selfridge (1950) college students were read word lists ranging in length from ten to fifty words each. The students' job was to repeat as much as they could from each list immediately after it was read. (This procedure is known as the method of *free recall,* and it is widely used in research on immediate memory.) Some of the lists were completely unorganized, consisting simply of a random collection of words unrelated to one another. Other lists were highly organized, since the words on them were taken directly from passages of written English. Between these two extremes were several lists that varied in the extent to which they approximated standard English sentences. The results of this experiment clearly indicated that accuracy of recall was directly related to the organization of the words within each list. That is, people found it much simpler to recall words that were organized into sentences than to recall an equal number of isolated words. Moreover, the more sentence-like the word list, the more readily it was recalled.

Deese (1959) has reported what is probably a related finding. In this study, eighteen different word lists were used. The lists varied in the extent to which the words on them were associated with one another. A list with a high degree of inter-item association included words like *moth, insect, wing, bird,* and *fly;* by contrast, a list of essentially unrelated words included the following: *lake, ride, tonight, enemy,* and *subtract.* Performance was much better on the lists that included words which were highly associated with one another. Such a list might reasonably be characterized as well organized, since its elements were systematically related to one another and were not simply a random sample of words from the dictionary. In explaining his results, Deese employed an associative version of the reconstruction hypothesis (see above). He reasoned that the subjects were probably able to remember only a small core of words (the "immediate memory span"), but they used these elements to generate other associated words in their attempted verbal recall. This procedure would yield reasonably good performance when the word list included many items that were indeed associated, but it would be less successful when the words on the list were essentially unrelated to one another.

Recall may also be facilitated if the material to be memorized reflects some underlying thematic consistency. Bousfield (1953) constructed a list of sixty words drawn from four distinct categories: animals, names, vegetables, and professions. The words were read in a random sequence; then the subjects attempted to recall (in order) as many words as they could. The results indicated that lists of thematically related words were recalled more readily than comparable lists of thematically unrelated words. Another important finding in this study was that thematically related words tended to be recalled in clustered sequences (*dog, cat, lion,* etc.), despite the fact that the words had not been presented in this order. Even though they had been instructed to recall the words in their original order, the subjects apparently reorganized the lists into thematic word clusters and then recited them one after another during the recall test. This finding is consistent with the hypothesis that the process of memory is often an active "effort after meaning," not just a passive retention of what has been presented.

Subjective organization

Although Bousfield's method for studying thematic clusters has often been used in immediate-recall experiments, his technique provides only a crude estimate of the degree of organization that is operative for any particular person on a given memory task. Thus, given a list of names of various animals, people, automobiles, and professions, one subject might organize this material into two main clusters: living versus non-living things; someone else might establish a more idiosyncratic categorization based on items that he *liked* versus those that he *disliked.*

Tulving (1962) devised a method for measuring the degree of organization that *each subject* imposes on a memory task. In Tulving's experiment a list of words was presented in several different orders; after each presentation the subject was to repeat, in any order he wished, all the words that he could recall. To assess subjective organization, Tulving searched for items that repeatedly appeared together during the subject's various recall attempts. If any two words (*canoe* and *book,* for example) were frequently recalled one after the other by a subject—despite the fact that the sequence of words had been changed from one exposure of the list to the next—Tulving assumed that these words were probably organized as elements within a single structure. Note that this conclusion was based solely on the sequence of the subject's recall attempts; the experimenter did not specify (or guess) *why* it was that certain pairs of words were frequently grouped together.

Tulving's results showed that subjective organization (as defined above) has a strong impact on memory performance. Thus, with repeated exposure to a word list, the amount recalled increases, and there is also clear evidence of an increase in subjective organization. These results suggest that in memorizing a list, the improvement in performance which results from repeated exposure may partly reflect the increasing structure that the subject perceives (or imposes). According to this hypothesis, we might assume that the individual recalls a *fixed* number of subjectively defined units, but that his performance improves as the list is presented over and over, because of the increased number of words included within each subjective unit.

A series of experiments by Mandler (1967) provides further support for the idea that memory is heavily dependent upon our ability to organize (or categorize) the material that we wish to retain. Mandler suggests that in memorizing a list of words, we will often be most successful if we can organize the elements of the task into a limited number of categories, making certain that no one category is "overloaded." During recall, he hypothesizes, we take advantage of this structure by first remembering the general categories that we have established and then reciting the individual items (words) within these categories. This hierarchical arrangement can presumably be extended for several levels (or layers); however, Mandler believes that most people can keep track of only a limited number of categories (five, perhaps) at any given level.

Conclusion

Many studies have shown the importance of organization as a determinant of memory; human subjects are far more successful in recalling organized materials than they are in recalling unorganized materials. It seems likely that this superiority in recall is based on the fact that one can recall a mass of organized details by memorizing the underlying rule (or structure) that holds them together; the structure serves as a kind of "shorthand" that is later expanded (or translated) into the concrete details of the task at hand. This generalization seems to have direct implications for memory in our everyday lives. Consider the student who is studying a body of new material, perhaps on the French Revolution. His recall may be enhanced if he can succeed in imposing some structure and coherence on this material—that is, if he perceives and understands the interrelationships among the various events cited. In contrast, we would predict poorer recall if he simply attempts to remember isolated facts and occurrences, without regard for the way in which these elemental units might be related.

Coding

Many of the techniques that people use to aid recall are related to the simple principle that *organization facilitates memory.* In order to remember the notes associated with lines in the treble clef (e, g, b, d, and f), children often memorize the sentence "Every good boy does fine." The notes associated with spaces of the clef (f, a, c, and e) may be even simpler to remember, since collectively they spell the word "face."

The type of technique in which the material to be remembered is "stored" in a modified form is often referred to as *coding,* an example of which is shown diagrammatically in Figure 5. Here we can see that the number of elements in the code is the same as the number of elements to be retained (that is, there is one word to be remembered for each note); but this type of coding will still facilitate memory, since it is easier to

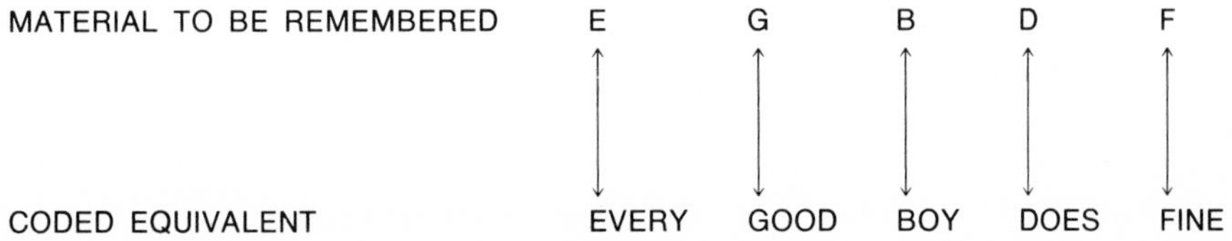

Figure 5

Example of coding in which each element to be remembered is stored in modified form.

recall the highly organized, meaningful sentence than it is to recall the less meaningful set of isolated letters.

In another type of code that increases memory performance, several of the items presented for memorizing are represented by a single item in the code. George Miller (1956) has reported an experiment in which the subject's task was to listen to a random series of "zeros" and "ones," which he was then to repeat in sequence. For example, he might be given the series 100111010101001010. Most people can successfully retain a series up to about nine digits in this type of experiment. However, by recoding the original series according to a system in which 000 = 0; 001 = 1; 010 = 2; 011 = 3; 100 = 4; etc. (see Figure 6), one of Miller's associates was able to recall series

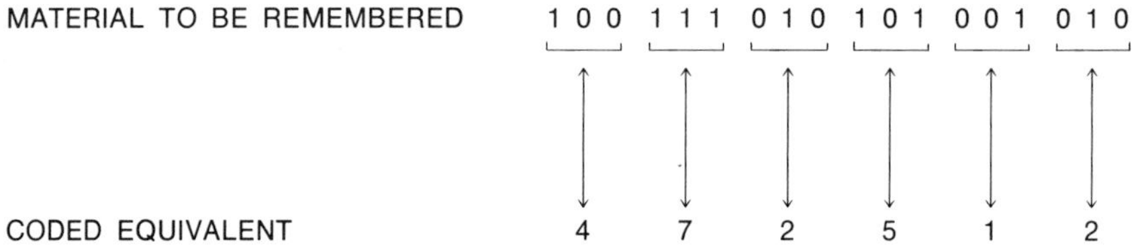

Figure 6

Example of coding in which three elements of material to be remembered are represented by one element in code.

over thirty digits in length. In this scheme, the subject first trained himself to respond to sets of three digits, which were represented in code by the numbers 0 through 7. If asked to remember the series 100111010101001010, he would break the series into six groups. As shown in Figure 6, the first three digits (100) would be symbolized by the number 4, the next three (111) would be symbolized by the number 7, the next three (010) by the number 2, and the final three triples by the numbers 5, 1, and 2. Thus, by retaining only six numbers—4, 7, 2, 5, 1, and 2—and translating each of these back into its "zero-one" (or binary) equivalent, one could correctly recite an eighteen-digit list. In the actual experiment, this three-to-one coding ratio enabled Miller's subject to recall about thirty digits; even better performance resulted from other coding schemes, in which each digit represented four or five elements in the original series of "zeros" and "ones."

Codes that are based on the "many-to-one" principle facilitate performance because they reduce the number of elements that must be remembered. In general, the *ease* with which we can symbolize something (as measured, for example, by the number of code units required for adequate symbolization) has a direct effect upon retention.

Glanzer and Clark (1963) reported an interesting experiment in which human subjects were presented with a series of eight black or white geometric figures (diamond, circle, square, etc.); for each trial, the eight figures were arranged in a horizontal array and projected on a screen for half a second. After viewing each array, subjects were given an answer sheet containing the geometric figures in the same arrangement in which they had appeared on the screen; the subjects were instructed to write either a B (for black) or a W (for white) on each figure. As you might expect, it was much easier to recall the colors in some arrays than in others. For example, when all eight figures were black, 98% of the subjects could correctly recall the colors of all the figures; other, more difficult arrays could be correctly recalled by only 20% of the subjects.

What has all this to do with coding? Glanzer and Clark tested a second group of subjects and found that the arrays most readily recalled could be verbally described in a relatively few words (for example, "all black"). Conversely, the arrays most difficult to recall were usually described in rather lengthy terms (for example, "first, fifth, and eighth are black"). These data suggest that subjects in the recall task translated the stimulus input into its equivalent verbal form (or code), which they held in memory, and then used this code to guide their final written response. When the input stimulus could be coded (verbally symbolized) by a brief description consisting of only a few words, it was successfully recalled; when the stimulus required a lengthy verbal description—that is, when it could not be efficiently coded—recall was less successful.

These data suggest that people with good memories may perhaps be blessed with relatively efficient coding systems for recalling the items that they wish to remember. They may be especially skillful in representing the material to be recalled with relatively few verbal symbols; ideally, these verbal symbols should be organized into a meaningful structure. Devices of this sort provide a practical technique for improving memory, and they are probably responsible for the unusual feats of the so-called "memory expert."

Coding and reconstruction

According to the reconstruction hypothesis (see above), we rarely attempt to remember a body of material in its full detail; instead, we schematize what is given to us and frequently store it in coded terms. The code that we use often involves a heavy reliance on *names* or *labels*. A famous experiment by Carmichael, Hogan, and Walter (1932) showed how the verbal labels that were used to represent a set of ambiguous figures could influence the subjects' recall and subsequent reproductions of these stimuli. In this study, half the subjects were given one set of labels for the various experimental figures, and the other half were given a second set of labels. Figure 7 shows some of the original stimuli, the different labels associated with each stimulus, and some schematized versions of the subjects' reproductions. The results of this study, showing the impact of verbal labels upon memory, nicely paralleled Bartlett's view that we typically retain only a core schema in memory (presumably a verbal label in this case), from which we attempt to "reconstruct" the original. A more recent study (Herman, Lawless, and Marshall, 1957) has suggested that even if subjects are not given verbal labels for the various stimuli, they will implicitly "name" the figures on their own, and these labels too will influence their subsequent reproductions.

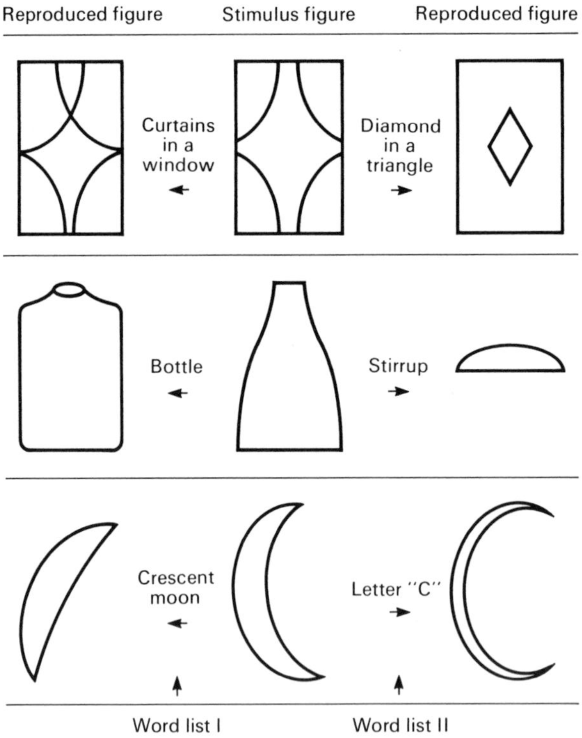

Figure 7

Effect of verbal labels on later reproductions of several ambiguous figures.

A series of experiments by Conrad (1959, 1962, 1964) provides additional evidence for the hypothesis that memory is highly dependent on verbal coding. Conrad's studies showed that in any subject's attempt to recall a series of letters that are presented *visually*, there will normally be a fair number of *substitution errors*— errors in which the subject will "recall" a letter that *sounds* like the code name for one of the original visual stimuli. These results suggest that the printed letters are coded and stored in the form of verbal equivalents (e.g., S = "Ess"), which may then be confused with similar-sounding letter names (e.g., "Ex") when the subject attempts to repeat the series that he has been shown. Wickelgren (1965, 1966) has carried this work still further by showing that the effects of retroactive and proactive inhibition are amplified, in a task involving *visual* presentation, if the interfering letters merely *sound* like those which are to be remembered.

Motivation and memory

In studying the cognitive processes of his patients, Sigmund Freud noted that they were often unable to recall anxiety-provoking events, or events associated with fearful occurrences. He hypothesized that these memory lapses represented the operation of a mechanism he termed *repression*, through which anxiety-provoking materials were sometimes automatically "banished" from consciousness despite the individual's conscious efforts to recall them. While we are concerned here with the relationship between repression and memory, we should note that the term *repression* can also refer to the individual's lack of awareness regarding the motives that guide him. Thus, according to Freud, we may employ repression not only to prevent us from consciously recognizing some of the antisocial motives that underlie much of our everyday behavior but also to prevent conscious recall of unpleasant events.

While contemporary psychologists generally accept the view that anxiety-provoking events are often difficult to recall, they have been critical of the relatively impressionistic data that are obtained in the course of clinical practice and have therefore attempted to investigate the process of repression experimentally. While some of the laboratory studies of repression have been criticized as being either poorly designed or naïve regarding psychoanalytic theory, some interesting results have been reported.

Stagner (1931) conducted one of the early experiments in this area. In this study, a group of college students who had just returned from vacation wrote a description of one pleasant and one unpleasant incident that they had experienced. Below each description, they then wrote a list of things that they had associated with each of the two incidents. Two weeks later, they were unexpectedly given copied versions of their descriptions and were asked to recall the associations that they had given previously. The results indicated that the average student could recall more things associated with the pleasant incident than with the unpleasant incident. It should be noted, however, that experiments of this sort do not rule out the possibility that the obtained differences in recall might have been caused by *rehearsal*; that is, the students may have done more thinking and talking about the pleasant event than the unpleasant one, and consequently the obtained effects may be explainable in these simple terms, without involving a complex mechanism like repression. (In psychological experimentation, as in other scientific fields, the sophisticated investigator tries to be conservative in interpreting his findings. He attempts to explain a given set of results by turning to the most simple explanatory principle that proves sufficient; complex explanations are accepted only when the simple accounts prove inadequate.)

In another investigation, Zeller (1950) suggested that a successful demonstration of repression requires not only that the imposition of some threatening experience should produce forgetting of related memories but also that the removal of the threat should be accompanied by a recovery of the previously repressed materials. Following this line of thought, Zeller arranged an experimental situation in which one group of students was subjected to a personal failure experience shortly after they had successfully mastered a list of nonsense syllables. In a subsequent test of recall, these subjects performed more poorly than a control group who had experienced success, rather than failure, following their initial learning experience. These results were attributed to repression, on the assumption that the experimental group had associated the nonsense syllables with failure (and anxiety) and had thus forgotten the syllables. When these subjects were subsequently given an opportunity to succeed on the task that they had previously failed and were then tested for retention, they showed improved recall of the nonsense syllables. To the extent that this experiment is relevant to the Freudian concept, these data suggest that repression may not be permanent but may be reversed when the material to be remembered is no longer associated with negative effects.

Intentional forgetting

According to psychoanalytic theory, repression is an automatic mechanism that may speed the process of forgetting, despite the individual's conscious attempts at recall. Nevertheless, Freud at one time believed that "the essence of repression lies simply in turning something away, and keeping it at a distance, from consciousness (Freud, 1915, p. 147)." This suggests that there may be some relationship between the phenomenon of repression and our more conscious efforts to suppress (or forget) disturbing memories. Starting from this conception, Weiner (1968) conducted a series of experiments to see if subjects who were *instructed* to forget a nonsense syllable would indeed show impaired memory when they were subsequently tested for recall. His results strongly supported the notion that a subject can intentionally facilitate the forgetting process, even though he is motivated to remember (when he is tested for recall) and is not deliberately "withholding" information. This finding nicely complements some earlier research by Weiner (1966, 1967), which showed that *retention* may be enhanced if the subject has been specially motivated to remember.

Weiner's results, showing that forgetting may be hastened by the instruction to forget, received additional support from Bjork, LaBerge, and Legrand (1968). These investigators designed a study in which several series of digits were presented visually; each series also contained either one or two consonant quadragrams (for instance, CRLF or MPRT). The subjects were to read aloud the numbers and letters within each series and were subsequently to recall (if possible) one or both of the quadragrams. There were three experimental conditions. In several lists only one quadragram appeared. The subjects' recall of this single test item was compared with the recall performance of subjects in a second condition, where the test item had been preceded by a different quadragram; in this second condition, the subjects were instructed to recall *both* consonant items, reciting the second (or test) item first. The results showed clear evidence of proactive inhibition among subjects in the second condition, in that recall of the test item was significantly poorer when both quadragrams were to be recalled. This was not a surprising finding, for it paralleled earlier demonstrations of proactive inhibition. The most interesting results of the study, however, were obtained from a third condition, where the subjects were again exposed to the lists containing two quadragrams; in this condition, however, shortly before the exposure of the second (or test) quadragram, a signal was given to indicate that the next item was the *only one* which was to be repeated during the test for recall. Within this third condition, then, the subjects essentially were instructed to *forget* the quadragram that had previously been shown to them and to concentrate on the item that followed. This instruction had a significant impact on recall, for the results showed less evidence of proactive inhibition than there was when both quadragrams were to be retained. The instruction to forget was not completely successful, however; that is, recall of the test item was somewhat poorer than was obtained in the lists that included only one quadragram. Figure 8 presents these results in graphic form.

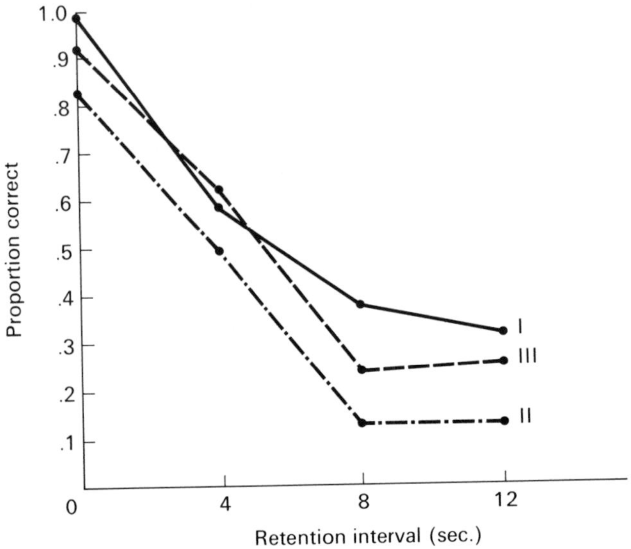

Figure 8

Proportion of correct recalls. Condition I: only one item presented and recalled. Condition II: two items presented, recall both. Condition III: two items presented, recall second only. (Adapted from Bjork, R. A., LaBerge, D., and LeGrand, R., 1968, with permission of the publisher, Psychonomic Journals, Inc.)

Bjork (1970) has theorized that intentional forgetting results from two related mechanisms. First, the instruction to forget may enable the subject to organize the items that he is to remember in a group that is functionally segregated from the items that can be forgotten. Once this grouping has been established, the memorizer can then concentrate his rehearsal efforts on those items that must be recalled (and ignore those items that can safely be forgotten). Bjork has obtained some support for this analysis in an interesting series of experiments. On the other hand, there appear to be some circumstances in which the "forget" instruction works effectively but does *not* seem to depend on the private repetitions and rehearsals that are so central to Bjork's theory. For example, in an experiment by Weiner and Reed (1969; Experiment II), the subjects were instructed at varying intervals to forget the consonant trigrams which they had been shown. If differential rehearsal was the main factor underlying their results, we would expect that the instruction to forget would be most effective—that is, it would minimize rehearsal—when it was given immediately after the presentation of the trigrams. The results of this study did not, however, support the rehearsal theory. That is, the instruction to forget was equally damaging to recall, whether it appeared early or late in the retention interval.

Although it is difficult to trace the specific processes involved here, the results of these experiments support the notion that memory effects can be partly controlled by the individual's motives and conscious intentions. The fact that the "forget" instructions are not, as a rule, fully effective is similar to the carryover phenomenon (see page 95). In brief, if people are instructed to forget about something which they have just learned, they may not be completely able to do so, although this instruction will have a significant impact on their subsequent memory and behavior.

The Zeigarnik effect

In studying the impact of motivation upon memory, some investigators have postulated that people who are actively working on a task develop "task tensions" that do not dissipate until the job at hand has been completed. If the task is not completed because of some interruption, this tension remains and the individual should, according to theory, continue to think about the incompleted task and should be motivated to complete it, if given an opportunity.

In a classic test of this hypothesis, Zeigarnik (1927) had a group of subjects attempt a series of twenty simple tasks, such as naming twelve cities beginning with the letter "K," punching holes in a sheet of paper, molding an animal from clay, etc. On half of these tasks the subjects were "accidentally" interrupted before completion, but they were permitted to finish the other half.

When the series was over, the subjects were asked to recall the names of as many tasks as they could. The results indicated that 80% of the subjects recalled more of the incompleted than of the completed tasks—a finding now known as the *Zeigarnik effect*. As indicated above, this phenomenon is generally attributed to the presence of undissipated tensions associated with the interrupted tasks. A further finding in support of this interpretation is that subjects often return spontaneously to the incomplete tasks when given an opportunity to do so.

At first glance, the Zeigarnik effect seems somewhat inconsistent with the concept of repression. If we assume that people prefer to complete the things they start, we might anticipate that they would repress their memory of tasks left incomplete. This argument gains still greater force if, for some reason, the subject interprets the experimenter's interruption as a sign that he has failed to complete a problem within its allotted time. How might this apparent conflict be resolved?

Some investigators (Rosenzweig, 1943; Lewis and Franklin, 1944) suggest that the issue may hinge upon whether the subjects in the experiment are task-oriented or ego-involved (i.e., concerned about their *personal* success in the experiment). As an inducement to task orientation, Rosenzweig's subjects were led to believe that their main job was to help the experimenter standardize his procedures; by contrast, in ego-involvement, the experimenter's instructions suggested that the subject's performance would reflect his intellectual ability. When the standard interruption procedures were applied under task orientation, Zeigarnik's original result was obtained; that is, subjects showed superior recall of the incompleted tasks. However, when the subjects were ego-involved, the interruptions were presumably interpreted as failures, and subjects showed superior recall of the completed, "successful" problems—presumably because they had repressed recall of the incompleted problems, the problems they had "failed." Unfortunately, this tidy pattern of results has often proved difficult to replicate in subsequent experiments (see Butterfield, 1964, for an extensive review of this literature).

Atkinson (1953) has reported an interesting study concerned with the Zeigarnik phenomenon. Among subjects who showed little "motivation to achieve" (and who were presumably concerned about avoiding failure), his results were similar to those obtained by Rosenzweig (see above). Because of their need to avoid failure, Atkinson's subjects recalled relatively *few* of the incompleted tasks when the experimental situation was ego-involving. On the other hand, among those who were *highly* motivated to achieve, the interrupted tasks were recalled *better* when the situation was presented in an ego-involving manner. Atkinson interpreted this as a sign that those who had a strong need for achievement were particularly focused on the incompleted tasks when they were led to believe that successful performance on the various "tests" might be considered a sign of personal accomplishment.

Summary

1. Ebbinghaus inaugurated the scientific study of memory. He invented the nonsense syllable and the method of savings, which are techniques still widely used in memory research.

2. Forgetting does not proceed at a uniform rate. Immediately after learning, we are likely to forget rather rapidly; as time goes on, however, we forget at a slower rate.

3. Some theorists have suggested that two different memory systems affect our capacity for (a) short-term and (b) long-term memory. According to this view, recently memorized materials will be quickly forgotten unless they are constantly practiced, but older, better-consolidated memories may be maintained without the benefit of further practice or rehearsal.

4. Once something has been memorized, the amount that we subsequently forget is importantly affected by the things we do and learn following the original memorization session. *Retroactive inhibition* is the phenomenon whereby the activities we engage in, subsequent to learning, tend to interfere with or inhibit the recall of material memorized earlier. *Proactive inhibition* refers to the fact that some of the things learned in the past may make it more difficult to remember the materials that we are currently attempting to memorize.

5. Material that is highly organized is easier to memorize than material that is lacking in structure. Moreover, in attempting to recall things, people will often *spontaneously* organize the material presented to them, even though they have not been instructed to do so. In memory, then, we do not simply receive and retain the information that has been presented; more typically, we restructure the material to be recalled in ways which reflect our previous experience.

6. In memorizing a body of material, we rarely attempt to recall all of the details in their original form. Instead, we schematize what is given to us and store it in *coded* terms. We then use this code (which is often based on *verbal labels*) to reconstruct the original information.

7. Clinical data suggest that people often find it difficult to remember anxiety-provoking incidents because of the automatic operation of the mechanism known as *repression.* Some laboratory studies support this conclusion. There is also evidence to suggest that forgetting may be hastened by conscious *suppression* of that which has been learned.

8. People often find it easier to remember tasks they have worked on but have not completed (due to interruption) than tasks they have finished. This phenomenon, known as the *Zeigarnik effect,* is generally attributed to "task tensions" that are assumed to remain active until the individual has completed the task at hand.

Supplementary reading

Adams, J. A. *Human memory.* New York: McGraw-Hill, 1967.
Mandler, G. Verbal learning. In T. M. Newcomb (Ed.) *New directions in psychology III.* New York: Holt, Rinehart & Winston, Inc.
Norman, D. A. *Memory and attention.* New York: Wiley, 1969.

3 Conceptual behavior

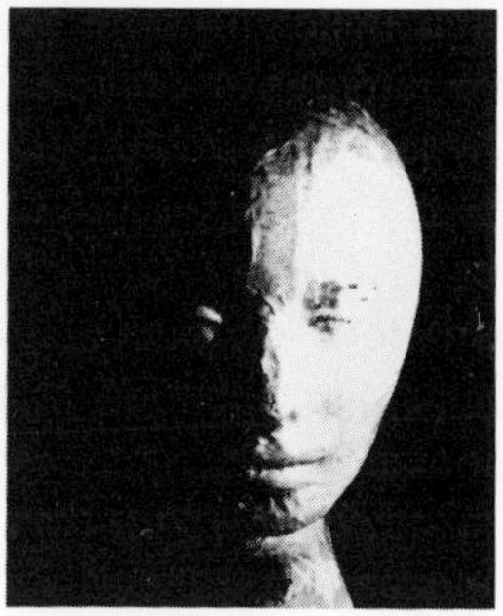

Consider the problem that a child faces as he learns to use the word "dog." For our present purposes, this word may be considered as a label or name that the child must learn to apply appropriately. The immediate problem that he faces is this: Which of the many things and objects around him may he properly label as dogs? Notice that we expect him to attach this *identical label* ("dog") to a variety of rather *individualized* animals (some short, some tall; some brown, some spotted; some long-haired, some short-haired). Moreover, once the child has completely mastered the word, we expect that he will be able to apply it correctly to new animals that may differ noticeably from those he has seen before. For example, if we show him an exotic breed with rather unique markings, we expect that our knowledgeable child will correctly identify it as a dog, even though he has never seen an animal quite like it before. This example illustrates some of the features that characterize *concept formation.*

Perhaps the most basic aspect of concept formation is that it involves a single response (for example, a single label or action) that is to be associated with a variety of distinguishable stimuli (for example, objects or events).

In a sense, our ability to classify the world into conceptual *categories* such as dogs, fires, friends, justice, etc., is a considerable advantage, for it often enables us to apply past reactions to the new things and events that we encounter every day. It may be argued, for example, that we never encounter exactly the same event twice. The fact that a variety of objects may properly be given the same label (dog) will thus enable us to make an appropriate adjustment (cautious friendliness, perhaps) in our first encounter with a particular dog. This type of transfer can best be understood if we relate it to our earlier comments concerning mediating responses and proprioceptive (self-produced) stimulation (see Chapter 1). In the present case (see Figure 1) we have assumed that, in the past, the overt response of cautious friendliness has been associated with animals that overtly or implicitly elicited the mediating label (r_m) "dog" and its resulting feedback pattern ($S_{m_{dog}}$). When a strange animal (dog_x) elicits the familiar label, the resulting feedback ($S_{m_{dog}}$) leads to the usual overt behavior, despite the absence of any previous contact with the dog in question. We should hasten to add that an overly broad conceptual system for categorization may often be maladaptive; failure to differentiate between a diseased dog and run-of-the-mill dogs may have unfortunate consequences.

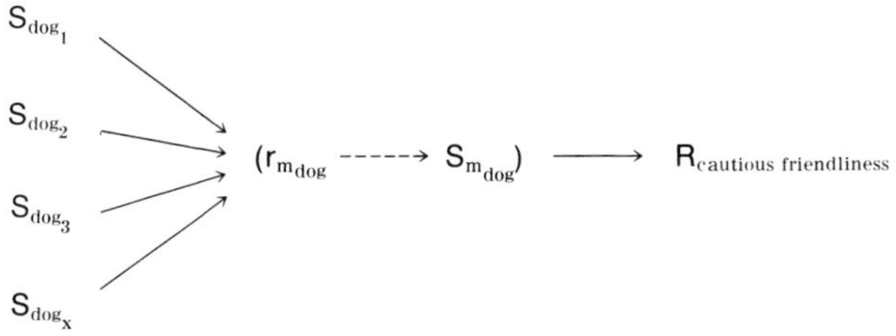

Figure 1

Response transfer due to presence of common mediating label (r_m) elicited by variety of dogs.

Laboratory studies of concept formation

Perhaps the earliest laboratory study of concept formation was conducted by Clark Hull (1920). In Hull's experiment, subjects were presented with twelve decks of cards, each card containing several Chinese symbols. The subject's task was to learn the nonsense syllable to be associated with each card. Since the same set of syllables served as responses as the subject progressed from one deck of cards to the next, each response (label) eventually came to be associated with several cards (stimuli). Moreover, although Hull's subjects were not aware of it in advance, each card contained a crucial element that was consistently associated with a particular response. For example, all cards that contained a check-like design were to be called "oo," regardless of the remaining content of the card and regardless of the deck in which the card appeared. Similarly, the presence of a "P-shaped" structure consistently signified that the card was an exemplar of the "na" concept. Hull observed that, with practice, his subjects were able to learn the various concepts in the deck; that is, *they could correctly label new instances of the concept when they were first presented.* One interesting and surprising observation was that some of Hull's subjects who had successfully learned to apply the concept labels were nevertheless unable to verbalize the cues to which they were responding. These subjects could apparently behave in accord with the labeling rules that the experiment required, and yet they were seemingly unaware of just how they went about doing this.

Following Hull's lead, experiments in concept formation have typically employed complex stimuli, each containing several irrelevant cues and some crucial (or relevant) cues that could be used to label properly each exemplar. The stimuli might thus be wooden blocks varying in shape (round versus square), in color (red, yellow, and green), and in size (large versus small). The subject's task would be to place each block in one of two categories, which might be arbitrarily labeled as DAKs and non-DAKs. The experimental session might proceed in the following manner: The different blocks (stimuli) would be presented one at a time, and the subject would attempt to label each one appropriately. Following each trial, the subject would be informed whether his response was "right" or "wrong." The experimenter might reinforce the subject when his responses conformed to some preselected rule—for instance, green stimuli = DAK; all others = non-DAK. In a system of categorization such as this, the exemplars included in the DAK class are termed *positive* instances, since they exemplify the essential attribute(s) of the concept; the non-DAKs are considered *negative* instances.

An early study by Smoke (1933) indicated that negative instances were relatively ineffective in conveying the concept that was to be mastered. Hovland (1952) suggested that this finding might derive from two rather different sources:

(a) In many situations, he noted, negative instances may contain less information (in a *logical* sense) than positive instances. For example, if I am informed on the one hand that a large red triangle is a non-DAK, but know nothing beyond this, I cannot infer the essential characteristics of the DAK category until I am given further information concerning the range of possible shapes and colors in the total array of stimuli. On the other hand, if I know (in addition) that *all* the stimuli are large triangles, and that they come in but three colors (red, yellow, and green), I can more readily deduce the characteristics of the DAK category: If the large red triangle is *not* a DAK, the DAKs must include either the yellows, or the greens, or both.

(b) Assuming that our situation is one in which positive and negative instances are equally informative (in a *logical* sense), it is nonetheless conceivable, Hovland noted, that the average subject finds it difficult (*psychologically*) to assimilate information from negative cases. Hovland and Weiss (1953) subsequently reported several experiments that pointed to this conclusion in a task that was constructed in such a fashion that the same amount of information was logically implicit in the positive and negative instances.

Subjects apparently find it difficult to infer the relevant attributes of a conceptual category when they are forced to proceed from negative instances. However, an experiment by Freibergs and Tulving (1961) showed that this difficulty can be largely overcome through extensive practice. Subjects in this study were presented with twenty successive conceptual tasks in which geometric forms served as stimuli. Each task could logically be solved if the subject was shown either four positive instances or four negative instances. One group of subjects was given four positive instances on each problem, and the other was given four negative instances. Both groups were to study the information and to describe the relevant feature of each concept as soon as they could. Figure 2 shows the median time that each group required for solution of the successive problems. Note, first, that subjects who were shown the negative instances failed to solve problems 1 through 4 within the $3\frac{1}{2}$ minutes that the experimenters had allotted; those who were shown the positive instances reached solution in about 2 minutes. Given additional practice, both groups were able to solve the problems more quickly, with the negative-instance group showing particularly rapid

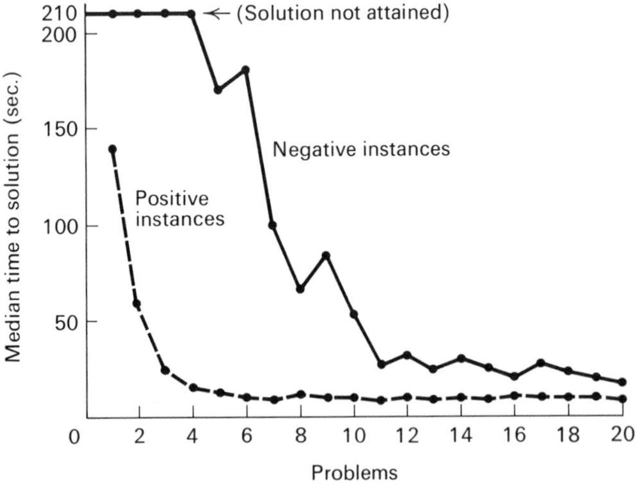

Figure 2

Median time to solution of 20 consecutive problems for subjects working with only positive or only negative instances. (Data from Freibergs and Tulving, 1961.)

improvement, until the difference between the two conditions was almost completely eliminated at the end of the experimental series. This result suggests that the difficulties most people exhibit when reasoning from negative instances may be due largely to their limited experience with problems of this type, rather than to some unchangeable aspect of the human cognitive apparatus.

Conjunctive concepts

Several different types of concepts, based on different labeling systems, have been studied by psychologists. The *conjunctive* concept is perhaps the most widely researched, and it is well exemplified both by the "dog" example and by Hull's experiment. In conjunctive concepts, the labeling rule is that all the exemplars of a given concept must have a *single common attribute* or *several common attributes.* The important thing to remember is that—in at least one way, and perhaps in several ways—all exemplars of the concept are alike. Thus, in learning the concept "dog," the learner's main problem is to recognize those features essential in determining the "dogginess" of a particular animal (number of legs, tail, fur, and so on) and to ignore irrelevant features (hair color, length of tail). In studying such a problem in the laboratory (see above), an experimenter might set up a conjunctive concept that included all *red* blocks (all other features, such as size or shape, would be irrelevant) or all *red squares,* regardless of size.

Disjunctive concepts

In a *disjunctive* concept, the constituent exemplars do not all share any single characteristic or group of characteristics. Instead, there may be several *alternative* characteristics—any one of which will justify the inclusion of a given exemplar within the concept. For example, consider the concept of a "strike" in baseball. A pitch may be classified as a strike if it exhibits any one of the following characteristics: (a) a pitch that crosses home plate between the batter's shoulders and his knees, (b) a pitch that results in a foul ball, or (c) a pitch on which the batter swings and misses. Psychologists have only recently begun to study the acquisition of disjunctive concepts. The little research that has been done suggests that concepts of this type are difficult to learn. Subjects often act as if they expect that the concept to be learned is organized conjunctively (rather than disjunctively), even though they are given no special reason to assume this. It is as if people generally expect that when different exemplars are given the same label, they must have some *common* underlying characteristic(s); thus, they find it difficult to accept the notion that two exemplars may both belong in the same category but for different reasons. For example, if we hear of two different cough medicines categorized as *effective remedies,* we ask what common features of these medicines explain their similarity rather than assume that the medicines may produce similar effects for different reasons.

Anisfeld (1966) has argued that the difficulty which experimental subjects often have in attempting to learn disjunctive concepts may result from the experimenter's failure to distinguish between the *underlying* attributes of a concept and the physical *manifestations* (cues) that permit proper classification of the exemplars. For example, if a disjunctive category includes all forms that are either square or red (or both), the various exemplars will bear no commonality beyond these particular manifestations (cues). While we can easily construct disjunctive concepts of this sort in the laboratory, Anisfeld contends that such concepts are difficult to master because they are unlike the real-world categories with which we are most familiar. In our everyday experience, while the external manifestations of a given concept may indeed be disjunctive, the exemplars normally share some common attribute(s) beyond these palpable cues. Thus, when considering the concept of a strike in baseball, we should note that the various types of strikes all stem from the batter's lapse in performance, and hence are alternative reflections of a common state of affairs. In brief, then, Anisfeld suggests that many real-world concepts which appear to be disjunctive *on the surface* are in fact basically conjunctive.

This analysis suggests that arbitrarily formed disjunctions (those that lack an underlying conjunctive base) may be difficult to learn because we lack prior experience with this type of conceptual category. Starting from this premise, Wells (1963) studied the possibility that disjunctive solutions might be more readily mastered if the subjects had previously been exposed to a series of other disjunctive problems. To test this notion, Wells presented a group of subjects with a series of disjunctive problems in which each problem contained two sets of stimuli (the "alphas" and the "nonalphas"); in each problem, the subjects' task was to find the difference between the two sets. The stimulus cards were composed of four geometric figures in a horizontal array. The "alpha" category was always based on a disjunctive rule, which might stipulate, for example, that "alphas" include all stimuli with a circle on the far left, or a square on the far right, or both.

Following two or four such *training problems,* all subjects were given an ambiguous *choice problem,* in which the stimuli presented as members of the "alpha" category were consistent both with a disjunctive rule and with a competing conjunctive rule. Subjects who had mastered prior disjunctive problems selected the disjunctive solution more often than those in a control condition, who had not mastered such problems. This result is reminiscent of Harlow's work on learning sets, in that the experimental subjects acquired increased facility in applying a general rule (disjunction), even though the particular cues that were relevant were changed from one problem to the next.

Relational concepts

In a *relational* concept, a single category can include quite diverse exemplars. Indeed, the exemplars of a relational concept are grouped together not because they share any particular feature (or features) but because each exemplar within the category shows some characteristic relationship. For example, in classifying two-digit numbers, we may employ a relationally defined rule that would include in a single category all cases in which the first digit was greater than the second. Such a category would include numbers such as 32, 51, 63, etc., because each of these exemplars exhibits the crucial (defining) relationship among its constituent digits. To date, there has been very little research on the acquisition or utilization of relational concepts. There is some evidence, however, that they may sometimes be no more difficult to learn than conjunctive concepts. This conclusion is suggested by a study in which subjects were presented with a group of geometric forms that could logically be described as representing exemplars from either (a) a disjunctive, (b) a conjunctive, or (c) a relational concept (Hunt and Hovland, 1960). As a means of determining which one of these "competing" conceptual rules had been detected in this situation where all three were possible, a subsequent series of test trials was presented; the subjects' task was to indicate *additional* stimuli that seemed to belong with the exemplars they had previously been shown. While relatively few subjects responded in terms of the disjunctive rule, conjunctive and relational solutions were used with about equal frequency. This suggests that, from the subject's viewpoint, relational rules may sometimes be logically indistinguishable from simple conjunctions. In Hovland and Hunt's experiment, for example, one relational category included all stimuli with the same number of figures in the upper and lower sections. While this rule requires that the subject attend to two primitive aspects of each exemplar, the relational rule based on "same number" may seem as straightforward and obvious to the average adult as a simple conjunctive concept such as "all red blocks."

The single-unit S-R approach to concept identification

Most research on concept formation has been concerned with the development of conjunctive concepts. Some of the early theorizing in this area was based on a simple extrapolation of the principles that had proven helpful in accounting for discrimination learning in experiments with rats and other subhuman species. The essential idea was this: as the subject gained more and more experience with the exemplars of a given concept, the cue (or cues) that characterized all members of the conceptual category would be strengthened in its capacity to evoke the response (usually verbal) which was to be associated with that concept. Thus, if all red stimuli (for instance) were members of the category VEC, there would be a continuous growth in the associative bond between "redness" and the desired response (VEC), resulting from the reinforcement ("right") that followed each correct VEC response. Note that this account makes no assumptions about such unobservable processes as *thinking* or *hypothesis-testing;* the learner is pictured as playing a rather passive role, and the associative link between external cues and overt responses is seen as developing rather automatically as a consequence of reinforcement.

Verbal concepts

Despite the elegant simplicity of this S-R formulation, it now appears inadequate and has been discarded by most active investigators in the field. There are several deficiencies in the simple S-R approach. For one thing, it fails to account for the fact that human subjects can easily master concept-formation tasks in which the exemplars of a given category are *totally dissimilar* from one another with respect to their physical attributes. For example, if the different stimuli to be categorized were *words,* the average adult could nevertheless master a categorization system even if the exemplars within a given class neither sounded nor looked alike. The words *milk, wine,* and *orange juice,* for example, might be classed together as "things to drink." There has, indeed, been a reasonably well-developed tradition of concept-formation research with verbal exemplars, and the results of this research have, in the main, closely paralleled those obtained in studies with *nonverbal* exemplars. Since it is clear that the mastery of a verbal concept cannot be based on a simple associative response to some unchanging physical property of the exemplars, it seems only reasonable to assume the existence of one or more mediating events (such as thoughts, mediating responses, or hypotheses) that occur *within* the subject and guide his overt response in learning *any* concept, whether the exemplars are verbal or not.

Delayed informative feedback

Another line of evidence pointing to the inadequacy of the simple S-R approach is derived from research on delayed informative feedback. If concept identification followed the pattern obtained in animal-learning experiments and in studies of human conditioning, we might anticipate that delayed feedback ("right" or "wrong") would interfere with concept identification in the same way that delayed reinforcement often impairs learning. Bourne and Bunderson (1963), however, found no systematic effect associated with delays up to eight seconds; this suggests that the linkage between exemplars and responses may not be an automatic consequence of feedback (reinforcement). On the other hand, these investigators did find a significant improvement in performance as they increased the interval between the experimenter's feedback and the presentation of the *next* exemplar. While this result may be attributable to some continuing consolidation process that is interrupted when the next stimulus is presented shortly after feedback, it seems more plausible to assume that the post-feedback interval provides an opportunity for the subject to revise his thinking (or hypotheses) on the basis of the information he has previously received. When the interval is short, he may have insufficient time to evaluate the evidence that has accumulated, and his performance may suffer.

Conceptual shifts

The study of conceptual shifts provides a final line of evidence that conflicts with the implications of a simple S-R approach. A subject who has been reinforced for placing red blocks in one category and green blocks in another may be shifted, without warning, to a feedback schedule that reinforces some *different* pattern of response. If concept acquisition followed a simple associative pattern, we might anticipate that such shifts would be particularly difficult when the original categorization scheme had been reinforced over a lengthy series of trials, for this would presumably have made the initially-acquired response pattern particularly resistant to extinction. While the results of these studies do not fall into *any* neat pattern, it is nevertheless clear that they deviate markedly from the simple trend that is sketched above. That is, a subject who has been reinforced for following one conceptual rule during a lengthy series of trials may, nevertheless, be quite capable of shifting his performance pattern quickly once a new conceptual rule is reinforced. Indeed, there is substantial evidence that in many situations, by increasing the subject's reinforced experience (number of trials) with one conceptual rule, we may make it *simpler* for him to discard this rule in favor of a rather different scheme. This type of facilitation seems to occur most commonly in adults of average or above-average intelligence (Wolff, 1967), although the effect may vary with the particular conceptual tasks that are involved.

The study of conceptual shifts has yielded still another finding that conflicts with a strict S-R model of concept formation. Consider a situation in which the initial conceptual rule has been the following: all green objects = DAK; all red objects = VEC. After a subject masters this concept, we may attempt to teach him a new conceptual rule. There are two basic types of conceptual changes. In one, termed a *reversal* (or *intradimensional*) *shift*, we would simply reverse the labeling scheme without telling our subjects; that is, while color would still be the dimension relevant to the conceptual rule, all green stimuli would now equal VEC (rather than DAK), and all red stimuli would equal DAK (not VEC). In a *nonreversal* (or *extradimensional*) *shift*, a dimension previously *irrelevant* would become *relevant*. For example, after learning to respond to color, subjects might now be required to learn a shape concept (square = DAK, round = VEC).

Normal adults find reversal shifts much simpler than nonreversal shifts (Kendler and D'Amato, 1955). This may seem surprising, since, as its name implies, a reversal shift requires a *complete change* in associations (for example; green stimuli now equals VEC, not DAK); in a nonreversal shift, by contrast, some of the stimuli maintain their original labels.

In an early attempt to defend the classic S-R position, Buss (1953) contended that the difficulties encountered in nonreversal shifts were probably due to partial reinforcement effects, which have long been known to retard the extinction of previously-learned behavior patterns. For example, following a nonreversal shift, a subject who had originally been reinforced for labeling shaded squares as DAKs (because of their *shading*) might *continue* to be reinforced for this same response if *shape* now became the relevant cue—that is, if DAKs now equaled all *squares* rather than all shaded objects. Figure 3 shows that, following this type of nonreversal shift, the responses associated with fully *50%* of the stimuli remain unchanged (thus, the shaded square continues to be a DAK, and the unfilled circle remains a VEC). Buss reasoned that the originally-learned response rule receives intermittent reinforcement on trials like these, thus interfering with the extinction of the "old" conceptual scheme and retarding mastery of the new task. In a reversal shift, on the other hand, the first-learned concept is never reinforced, for *all* of the initially-learned responses must be changed; as a consequence, Buss theorized, the solution to the first task is soon extinguished, and the reversal shift is learned relatively quickly.

This explanation implies that the two types of shifts might be equally difficult if the trials providing partial reinforcement could somehow be eliminated. One way of accomplishing this is to introduce a new set of stimuli for the second (or shift) problem. With new stimuli, the initially relevant cue (or cues) cannot re-evoke the particular S-R associations that were developed in the first task, and hence partial reinforcement is impossible—regardless of the outcome on any given trial. For example,

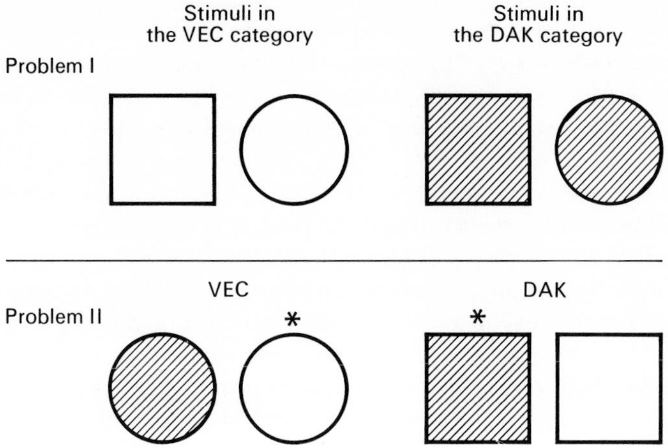

*The responses to these stimuli are unchanged from Problem I to Problem II; thus they provide partial reinforcement for the first-learned concept.

Figure 3

Partial reinforcement of an earlier solution following a nonreversal shift.

if the subject had originally learned to respond to shading (shaded figures = DAK; unshaded = VEC), we might switch him to a new set of stimuli, each of which was either red or green; we could then teach him to categorize by *shape* (a nonreversal shift) without providing partial reinforcement for the initially-learned concept. Similarly, an intradimensional shift could be applied by requiring the subject to continue responding in terms of *color*, with the two categories now being red stimuli versus green stimuli (rather than shaded versus unshaded).

Harrow and Friedman (1958) performed an experiment based on this general scheme and found that, despite the elimination of partial reinforcement, the reversal shift was still simpler than the nonreversal shift.

Multi-stage S-R theories

Results like those presented above have led most investigators to discard the classical, single-stage S-R model of concept formation, in which the external stimulus is assumed to exercise direct associative control over the subject's overt response. In its place, a variety of multi-stage models have been proposed. In these accounts, the externally presented stimulus is assumed to evoke one or more internal responses; these responses, in turn, have sensory consequences, which may either evoke additional internal reactions (and *their* sensory consequences) or trigger the overt response that is ultimately recorded by the experimenter.

Perhaps the most influential of these multi-unit S-R theories has been that proposed by Kendler and Kendler (1962). In this account, the mediating responses (r_m) that link the external stimulus to a subject's overt response are assumed to be largely verbal in nature. For example, having discovered color to be the relevant cue in a given task, a subject may respond to a particular exemplar with an implicit verbal label ("green"); the feedback from this response (s_m) is then assumed to guide the observed overt performance ("DAK"). In contrast to this verbal-mediation hypothesis, Zeaman and House (1963) have emphasized the role of *attentional* factors in concept identification. According to these theorists, the mediating activity that guides overt performance consists not of verbal responses but rather of dimensional observing responses, in which the subject attends closely to one or another of the stimulus dimensions (for example, shape or color) represented in the various exemplars.

In essence, both of these models attribute the difficulty of extradimensional (nonreversal) shifts to the fact that the "new" concept requires the subject to respond implicitly to (or attend to) a stimulus dimension that was previously irrelevant. In the learning of an intradimensional shift, on the other hand, the initially relevant dimension retains its importance, and the subject's only problem is to relearn the proper usage of the overt response alternatives; thus, while the color cue may still be relevant, the subject must learn that the stimuli previously called DAKs are now to be labeled as VECs (and vice versa).

When examined closely, the differences between a verbal-mediation theory and an attentional theory often seem to hinge upon the theorists' preferred terminology. While one investigator may emphasize the fundamental importance of the verbal mediational component, another may contend that these verbal mediators are important mainly because they accompany (or direct) the subject's orienting responses. In brief, it is often difficult to arrange a laboratory situation in which these two activities (verbal mediation and orientation of attention) function *distinctively* rather than in an interrelated fashion. Kendler, Kendler, and Saunders (1967), however, have reported an ingenious experiment that demonstrated the importance of verbal mediation in a setting where attentional factors seemed to play a minimal role. In this study, the subjects were presented with a series of words drawn from two distinct semantic categories; some words were associated with *furniture*, and others were associated with *clothing*. The subjects' task was to categorize these words into two groups that did not always follow the expected line of separation based on everyday usage. After learning to respond properly to each word, the subjects were required to learn an intradimensional shift, in which the initial sorting pattern was reversed. When the original sorting called for the "natural" categorization (furniture words in one group, clothing words in the other), the new concept was learned relatively quickly, presumably because the relevant verbal labels (*furniture* versus *clothing*) served as mediators. When the words initially grouped together were *unrelated* (and hence did *not* evoke a common mediating response), the reversal shift proved more difficult.

Concept shifts in animals and children

In contrast to the results typically obtained with normal adults, reversal shifts are more difficult for lower animals than nonreversal shifts (Brookshire, Warren, and Ball, 1961). This difference between the performance of human adults and that of animals is thought to reflect differences in their approach to conceptual tasks. According to the verbal-mediation theory, humans are strongly influenced by the cues that they produce as they symbolically respond to the critical (or relevant) cue in each exemplar. Since animals have less symbolic facility than humans, their overt responses are presumed to be more directly controlled by external stimuli. As a result, because they are *not* aided by an unchanging implicit response (the way the human adult is), they find the reversal shift particularly difficult, since they must extinguish an old habit completely and replace it with a new one.

The reasoning presented above suggests that children—who are less verbally facile than adults—should respond to shift problems more in the manner of the lower animals; reversal shifts should be more difficult for them than nonreversals (in contrast to the typical finding with adults). While the evidence here is not completely consistent (Wolff, 1967), this conclusion has nevertheless received substantial support (Kendler and Kendler, 1962). Moreover, it has also been demonstrated (Kendler, 1964) that the child's ability to master reversal shifts may be significantly enhanced if he is given specific training in verbally describing the relevant aspects of the stimuli that constitute his task. In one study, children were to choose between two stimuli that varied in shape (square versus round) and color (black versus white). If they chose the correct stimulus, they were reinforced with a marble. Some children were given verbalization training by having them precede each of their choices with the sentence "The black is the winner and the white is the loser" (assuming that color was the relevant dimension). Other children were presented with a similar concept-formation task but were given no special instructions about verbalizing the cues to which they were responding. After all the children had mastered this initial task, they were presented with a second task, with no ostensible break in the procedure. The children's performance in this second task indicated that the verbalization training had facilitated the ease with which a reversal shift could be mastered. While this study was concerned with the overt verbalizations of children, the adult's striking success in solving reversal shift problems is presumably related to the use of similar verbal mechanisms at a covert level.

Despite the successes sketched above, the verbal-mediation approach does not fully account for the available data on conceptual shifts. Two deficiencies stand out. First, although one might assume that deaf children would be less developed verbally than their age mates, there is no evidence that deafness affects their performance on conceptual shift problems (Rosenstein, 1960; Russell, 1964). Similarly, if the relative simplicity of the reversal shift is due to verbal mediation, we might anticipate that retardates would find this task particularly difficult (relative to nonreversal shifts) because of their linguistic deficiencies. However, a careful review of this literature (Wolff, 1967) fails to support the prediction. On the other hand, it is conceivable that the verbal skills called for in these tasks may be minimal (the verbal mediators need not be comprehensible to others, for example) and thus may be within the capacity of even these handicapped subjects.

Hypothesis-testing in concept identification

In contrast to the various S-R formulations presented above, some investigators (Bower and Trabasso, 1963; Levine, 1966) have suggested that concept identification might profitably be regarded as a situation in which the subject actively tests a series of *hypotheses*. For these theorists, each overt response is presumably guided by some hypothesis, such as "all the *tall* ones are VECs." The experimenter's subsequent feedback ("right" or "wrong") determines whether the hypothesis is retained for the next trial or is rejected in favor of a new hypothesis.

Continuity versus discontinuity

S-R approaches to concept identification are built on the assumption that concept learning (like other forms of learning) reflects a continuous, incremental process; it is assumed, for example, that the learner *gradually* comes to respond to color as the relevant cue in a given problem. Hypothesis-testing models, on the other hand, typically characterize concept identification as a *discontinuous* process in which the subject actively tests a series of discrete hypotheses in attempting to discover the correct categorization rule; at any given time in the process, the subject *learns only about the correctness or incorrectness of the particular hypothesis* (or hypotheses) *he is testing*.

The *discontinuity* approach suggests that if, say, color were the relevant dimension in a concept-formation task, this fact would have virtually no impact upon the learner during trials in which he was "trying out" other hypotheses (shape, for example). According to the continuity hypothesis, however, even if the learner was focusing his attention on the wrong hypothesis, he would be gradually building up a tendency to respond in accordance with the crucial dimension. Thus, according to the continuity theory, if our subject labels a *round green* block as a DAK (because he thinks shape is crucial) and is told that he is "right," this sequence of events should simultaneously strengthen his tendency to apply the DAK label (a) to subsequent round blocks and (b) to subsequent green blocks. If color is in fact the correct basis for labeling, our subject will eventually come to ignore the shape of the blocks in making his responses, since this cue would not lead to consistent success. As noted above, however, the continuity theory suggests that *throughout* the series of learning trials our subject will have *gradually* and *automatically* built up the association between the green stimuli and the DAK response, even though he may have been focusing on other, irrelevant dimensions during the initial steps of learning.

Although there is not complete agreement on the issue, recent evidence suggests that the discontinuity model may be more appropriate than the continuity model as a description of the concept-formation process in college students. On the other hand, several experiments suggest that the continuity approach may present a more faithful account of concept formation in animals and in children of average intelligence. What is the evidence for these assertions? Some investigators have studied the behavior of their subjects *before* they had fully mastered the concepts they were to learn. For example, many studies assume that a subject has completely learned a concept if he succeeds in responding correctly to ten successive stimuli. If concept learning is a continuous process, we should find that our subject's performance shows a steady improvement in the trials prior to his errorless run, as the crucial cue becomes more and more potent in guiding his response. On the other hand, if concept learning is discontinuous, we would expect that the subjects would perform at a *chance* level on trials preceding their discovery of the correct solution, because they would presumably be testing out incorrect hypotheses. However, when the correct hypothesis occurs to the learner, he should, according to the discontinuity view, shift *abruptly* from chance performance to his final, errorless level of performance. The hypothetical performance curves predicted by the two theories are shown in Figure 4, which illustrates expected performance trends for the trials preceding complete mastery of the task.

In a study of concept attainment in elementary and junior high school children, Osler and Fivel (1961a) examined the ten trials preceding each child's final errorless run and then classified their subjects as gradual or sudden learners, depending upon the number of correct responses achieved in this pre-solution series. Their results indicated that *bright* children (with IQs above 110) were most likely to be sudden learners, in that they showed relatively poor performance in the trials just preceding

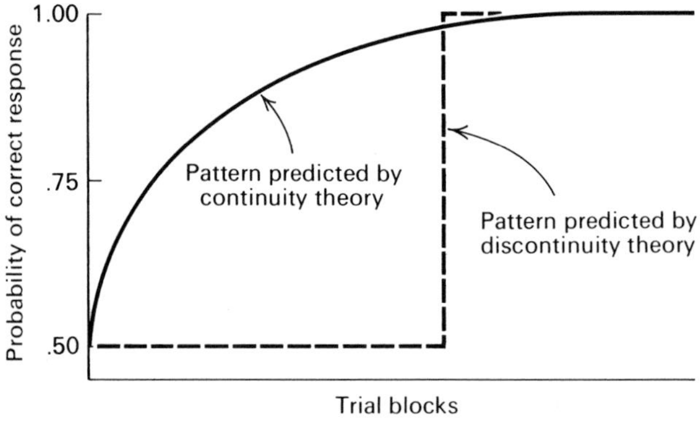

Figure 4

Performance curves in concept-formation task as predicted by continuity and discontinuity theories.

solution, while the *average* youngsters were less likely to learn suddenly. These data suggest that the bright youngster may solve concept-formation tasks by employing successive hypotheses, as outlined in the discontinuity theory; the average child, on the other hand, may rely on simple associative learning, as stressed by the continuity approach.

A subsequent study by Osler and Trautman (1961b) provides additional support for this conclusion. In this experiment, some children were presented with a rather simple concept-formation task in which they were to choose between two cards displaying different numbers of circles. One card of each pair contained two black circles positioned at random; the other card contained either one, three, four, or five circles. The children could earn marbles, which could later be exchanged for a prize, by consistently choosing the card with the two circles. A second group of children was presented with a similar but somewhat more complex task in which they were to choose between two cards with pictures (rather than circles). Each picture contained between one and five common objects of various sizes and colors. Once again, one card in each pair depicted the "two" concept (included two objects), and the children were reinforced for choosing this card—whether it contained two red cars, two walking boys, or any other group of two objects. Notice that in the simple task used with the first group, the stimulus cards differed from one another in only a few ways. The main differences between the stimuli involved the number of circles (the crucial cue) and the specific positioning of the circles. In the complex task, on the other hand, the stimulus cards differed in the number of objects depicted, in the specific objects shown, in color, in size, in the positioning of stimuli on the card, and in several other ways. If, as suggested above, a bright child generally approaches concept-formation tasks in the manner assumed by the discontinuity approach, he would successively try out each of the available possibilities, and we would expect him to learn the simple task rather quickly, since there would be relatively few incorrect alternatives for him to eliminate before he recognized that the number of circles on each card was crucial. In contrast, it should take a bright child considerably longer to learn the complex task, since he might try many reasonable alternatives before finding the correct solution. Osler and Trautman's study confirmed these hypotheses. The data clearly showed that the bright children solved the simple task in fewer trials than were required to solve the complex task.

The children of average intelligence learned the simple concepts in about the same time that it took them to learn the complex concepts. This result is consistent with the view that average children learn less by testing hypotheses than by steadily developing stimulus-response associations. For these children, then, regardless of the number of cues in the stimuli, there seemed to be a continuous development of association between the "twoness" concept and the subject's choice of response.

As you might expect from the results obtained with bright children, the available evidence suggests that college students typically solve concept-attainment tasks by the discontinuity approach. For example, Bower and Trabasso (1963) have examined the performance of students in a concept-formation task just prior to the achievement of solution. Their results clearly indicate that these subjects learn quite *suddenly* (presumably when they discover the correct hypothesis), because the data suggest that in the trials preceding solution, the subjects have been performing at about a chance level of performance and are right about as often as they would be through blind guessing. It seems reasonable to infer that they have been trying out one or more of the incorrect hypotheses before switching to the correct one.

The continuity-discontinuity controversy has also been studied through concept-shift experiments. Bower and Trabasso (1963) presented their subjects with reversal or nonreversal shifts *before* the initially reinforced pattern had been mastered. During his first 10 trials, for example, a subject might be given feedback supporting the following rule: Cue 1 → Response 1, Cue 2 → Response 2; on trial 11, the reinforced pattern was surreptitiously changed to: Cue 1 → Response 2, Cue 2 → Response 1. The continuity approach suggests that such shifts should retard the subject's mastery of the second task, for in theory, the subject must (a) extinguish the associative bonds that were incrementally developed during the initial phase of the experiment and (b) begin to learn the new, "reversed" conceptual rule. Bower and Trabasso's results failed to support this expectation, for subjects who had been shifted mastered the second conceptual task just as quickly as a control group that had never been shifted. These results imply that concept identification is an *all-or-none process*; it does not seem to depend on the gradual growth of associative bonds based on repeated consistent feedback, for changes in the reinforcement pattern do not seem to impede performance.

Redundant cues

The preceding discussion has focused on concept-formation tasks involving only one relevant cue (color, for instance). More recently, several investigators have explored problems that can be solved in more than one way. It is a simple matter, for example, to arrange the stimuli in a two-category problem so that the exemplars of the VEC category are all *red squares*, and the DAKs are *green circles*. In this setting, a subject could learn to perform perfectly by attending to either the color or the shape of the various stimuli. Since either of these relevant attributes would be sufficient to guide an errorless performance, psychologists speak of them as being relevant and *redundant*.

Trabasso and Bower (1968) have explored a variety of factors that affect performance in conceptual tasks involving redundant relevant cues. Their results indicate that most subjects learn to base their responses on only one cue and are typically quite unaware that the other relevant cue has any special significance. Moreover, subjects who can verbally identify only one of the relevant cues are typically unable to perform effectively when faced with *test trials* that require utilization of the "unchosen" cue. This last finding strongly favors a hypothesis-testing theory of concept formation, since many subjects appear to be unaffected by perfectly valid and perceptible cues that—while having been repeatedly reinforced—are extraneous to the hypothesis that has been tested and found to be "correct." By contrast, a strict continuity approach would lead to the expectation that through repeated reinforcement, the subject will eventually learn to base his response on *any* relevant cue that can be easily perceived, whether or not it is included in his verbal hypothesis.

In the design of a conceptual experiment, certain stimulus attributes may be *partially redundant*, because they usually (but not invariably) appear together. For example, square figures may typically be presented on a stippled background, while round ones are commonly shown against a cross-hatched background (see Figure 5). Suppose that a group of subjects was first reinforced for categorizing such stimuli on the basis of shape and that, when this task had been mastered, the reinforcement rule was then switched without any warning so that the background pattern was now the only relevant cue. If concept formation was a continuous incremental process, we would expect these subjects to adapt relatively easily to the new performance rule, provided that the figures on the stippled background were to be given the same label that was previously given to the squares. Thus, Figure 5 shows that in applying a square-round discrimination on Problem I (square = VEC; round = DAK), our subjects have been simultaneously (and inadvertently) reinforced, on 75% of the figures, for discriminating on the basis of background. This should, according to continuity

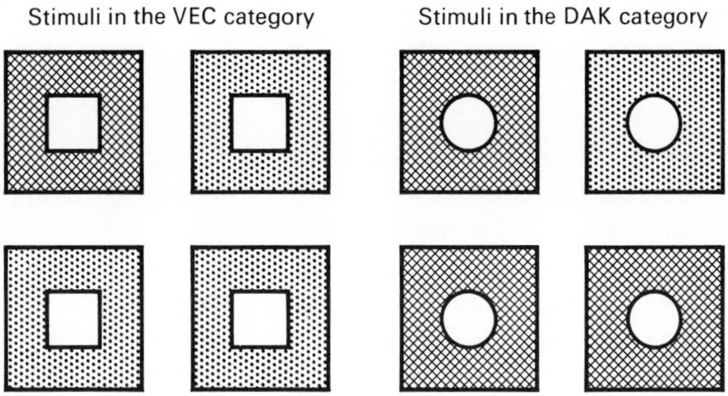

Figure 5

Stimuli for experimental test of continuity versus discontinuity. Note that most square stimuli have a stippled background, while the round ones have a cross-hatched background.

theory, facilitate subsequent conceptual learning according to the following principle: stippled background = VEC; cross-hatch = DAK.

Gormezano and Grant (1958) performed an experiment based on this reasoning (the details were somewhat different from those described above). Contrary to the continuity hypothesis, their results showed that the subjects' speed in mastering a second conceptual task was *unaffected* by the extent to which this new problem parallelled the categorization system they had previously learned. Subjects apparently concentrated on one hypothesis at a time; while learning one conceptual rule (square versus round, in the above example), they failed to note that the utilization of other cues (background pattern) would lead to near-perfect performance. At any rate, their speed in mastering a second concept did not appear to depend on the amount of "overlap" (or redundancy) between this new concept and the previously learned categorization.

In contrast to these results obtained with college students, Hall (1966) reports that animal experiments typically show the pattern predicted by continuity theory. That is, the solution of a second problem may be *facilitated* if it is intermittently reinforced while an initial categorization scheme is being mastered. This difference between the results obtained in parallel studies of humans and animals is reminiscent of the reversal-nonreversal shift literature (see above). In both sets of experiments, lower animals seem to behave more in accordance with a simple S-R model, based on direct associative connections between external stimuli and overt responses; in contrast, symbolic processes seem more important in determining the performance of the human adult.

This conclusion may be too simple, however. Kamin (1966) has shown that under appropriate conditions, laboratory rats may be *unresponsive* to a redundant cue that is easily perceivable. Moreover, an experiment by Guy, van Fleet, and Bourne (1966) suggests that stimulus redundancy may sometimes have an impact on *human* concept identification if the redundant cue is properly introduced into the experimental setting. In the study by Guy, et. al., the stimulus characteristics which were later to be crucial (stippled versus cross-hatched background) were added to the problem *after* the initial concept had been completely mastered. The experiment thus had three parts. (1) The subjects first learned a conceptual problem involving visual stimuli that were presented against a blank white background. (2) After the subjects reached a criterion of 10 errorless trials in a row, a new stimulus dimension was introduced—stippled versus cross-hatched background; however, the experimenter continued to reinforce the initial categorization rule. (3) In the final part of the experiment, the reinforcement rule was changed so that the *background* of the various stimulus cards then served as the only relevant cue. The results indicated that this second problem was solved most quickly when the stimuli presented in phase (2) showed substantial overlap (as in Figure 5) between the *initially* relevant stimulus dimension and the background pattern, which was *later* to serve as the sole relevant cue. These results are consistent, of course, with the continuity hypothesis, although it is interesting to note that even in this study, there was clear evidence that the second (or shift) problem had been mastered suddenly, rather than incrementally; hence, the shift problem seemed to reflect a hypothesis-testing process. It seems plausible to conclude that the availability of the "background" hypothesis was probably affected by its congruence with the reinforcement received in phase (2) of the experiment.

Novelty and redundancy

There is a striking contrast between Gormezano and Grant's "discontinuity" results (where the overlap between redundant attributes was present from the start) and the "continuity" pattern obtained by Guy et. al. (where the redundancy involved a *new* stimulus dimension which was introduced only after the subjects had mastered the first concept). A comparison of the two studies suggests that the subject's response to redundant attributes may depend on the novelty of the cue which is to be relevant. Thus, if a novel, attention-getting cue such as variation in background is suddenly introduced after successful solution of the initial conceptual task, the subject may be sensitive to the relationship between this new cue and the feedback (reinforcement) provided by the experimenter. In any event, once the previously acquired categorization scheme proves to be unworkable, a redundant cue that has recently been introduced into the problem will sometimes prompt an early testing of the newly introduced attribute.

Trabasso and Bower reported some related findings in an experiment where the subjects were first required to solve a conceptual task involving *one* relevant cue, and were then given a series of trials in which a previously irrelevant attribute was made relevant and redundant with respect to the first cue. For example, some subjects first learned to categorize geometric figures solely on the basis of shape (circles versus triangles). When this task had been mastered, a formerly irrelevant attribute was surreptitiously made relevant and redundant; thus—although the subjects were not informed of the change—every one of the "circle" stimuli now included a heavy black dot above it, while the triangles always had a dot below them. The original response rule (circles = "alpha"; triangles = "beta") was then reinforced for an additional series of 32 trials; during this period, of course, the shape of the figures and the location of the dots were both *relevant* and *redundant*, since either cue would enable the subject to respond appropriately. After a sequence of this sort, subjects showed no evidence that they had "noticed" the relevance of the dot location (the second relevant attribute). They were unable to respond correctly, for instance, when the stimulus to be classified was neither a circle nor a triangle, but a *square* with a dot below it. This phenomenon was quite striking, in that not one out of 86 subjects showed any sign that he had learned the significance of the "second" relevant attribute. Trabasso and Bower have referred to this phenomenon as "blocking." Similar results have been reported by Kamin (1966) in a series of experiments with rats. These results suggest that so long as some previously noticed cue continues to "work" (lead to reinforcement), the subject may simply focus on this cue and fail to note the significance of other cues that were initially *irrelevant*, but have more recently become *relevant*.

The "blocking" phenomenon can sometimes be overcome, however, if the newly relevant cue is *added* to the stimulus array after the initial learning series, rather than being a familiar cue that had originally been *irrelevant*. These results provide additional evidence that a second relevant cue is more likely to be noticed (and learned) if it has novelty value. Related findings have been reported in animal studies by Mackintosh (1965) and Terrace (1963).

Mackintosh compared two techniques for introducing a redundant brightness cue (black versus white) into a discrimination task in which his animals had initially learned to discriminate between horizontal and vertical rectangles. For some animals, the brightness cue was introduced *gradually*; after a learning series that involved rectangles of uniform grayness, the animals were exposed first to rectangles that differed only moderately in brightness-value and then to rectangles consisting of more extreme brightness contrasts. For other animals, the brightness variable was introduced *abruptly*; that is, after the initial learning series with gray rectangles, the animal was suddenly faced with rectangles that were either black or white. The results of a subsequent test series, involving *square* stimuli (rather than rectangles), indicated that the brightness cue was learned most effectively when it was introduced abruptly rather than gradually. The sudden introduction of black versus white stimuli presumably led to a heightened level of attention and learning. Terrace (1963) showed that a related phenomenon could be produced if an originally relevant color cue (red versus green) was gradually *faded out* thus reducing the salience of color and forcing the animals to rely more and more on the redundant cue that had been added to the problem after the initial mastery of the color discrimination. The fading procedure yielded superior performance as compared with an abrupt transition, when the animals were presented with test stimuli from which the originally relevant color cue had been removed.

Confirmation and disconfirmation of hypotheses

In most hypothesis-testing theories it is assumed that a given hypothesis will be maintained without change so long as it leads to correct overt responding. When the response is *not* reinforced, the underlying hypothesis is presumably discarded and another hypothesis is selected—one based on perceptual salience (Trabasso and Bower, 1968), sheer chance, or some combination of the two. Levine (1966) has developed a procedure which permits the experimenter to infer the hypothesis guiding the subject's response, and his data strongly support the "no-change-if-no-error" postulate. In Levine's experiment, subjects were presented with a series of stimulus cards, each of which contained two letters: an "X" and a "T." The various cards differed, however, in the *position* of these letters (left versus right side of the card), their *size* (large versus small), and their *color* (black versus white). On each card, the subject was to identify the letter that he thought was "correct." In contrast to the usual concept-identification task, however, the experimenter provided feedback only on certain selected trials. By checking the subject's response to the succeeding "no-outcome" trials, Levine could infer the underlying hypotheses then being employed. For example, if the subject was reinforced ("right") for choosing a large black "X" that was located on the left of the card (rather than the small white "T" that was on the right), he might subsequently choose letters that were either (a) large, (b) black, (c) "X's," or (d) on the left, until he received further feedback that conflicted with his chosen hypothesis. By examining the choices that followed a particular feedback trial, Levine was able to infer the specific hypothesis then being tested. On over 90% of the no-outcome trials, his subjects responded in a systematic and interpretable pattern; within a given series of no-outcome trials, for example, a certain subject might consistently choose the *black* stimulus. The pattern of responses that followed each of the feedback trials also permitted a check on whether or not the subject had changed from the hypothesis he had previously been testing. Levine found that hypotheses were changed only about 5% of the time following a reinforcement ("right"). "Wrong" responses, however, led to a change of hypothesis 98% of the time. These results provide strong support for the assumption of "no-change-if-no-error," although other investigators have reported experiments in which this assumption proved somewhat less tenable (Suppes and Schlag-Rey, 1965).

While most theories of hypothesis-testing agree on the notion that positive feedback ("right") leads to a continued use of the hypothesis previously under consideration, there are conflicting views of what happens when the feedback is negative ("wrong"). One important difference among the theorists concerns the amount of intelligence that each theorist implicitly attributes to the concept learner. In Restle's model, for example (1962), the learner is presumed to be of rather limited intelligence: it is assumed that he selects hypotheses *randomly* from a pool of possibilities suggested by the experimental situation. If a particular hypothesis proves to be wrong, it is returned to this pool of "possibilities" and may indeed be re-sampled (that is, selected for testing once again) *on the next trial*. This would imply that even though a subject might reject a hypothesis he had been following if he were told it was incorrect, he might—through sheer chance—elect to test that very same notion on the succeeding trial. A subject who followed such a pattern would obviously be rather stupid, and, fortunately, there are data to suggest that humans rarely follow such a course. Levine, for example (1966), showed that the re-selection of a hypothesis which has just been disconfirmed occurs quite rarely—far less often than Restle's model would predict.

Bower and Trabasso (1963) assume that the concept learner has somewhat more intelligence (but not much more). They suggest that after receiving negative feedback ("wrong"), the learner selects a hypothesis that is consistent with the information he has just received. Thus, in this model, if the subject is informed that the large red square is a DAK (rather than a VEC, as he had previously assumed), he will randomly select one of the immediately plausible alternatives (DAK = large, or DAK = square, or DAK = red) to be tested on the next trial, but he will be unaffected by the feedback received on *earlier* trials. Notice that while this model prevents the subject from re-sampling a hypothesis he has *just* rejected, previously rejected hypotheses are not *permanently* eliminated from consideration. Indeed, a hypothesis (call it H1) that has proved incorrect on trial 1 may nevertheless be selected for re-testing as early as trial 3, provided (a) that an error has occurred on trial 2 and (b) that hypothesis H1 is logically consistent with the feedback from trial 2. In brief, then, while Bower and Trabasso assume that the selection of a hypothesis is constrained by the information received on the preceding error trial (this has been called "local consistency"), the subject's memory is not presumed to stretch back much further than this, since he may re-select hypotheses that have previously been tested and found wanting.

The theories proposed by Restle (1962) and by Bower and Trabasso (1963) both include the notion that incorrect hypotheses are not permanently eliminated from further consideration; rather, they remain within the pool of "possibilities" from which the subject makes his choice. According to these theories, the hypothesis pool should thus remain roughly constant in size as the subject continues to search for a solution, and the chances of selecting the *correct* hypothesis should be relatively unchanged—regardless of how many different hypotheses have previously been tried and found wanting. Bower and Trabasso (1963) have reported experimental results that strongly support this notion. Other investigators, however, have suggested that when hypotheses are disconfirmed, they may be eliminated (either temporarily or permanently) from the pool of "possibilities" that the subject is considering. As a result, if the correct hypothesis is included in the initial pool of possibilities, there should be an increased likelihood that it will be selected as more and more "false" hypotheses are eliminated through disconfirmation. Levine (1966) has shown, for example, that if a given hypothesis (call it H1) proves incorrect, it is very unlikely to be tried again either as H2 or as H3. His subjects did *not* re-sample hypotheses that had previously been revealed as inadequate; rather, they eliminated them from the pool of alternatives and showed an increasing likelihood of selecting the correct hypothesis.

While Levine's subjects showed a clear-cut tendency to take account of the disconfirmed hypotheses that they had tested, it is interesting to note that they were even more successful in following the implications of feedback trials on which they were "right." For example, a subject who was reinforced for choosing a large black "X" (located on the left side of the stimulus card) was better able to make use of this feedback than was a subject who had chosen the alternative stimulus (the small white "T" that was on the right) and had received *negative* feedback. While these two outcomes are *logically* equivalent, both providing support for a particular set of hypotheses (large, black, "X," and left side), they apparently differ *psychologically.* This result is reminiscent of our earlier discussion concerning negative and positive instances (see pp. 53–55). In both cases, the data suggest that it may be difficult for a person to proceed logically when he receives information in a negative form. Upon learning that a given hypothesis is "wrong," we are seemingly unable to utilize fully the logical implications of this feedback; similarly, it is hard for us to proceed effectively when presented with a particular stimulus as a "non-example" (or negative instance) of a concept whose boundaries are to be discovered. These phenomena may both reflect our limited ability to recognize the *positive implications* of negative information. If a certain hypothesis (or set of hypotheses) is incorrect, it logically implies that the correct solution must lie among the remaining alternatives; but we are apparently rather clumsy in making this inference.

Strategies in concept attainment

Levine's approach to hypothesis-testing (1966) relies heavily upon the subject's use of intelligent deduction as he proceeds from one hypothesis to the next, in quest of a solution. Bruner, Goodnow, and Austin (1962) were perhaps the first to focus on the "strategy" of the concept learner—the overall manner in which he develops hypotheses during the course of concept formation.

Consider the problem faced by the clinical neurologist seeking to discover the areas of the brain that are essential for speech. In the course of his daily practice, he encounters many patients suffering from aphasia (impairment of speech). These patients do not show *identical* patterns of brain damage, and our neurologist is thus faced with the problem of discovering the "crucial" areas that, when damaged, lead to aphasia. How shall he proceed?

Suppose that the first aphasic he encounters shows extensive brain damage encompassing areas I through VI. One strategy he might employ—one often employed by college students when they are faced with a laboratory analogue of this problem—may be termed a *wholist* approach. In our present example, this would take the form of initially adopting the hypothesis that all six of the damaged areas are essential to speech. So long as our neurologist continued to meet aphasics who showed damage in all six of these areas, he would maintain his initial hypothesis. Suppose, however, he were to find one aphasic—or, better yet, several aphasics—who showed damage in areas I, II, III, and VIII. A strict follower of the wholistic approach would then alter his hypothesis in order to account for features that the old hypothesis and the present instance(s) have in common. The new hypothesis would assert that aphasia results from damage to areas I, II, and III.

By adopting this approach, our neurologist will generate hypotheses that become increasingly "focused." He may, for example, continue to hypothesize that areas I, II, and III are all essential for the maintenance of normal speech, until he encounters an aphasic patient (or group of patients) who fails to show damage in all three of these areas. If he were to examine an aphasic who did *not* show damage in area II, the neurologist might focus his hypothesis still further and assert that only areas I and III are essential to speech. This is a slow and steady strategy, and one of its main virtues is the relative ease with which it can be executed. It is particularly undemanding in its memory requirements, for the learner need only recall his most recent hypothesis (in the present example, the neurologist's hypothesis is always a summary of features common to *all* the aphasics he has thus far encountered).

It is important to note that the wholist approach differs from the models we have previously considered in its explicit assumption that the subject starts out with a complex *conjunctive* hypothesis, in which several attributes are *all* presumed to be critical in defining the concept. As information accumulates, more and more attributes are shown to be irrelevant and are "dropped." The process may indeed end with *only one attribute* being regarded as essential. On the other hand, the models discussed previously assume that the subject considers *simple* hypotheses (such as shape, or color), rather than a conjunction of attributes. Indeed, the experimenter may *instruct* his subjects to look for this type of solution so that they will attack the problem from the starting point that his theory assumes.

Scanning strategies present an interesting contrast to the wholist approach, and they more closely resemble the hypothesis-testing theories considered earlier. Here, the subject is presumed to select one attribute (or more than one) as being critical, even before he has eliminated more complex conjunctive possibilities. A neurologist who followed a scanning approach in his study of aphasia would, essentially, "bet" on some area (or areas) as being crucial for speech. For example, if his initial aphasic patients showed damage in areas I through VI, our scanner might hypothesize (largely on the basis of a "hunch") that aphasia was produced by damage to areas I, IV, and VI, and that areas II, III, and V were irrelevant. If this hypothesis conflicted with his subsequent experience, it would, of course, be changed. Ideally, the new hypothesis would be consistent with all the instances previously seen. However, in reformulating his hypothesis, our scanner (or partist) must rely heavily upon his memory, for the partist's hypothesis is *not* an up-to-date summary of features consistently associated with aphasia. As a result, when the partist is forced to revamp his hypothesis, he must attempt to recall all the individual aphasics he has previously encountered. Perhaps as a result of the heavy reliance on memory, this type of approach tends to be particularly inefficient if the learner is placed under time pressure. Under these conditions, laboratory studies suggest that the partist is often unable to execute successfully the rather complex cognitive activities that his strategy calls for. The more mechanical wholist approach, on the other hand, is less markedly affected by such forms of cognitive stress (Bruner, Goodnow, and Austin, 1962).

There is also evidence that in the usual concept-identification paradigm, subjects who are efficient in finding the solution tend to follow a wholist (or focusing) strategy. In one study (Bourne, 1965), subjects were required not only to categorize each exemplar that was presented but also to verbalize their then-current hypotheses. Those who performed most effectively seemed to follow a focusing strategy, in that the hypotheses they tested *first* included more attributes than was true for the slow learners;

after disconfirmation, moreover, the fast learners tended to make simpler, more systematic changes in their hypotheses.

Focusing and scanning strategies are not only applicable in the realm of concept identification. Closely related cognitive approaches may be observed in such games as "Twenty Questions," where one may simply emit successive unrelated guesses ("Is it a shoe?" "Is it an airplane?" and so on) in a manner that suggests the scanning strategy, or gradually "narrow in," as in the focusing strategy. To test the possibility that these contrasting approaches might be systematically affected as the child developed cognitively, Mosher and Hornsby (1966) conducted an experiment in which children of different ages were shown a photographic array that included 42 pictures of familiar objects; they were instructed to try to determine the "correct" picture by asking the experimenter questions that could be answered with a simple "yes" or "no." An analysis of the questions that were asked by 6-year-old children (the youngest group tested) indicated that they simply emitted guesses, one after another, without any apparent plan. Children of 8 and 11, on the other hand, showed an increasing tendency to use a focusing-like approach. Their initial questions, for example, tended to be more general ("Is it a tool?" rather than "Is it a saw?"). They also showed a tendency to "narrow in" by asking several logically related questions before assaying a particular guess.

These two idealized strategies, focusing and scanning, are rarely followed in a deliberate, detailed fashion, although there is evidence that people rather consistently act in general accord with one or the other of these approaches on a variety of concept-formation tasks. The wholist (focusing) strategy is, however, more widely employed than the partist (scanning) approach when bright college students are faced with the type of "neutral" concept-formation materials typically employed in the laboratory (for example, designs that vary in size, shape, color, etc.). However, in tasks of this sort, it is unlikely that the learner will enter the situation with strong biases and expectations based on previous experience. If we were to present our learner with complete descriptions of several hypothetical people—some of whom were known to be excellent salesmen—and his task was to learn the essential characteristics of this group, such "compelling" and "reasonable" attributes as intelligence or friendliness or physical appearance might be adopted as tentative hypotheses in the manner of the partist, even before such undramatic possibilities as place of birth or number of siblings had been systematically eliminated from consideration through the cautious focusing approach. In short, when the learner is presented with familiar, meaningful materials, problem solving is likely to start with hypotheses that have previously been reasonable and useful, rather than with the more neutral and uncommitted wholistic strategy.

Summary

1. Through concept formation, the individual learns to apply a single label to a variety of distinct but related instances (or exemplars). For example, when a child has successfully mastered the concept "dog," he will have learned to apply this same label to a variety of clearly distinguishable animals. He will, moreover, be capable of applying the appropriate label to dogs he has not previously encountered.

2. There are three main types of concepts: (a) In a conjunctive concept, the different instances (or exemplars) of the concept must all share one or more common attributes. (b) In a disjunctive concept, the different exemplars need not share any common characteristic; instead, they may be included in the same concept for one of several reasons (for example, a strike in baseball may be a case in which the batter missed the ball completely or it may be a "called" strike). (c) In a relational concept, the different exemplars are placed in the same class because they all show some particular relationship among their constituent attributes. For example, social interactions between pairs of siblings may be classed as symmetric if the interacting children respond similarly to one another, whether they are friendly, unfriendly, or withdrawn.

3. Most research on concept formation has dealt with conjunctive concepts. Several competing theories have been advanced to account for the available data. The single-unit S-R approach is based on a simple extrapolation of the learning principles that were originally developed to account for discrimination learning. This theory attempts to explain concept formation as resulting from the associative connections that are established between external cues (such as the color or shape of a stimulus) and the desired response; it does not make any assumptions regarding such unobservable processes as thinking or hypothesis-testing.

4. Despite the simplicity and presumed generality of the single-unit S-R formulation, it now appears inadequate. As a result, some investigators have proposed *multi-stage S-R* theories, involving one or more internal responses which are assumed to trigger the overt reaction that is ultimately recorded by the experimenter. Other researchers have emphasized the importance of *hypothesis-testing* as an essential aspect of most concept-formation studies. This approach is based on the assumption that concepts are learned rather abruptly, as the individual tries out one hypothesis after another in an attempt to learn the correct labeling rule. Present evidence suggests that the S-R approaches may provide a reasonably accurate characterization of concept formation in young children of average intelligence and in animals. On the other hand, gifted children and college students seem to learn concepts in accordance with the hypothesis-testing approach.

5. Two rather distinct approaches (or strategies) have been identified in concept formation. In the wholist approach, the learner first attempts to label the exemplars by means of the most general hypothesis (or rule) that is consistent with his experience; then as he views more and more exemplars, he gradually and systematically narrows his hypothesis. On the other hand, in the scanning (or partist) approach, the learner follows his hunches and successively attempts to select the correct labeling rule without proceeding in the systematic and increasingly focused manner that characterizes the wholist approach.

Supplementary reading

Bourne, L. E. *Human conceptual behavior.* Boston: Allyn and Bacon, 1966.

4 Behavior without awareness

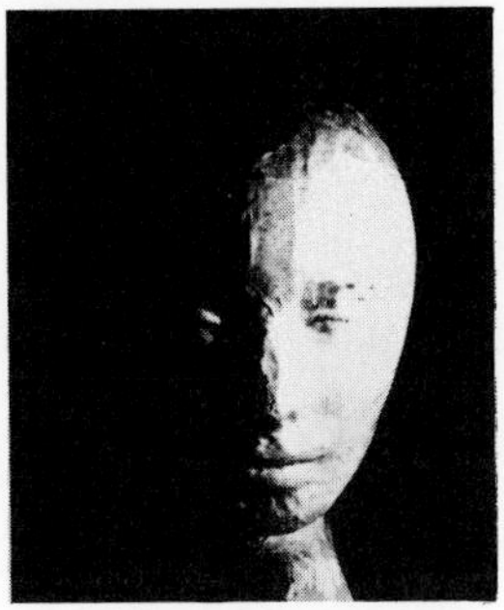

Psychologists have long been fascinated by a variety of phenomena that may roughly be described as instances of behavior without awareness. Although this field of investigation has borrowed both directly and indirectly from Freud's pioneering clinical insights, much of the recent emphasis has grown out of laboratory studies concerned with the mechanisms of perception, learning, and performance.

Stated most simply, the behavior-without-awareness controversy revolves about the importance of the individual's *conscious, deliberate intentions* as determinants of his overt behavior. In contrast to traditional views, which emphasized the importance of man's conscious and deliberate decisions as determinants of his actions, some theorists have suggested that these "mentalistic" concepts add little to our understanding of human behavior. They contend, instead, that most, if not all, behavior is carried out rather *automatically,* in response to the cues and reinforcements that the environment provides. According to this view, notions such as *conscious intention* and the like are not *causally* related to our actions, but instead, represent processes that often occur after-the-fact, after the behavior-to-be-explained has been completed, and are, in any case, of minor significance in controlling the individual's overt behavior.

What do we mean by the elusive concept of awareness? Awareness, of course, is not the sort of thing that one can observe *directly* when studying the behavior of others (I cannot see your field of consciousness); hence, it presents certain difficulties for the would-be researcher. While recognizing the complexities involved in a conceptual definition, most investigators have implicitly assumed that awareness may be equated with *verbalization,* for the presence or absence of awareness has almost always been determined by *verbal inquiry.*

Unfortunately, the assumption of "faithful verbalization" does not appear to be completely satisfactory. For example, if we equate *conscious awareness* with *verbal awareness,* we will find it difficult to investigate these problems with retardates or with those who are too young to have achieved mastery of language. Moreover, if we admit that there are cases in which the subject's conscious awareness may be inaccessible to verbal inquiry, we raise a more general problem: when *can* we feel confident that verbalization provides an adequate measure of awareness? Current practice suggests that most investigators are willing to assume that an adult subject can be "trusted" to verbalize his awareness if the required verbalization is (a) relatively simple and (b) socially acceptable (it should not require the use of taboo words or other embarrassing statements). Despite the weaknesses in this approach (Eriksen, 1958), the absence of a clear, workable alternative has led most researchers to rely upon verbal inquiry as a means of assessing awareness.

Perceptual and attentional factors in awareness

The concept of unawareness has traditionally been used in at least two relatively distinct ways. In some situations, relevant cues may not be consciously perceived (or recognized) because of *stimulus impoverishment.* For example, we may be unable to recognize a word due to its brevity of exposure (when a verbal stimulus is flashed on a screen for one one-thousandth of a second) or to its limited intensity (when a recorded message is presented very softly, at a loudness that is below threshold). Awareness in this sense has been studied most carefully in the perceptual realm, although, as we shall see, it has also been of interest in some learning experiments.

In addition to the unawareness that results from stimulus impoverishment, some investigators have focused on situations in which lack of awareness may be attributed to the individual's failure to recognize the *significance* of certain clearly perceptible cues. In these situations, although the relevant stimuli may be readily detectable (above threshold), they may not be in the focal field of consciousness, due to the misdirection of attention or to faulty comprehension.

Lack of awareness due to stimulus impoverishment

Starting at the most primitive biological level, it is clear that a great many bodily responses, such as changes in heart rate, respiration, and pupillary dilation, are controlled quite automatically, without any conscious effort. Note that many of these automatic adjustments are not reflected in consciousness; thus, changes in skin conductivity (GSR) or in the EEG not only may be triggered without any deliberate intent to respond but also may occur without any conscious recognition that a behavioral adjustment has taken place. In some instances, moreover, the stimuli that control these automatic reaction patterns may be outside the field of consciousness in the *perceptual* sense. For example, respiratory responses may be stimulated by increasing the concentration of CO_2 in the blood, even though the receptors that are involved here do not normally produce conscious concomitants. In other cases, we may respond to an above-threshold stimulus, but without any deliberate intention to do so; thus, following a near-accident, the lucky motorist may suddenly become aware of the rapid and vigorous activity of his heart. Or, to cite another familiar example, I may reflexively pull my hand away from a hot stove, without consciously deciding to do so.

Behavior without awareness at this reflexive level appears to be incontrovertible and has not been subject to much discussion. The issue becomes more lively, however, when we focus on behavior patterns that reflect *learned* modes of adjustment rather than built-in reflexes.

Conditioning and learning

Consider the problem of conditioning. In the experimental arrangement devised by Pavlov, the conditioned stimulus (a tone) is presented just prior to the onset of an electric shock. After conditioning has taken place, the presentation of the tone *by itself* elicits a response pattern similar to the reaction originally evoked by the shock (an increase in heart rate, withdrawal of the hand from the shock apparatus, etc.). What is the role of awareness in this paradigm?

Unfortunately, it is impossible to give a single answer, for this question may be interpreted in several ways. We may ask, for instance, if it is possible to condition *responses* that normally occur without awareness. Here, the evidence is clear, for successful conditioning has been reported of responses—like the GSR, or pupillary dilation—that normally occur without conscious registration. How about the stimuli—must the subject be aware of the conditioned or the unconditioned stimulus (CS and UCS)? Here the answer is more complex. Kimble (1961) cites a Russian experiment on *interoceptive* conditioning, in which various liquids were directly introduced into a dog's intestines by means of a tube. These liquids were used as conditioned stimuli and their delivery preceded the presentation of a shock (UCS) to the left hind paw.

Despite the fact that there is no known sensory representation for specific chemicals introduced in this interoceptive manner, the dogs were able to form a discrimination between such liquids as hydrochloric acid (which served as the CS, preceding the shock) and a saline solution of similar temperature and volume (which had not been paired with the shock). Thus, following a series of training trials, the introduction of the hydrochloric acid led to consistent leg-flexion, while the saline solution did *not* evoke this response.

In a somewhat more traditional conditioning experiment, using *exteroceptive* stimuli, Newhall and Sears (1933) were able to condition human subjects when a subliminal visual stimulus (CS) was paired with an electric shock to the hand (UCS). However, the results here were weak and unstable. Other investigators, following an early report of success by Baker (1938), attempted to establish subliminal *tones* as conditioned stimuli, but with largely negative results. Summing up, then, we may tentatively conclude that conditioning can be established using a conditioned stimulus (CS) which is not represented in awareness, if the CS is applied *interoceptively*. On the other hand, there is no firm evidence that conditioning can be established when a subliminal CS is presented *exteroceptively.*

The studies reviewed above have all focused on the attempt to establish conditioning using a subliminal *conditioned* stimulus. There appears to have been less interest in the possibility of conditioning based on a subliminal *unconditioned* stimulus, perhaps because it is difficult to elicit reliable unconditioned responses in this manner (an unreliable linkage between the unconditioned stimulus and its associated response would severely hamper conditioning under *any* circumstances, whether the UCS was subliminal or supraliminal). In a related area of investigation, however, Jones, Manis, and Weiner (1963) conducted a series of studies using subliminal verbal reinforcements ("Right" and "Wrong"). Unfortunately, the results were inconclusive.

Performance

Despite past difficulties in developing stable conditioning or learning using subliminal stimuli, there is some evidence that such stimulation may activate *previously* acquired responses. In a famous experiment by Lazarus and McCleary (1951), five nonsense syllables that were presented well above threshold were repeatedly paired with shock, while another five syllables were *not* paired with shock. Following this acquisiton experience, the ten syllables were tachistoscopically presented, one at a time, for very brief exposure intervals. The results indicated that even when the subject could not identify the particular stimulus being shown, presentations of the syllables that had been associated with shock produced greater changes in skin conductivity (GSR) than did the unshocked syllables. It is possible, however, that this so-called subception effect might be drastically reduced (and perhaps eliminated) if the experimenters' method for assessing awareness had included the possibility of partial awareness. The main point here is that a subject may fail to identify a particular syllable and yet recognize one or more of the component letters; this partial recognition might, in turn, trigger a change in GSR, if the "fragmentary perception" was sufficiently similar to a syllable that had been paired with shock. Unfortunately, the results of the Lazarus-McCleary experiment do not permit us to assess this hypothesis, for on each trial, if the subject failed to name the particular stimulus being shown, he was simply scored "unaware" without regard for any partial recognition that may have taken place.

In discussing experiments of this type, Eriksen (1958) has suggested that the verbal recognition response may not be a perfect indicator of awareness. He hypothesizes that, on a given trial, the presentation of a stimulus may evoke a perceptual response but may nevertheless *fail* to elicit the expected verbal report ("I see the syllable 'VEC' "); nevertheless, Eriksen theorizes, the fleeting unverbalized perception may be sufficient to trigger the GSR. Note that this explanation assumes that the perceptual response (awareness?) need *not* be reflected in the subject's verbal report, contrasting with the widespread assumption that a verbal report provides an acceptable reflection of perceptual awareness.

Despite the controversy that surrounds the subception effect, there is considerable evidence that human performance can often reach surprising levels of accuracy under conditions of severe stimulus impoverishment. Adams (1957) notes that, in many situations, subjects can make discriminatory judgments that are far better than one might expect from pure chance, even though their responses may subjectively appear to be "guesses." In one experiment, for example, a subject was asked to indicate whether a number or a letter was printed on a card that was displayed at a considerable distance (Sidis, 1898). Although the observer had no subjective confidence in his ability to respond accurately, he was correct on 67% of the trials, while his chance likelihood of being correct was 50%. Similarly, this subject also succeeded in identifying specific numbers and letters at above-chance levels, although his introspective report suggested that he was not consciously aware of any noticeable difference between the various stimuli, and he felt that he was simply guessing. Results of this sort have been reported in several sensory modalities, ranging from weight judgments to the identification of letters presented in a whisper.

While these effects seem highly replicable, one can speculate that they may mainly testify to the overextended use of phrases such as "no confidence" and "pure guessing"; that is, these terms may sometimes be applied despite the presence of minimal, *consciously detectable* cues. If this is true, the results that are typically obtained in "guessing" experiments like those reviewed above could not be confidently interpreted as evidence for discrimination without awareness; a subject who said he was "just guessing" and yet performed at an above-chance level might actually be responding to some consciously perceived (but unverbalized) cue.

Lack of awareness due to faulty comprehension

In the view of many psychologists, the most important evidence supporting the behavior-without-awareness doctrine does not come from studies involving subliminal stimuli, but is, instead, derived from the fact that behavioral changes often occur in the absence of "cognitive" awareness or intentions, in situations where the relevant stimuli may be well above threshold values.

Classical conditioning

Although it has been widely assumed that conditioning develops rather automatically, whether or not the individual recognizes that presentation of the CS always precedes the onset of the UCS, the evidence here is far from clear. In one study (Lacey and Smith, 1954), subjects were presented with a chain association task; they were given several stimulus words and were instructed to free-associate to each one for fifteen seconds. One group received a severe electric shock following free association to the stimulus word *cow*, while the other group was shocked following associations to the stimulus word *paper*. These contrasting shock-schedules led to significant differences in autonomic reactivity upon presentation of the critical stimulus words. The investigators report, moreover, that this conditioning occurred despite the subjects' inability to verbalize the relationship between the CS (the word *cow*, for example) and the UCS (shock). This study also revealed evidence for *generalization* without awareness, for the subjects in the *cow-shock* group showed a clear-cut autonomic response to other "rural" words, such as *corn* and *harvest*. However, in a followup to the Lacey and Smith experiment, Chatterjee and Eriksen (1962) used a more detailed method for determining their subjects' expectations of shock and reported that they could find *no evidence* for conditioning among subjects who failed to notice the relationship between the word that served as the CS and the UCS (shock) that always followed it. Similarly, they found no evidence of generalization without awareness.

Staats and Staats (1957) developed an unusual application of the classical conditioning procedure in an attempt to alter their subjects' verbal reactions to selected nonsense syllables. This study was presented to the subjects as one in which two types of learning would be studied simultaneously—one learning task involved nonsense syllables, while the other concerned the learning of words. During the experimental session, six nonsense syllables were repeatedly shown, one at a time, in random order; about one second after each such presentation, the experimenter pronounced a different word. The subjects were instructed to look at the nonsense syllables and to repeat the various words aloud as they were read by the experimenter. Although the presentation of words and syllables appeared to be unrelated, in one group the syllable *XEH* was consistently followed by words that had *negative* connotations (for example, *sick, worthless, sour, stupid, thief,* etc.), while the syllable *YOF* was always followed by words having *positive* meaning (*sweetly, healthy,* etc.). At the end of the experimental session the subjects were told that it was necessary to see how they *felt* about each syllable, since this may have affected their recall scores. Each subject's response to each syllable was then rated on a 7-point scale that ran from *pleasant* to *unpleasant.* The results indicated that if a syllable had consistently been followed by negative words, it was rated less favorably than a contrasting syllable that had been paired with positive words. These results were interpreted as reflecting a conditioning process in which the nonsense syllables served as *conditioned stimuli*, while the pleasant (or unpleasant) words functioned as *unconditioned stimuli* that elicited positive (or negative) meaning responses. Through successive pairings, a given syllable (CS) eventually acquired the capacity to elicit the meaning response (positive or negative) with which it had been associated. Most important for our present concern is the fact that these results did *not* appear to hinge on the subjects' awareness of the CS-UCS relationship that the experimenters had established. This claim has, however, been challenged by Page (1969), who suggests that the apparent conditioning effect in this experiment was in fact *consciously* mediated, rather than the consequence of an automatic learning process.

Although these experiments provide mixed evidence for the assertion that conditioning can occur in the absence of conscious awareness, it is clear that the development of insight does not, *by itself,* guarantee that conditioning will be successful. Kimble notes, for example (1962), that in the typical eyelid conditioning experiment, the subject may recognize the relationship between the conditioned stimulus (tone) and the unconditioned stimulus (air puff) after only a few trials, but the appearance of an anticipatory conditioned eyeblink may not occur until many more trials have taken place. Similarly, if the interval between the CS and the UCS is extended from .5 second (an interval which produces optimal conditioning) to 1.5 seconds, the resultant level of conditioning is lowered appreciably, although there is virtually *no* impact on the subject's ability to verbalize the CS-UCS sequence that he anticipates. These observations indicate that successful *conditioning* is not an automatic consequence of *awareness.*

Concept formation

Behavior without awareness has often been reported in studies of concept formation; a subject who has apparently discovered the relevant "response rule" in a concept-formation task may, nevertheless, be unable to verbalize the cues to which he has been responding. Hull's research on concept formation is a classic example (see p. 52), for many of his subjects learned to classify the experimental stimuli (Chinese symbols) in accordance with the system that was being reinforced, but they could not specify the relevant cues.

Although reports of this sort have been common in concept formation research, the evidence here is far from conclusive, for such results may reflect the operation of *correlated hypotheses*. That is, in some instances, the hypotheses that subjects verbalize (or otherwise communicate) may provide reasonably successful means for differentiating the various stimuli, even though they have been formulated in rather different terms than those favored by the experimenter. Thus, in Hull's study, the subjects' "inadequate" drawings of the elements which they felt were crucial in the guidance of their performance *may* have been a sufficient basis for differentiating the various groups of stimuli. Similarly, in experiments where awareness has been assessed by purely verbal means, the verbalizations of "unaware" subjects—no matter how much they differed from the experimenter's *preferred* verbalization—may indeed have been useful as a guide to behavior.

A study by Manis and Barnes (1961), however, included a check on this correlated hypothesis explanation, and the results supported the inference of behavior without awareness. In this experiment, the subjects played the role of "plane spotters"; they were shown a series of stimuli that were presented as "airplane ensignia" and were instructed to classify each "plane" as "friendly" or "enemy." Following each response, the subjects were told whether they were right or wrong. Each stimulus (insignia) included the Arabic numbers 2, 3, 4, and 5 arranged in a cross-shaped pattern; while each insignia included the same four numbers, the positions of these digits varied from one "plane" to the next, with the restriction that a *two* (for friendly planes) or a *five* (for enemy planes) always appeared on the left. When this concept-formation task had been mastered, generalization was assessed by presenting a new series of insignia in which each Arabic numeral was replaced by a corresponding number of circles (for example, *two* circles replaced the number 2, *three* circles replaced the number 3, and so on). These substitutions were fully explained and the subjects were instructed to use the same approach (hypothesis) that had worked successfully in the initial series. Following a test for retention with the original stimuli, the subjects were then interviewed to see if they were verbally aware of the relevant response rule. The results indicated that subjects who had been unable to state the rule that was used to determine reinforcement had nevertheless performed at an above-chance level on the generalization series. To check on the possibility that this may have been a simple reflection of various correlated (partially correct) hypotheses, the experimenters made a comparison between (a) the observed generalization performances and (b) the performance levels that would have been achieved if each subject had consistently followed the response rule (or rules) that he had verbalized. This comparison revealed that over 85% of the subjects were more successful in the generalization task than was anticipated from the hypotheses they had verbalized in the interview.

Awareness in language behavior

The complex patterns that constitute our everyday speech provide another example of behavior without awareness, for while we have all learned to speak with reasonable grammatical correctness, only a few of us are aware of the "rules" that govern our choice of words as we participate in a conversation. We can, for example, choose the proper words to create a meaningful sentence and yet be unable to explain why a given word order or verb form was used. Similarly, at a less complex level, we follow certain pronunciation rules quite consistently, without recognizing the patterns that are involved.

The rules governing the pluralization of English nouns provide a good illustration, for while we may recognize that the most common method of pluralization involves the addition of a final *s*, we are rarely aware of the fact that these *s*'s are pronounced in different ways, depending upon the terminal sound of the noun to be pluralized. Thus, singular nouns that end with a voiced consonant (*bug, fad, lab,* and so on) are normally changed into plurals by adding a final *z*-sound (bug-*zz*, fad-*zz*, lab-*zz*). In contrast, singular nouns that end in a voiceless consonant (such as *cat* or *cap*) are pluralized through the addition of a voiceless hissing *s*-sound (cat-*ss*, cap-*ss*). We need not outline all the pluralization rules at this point, for our main purpose is simply to document the fact that the experienced speaker of English follows these patterns quite automatically, without consciously intending to do so. The fact that these are indeed behavioral "rules" and not a series of items that are retained through rote memory is revealed by the fact that we will readily follow these same patterns if we are faced with the task of pluralizing a nonsense syllable that we have never heard in plural form. Thus, if there were an object known as a ***wug***, we would all agree that a set of them would be referred to as a group of wug-*z* (not a group of wug-*s*; see p. 133, also Berko, 1958). Finally, we should note that our present, seemingly automatic, approach to pluralization is *not* a skill that was once firmly embedded in consciousness, but has now been forgotten, for it is highly unlikely that the young child is ever aware of these pronunciation rules, even when he is first learning to speak (and there is good reason to believe that these patterns are learned, and not innate). (See p. 134.)

Mechanistic versus cognitive interpretations of verbal reinforcement

Although there is widespread agreement concerning the empirical consequences of such verbal rewards as "Good" or "That's right" in studies of human learning, the proper interpretation of these reinforcement effects remains controversial. Thorndike asserted in his *Law of Effect* that rewards operate in an automatic fashion to strengthen the responses that precede them; moreover, this strengthening is said to be independent of the learner's "understanding" of the situation. In contrast to this view, cognitive theorists have emphasized the information-giving aspects of a reward (it simply informs the learner that a given response has been correct). Note that both of these accounts are consistent with much of the available evidence. For example, they are both consistent with the facts that rewarded responses tend to be repeated, and that learning is virtually impossible in the absence of knowledge of results. While most laymen might prefer the cognitive interpretation because of its greater compatibility with a humanistic conception of man, scientific conclusions are not ideally based on considerations of this type, and hence several lines of experimentation have been pursued in an attempt to gain more adequate understanding.

Incidental learning

Pursuing Thorndike's mechanistic line of thought, many experimenters have been concerned with the effectiveness of rewards in *incidental learning* situations. In these studies, the experimental setting is such that the subjects are not consciously motivated to repeat responses that have previously been identified as "correct." Postman and Adams (1954), for example, employed what was presented as an extrasensory perception (ESP) task. Their subjects were shown a series of words and were to guess the number between 1 and 10 which the experimenters had arbitrarily paired with each word. After each guess, subjects were told whether they had been right or wrong; however, since the experimenters were not truly interested in ESP, the feedback followed a prearranged pattern and did not depend upon the accuracy of the subjects' guesses. Following the first presentation of the word list, the guessing procedure was repeated, and the subjects were instructed again to guess the numbers associated with each word; on this trial, however, there was no feedback from the experimenter. Most importantly, the subjects were instructed that the word-number pairings would be randomly changed, so that a number that had initially been "correct" for a given word would not necessarily be correct on the second presentation of the word list.

If rewards operated in a purely mechanistic fashion to strengthen the stimulus-response associations that they followed, we would expect that many guesses which had initially been followed by a reward ("right") would be repeated, despite the subject's knowledge that the original word-number pairings were often to be changed. Similarly, we would expect relatively few repetitions on items that had been followed by punishment ("wrong"). According to a cognitive interpretation, on the other hand, we would anticipate a rather different pattern of results; since the subjects had been led to believe that the feedback they had previously received could *not* be used to guide future performance, the cognitive theory suggests that their subsequent guesses would be unaffected by the previous pattern of rewards and punishment. Several experiments of this sort have been conducted to date; the results have generally shown the trends predicted by Thorndike's mechanistic theory. That is, on the second presentation of the word list, responses that had initially been associated with reward have tended to reappear. Moreover, when asked to recall the number responses that they originally gave to each word, subjects have typically been more successful in recalling the rewarded responses than the responses that were initially unrewarded.

Some studies of incidental learning have investigated the effects that are produced when the subject is reinforced according to a *systematic pattern*. In these studies, the subject's task appears to involve a series of relatively independent trials and thus discourages the conscious search for a consistent response rule. In one experiment, Thorndike (1932) presented his subject with a series of Spanish words and instructed them to underline the correct translation of each word from a set of five alternatives. Following each trial the subject was told whether he was "right" or "wrong." The word lists were arranged so that the correct response most commonly appeared on the far right, while the word in the second place from the right was less commonly correct, and so on, with the word on the extreme left being correct on only a few trials. The resulting data showed clear-cut evidence of learning without awareness. Subjects who seemed unaware of the positional bias (in a post-experimental interview) nevertheless showed an *increase* in the frequency with which they chose words in the two positions on the right and a *decrease* in their selections from the left. Related results have been reported by Rees and Israel (1935) in a study involving the establishment of an unconscious "set" (or mode of approach) to the solution of anagrams.

These experiments suggest that systematic reinforcement may produce behavior without awareness when the experimental task is somewhat ambiguous and uncertainty exists concerning the correct response on any given trial. Under these conditions, the behavior pattern that has previously been reinforced will often be maintained, even though there may be no conscious intention to do so.

Verbal operant conditioning

Another line of research which bears on the role of awareness in the reinforcement process derives from the operant conditioning paradigm. One of the earliest studies in this tradition was conducted by Greenspoon (1955); subjects in this experiment were simply instructed to say all the words they could think of, without using any phrases or sentences, and without counting. Without telling his subjects that there were any right or wrong responses, Greenspoon attempted to reinforce the use of plural nouns by a simple expedient of saying "mmm-hmmm" whenever a plural was emitted. His results indicated that this procedure led to an increased usage of plural nouns. However, more interesting than this straightforward demonstration of the efficacy of verbal reward was the fact that when his subjects were questioned at the end of the experimental session, only ten out of seventy-five were able to verbalize the relationship between their responses and the experimenter's reinforcing behavior ("mmm-hmmm"). Moreover, these ten subjects did not respond differently from the sixty-five subjects who were "unaware" of the experimental manipulations, suggesting that the experimenter's reinforcements had been equally effective regardless of the subjects' "insights" into the situation.

Many more studies of this sort have been conducted to date. The vast majority show that it is indeed possible to alter people's verbal behavior by having the experimenter say such things as "Good," "Right," etc. There is considerable controversy, however, concerning the claims that learning can occur in these situations without awareness. For example, it has been argued that in the Greenspoon study and others conducted shortly after it, the post-experimental interviews were too brief and superficial, and thus failed to detect awareness on the part of many subjects who did, in fact, have insight into what the experimenter was doing (Spielberger, 1962; Spielberger and DeNike, 1966). These critics have gone on to show that when the subjects' awareness is assessed by a more adequate set of probing questions, a substantially greater proportion are judged to have awareness; more important, these critics maintain, is the fact that subjects who are "truly" unaware rarely show evidence of having learned anything in these experiments.

Some critics have focused on the problem of *correlated hypotheses* (see above) in the operant conditioning paradigm. For example, Dulany (1961, 1962) has shown that in a continuous association task such as Greenspoon's, the subjects often believe that when they are reinforced they should continue with additional responses from the "same" semantic category. When this strategy is followed and the experimenter reinforces plural nouns [for example, shoe, house, car*s*, (Umhmmm), boat*s*, (Umhmmm), ship*s*, (Umhmmm), . . .], the resulting associations normally show an increasing frequency of plurals. That is, the search for a semantic associate will typically yield a response that agrees in *number* with the preceding word in the chain; hence, if the word just reinforced has been a plural and the subject searches for a semantic associate, he usually responds with another plural because of the constraints imposed by our everyday linguistic habits.

For a variety of reasons, therefore, the critics assert that there is no convincing evidence for verbal operant conditioning without awareness, and they conclude that previous reports of this phenomenon have been based on faulty experimentation. This is not, however, the end of the controversy. It has been suggested, for example, that the almost exclusive reliance on *college students* as experimental subjects in this domain has had a profound effect on the results. Lanyon and Drotar (1966) report that in a survey of more than 200 verbal conditioning studies, a major determinant of the achievement (or nonachievement) of verbal awareness was the educational level of the subjects. College students systematically showed a higher incidence of awareness than those with fewer years of education. In part, this is undoubtedly due to differences in verbal intelligence, for several investigators have reported that above-average intellectual ability may enhance the likelihood of awareness—even if we compare intelligent and unintelligent subjects who have shown similar performance gains in verbal conditioning (McCullough, 1962; Crowne and Strickland, 1961; Lanyon and Drotar, 1966).

These results suggest that the evidence for learning without awareness might be more consistent if more studies were conducted with subjects of average, or below average, intelligence. There are some difficulties here, however, for a skeptic might contend that an unintelligent subject who *was* aware of the response-reinforcement contingencies might nonetheless have difficulty giving an adequate verbal report of his cognitive processes; consequently, he might be mislabeled as "unaware." It is thus essential in this research that the subjects be readily capable of verbalizing any insights that they may have.

The "open" versus "masked" nature of the experimental task is another variable that must be considered in evaluating the evidence for learning without awareness. In some studies, the subject's task has been to make up a series of sentences, each beginning with one of six pronouns; the experimenter then reinforces all sentences beginning with "I" or "we." Dixon and Oakes (1965) have suggested that the *simplicity* of this widely used paradigm has been an important factor in contributing to the frequent reports of awareness. It seems quite likely that this virtually "meaningless" task would encourage the subject to determine what the experimenter is "really" interested in; thus, the task may stimulate a more self-conscious search for some guiding response rule (hypothesis) than might otherwise be the case. To get around this problem, Dixon and Oakes developed a technique to interfere with the process of hypothesis formation. Between trials in their experiment, some of the subjects were required to name a series of colors presented in rapid succession. For these subjects there was *no relationship* between the amount of behavior change induced by the reinforcements and their verbal awareness of the response-reinforcement contingency. In contrast, subjects who did *not* participate in the color-naming task showed the usual correlation between awareness and conditioning (those who had developed insight showed the strongest conditioning effects). Dixon and Oakes concluded, therefore, that there is no *necessary* relationship between awareness and learning. They reasoned that even if the experimental arrangements prevent the effective formulation of hypotheses, learning may be unaffected, and may, moreover, be unrelated to the subject's degree of verbal awareness.

Lanyon (1967) has focused on a related aspect of verbal operant conditioning. He suggests that since most of the studies in this area were conducted with students drawn from introductory psychology classes, the subjects were doubtless motivated to determine the main goals of the experimenter and the "true" nature of the experimental situation. Lanyon theorized, however, that this hypothesis-testing, questioning approach should be less common among students not enrolled in psychology classes, and he reported strong evidence for learning without awareness with a sample of this type. Following this same line of approach, Krasner (1967) has emphasized the importance of experimental subtlety in minimizing the effects of conscious problem-solving. He cites a variety of studies where positive results were obtained when reinforcement was provided for such complex and "non-obvious" behaviors as the use of human movement and animal responses in reaction to ink blots (Dinoff, 1960).

This brief survey of the verbal operant conditioning literature suggests that learning without awareness may be difficult to demonstrate when an intelligent subject is faced with a puzzling task that arouses his suspicion and evokes self-conscious hypothesis testing in the search for an adequate understanding of the experimenter's aims. On the other hand, when the subjects are less gifted intellectually or are given a reasonably interesting task that does not alert their suspicions, the phenomenon seems amply demonstrated (Rosenfeld and Baer, 1969).

The carryover effect: The maintenance of behavior in the absence of intention

Given the fact that a certain behavior pattern has been learned (either with or without awareness), several investigators have studied the extent to which this prior learning can be "turned off" when the individual is instructed to disregard his prior experience. The fact that a previously learned response may often be maintained *despite* a conscious effort at change indicates that overt behavior and verbal insight (or intention) often operate somewhat independently. A good example of this phenomenon was reported in a study by Bridger and Mandel (1965). In this experiment the galvanic skin response (GSR) was classically conditioned to a flash of light (CS), which had been paired with a series of electric shocks (UCS). For some subjects this conditioning was established under a continuous reinforcement schedule, while for others, the shocks were intermittent, occurring on only 25% of the trials. Following a series of acquisition trials, half the subjects in each group were then *informed* that there would be no more shocks; moreover, the shock electrodes were removed at this point. Despite this assurance, however, among those informed subjects who indicated (in a post-experimental inquiry) that they were "positive" there would be no more shocks, presentation of the light (CS) on five succeeding extinction trials continued to elicit the GSR response. This result suggests that the GSR conditioning was partly independent of the subjects' conscious anticipation concerning the light-shock sequence.

The Bridger and Mandel experiment also revealed that within the *informed* groups, extinction occurred with equal speed, whether the original conditioning had been established under a continuous or partial reinforcement schedule. By contrast, when subjects were *not* explicitly informed that the shock series was finished, the classic extinction pattern was observed. That is, the GSR reaction extinguished more slowly in the group that had been *partially* reinforced than it did in the continuously reinforced group.

This pattern of results following partial reinforcement was interpreted as favoring a discrimination hypothesis. According to this view, the marked resistance to extinction—which is a normal consequence of partial reinforcement—results from the subject's difficulty in detecting the switch from *acquisition* to *extinction* (where the proportion of the reinforced trials is merely decreased to 0%!). For the continuously reinforced subject, on the other hand, the switch to extinction should be more readily detectable, for the acquisition series has not included any trials in which reinforcement was omitted, and hence the start of the (nonreinforced) extinction series abruptly signals a change in experimental conditions.

Bridger and Mandel interpreted their results as indicating the presence of two components in conditioning: (a) a simple conditioning process that presumably operates rather automatically, independent of verbal expectations, and (b) a mediated (presumably conscious) process that accounts for the partial reinforcement extinction effect. A related conclusion seems warranted by Bridger and Mandel's prior finding (1964) that the GSR could be conditioned to a light (CS) simply by informing subjects that they would receive two painful shocks in association with the designated CS (no shocks were actually delivered, however). The overall performance of this "threatened" group in response to a series of CS presentations did not differ appreciably from that shown by a *threat and shock* group, who were also informed of the association between light and shock, and in addition, *experienced* twenty trials of the anticipated CS-UCS pairing. The significant responsivity shown by the *threat* group suggests that conditioning may indeed be partly dependent on conscious verbal processes. The presence of an additional, *non-mediated* (automatic) component is shown by the fact that the *threat* subjects showed a more rapid rate of extinction than the *threat and shock* group when the subjects were informed that the shocks would no longer be presented and the shock electrodes removed.

Manis and Ruppe (1969) found that automatic carryover effects could also be obtained with a *voluntary* response, not just with the involuntary GSR. Subjects in this experiment were presented with pairs of nouns; on each trial, they were to make up a sentence using one of the two given nouns as the subject. Each pair of nouns included one word in the singular form and one in the plural. In the acquisition series, half the subjects were verbally reinforced ("right") for using the singular noun and half for using the plural. When this task had been fully mastered, the subjects were instructed to search for a *new* basis for constructing their sentences; it was emphasized that the old response rule was no longer operative and that the correct solution was unrelated to the previous reinforcement pattern. In fact, however, there was no solution possible, for the subsequent trials were *randomly* reinforced. The results revealed strong evidence for the carryover effect, for the subjects tended to maintain the response pattern that had previously been established. This carryover effect was present even among those who indicated (in a post-experimental interview) that they had *not* consciously re-tested the "old" response rule while searching for a "new" solution. Note the similarity between these results and the findings reported by Postman and Adams (1954) in their "ESP" experiment (see above), where subjects tended to repeat their previously reinforced responses even though they had received explicit instructions that these responses would not necessarily be reinforced again. The two experiments differ mainly in the *specificity* of the responses that were studied, for Manis and Ruppe's subjects carried over a rather general response class (sentences with singular or plural subjects), while Postman and Adams studied the repetition of specific number-responses.

Summary

1. The behavior-without-awareness controversy revolves about the importance of the individual's ***conscious, deliberate intentions*** as determinants of his overt behavior. In contrast to traditional views that emphasize the importance of man's conscious decisions as determinants of action, some investigators contend that much of our behavior is carried out rather *automatically*, in response to the cues and reinforcements that the environment provides.

2. The concept of unawareness has traditionally been used in at least two distinct ways. In some situations relevant cues may not be consciously perceived (or recognized) because of *stimulus* impoverishment. In other instances, lack of awareness may be attributable to the individual's failure to recognize the *significance* of certain clearly perceptible events.

3. At the most primitive biological level, many of our bodily responses, such as changes in heart rate and respiration, are controlled without any conscious effort. Moreover, there is some evidence that conditioning can be successfully established using an *interoceptive* conditioned stimulus (CS) that is not represented in awareness. On the other hand, there is no firm evidence that conditioning can be established using a subliminal conditioned stimulus that is presented *exteroceptively.*

4. People can often make discriminatory judgments that are far better than one might expect from pure chance, even though they believe that their responses are "sheer guesses." For example, a subject may succeed in visually identifying

various numbers under viewing conditions that do *not* generate consciously detectable cues.

5. Behavior without awareness has often been reported in studies of concept formation. That is, a subject who has apparently discovered the relevant "response rule" may, nevertheless, be unable to verbalize the cues to which he has been responding.

6. The verbal operant conditioning paradigm has frequently been used in studies of behavior without awareness. Despite conflicting claims, the phenomenon seems amply demonstrated (a) among subjects who are of average or below-average intelligence and (b) in settings that present the subject with an interesting task that does not elicit a self-conscious hypothesis-testing approach.

7. Several studies suggest that previously learned responses are often maintained despite the absence of any conscious intent to do so.

Supplementary reading

Eriksen, C. W. (Ed.) *Behavior and awareness.* Durham: Duke University Press, 1962.

Krasner, L. Verbal operant conditioning and awareness. In K. Salzinger and S. Salzinger (Eds.), *Research in verbal behavior and some neurophysiological implications.* New York: Academic Press, 1967.

Spielberger, C. D. and DeNike, L. D. Descriptive behaviorism versus cognitive theory in verbal operant conditioning. *Psychological Review,* 1966, **73**, 306–326.

2 Language

5 Associative and statistical approaches to language

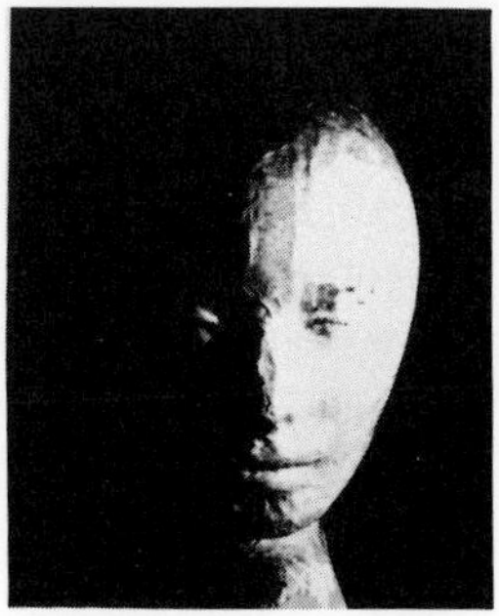

The development of language is widely regarded as man's most distinctive, important, and complex cognitive achievement. Moreover, it is an achievement that anthropologists report to be universal among human groups, regardless of their geographic or cultural surroundings. Despite its importance and universality, however, the development of language is but dimly understood at the present time.

Learning and language

The psychological study of language has often proceeded from the assumption that linguistic skills might ultimately prove to be explainable in terms of the basic learning mechanisms that have been explored so intensively since the pioneering works of Pavlov and Thorndike (see Chapter 8). While this point of view has never advanced beyond some rather generalized and schematic accounts of the way in which speech production and comprehension *might* develop, it has, nevertheless, enjoyed immense popularity among American psychologists, and was virtually unchallenged until the late 1950s.

Speech as a verbal operant

B. F. Skinner (1957) has attempted to account for the complexities of speech by ingeniously applying to language the principles of operant conditioning—principles originally developed in the study of animal behavior. Skinner primarily stresses the extent to which verbal behavior is shaped by the *reinforcements* and *discriminative stimuli* that the environment provides. His approach can perhaps best be understood if we first review the meaning of these concepts (see Walker, E. L., *Conditioning and Instrumental Learning,* for a more complete account).

Responses that are reinforced (that result in "positive" consequences) tend to be repeated in the future. Thus, in a very simple case, a rat may be deprived of food and placed in an experimental chamber that contains a lever connected to a food-delivery mechanism. If the apparatus is arranged so that bar pressing results in the delivery of food pellets, bar-pressing responses will occur with increasing frequency. Conversely, if bar pressing does not produce reinforcement, it will not gain in strength and may indeed appear with decreased frequency in the future (extinction).

Many experiments at least suggestively related to the bar-pressing example demonstrate the influence of social reinforcements upon verbal behavior.

Early vocalizing and babbling

For the first month or so after birth, the infant's vocalizing consists largely of cries, clucks, and squeaks. As he matures, however, he produces more and more sounds—such a variety, in fact, that some observers (for example, Osgood, 1953) think the young infant produces the full range of sounds that can be produced by the human vocal apparatus.

Starting with this relatively unstructured pattern of verbal behavior, learning theorists have attempted to account for linguistic development by emphasizing the effects of reinforcement. For example, Rheingold, Gewirtz, and Ross (1959) applied operant conditioning techniques to a group of three-month-old infants in order to demonstrate the "shaping" effects of the environment on the child's vocalizations. After observing the infants' rate of vocalizing during an initial baseline period, these investigators reinforced subsequent vocalizations by clucking, by smiling, and by lightly squeezing the children's abdomens. These procedures effectively strengthened the vocalizing response, for vocalizations occurred more frequently than in the baseline period; moreover, in accordance with the pattern commonly observed in other response classes, the infants' rate of vocalization decreased significantly when the experimenters withheld reinforcement during a final *extinction* phase.

Starting at about the fifth month after birth, the child's vocalizing and crying is gradually replaced by babbling utterances that are more syllabic in character, although still quite incomprehensible. Here are some examples originally observed by Shirley (1933): "a-bah-bah," "luh-luh-lah," "adhu-ajuh." The significance of this babbling stage in the development of later linguistic competence is presently something of a controversy. Some observers (Osgood, 1953; Staats and Staats, 1963) have suggested that babbling represents an early approximation to adult speech, and that both babbling and mature speech may ultimately be explained through an extrapolation of basic learning principles.

Learning theorists assume that when an infant is being fed or comforted, he is commonly being *talked to* by a parent; thus, parental speech sounds acquire secondary reinforcing properties (that is, they tend to "sound good") because of their association with primary comforts. Given this background, it is assumed that when the child now engages in vocal activity, some of the resulting sounds resemble parental speech. Vocal movements of this type are thought to be self-strengthening, because they are invariably followed by English-like sounds (the speaker hears what he has said) that have presumably acquired secondary reinforcing properties through previous conditioning. Parental praise and attention ("Listen to what Johnny just said") would constitute yet another source of reinforcement for these responses. Through these mechanisms, the content of the child's vocalization is thought to change gradually; as the sounds that resemble parental speech are repeatedly reinforced, they come to dominate his verbal output. Note that this account suggests a different progression of babbling behaviors in diverse linguistic communities. For example, the guttural sounds of German would be established as secondary reinforcers in a German home and would thus occur more and more frequently in the output of a German child; a different progression would occur in the development of an American or English youngster.

Staats and Staats (1963) contend that there is a gradual progression from the babbling responses of the infant to the first appropriately patterned speech responses. This progression is presumably "shaped" through a series of successive approximations, until the child's speech closely matches that of his parents.

In contrast to this account of babbling behavior, based on the concepts of learning theory, other investigators have suggested that babbling may be largely innate and of little significance in the later development of language. For example, Carroll (1964, p. 31) states:

> "There is some ground for thinking that this stage is biologically determined, since it occurs in many babies who are subsequently found to be congenitally deaf. . . . Although certain trends can be observed in the kinds of sounds emitted by an infant in the babbling stage, these sounds have little bearing on the phonemes of the language the child is to learn."

Verbal operant conditioning

Operant-like effects have also been obtained in studies with adult speakers. In one experiment (Cohen, Kalish, Thruston, and Cohen, 1954) subjects were presented with a series of cards on which there appeared six pronouns ("I," "he," "she," "we," "they," and "you") and a verb, such as *swim,* or *read.* The same pronouns appeared on each card, although the verb was changed from one card to the next. Subjects were instructed to compose a sentence for each card by using one of the pronouns and the verb. The experimenters' main interest was in increasing the number of sentences that included the pronouns "I" or "we"; consequently, they reinforced the use of these pronouns by saying "good" whenever one was used in a sentence. Through this simple procedure, it was possible to "control" partially the subjects' verbal behaviors: the results of the experiment indicated that the reinforced pronouns ("I" and "we") were used with increasing frequency. While studies like this suggest that verbal responses may be strengthened through the operation of verbal reinforcements ("good"), a fair amount of evidence suggests that human behavior in this type of experiment may often be controlled by conscious plans and hypotheses rather than by the automatic operation of reinforcements (see pp. 92–93; also Spielberger, 1962, for a more complete discussion of this issue).

Skinner uses the concept of the *discriminative stimulus* to account for the fact that, through appropriate training, a hungry rat can be taught to press a bar under certain *specific conditions* rather than indiscriminately. For example, if bar pressing results in food pellets while a signal light is on (and not when it is off), the rat will soon learn this discrimination; he will engage in bar pressing when the light is on and refrain from this behavior when it is off. A similar process, says Skinner, seems to occur in language behavior. A child can be trained so that he will say "thank you" only on certain occasions. As with the rat, discrimination training is accomplished by reinforcing the response when it occurs under appropriate circumstances (for example, when the child has just been given a candy bar) and withholding reinforcement if the response occurs when it is inappropriate.

Skinner's theory of verbal behavior

If, as Skinner asserts, language can be adequately explained through an application of the same laws that apply to other forms of behavior, we might well ask if verbal behavior has *any* unique characteristics. Skinner feels that there is indeed one distinguishing hallmark: verbal behavior does not operate *directly* upon the environment to produce reinforcements, as the rat does when he presses the bar in his experimental chamber. Instead, verbal behavior most typically leads to reinforcement through an *indirect* medium involving the actions of *others.* For example, when eating dinner I may be faced with the problem of getting cream for my coffee. I can obtain this goal quite directly through the nonverbal act of reaching; alternatively, I may verbally request the cream and find that this response will also result in reinforcement—this time, however, because of the effects of my behavior ("Please pass the cream") upon the behavior of others. Note that Skinner's definition does not limit verbal behavior to any limited group of responses, such as those involving the vocal tract. Nonvocal actions (gestures, facial expressions, etc.) often enable us to gain our ends through the behavior of others and hence qualify as verbal (but not vocal) behavior.

Skinner continually attempts to point out how a given class of verbal behavior might plausibly be explained in terms of some discriminative stimulus and reinforcement that jointly "control" the behavior (determine when it will occur). He attempts to classify verbal behaviors by noting the various types of discriminative stimuli that "signal" the occasions when a given verbal response will be reinforced.

Mands are perhaps the simplest class of verbal behaviors in Skinner's system. Verbal statements such as *demands, commands,* or requests would all be classified as mands. A specific mand might be our example above: "Please pass the cream." In this brief episode, the verbal response is presumed to be controlled partly by the speaker's need for cream and partly by the presence of an audience. (The audience is regarded as a uniquely important discriminative stimulus. When there is no audience, when others are not within listening range, verbal behaviors are rarely if ever reinforced; hence, they rarely occur under these circumstances.) In attempting to account for the occurrence of the speaker's verbal response, Skinner would thus point to the probability that it had previously been successful in gaining reinforcements (cream) under similar circumstances and hence had gained in strength. Following this same approach, Skinner notes that if the use of polite words ("please") has typically increased the likelihood that a mand will yield reinforcement, words of this sort will probably accompany future mands ("Please pass the cream"); if words like "please" have not generally enhanced the likelihood of reinforcement, they may well be omitted from the child's behavioral repertoire.

The *tact* represents a second major class of verbal behaviors. In the case of the tact, the physical environment acts as the discriminative stimulus. That is, the reinforced occurrence of the response depends upon certain characteristics of the environment. For example, Junior may call to his mother, who is working in the yard, "There is a telephone call for you." The parent will generally reinforce this statement ("thank you") if, in fact, there has been a call; otherwise, the speaker's response will probably result in punishment rather than reinforcement. Thus, the physical environment partly determines Junior's verbal behavior; he learns to "match" his words with the state of affairs around him.

While a mand has obvious advantages for the speaker, the tact seems mainly to benefit the listener, since it may extend his knowledge of the environment (without the speaker's announcement, in the above example, the listener would miss his call). Since tacts often provide him with valuable information, it is to the listener's advantage to reinforce them when they are properly executed. In this way, he may effectively strengthen the speaker's "informative" tacting behaviors and increase the frequency of their occurrence. However, there are many "true" tacts that the speaker will rarely emit, perhaps because in the past they have not benefited his listening audience and hence have not been strengthened by reinforcements. For example, the speaker will usually refrain from "obvious" tacts that are uninformative to the listener ("The chair has four legs"), since this behavior is not likely to have been reinforced in the past.

Some verbal behaviors are controlled by verbal stimuli. *Echoic* responses refer to those instances in which one individual is reinforced for imitating the behavior of another. Skinner notes that the development of an echoic repertoire in children may be helpful in the acquisition of further verbal skills. Thus, a child who has had extensive reinforcement for a variety of echoic behaviors will presumably say "Rover" following the verbal stimulus (request): "Say 'Rover' "; this may prove to be a significant help in teaching the child the proper name for the family pet.

Intraverbal behaviors constitute another class of responses in which the speaker's behavior is determined by prior verbal stimulation. The question "How are you?" often elicits (is an occasion for) the response "Fine"; or the stimulus "Two times three" elicits "Six." Sometimes the speaker may supply his own stimulus for an intraverbal response, as when a singer, in attempting to recall a line somewhere in the middle of a song, finds it necessary to start from the beginning to get a "running start."

Textual responses represent still another category of behavior that is controlled by verbal stimulation. Textual behaviors denote those instances in which a passage of written material serves as the discriminative stimulus that controls the speaker's utterances. In short, textual behavior refers to *reading,* a situation in which the speaker's responses are determined by the text to which he is exposed—presumably because of the reinforcements that may be gained through such behavior. Thus, if a child says "shoe" when looking at the letters s-h-o-e, his teacher may praise him publicly.

A critique of Skinner's approach

Skinner's theory of verbal behavior was eagerly received by many, not only because of its emphasis on the basic principles of operant conditioning as an explanation for the complexities of speech but also because of its apparent objectivity and its deliberate rejection of such "mentalistic" concepts as *meaning* and *reference.* Moreover, by forcefully rejecting such traditional concepts as *intention* or *purpose* as outmoded and unscientific, Skinner posited a speaker who contributed little of "his own" to the process of verbal behavior; the speaker in the Skinnerian model was assumed to be strictly controlled by his past reinforcement history and by the stimuli in his environment. As a consequence, speech was readily manipulable, in principle, through these "external" factors.

Despite the confident and objective aura of Skinner's approach, it has met with severe criticism. Some critics have questioned Skinner's assertion that the various categories of verbal behavior are mechanically developed, independent of one another. Thus, it has been suggested that there must be some *central representational process* accompanying the use of a word such as "water"—a process that would facilitate the transfer of this response from situations where, for example, "water" functions as a *mand* (cases in which deprivation plays an important role) to situations where "water" functions as a *tact* (when the speaker is describing some feature of his environment).

Noam Chomsky, a linguist, has doubtless been the most severe of Skinner's critics (1959). He has raised serious questions regarding the apparent objectivity of the entire approach, suggesting, for example, that the concept of reinforcement is used so loosely that its original, concrete meaning is almost completely destroyed. Thus, in contrast to the laboratory situation in which a food-deprived animal may be reinforced with food pellets, Skinner suggests that verbal behaviors may sometimes be strengthened either through such fanciful procedures as *automatic self-reinforcement* (when the child reinforces his own "successful" echoic behavior) or through events that may occur in the rather *distant future* (in the case of the writer who is presumably reinforced by the hope that his work will ultimately be well received). Chomsky suggests that through such extensions the original specificity of the reinforcement concept is lost; thus, the word "reinforcement," replete with its connotations of scientific objectivity, simply replaces more conventional terms such as *liking* and *wanting.* For example, rather than saying that children often *like* to imitate their parents' speech, a Skinnerian might explain that they derive *self-reinforcement* from echoic responses; similarly, the writer who works long hours because he *wants* his work to be favorably received might be said to *gain reinforcement* for his present efforts through the as-yet-unrealized reactions of others. While it is always easy to characterize scientific terms as "jargon," it seems legitimate in these cases to wonder whether the reinforcement terminology has, in fact, led to a more satisfactory understanding of the behaviors in question.

Chomsky also takes issue with the way in which Skinner extends the concept of *stimulus control* to the domain of verbal behavior. In principle, the operant conditioning approach asserts that the individual's verbal responses are determined in large part by the physical stimuli in the speaker's environment; thus, according to the theory, if the discriminative stimuli are skillfully manipulated, the speaker's utterances may be controlled. In reply to this assertion, Chomsky notes that it is usually impossible to determine *which aspect* of a given situation will, in fact, have an impact upon the speaker until *after* he has completed his utterance. If the speaker is looking at a painting, for example, he may respond to any number of things: the painting's color, shape, frame, subject matter, or the associations that are elicited by one or more of these features. This means that the *effective stimulus* is not in fact a readily manipulable aspect of the environment, but is, in a sense, "selected" by the speaker from a multitude of possibilities.

Once again, Chomsky argues, a concept derived from a carefully conceived experimental background has been overextended, for the concept of the discriminative stimulus is often used by Skinner in place of such traditional terms as *reference,* with little evidence of scientific gain. For example, in place of the rather forbidding assertion that the speaker's remarks were *under the discriminative control of* the subject matter of the painting, it could simply be said that the speaker *referred to* the subject matter of the painting (when he said: "It looks like a circus.").

The associationist approach

The associationist approach represents a long-standing and still vigorous tradition in the psychological study of language. The associationists have repeatedly emphasized the lawfully structured (nonrandom) nature of our verbal associations, and they have sought to show the impact of these verbal habits on such fundamental processes as cognition, learning, perception, and communication.

Word-association studies have had a long and varied history. In the simplest and most classic form of the word-association test, the subject is presented with a series of stimulus words; he is instructed to respond to each one with the first word (or words) that occur to him. Sir Francis Galton was the first to introduce this technique. Serving as his own subject, Galton was so vividly impressed by the very personal nature of his reactions that he refrained from publishing the results of his experiment. Following Galton's work, there have been two main lines of research in the study of word associations. Starting from the time of Jung (1918), psychologists working in the clinical tradition found the technique useful as a means of assessing the emotional reactions of individual patients; experimental psychologists have also used the word-association method as a means of studying thought processes from a more generalized point of view.

The clinical approach. Jung reasoned that the emotional complexes and resistances of patients could be identified by noting the stimulus words that led either to unusual responses or to responses that were produced after some delay. As we will see, these two response indicators, *response frequency* and *response latency,* tend to be related; common responses are usually produced rather quickly, while uncommon ones take somewhat longer. Present-day clinicians have been particularly interested in interpreting responses that seem *idiosyncratic* and thus indicative of the respondent's unique psychological characteristics. Thus, the patient who responds with *tyrant* to the stimulus word *father* has presumably given us a reasonably clear indication of certain underlying attitudes. Most responses are not so direct and readily interpretable, however, and the clinician is more typically faced with the problem of *interpreting* his patient's associations. In performing this task, he is likely to proceed in a manner reminiscent of the psychoanalyst; he will assume that the patients' overt responses are indirect and symbolic representations of emotional reactions, much as the manifest content of a dream symbolically reflects the latent content.

The clinician's interest in word associations is mainly focused on unique responses, on the assumption that only these can provide a basis for understanding how one person differs from another. Parallelling this premise is the clinician's belief that the patient's deviant responses reflect ego weakness, for they are presumably manifestations of a temporary "breakdown" in the censoring mechanism that normally blocks the expression of unsocialized reactions. Since weak ego strength is characteristic of the severely disturbed psychotic individual, we are logically led to the expectation that psychotics should produce an above-average number of deviant (uncommon) free-association responses. Early research by Kent and Rosanoff (1910) confirmed this expectation. These investigators compared the free associations of 247 psychotics with those produced by a sample of 1,000 control subjects. Defining an *individual reaction* as one which appeared less than twice in their sample of 1,000 normal subject, Kent and Rosanoff reported that over 26 per cent of the responses in the psychotic group were individual reactions, as compared with less than 7 per cent of the responses in the normal group.

Experimental studies of word association. The word-association task has also evoked continuing interest among experimental psychologists. Following the example of Kent and Rosanoff (see above), experimental psychologists have developed a variety of *word-association norms* in order to provide a firm basis for examining the popularity of different responses. The most extensive of these norms were collected by Russell and Jenkins (1954), who presented the 100 stimuli from the Kent-Rosanoff list to a group of 1,008 students at the University of Minnesota. An example of the sort of information that may be found in such norms is presented in Table 1, which shows the obtained frequency of various responses to the stimulus word *table.*

Table 1

Frequency of different free associations to the word *table.* (Data from Russell and Jenkins, 1954.)

	Table		
Response	Frequency	Response	Frequency
Chair	691	Salt	4
Food	59	Flat	3
Desk	33	Plate	3
Top	30	Tablecloth	3
Cloth	29	Cards	2
Eat	23	Chairs	2
Leg	11	Dark	2
Dish	8	Eating	2
Lamp	8	Maple	2
Legs	7	Round	2
Wood	7	Tennis	2
Kitchen	6	Big	1
Fork	5	Book	1
Spoon	5	Floor	1
Brown	4	Large	1
Dinner	4	Sat	1
Dishes	4	Silverware	1
		Sit	1

Comparisons between the Kent-Rosanoff norms (established in 1910) and those collected more recently have generally shown a tendency toward increasing *commonality* (or sterotypy) of response. That is, in the more recent data, the most popular responses to the various stimulus words tended to be given by a greater percentage of the subjects than was the case in 1910. This trend has been obtained in studies of both children and adults, and it is usually attributed to the increased availability of mass-communication media such as magazines, television, and radio, which have served to "homogenize" our verbal environment to a large extent.

A study by Palermo and Jenkins (1965) reveals another interesting change in the free association norms of the 1960s; these researchers compared the free associations of fourth and fifth graders, as reported in a 1916 study, with those collected from similar age groups in 1961. Apart from the trend toward increased uniformity of response, the Palermo and Jenkins study revealed an increased number of *paradigmatic* response words—associations drawn from the same part of speech as the stimulus; for example, the stimulus word *table* (a noun) might elicit another noun (*chair*). Paradigmatic responses are given more often by adults than by children; children more typically produce *syntagmatic* responses—responses drawn from a different grammatical class than the stimulus word (as in the example *table-eat*). The increased frequency of paradigmatic responses within the sample of children tested by Palermo and Jenkins led these investigators to conclude that this group was probably more precocious in a linguistic sense than their counterparts 45 years earlier. This interpretation was strengthened by the fact that *all* of the observed differences between the two samples were consistent with the "precocity" hypothesis.

Marbe's law. What is the relationship between group norms and the associative behavior of the individual? Can we assume, for example, that the associative bond between the stimulus and response words is particularly *strong* for an individual subject who produces a relatively popular response (as defined by group norms)? To answer this question, several investigators (see Woodworth and Schlosberg, 1954) have correlated response *frequency* with response *latency* (speed of response). The results of these studies clearly indicate that the popularity of a response (as determined from group data) is indeed a good indicator of response availability for the individual, since popular responses tend to be emitted rather quickly in comparison with those that occur less frequently. This principle has been termed *Marbe's law*, in honor of a pioneering investigator of the phenomenon (Thumb and Marbe, 1901). A result closely related to Marbe's law has been reported by Bousfield and Barclay (1950), who used a type of *restricted* word-association test. In this study, subjects were instructed to list all the *animals* they could think of; the results indicated that the animals that were listed most frequently (for example, *dog* or *cat*) tended to appear relatively early in the sequence of responses, as contrasted with the animals that were named infrequently (for example, *armadillo*).

The relationship between response *frequency* and response *speed* suggests that the familiarity (or frequency) of the *stimulus* word may also play a significant role in the association process. One study indicated that *common* stimulus words (those that appear frequently in samples of written English) evoke fewer *different* responses than do uncommon words (Postman, 1964); this means that common stimulus words normally evoke relatively popular responses. Moreover, since popular responses are usually emitted rather quickly, and since common stimulus words lead to popular responses, we might anticipate that the latency of response to these common words might be rather short. The available results do, indeed, support this expectation. Cofer and Shevitz (1952) studied subjects' continous associations to stimulus words of varying frequency, and they found that the number of associations generated within a fixed time interval was significantly affected by the frequency with which the stimulus word appeared in normal English prose. Since the common stimulus words elicited more associations in the allotted time than the uncommon words, we are led to conclude that the average speed of response to the common words must have been higher.

Word association and natural language. Although it is clear that word associations are far from random, and that they may have far-reaching effects upon the individual's performance in laboratory studies of learning and perception, the relationship between word associations and everyday speech (or writing) is rather complex. One of the earliest studies of this topic was conducted by Davis Howes (1957), who compared the frequency with which various words were used in written language (as tabulated by Thorndike and Lorge, 1944) with the frequency of occurrence for these same words as word-association responses (as listed in the Kent-Rosanoff norms). Howes' results indicated that there was a high correlation ($r = .94$) between these two sets of data; words that occurred frequently in written language also appeared frequently as word-association responses. It should be noted, however, that in conducting this study, Howes considered only *contentive* words (such as nouns, verbs, and adjectives); although *connective* words (conjunctions, articles, pronouns, and auxiliaries) appear quite frequently in samples of written language, they rarely occur as word associates—probably because of the subjects' implicit understanding of the task.

Despite Howes' results, which suggest some underlying equivalence between word associations and everyday speech, it is clear that the stimulus-response pairs that emerge in association norms do *not*, in the main, reflect common verbal sequences. For example, a strongly associated pair of words such as *up-down* would rarely appear as adjacent words in normal speech. Similarly, associations such as *green* (in response to *grass*) or *blue* (in response to *sky*) invert the word order of grammatical English, for adjectives normally precede the nouns that they modify (as in *green grass* or *blue sky,* as opposed to *grass-green* and *sky-blue*).

Word associations and grammatical classes. Linguists classify the words of a language into relatively homogeneous syntactic classes by noting their "privileges of occurrence" (the verbal contexts in which they may grammatically appear). For example, there is a vast array of nouns that can be placed in the sentence frames: "See the ______," "I own a ______," "This ______ is mine." This method of grammatical classification is preferable to that based on the traditional parts of speech (e.g., a noun is the name of a person, place or thing), in part, because the traditional definitions are rather imprecise. Moreover, the privileges-of-occurrence idea provides us with an important insight regarding the development of language; it suggests that when a new word is introduced in a sentence, two things may occur: (1) the syntactic class to which it belongs may well be revealed by the words that surround it, and (2) the reader may immediately recognize other grammatically acceptable ways of using the new word. For example, if I hear that someone wants a *huft,* I realize from the verbal context that it would be grammatically correct to use the word *huft* as a noun, in sentences like: "I once had a huft," "Look at the huft," "That huft is nice," etc., even though it might later turn out (when I learn the exact meaning of *huft*) that some of these sentences are silly or untrue.

In an ingenious experiment with grade school children, Roger Brown and Jean Berko (1960) set out to explore (1) the child's increasing ability to manipulate these implicit rules of syntax and (2) the relationship between these skills and the child's word associations. One part of the study required that the children apply their syntactic knowledge to a series of nonsense words (like *huft, niss, wug,* etc.). On each problem, the child was shown a picture and was presented with a query of the following type: "Do you know what a wug is? This is a picture of a little girl thinking about a wug. Can you make up what that might mean?" This context served to identify *wug* as a noun, and the experimenters carefully checked each child's response to see if it was consistent with this fact. For example, if the child said "She is thinking about her favorite wug, which was a gift from her aunt," or if she volunteered that "A wug is a doll," she was credited with having correctly utilized the part of speech implied by the introductory verbal context. Using this method, the researchers constructed test materials to assess the children's ability to use nonsense words whose verbal contexts identified them as nouns, adjectives, adverbs, transitive verbs, and intransitive verbs. The performances of first-grade, second-grade, and third-grade children were compared with those of a group of adults. The results showed a consistent tendency for performance to improve with age.

In a second part of this same study, the four groups of subjects were given a *free-association* test; they were given six stimulus words representing each of the parts of speech that were central to the nonsense-word task, and were asked to say another word in response to each stimulus. One important finding was the fact that *performance on the nonsense-word task* (see above) *was significantly related to performance on the free-association task*; within each age group, the parts of speech that most frequently led to paradigmatic responses in the free-association task were usually the parts of speech that were handled most successfully in the task that required the grammatical usage of nonsense words. These results suggest that the child's increasingly paradigmatic associations may signal a developing tendency to organize his vocabulary into *syntactic classes* (parts of speech), as opposed to an organization based on contiguities (like *table-eat* or *dark-night*) and phrase completions (to *send-mail*).

This analysis implies that for the adult, associated words may often enjoy similar privileges of occurrence. That is, although associated pairs may not reflect acceptable verbal sequences, they may nonetheless have the *potential* of being used in the same verbal environments. The associated words *black* and *white*, for example, may both appear in sentences like "My dog is ______," "She wore a ______ sweater," and so on. While it is conceivable that associated paradigmatic pairs commonly appear in identical (or closely related) verbal contexts, the relevant data to support this point are simply not available. As a best-available approximation, Jenkins and Palermo (1964) report that if subjects are instructed to write sentences that include a pre-selected "key word" and are then asked to replace the key word with another, the substitute is often a high-frequency associate of the word being replaced. This line of reasoning suggests that word associations (between *black* and *white*, for example) may develop through a sequence reminiscent of response equivalence. Thus, if a common set of sentence frames has been used in combination with the words *black* and *white*, the existence of these mutually shared verbal contexts (as stimuli) should lead to the development of an associative bond between the responses *black* and *white*. (See Deese, 1966 and Jenkins and Palermo, 1964, for a more extended discussion of this viewpoint).

Word associations and reading performance. The considerations noted above have all revolved about the similarity between word associations and the observed verbal behavior of an accomplished *speaker*. Let us now change our orientation and consider word associations from the standpoint of the message *recipient*. Samuels (1966) has reported two experiments showing the impact of word associations on reading speed and information recall. In these studies, fifth and sixth graders, as well as a class of college juniors, were given the task of reading either high-association or low-association paragraphs. The high-association paragraph included such associated word pairs as *moon* and *stars, green* and *grass*; in the low-association paragraph, one member of each pair (the response word) was replaced by some other, *unrelated* word, which was nevertheless meaningful in the paragraph and equally familiar to the readers. For example, in the high-association paragraph one sentence read "Outside, the *moon* and *stars* shone brightly in the June sky, and the *green grass* sparkled in the night." In the low-association condition this sentence was altered as follows: "Outside, the *moon* and *lake* appeared clearly in the June evening, and the *green house* sparkled in the valley." Samuel's results indicated that the high-association paragraph was read more quickly than the low-association paragraph; moreover, when the subjects were given a series of multiple-choice questions based on the paragraphs they had read, the high-association group again showed superior performance. These results are unique in demonstrating the role of word associations in a realistic, everyday activity.

Word associations and meaning. Psycholinguists have long been interested in *semantics*, the relationship between verbal utterances and the meanings (or ideas) that they signify. Since speech is most typically used to transmit meaning, some investigators have suggested that it might be fruitful to regard the listener's response(s) to any utterance as an index of the *meaning* of that utterance. Despite the plausibility of this conception, it is difficult to test directly, since the listener's (or reader's) response to a given linguistic stimulus may, under normal circumstances, be quite unremarkable—it may be wholly internal. There is the possibility, however, that free-association techniques may be used to externalize at least *some* of the reactions evoked by linguistic stimuli—notably the listener's *verbal* reactions (as contrasted with the images, motivational states, and so on that language may stimulate). This associative approach to meaning is somewhat strengthened (but not *proved*) by the fact that word associations generally have evaluative connotations that are similar to those of their eliciting stimuli. That is, despite the frequency of contrast or oppositional responses (e.g., *clean-dirty*), there is a general tendency for stimulus words with favorable connotations to be associated with positively valued responses such as happy, healthy, and so on (De Burger and Donahoe, 1965).

How do words become associated with the things they signify? Charles Osgood suggests (1957) that this occurs in two ways. At the most primitive level—that of the child—we have what Osgood terms *sign learning*. In sign learning, the child is assumed to have repeatedly heard a given word ("cat") in the presence of a specific object (the household cat). Through a process of conditioning, the word eventually comes to elicit some part of the child's response to the object (cat). While it is clear that we do not overtly respond in the same manner to the word and the object to which it refers, Osgood hypothesizes that the word normally tends to elicit "lightweight" (that is, relatively easy-to-perform) components of the total response complex originally associated with its referent, as shown diagrammatically in Figure 1. For example, while the *object* cat may elicit playful stroking behavior on the child's part, the word "cat" may result in an internal pattern of neural discharge (r_m) similar to that which accompanies the overt response (R_T) to the object cat. The proprioceptive feedback (s_m) from these lightweight responses presumably plays an important role in guiding the child's overt reaction (R_o) to any given word, as discussed in our earlier discussion of mediated generalization (see p. 15).

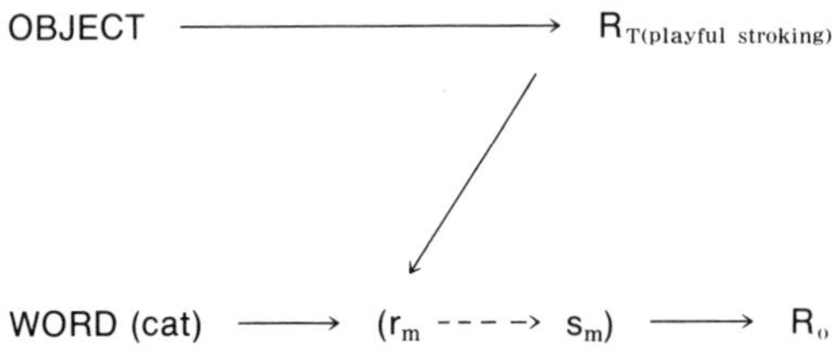

Figure 1

Osgood's theory of meaning. Following learning, the word "cat" elicits part of response complex originally associated with object cat. (Adapted from Osgood, C. E. *Method and theory in experimental psychology.* New York: Oxford University Press, 1953.)

In addition to sign learning, Osgood postulates that words often acquire their meaning through association with other signs whose meaning is already known; this is known as *assign learning*. He notes, for example, that most five-year-olds understand the word "zebra," although they may never have been in the presence of a zebra. They have, however, been told of the zebra's various characteristics (size, shape, striped appearance, etc.). According to Osgood's theory, the reactions that the child has previously learned to associate with these different characteristics are now "assigned" (through further learning) to the new word "zebra." Osgood assumes that a similar process is involved in learning the meaning of signs and assigns; "lightweight" responses previously elicited by an object (in sign learning) or by a familiar symbol (in assign learning) now come to be associated with the new stimulus word, through conditioning.

According to Osgood's theory, the mediating responses (r_m) associated with various words constitute their meaning. As shown in Figure 1, proprioceptive feedback (S_m) from these responses guides our overt reactions (R_o) to these language symbols. Unfortunately, the theory is quite vague in specifying the content and locus of these mediating responses, many of which may occur at a physiological or neurological level. Consequently, it has thus far been impossible to investigate the meaning process through direct observation.

Osgood's theory of meaning has often been criticized for confusing the related concepts of *meaning* and *reference*. According to the theory, the "meaning" of a word develops through an associative linkage of the word and the thing it represents (the *referent*). It has been argued, however, that the referent of a word or phrase should *not* be confused with its meaning, since these are distinct entities. For example, two statements may have the same referent, even though they mean rather different things. While the name "Sigmund Freud" may *refer to* the same individual as the phrase "the founder of psychoanalysis," these two utterances clearly have different *meanings*. The sentence "Sigmund Freud was the founder of psychoanalysis" is thus not a pointless one; if the two utterances in question had the *same meaning*, the above sentence would be as uninformative as the statement "Sigmund Freud was Sigmund Freud." Another point worth considering is the fact that a sentence may be meaningful even though its referent is non-existent, in a physical sense. Thus, the statement "Leprechauns are more mischievous than angels" is meaningful even though the entities to which it refers cannot be experienced in the same way that we can see, touch, and point to the objects signified by such words as "car," "house," and "boulder." Finally, such words as "but," "very," and "or" are clearly loaded with meaning, even though it is difficult to see how Osgood's theory would account for the child's ability to comprehend these terms, through either sign learning or assign learning.

The semantic differential

In addition to his theoretical writings on the concept of meaning, Osgood and his associates (Osgood, Suci, and Tannenbaum, 1957) have spent many years developing a procedure known as the ***semantic differential.***[1] Their aim has been to assess quantitatively the connotative meaning of various words and other symbols. Before describing the essentials of this technique, we should note the important distinction between ***connotative meaning*** (the associations that are called up when we are presented with various symbols) and ***denotative meaning*** (the objects and actions that these symbols represent in the real world). Thus, while the words "nurse" and "teacher" may have similar connotations (helpful, kind, etc.), they denote persons in quite distinct occupational roles.

The semantic differential might best be described as a controlled association method for measuring connotative meaning. In a study of the connotative meaning of a word such as "justice," subjects might be asked to rate this word on a series of seven-step adjectival scales such as those shown in Figure 2. The responses (X's) in this example

JUSTICE

CRUEL	___	___	___	___	X	___	___	KIND
CURVED	___	___	___	___	X	___	___	STRAIGHT
MASCULINE	___	___	X	___	___	___	___	FEMININE
ACTIVE	___	___	___	___	X	___	___	PASSIVE
SAVORY	___	X	___	___	___	___	___	TASTELESS
UNSUCCESSFUL	___	___	X	___	___	___	___	SUCCESSFUL

Figure 2

Responses to the concept of "justice" on several scales of semantic differential.

represent the average ratings of 540 students at the University of Minnesota. It is assumed that the respondents' ratings indicate the extent to which they associate the different words being rated ("justice," in this case) with the various polar adjectives. In order to quantify such data it is common to assign the numbers 1 through

[1] Snider and Osgood (1969) is a recent collection of papers concerned with the semantic differential.

7 to the responses, depending upon the rating categories in which they fall; thus, if the value 1 was given to the "kind" end of the first scale, the concept "justice" would have a rating 3, while a neutral rating would be assigned a score of 4. Note again that this method does not enable us to determine the denotative meaning of justice, nor does it give us a good idea of what the dictionary definition might be. It does, however, indicate the attributes that our respondents associate with the concept of justice, and how strongly they hold to these associations. For example, within the Minnesota sample, justice is regarded as moderately kind (rather than cruel), moderately straight (as opposed to curved), moderately masculine, and so on.

An almost infinite variety of scales could be constructed by simply listing all the adjective-opposite pairs in a given language (for example, bright-dark, democratic-undemocratic, happy-sad, etc.). Fortunately, however, Osgood, Suci and Tannenbaum (1957) have shown that different scales often elicit similar responses. For example, concepts rated as healthy (as opposed to sick) also tend to be rated as nice (rather than awful) and beautiful (rather than ugly). This cluster of scales and others like them are generally regarded as representing an *evaluative* factor, which essentially indicates how good versus bad a given concept seems to be. Thus "justice" would be rated as healthy, nice, and beautiful, while "disgust" would be rated as sick, awful, and ugly. In addition to the evaluative cluster of scales (which seem to be the most numerous of all), Osgood and his collaborators have discovered two other important clusters representing *potency* and *activity*. The potency factor includes such scales as large-small, strong-weak, and heavy-light, while the activity cluster includes sharp-dull, hot-cold, and active-passive. Although recent research indicates that the realm of connotative meaning may include additional scale clusters (or dimensions) beyond the three listed, these three—evaluation, potency, and activity—represent important aspects of connotation in a wide variety of languages.

While the semantic differential has proven to be a useful and popular research tool, it has several shortcomings. One of the most serious problems is that the concept being rated at a particular time may influence the interpretations placed upon the various rating scales. For example, while the scale healthy-unhealthy is usually interpreted figuratively and thus elicits ratings that correlate with the evaluative cluster (good-bad, kind-cruel, etc.), one can picture a respondent, who, being called upon to rate a specific concept (*my father,* for example), may interpret the scale in its *denotative* sense (presence versus absence of physical well-being); our hypothetical subject may, accordingly, characterize his ailing father as being unhealthy, but kind, honest, and so on. This example—showing the impact of a particular concept on the interpretation placed upon a given rating scale—may be quite common, leading us to wonder if the semantic differential does, in fact, measure "pure" connotation; it seems more plausible to assume that it elicits an unknown mixture of connotative and denotative reactions. Considerations of this sort also lead to questions regarding the generality of the three-dimensional meaning space, for it has been suggested (Carroll, 1959) that by altering the sample of scales and the sample of concepts presented for rating, we may drastically affect the number and character of the semantic dimensions that appear. Despite these limitations, the semantic differential has proven to be a very flexible research tool. Some of its uses are described below.

Mediated learning. An interesting experiment by Ryan (1960) indicates that mediated facilitation may be demonstrated in a learning situation if the critically related pairs are selected because of their similar semantic profiles (in contrast to earlier studies showing transfer between words that are *directly* associated, such as *hot-cold*). In Ryan's study, subjects first learned a paired-associate list including a pair like X-ZUG; this prior learning significantly facilitated the learning of X′-ZUG on a second list (where X and X′ were words with similar profiles on the semantic differential, but were *not* associatively related to each other). This result is presumably attributable to some form of stimulus generalization (see p. 14); that is, the development of association between ZUG and X is apparently accompanied by a generalized association between ZUG and other words (such as X′) which are *meaningfully* related to X, although they do not sound or look like X, nor are they directly associated with it.

Semantic satiation. Continued repetition or inspection of a word is often accompanied by a loss in the word's meaningfulness. You can informally investigate this phenomenon yourself by looking at and concentrating on any of the words on this page (the word "page," for example).

To investigate this semantic satiation more systematically, some experimenters (Lambert and Jakobovits, 1960) have turned to the semantic differential. They reasoned that if continued inspection or repetition of a word leads to a loss in meaningfulness, this should be detectable in the semantic differential ratings elicited by the word. In particular, if a word loses its meaningfulness, it should be rated in more neutral terms than it was before the satiation procedure, since it would presumably become relatively devoid of connotative associations. Results of this sort have, in fact, been obtained in a series of studies (Amster, 1964).

Some related effects have also been observed. For example, if subjects continuously repeat a given word and are then asked to rate a synonym, satiation effects may also be obtained for the synonym. This suggests that the satiation phenomenon has rather general cognitive ramifications, rather than being limited to single, isolated words. Also, where satiation procedures were applied to numbers which were then included as elements in various addition problems, the time required to solve these problems was effectively lengthened. In this case, presumably, satiation temporarily reduced the meaningfulness of the numbers and thus interfered with the subjects' ability to respond to the numbers appropriately in the test problems.

How are these results to be explained? Several conflicting explanations have been offered, perhaps the most popular being an inhibitory interpretation. This account emphasizes that most responses (verbal or otherwise) become temporarily less available immediately after they have been performed. Thus, if a rat has just turned left at the choice point of a T-maze, and is immediately returned to the maze, the probability of his turning left again will be somewhat reduced. Moreover, if he has just been forced to take several left turns, the likelihood that he will turn left again will be still lower. Analogously, if we assume (as discussed earlier) that words and other symbols automatically result in certain internal mediating responses that constitute their meaning, we are led to anticipate that these meaning responses will be somewhat weaker and less available if they have just been repeatedly elicited. Thus, repetition of a word may make its associated meaning response less and less available, which would be reflected in (a) a relatively neutral semantic profile and (b) a significant decrement in the capacity to solve problems requiring the use of these words.

Psychotherapy. O. H. Mowrer used the semantic differential to quantify the changes in connotative meaning that accompanied psychotherapy (cited in Osgood et al., 1957). Two patients were represented in this exploratory study, a young man and a young woman. They were administered semantic differential forms on three occasions: near the start of therapy, at about the middle of the therapy process, and shortly after successful therapy had been terminated. The same eight concepts ("me," "mother," "father," "baby," "lady," "God," "sin," and "fraud") were rated in each of the three test sessions. By observing the similarity in the rating given to the concepts "me," "father," and "mother," it was possible to assess the patients' identifications (did the young lady rate herself as being more similar to her father than to her mother?). In Mowrer's cases, the young man initially saw himself as closely resembling his mother; the young woman saw herself as resembling her father. By the end of the therapy, however, the young man identified with his father, and the young woman with her mother. Since these results agreed with the therapist's clinical observations, this seems a promising approach to clinical research.

Associative overlap

Following Osgood's pioneering efforts, other investigators have applied associative techniques to the task of measuring meaning. One of the more recent approaches is exemplified by the work of James Deese (1966), who has attempted to assess the extent to which various word-pairs elicit common associations in the standard word-association procedure. For example, consider the words *wing* and *bird.* At an intuitive level they appear to be closely related, and this is reflected in the fact that these words elicit several common associations when presented as associative stimuli; thus, in addition to the fact that *bird* and *wing* are *directly* associated with each other, both words lead to the response *butterfly.* Deese has worked with a measure of "associative overlap," known as the *intersection coefficient,* which quantifies this similarity of response; intersection coefficients range from 0.00, signifying no commonality of response, to a theoretical high of 1.00, which would be obtained if the two words in question led to identical response distributions. Table 2 presents intersection coefficients for the words *woman, man, girl,* and *boy* and shows, for example, that the words *man* and *woman* are more closely related (an intersection coefficient of .68) than the pair *man* and *girl* (.08)—a result that conforms with common-sense expectations.

Table 2

Intersection coefficients showing the "associative overlap" between the words *woman, man, girl,* and *boy.* (From Deese, 1966, p. 57.)

	Stimulus		Response	
	Woman	Man	Girl	Boy
Woman	1.00	.68	.16	.12
Man		1.00	.08	.04
Girl			1.00	.73
Boy				1.00

An interesting adaptation of Deese's approach to meaning was reported by Feldman (1962) in a study concerned with the associative correlates of attitude. Feldman selected two groups of students who differed in the salience of their religious convictions; one group showed strong religious values (as assessed by the Allport-Vernon-Lindzey inventory), while the other was relatively non-religious. Free associations were obtained from both groups, using a series of fifteen religious-value stimulus words (such as *sermon, clergyman, religion,* and *faith*), and intersection coefficients were calculated separately for the two groups. A comparison of these coefficients revealed that the various religious terms seemed to form a more tightly-knit structure in the group with strong religious values than they did in the group with less pronounced religious convictions; that is, the religious students exhibited systematically higher intersection coefficients than the agnostics. Apparently, the religious words were relatively similar in meaning from the religious students' point of view, but they seemed rather diverse to the subjects with less salient religious values.

Deese's technique has also been used to analyze the associative relationships existing within a sample of *structural* (or connective) words—words that have no denotative meaning of their own, but mainly serve to connect other words that do. In this study, free associations were first obtained to a collection of verbal auxiliaries (like *be, are, was,* and so on), and intersection coefficients were computed for the various pairs of stimulus words. Factor-analytic techniques were then applied, in order to identify (by strictly mathematical means) those clusters of words that were most closely related. These procedures yielded an intuitively satisfactory grouping of auxiliaries. There were two pairs of contrasting clusters. One cluster consisted of the words *do, does, can,* and *will* as opposed to *might, would*, and *could*. Another cluster included various forms of the verb *to be* (*been, be, is, was,* and *are*), as contrasted with a *to have* cluster (*has, have,* and *had*). This study shows that associative data may yield important insights concerning functional (connective) words, in addition to their utility in the analysis of words that have semantic (referential) meaning.

Statistical approaches to language

The study of language usage reveals certain statistical regularities that seem to derive from underlying constraints imposed both by the laws of grammar and by the behavioral dispositions of language users. These regularities are often uncovered by simply counting the relative frequency with which different words appear in a given language. Thorndike and Lorge (1944), for example, conducted an important survey of this type, analyzing a large sample of printed English; Davis Howes (1966) has reported a similar study of spoken English, based on speech samples obtained in an interview situation. Norms of this sort are extremely useful in laboratory studies that use verbal materials, for familiarity plays an important role in verbal learning and perception.

Zipf's law

One of the more important findings uncovered through the word count method is Zipf's Law of Least Effort (1949). According to this law, the more effort involved in emitting a given word (or sound), the less frequent the appearance of that word in everyday discourse. One index of "word effort," of course, would be the length of the word; in general, we may assume that long words require more effort than short ones. The law of least effort thus suggests that, on the average, short words will be used more often than long ones. This relationship between word length and word frequency has in fact been verified in Chinese, Latin, and English, suggesting that it is probably characteristic of all languages.

In interpreting these data, Zipf argues that frequent usage causes the shortening of words. Examples such as the shortening of "moving pictures" to "movies" and "automobile" to "auto" or "car" illustrate this trend. Another example is the widespread use of abbreviations for the various government agencies—a trend that is particularly prominent among federal employees in Washington, D.C. As you might guess, the everyday activities of government workers require them to talk about these agencies on many occasions. Hence, according to Zipf's law, they should show a strong inclination to shorten the formal names of the agencies. The Department of Health, Education and Welfare is thus colloquially referred to as HEW, while the Organization of American States is abbreviated as OAS. The development of slang and specialized scientific jargon often seems to follow a similar pattern. Note, for example, the use of the term GSR, rather than galvanic skin response, among experimental psychologists.[2]

An experiment by Krauss and Weinheimer (1964a) provides perhaps the clearest example of the condensation process that lies at the heart of Zipf's law. In this study,

[2]Sapir (1916) argued that the length of a word also gives us a clue about the age of the word. In particular, Sapir suggested that short words are generally old ones, while new words are more likely to be long "compounds" formed by the combination of several short "kernels." For example, short words such as "knight," "good," and "sun" have doubtless been a part of the English language for a considerable time, as contrasted with words of more recent origin like "delicatessen." If Zipf is correct, we may expect that such new, rather long words will eventually become shorter—at least among those who have occasion to use them frequently. Perhaps we are already seeing the start of this process in the emergence of such colloquial terms as "delly."

pairs of subjects who were visually separated from one another attempted to solve a problem in which they had to communicate about several unusual designs for which there were no common, standardized names. Each subject was given six designs which were labeled from A to F, or from 1 to 6. The subjects in each pair then attempted to determine the letter-number pairings for the various designs. That is, a subject whose figures were *numbered* was faced with the task of determining the *letters* that his partner had assigned to these identical designs.

As the experimental session proceeded, the investigators noted that there was a systematic decrease in the number of words used in referring to the various designs. For example, a figure that was initially described as "an upside-down martini glass in a wire stand" was shortened first to the phrase "inverted martini glass" and ultimately to the word "martini." By the end of the experimental session, the designs that were mentioned frequently were denoted by relatively short names; those that were mentioned less often required longer phrases of reference.

In a subsequent experiment (Krauss and Weinheimer, 1964b), this same matching task was attempted with each subject's output being tape recorded for *future* playback, rather than emerging in the course of a continuous two-person conversation. In this case, the reference phrases were substantially longer than they were when interaction was possible. Moreover, the abbreviation process was much reduced in magnitude. These results suggest that the abbreviation process is partly controlled by feedback from the listener; condensations seem to be avoided, unless the speaker can be reasonably confident (based on past experience) that communication will proceed effectively despite his use of abbreviated reference phrases.

Mere exposure and the Pollyanna hypothesis

Word counts have been completed in a number of different languages. An unexpected phenomenon that has turned up with remarkable regularity is the fact that words with "good" connotations occur far more frequently than "bad" words. In English, for example, according to the Thorndike-Lorge word count, the word "happiness" occurs more than 15 times as often as the word "unhappiness," and the word "beauty" is used 41 times more frequently than the word "ugliness." Zajonc (1968) has presented evidence that this bias towards "goodness" occurs quite consistently in English, French, German, and Spanish; and Boucher and Osgood (1969) have reported similar effects in 10 additional languages. To account for this phenomenon, Zajonc suggests that the "mere exposure" to novel stimuli (both verbal and nonverbal) leads people to evaluate those stimuli in increasingly positive terms. He has found, for example, that human subjects will show an increasingly positive reaction to (a) nonsense syllables, (b) "Chinese" characters, and (c) pictures of unfamiliar people, if these stimuli are simply presented to them repeatedly, so as to increase their familiarity. The exposure thesis thus implies that common words acquire "good" connotations if they are simply used often enough.

Boucher and Osgood (1969), on the other hand, interpret the frequent appearance of "good" words as evidence for a universal "Pollyanna" tendency, which leads people to talk about "good" things more often than "bad" things, and to learn "good" words at an earlier age than they learn "bad" ones. They suggest that the value-enhancing effects of mere exposure may be limited to stimuli that are either *meaningless* or *unfamiliar;* a stimulus that is already meaningful and familiar may, indeed, be evaluated in increasingly *negative* terms if we are exposed to it so often as to generate boredom (Maddi, 1968). While it is clear that the mere exposure hypothesis can account for our positive reaction to such high-frequency words as *health* or *wisdom* (as opposed to *sickness* and *stupidity*), Jakobovitz (1968) suggests that this explanation is incomplete, since it fails to tell us why it is that these high-frequency words refer to *non-verbal* states that are themselves intrinsically valuable. Zajonc's basic thesis is, however, an intriguing one that relates the word-count data to a broad behavioral principle which has proven useful in studies of both humans and animals (Zajonc, 1968). The conditions under which it can most fruitfully be applied remain to be determined in future research.

Redundancy in language

Since syntactic rules require that the speaker's utterances must conform to certain conventions of word order, and since these utterances will generally bear some sensible relationship to the "real world," it is often possible for the listener to guess some of the words that a speaker has used, even if he fails to hear exactly what has been said. By knowing the rules that guide the speaker's verbal behavior, the listener can thus infer what he has missed. For example, here is a passage from a contemporary novel in which every fifth word has been deleted. See if you can guess the words deleted.

> The glory of Manhattan __(1)__ Willie had seen from __(2)__ airplane was nowhere visible __(3)__ Broadway and Fiftieth Street __(4)__ he came up out __(5)__ the subway. It was __(6)__ same old dirty crowded __(7)__ :

here a cigar store, ___(8)___ an orange-drink stand, ___(9)___ a flickering movie marquee. . . .[3]

As you can see, in this ordinary passage of English text, many of the constituent words are readily predictable from the context in which they appear. Words that can be successfully guessed from their context are termed redundant, since the presence of these words does not convey much beyond what is implied by the surrounding verbal context. Languages generally contain a great deal of redundancy. This often enables the speaker to convey his meaning even though some parts of his message may have been lost in transmission due to noise, faulty pronunciation, or his listener's inattention.

Two types of experiments provide clear evidence that redundancy tends to eliminate errors in communication. One study (Miller, Heise, and Lichter, 1951) was concerned with the effect of redundancy on the intelligibility of speech. The subjects were presented with a series of words tape-recorded against a noisy background. The subjects simply had to indicate the words they heard. The results showed that words were easier to understand and correctly identify when they were presented in a meaningful sentence than they were when presented in random order. When a word is placed within a sentence, such as, "Apples grow on ______," there is a limited range of possibilities for the missing word. Even a vague impression of the last word enables the listener to make a fairly good guess. On the other hand, when words are presented in isolation there is no redundancy, and the listener finds it difficult to guess correctly when he is uncertain of a word, for the range of possibilities is virtually limitless.

A study by Taylor (1953) suggests that redundancy also affects the receiver's ability to comprehend a message; that is, highly redundant messages are more apt to convey successfully their meaning than are messages low in redundancy. Taylor's study was conducted as follows: In order to measure the redundancy of several written passages, he employed a procedure known as the "Cloze" technique (derived from the Gestalt concept of closure; see Weintraub and Walker, *Perception,* 1966). As shown in our passage above from *The Caine Mutiny,* Taylor simply deleted every fifth word of the original material and had a group of students attempt to fill in the missing words. For passages that were readily understandable, it was relatively easy to replace the deleted words; for other passages—particularly those that were difficult to comprehend—the missing words were hard to guess. Taylor's results thus

[3]The correct answers are: (1) which, (2) the, (3) on, (4) when, (5) of, (6) the, (7) street, (8) there, (9) yonder. From *The Caine Mutiny* by Herman Wouk. Copyright 1951 by Herman Wouk.

indicated that the readability of a written passage was related to its redundancy. The passages that were most readable (easiest to understand) were more redundant than those that proved to be relatively difficult.

On comprehensible writing

Taylor's findings concerning the relationship between verbal redundancy and readability warrant further amplification, since many people are concerned with making their writing more comprehensible. At a practical level, we might inquire into some of the characteristics that typically appear in prose that is easy to understand. In brief, how can the writer tell when his prose is reasonably redundant (and hence comprehensible) without subjecting it to the complexities of the Cloze procedure?

Two main factors seem to play an important role here. One of these is the writer's use of familiar words. Not surprisingly, familiar words are relatively easy to understand; and, generally speaking, the more familiar the words, the more comprehensible is the passage. Familiar words also make for redundancy. Consider a passage that contains many difficult words like "amanuensis" or "ubiquitous." When uncommon words of this sort are deleted in the course of the Cloze procedure, most readers will find it difficult to guess what has been omitted. Consequently, passages that contain many difficult words turn out to be low in redundancy; and, as we have seen, low redundancy usually leads to poor comprehension.

A second factor that affects both redundancy and reading comprehension is the average sentence length within the passage. Long sentences tend to produce passages that are low in redundancy and difficult to comprehend. "Long sentences often arrange words in patterns that are strange to the reader's verbal habits, whereas short sentences cannot. In a long sentence the qualifications can split apart words that function together. The reader's memory span is limited, and he is apt to forget the noun before he discovers the verb that goes with it (Miller, *Language and Communication,* p. 137)."

Several methods have been devised to provide the writer with systematic help in determining the readability of his prose. These techniques typically require a careful analysis of word familiarity and sentence length, among other factors. The so-called Flesch count is perhaps the most widely used of these procedures.[4]

[4]The Flesch count is computed by randomly selecting several sample passages—each containing 100 words —from the material being scored. The average number of syllables within each 100-word passage is then determined; this provides an indirect measure of word familiarity (W), since—as noted in Zipf's research de-

Summary

1. The psychological study of language has often proceeded from the assumption that linguistic skills might ultimately prove to be explainable in terms of basic learning mechanisms.

2. B. F. Skinner has sought to explain verbal behavior by stressing the importance of such concepts as *reinforcement* and *discriminative stimulation,* which have previously been identified as important determinants of nonverbal behavior. For Skinner, the main difference between verbal and nonverbal behavior is that verbal responses are typically reinforced because of their effects upon another person, while nonverbal behavior operates directly upon the environment. Skinner's approach has been criticized, however, because of its vague and overextended application of learning concepts, which often seem rather remote in the context of speech and communication.

3. Some psychologists have emphasized the lawfully structured character of our verbal associations and have attempted to show the impact of these verbal habits in a variety of areas, ranging from clinical psychology to experimental studies in learning and perception. Although it is clear that word associations may have far-reaching effects, there is relatively little evidence relating association patterns to the phenomena of everyday speech. Thus, despite some studies relating association norms to the individual's performance in tasks involving free speech and reading, associated word pairs do *not,* in the main, reflect common verbal sequences.

4. Charles Osgood has stressed the way in which verbal meanings are developed through the association between words and things. His theory assumes that, through conditioning, a word eventually comes to elicit a part of the total behavior initially associated with the thing it signifies. This theory has been criticized, however, for confusing the concepts of meaning and reference; for example, words such as "but" and "or" are clearly quite meaningful, although it is difficult to specify what they refer to (in contrast to words like "dog" or "house").

5. To investigate the process of connotative meaning, Osgood developed an instrument known as the semantic differential, which is essentially a controlled-association technique that may be used to quantify the individual's symbolic reactions to verbal (or nonverbal) stimuli. The semantic differential measures three aspects of connotative meaning: evaluation, potency, and activity. It has proven to be a useful tool in a great range of investigations.

6. The study of language reveals a number of statistical regularities that probably derive from the constraints imposed by grammar and the behavioral dispositions of

---

scribed earlier in the chapter—unfamiliar words tend to be long and have many syllables. The average number of words per sentence (S) within these 100-word samples is also computed. Reading ease is then quantified by the formula:

$$\text{Reading ease} = 206.84 - 0.85W - 1.02S$$

Passages that score below 60 on this measure are fairly difficult to read, and scores around zero indicate impossibly difficult material. Scores of 80 and above generally indicate easy reading.

language users. For example, short words tend to occur more frequently than long ones. In his Law of Least Effort, Zipf contends that frequency of usage eventually affects the length of a word—rather than vice versa—and there is some experimental evidence to support this interpretation. There is also some evidence that words which appear frequently have "good" connotations, although the proper interpretation of this phenomenon is presently unclear.

7. Since the rules of grammar require verbal utterances to conform to certain conventions of word order, it is often possible to guess some of the words that a speaker will use from the verbal context in which they appear. Words whose occurrence can be successfully anticipated from their context are termed *redundant.* Redundancy facilitates communication, since it often enables the listener to infer what the speaker is saying, even if he fails to hear some of the words in the message. Redundancy also makes messages easier to understand.

Supplementary reading

Cramer, P. *Word association.* New York: Academic Press, 1968.

Jakobovits, L. A. and Miron, M. S. (Eds.) *Readings in the psychology of language.* Englewood Cliffs, N. J.: Prentice-Hall, Inc., 1967.

Staats, A. W. and Staats, C. K. *Complex human behavior.* New York: Holt, Rinehart & Winston, 1963.

6 Linguistic structure and the psychology of language

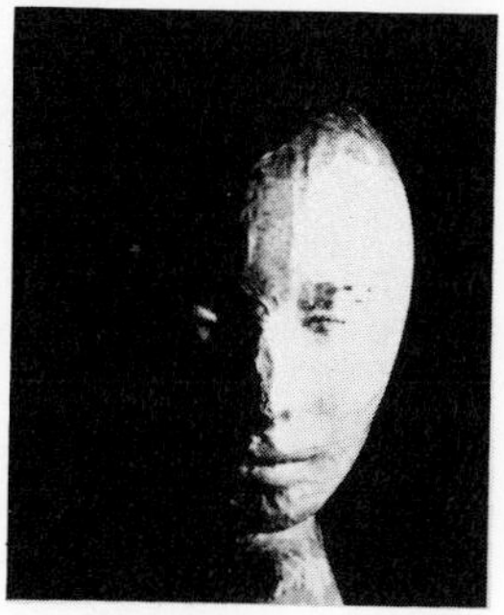

Everyday speech is based on a variety of abstract rules (or regularities). Most of us, however, are quite incapable of describing these underlying patterns, even though they are automatically reflected in our speech (if it is at all meaningful). The identification and description of these linguistic patterns (or structures) is a complex task that constitutes an important goal for the linguistic scholar.

In contrast to the traditional grammar teacher, linguistic researchers are not particularly interested in the *prescriptive* rules that are presumed to result in "good usage." Instead, they are mainly concerned with uncovering *descriptive* rules (or regularities) that are reflected in normal speech patterns, whether or not these patterns are regarded as "proper" by some educated elite.

Overt speech does not always conform to the abstract patterns that the linguist has identified, however. It has therefore become customary to distinguish between linguistic *competence* and linguistic *performance.* The basic notion here is that while we all have an implicit knowledge of certain rules that are embodied in our everyday speech (that is, we all have linguistic *competence*), we often express this competence rather imperfectly, due to such factors as fatigue, lapses of attention, and so on. Verbal performance does not, as a consequence, provide an unblemished expression of the competence that underlies it. In the main, linguists have sought to characterize the idealized patterns that are embodied in linguistic competence and have been less concerned with the study of everyday language performance and the mechanism whereby it is achieved. Psychologists, on the other hand, have been more attentive to the study of language performance.

Given the basic distinction between linguistic competence and performance, we may ask if the rules and patterns discovered by the linguist have any psychological reality. Do they provide us with an increased understanding of the psychological processes actually involved in speech production and comprehension? Or, alternatively, should they more properly be conceived as convenient "fictions" that have been abstracted from everyday speech patterns but are only dimly reflected in the concrete actions of mature speakers? Several experiments have been designed to answer this question; the results suggest that the patterns uncovered by linguistic analysis often reflect psychologically meaningful processes that operate in a variety of situations. Some examples of this research are reviewed below.

Morphological (word-forming) rules

One type of "rule" that is operative in English, and in all other languages as well, governs the sequences of elementary sounds (what the linguist calls *phonemes*) that are "permissible" in forming meaningful words. For example, any English word that begins with a *d* must be followed either by a vowel or by a *w* or an *r* (as in words like *dot, drip,* and *dwindle*). Morphological rules of this type can be used to generate two classes of sounds: (1) those that we accept as meaningful words and (2) those that are consistent with the morphological rules but do not actually occur in English words. Thus, meaningless sound sequences like *dwill, dup,* and *drem* are perfectly consistent with the "*d* rule" that is outlined above.

Greenberg and Jenkins (1964) found that college students have an intuitive but unverbalized familiarity with morphological rules of this type. In an impressive series of experiments, these investigators showed that when students are asked to rate the similarity to English of meaningless sound sequences, they can recognize the distinction between the sequences (such as *lut* or *swit*) that are consistent with the rules of English morphology and the sequences (like *gvsurs*) that are inconsistent with those rules.

If experienced speakers have implicitly grasped the morphological rules that govern the structure of English, we might further anticipate that this should have a marked impact on their perceptual and associative response to various sound sequences. The available evidence supports this view. In an experiment on auditory perception, for example, Brown and Hildum (1956) found that "lawful" but meaningless syllables (like *throop,* and *skice*) were accurately identified more often than were "unlawful" syllables (like *zdrall* and *tlib*). Underwood and Shultz (1960) have reported a closely related phenomenon: nonsense syllables that are readily pronouncible (presumably because they are consistent with English morphology) can be more easily retained in memory than syllables that are more difficult to pronounce. Finally, Greenberg and Jenkins (1964) showed that in a continuous free-association task involving meaningless auditory stimuli, subjects produced more verbal associates in response to stimuli that were consistent with English morphology than they did in response to stimuli that were not. These experiments indicate that our mastery of English includes an implicit familiarity with the morphology of the language, for our reaction to meaningless sound sequences may be reliably affected by the "goodness-of-fit" between these sequences and the morphological patterns that underlie our everyday speech.

Pluralization

Many words in English are constructed from the combination of smaller meaningful units (the linguist calls these units *morphemes*). Thus, the word *dogs* is composed of two morphemes: *dog* and *-s*. The morpheme *-s* may be used in a relatively regular and systematic manner to convert many singular nouns to their plural form. Thus, upon first exposure to a cartoon figure called a *Schmoo*, one knows immediately that a collection of such characters will be referred to as a group of *Schmoos* (even though Al Capp, the creator of the cartoon, originally attempted—without success—to disregard the usual rules by specifying the plural form as *Schmoon*).

English plurals follow a more complex system than the simple spelling rule "add an *s*" would suggest. For nouns like *rug* or *cab*, where the singular forms end in a so-called "voiced" consonant, the plural is formed by adding a terminal *z* sound, to yield *rug-z* and *cab-z*; the *z* ending is also used to pluralize words terminating in vowel-like sounds (*bee* becomes *bee-z*, and *row* becomes *row-z*). With words like *bat* or *cap*, which end in unvoiced consonants, pluralization involves the addition of a voiceless *s*, to produce words like *bat-s* or *cap-s*. Lastly, there is a final class of nouns with endings like those in *horse* or *judge*, where the plural is formed by adding an *ez* sound, as in *horse-ez* or *judge-ez*. To clarify the difference between these plural endings, compare the pronunciation of the final *s* in the words *rugs*(z), *bats*(s), and *horses*(ez).

Berko devised a task to assess the child's developing knowledge of these rules; she tested children ranging from pre-school age through the third grade. The test itself was rather simple. Each child was shown a series of imaginative drawings, like the one shown in Figure 1, and was presented with problems like the following: "This is a wug. Now there are two of them. There are two ________." The child's task was to complete the experimenter's sentence. Note that the problem involves an "artificial"

This is a wug.
Now there is another one.
There are two of them.
There are two ________.

Figure 1

Adapted from Berko, J. The child's learning of English morphology. *Word,* 1958, **14**, 150–177.

word (*wug*) and hence cannot be answered appropriately unless the child has mastered the relevant pluralization rule; he cannot simply rely upon rote memory or imitation. Berko's subjects were tested on singular "nouns" that called for all three types of terminal *s*'s; thus, in addition to the *wug* (plural: *wug-z*), one animal was termed a *bik* (*bik-s*), and another a *niss* (*niss-ez*). The results indicated that even first-grade children were well-acquainted with the rules of pluralization and were quite capable of providing proper endings to the various singular forms. Thus, it is clear that the rules governing pluralization are mastered at an early age.

Might these results be due to a "built-in" vocal mechanism that leads us *automatically* to pluralize properly? While there has been no systematic investigation of this possibility, such an explanation seems unlikely. There are, for example, many words (but not *plural* words) in which consonants such as *r* or *l* may be followed either by a voiced *z* (as in *purrs* or *pulls*) or by an unvoiced *s* (as in *purse* or *pulse*). In the formation of plurals, on the other hand, there is no "option"—nouns that end in *r* and *l* use the voiced *z regularly*, as in bear-*z* or pill-*z*. Observations such as this suggest that the selection of a particular plural form depends not on some innate vocal mechanism for "natural" sound sequences but on an acquired knowledge of English pluralization patterns.

The structure of sentences

In recent years the learning theorists' accounts of language behavior have come under sharp attack. The critics have contended, among other things, that psychologists have misconstrued the basic nature of language and have thus formulated overly simple models. Starting from a stimulus-response orientation, learning theorists have found it simplest to assume that verbal sequences are generated from "left to right"; that is, they have assumed that the *proprioceptive feedback* from each word serves as the cue for its successor. According to this scheme, our syntactic habits result from inter-word associative "chains" that have been formed in the past.

For several reasons, however, attempts to account for everday speech in terms of inter-word associative chains have been severely criticized. Lashley (1951) argued that in many forms of serial behavior, such as that exemplified by a skilled violinist playing a rapid passage of music, there is insufficient time between the successive finger strokes to permit the proprioceptive sensory control that the chaining theory postulates; similar constraints would presumably operate in normal speech. Moreover, Lashley noted, a new pronunciation scheme can often be imposed on our language (thus producing a novel pattern of proprioceptive feedback) without noticeable difficulty; in "pig Latin," for instance, words are transformed by placing the initial sound at the end of the word and adding a long *ay* sound to produce sequences like: e-thay ucks-day ere-way wimming-say on-ay e-thay ond-pay. If each word is triggered by its predecessor, as the chaining theory contends, it is difficult to explain the relative ease with which we can speak pig Latin; theoretically, the novel verbal units should prove ineffective in their hypothesized cueing function, and there should be great difficulties in simply forming the "strange" words required by our adopted dialect.

Considerations like these led Lashley to the suggestion that speech is somehow controlled by a central "planning" mechanism, which readies the successive words before they are overtly enunciated, rather than having each word cued by its predecessor. As further evidence that verbal units are readied for use before they are actually spoken, Lashley noted the verbal contaminations known as *Spoonerisms*, in which there may be an inversion of word order ("Let us always remember that waste makes haste") or a transposition of word parts ("Our queer old dean" instead of "Our dear old queen").

Left-to-right sequencing systems are particularly hard-pressed to account for the *nested dependencies* that often appear in English and other languages. For example, we can readily construct sentences in which other sentences are embedded, as in the following: "The student who said, 'I've got an exam tomorrow' left shortly after dinner." In this example, the sentence "The student . . . left shortly after dinner" maintains its meaning even though it involves a grammatical dependency that extends across another fully meaningful sentence. If each word was elicited by its immediate predecessor(s), it would be quite difficult to continue the sequence beyond the embedded quote, for the concluding words ". . . left shortly after dinner" are most closely related, in a linguistic sense, to the beginning of the sentence ("The student . . ."). Considerations like this have led to a widespread rejection of left-to-right models of speech and have resulted in the construction of complex models based on linguistic structures that operate in a *hierarchical* fashion. Thus, in our embedded sentence given above, the string "I've got an exam tomorrow" has been placed in a subordinate role with respect to the total utterance.

Syntax and linguistic productivity

Noam Chomsky and his followers have focused particular attention on the *productive* aspects of language—on the fact that adult mastery of a language enables the individual to speak and understand "original" sentences, sentences he has neither heard nor used before. This productive characteristic, which is presumably achieved through our ability to organize words into more complex structures (such as phrases and, ultimately, sentences), has led to an emphasis on the syntactic rules that play such a fundamental role in language.

It is important to remember that syntactic rules do not merely guard against awkward and unesthetic speech; they are absolutely essential in helping the speaker to convey his intended meaning, whether or not his words seem to accord with traditional notions of "proper usage." Consider the sentence "The boy hit the ball." These same words can be rearranged to produce several quite distinct sentences—for example, "Hit the boy the ball," "The ball hit the boy." This simple example indicates that the total linguistic meaning of a sentence is based on more than just the *lexical* (dictionary) meaning of its constituent words; the *structure* of the sentence, as conveyed through word order and other mechanisms, must also be considered.

Chomsky has argued that the rules of syntax may be divided into two major classes: those that determine the *surface structure* of the various sentences in the language and those that determine the *deep structure* underlying the manifest content that we hear.

Surface structure

The surface structure of a sentence reflects the relationships among its component parts. For example, the sentence "The tall boy saved the dying woman" is composed of a noun phrase ("the tall boy") and a verb phrase ("saved the dying woman"); these, in turn, can be further analyzed into constituent parts. Analyses of surface structure show that a sentence is not just a string of words; rather, it is constructed of phrase-like segments whose constituent words are closely related to one another.

In normal speech, surface structure can often be inferred from the location of *function* words (like *in, the, but,* and so on). These words have little substantive significance when compared to nouns and verbs, but nevertheless, they exert a powerful influence on meaning; compare, for example, *the ship sails* with *ship the sails*. The speaker's pattern of stresses and pauses plays a similar role in conveying phrase structure.

If we cannot determine the phrase structure of a sentence, we may be uncertain as to the speaker's intended meaning. For example, the sentence "They are eating apples" is difficult to understand if we do not know which of the last two words should receive the stress (they are eating *apples,* or they are *eating* apples); the pattern of stress indicates whether the word *eating* is a modifier in the phrase *eating apples,* or if it functions as a verb in the sequence *are eating.*

Phrase structures have not only proven helpful to the linguist as a means of characterizing the relations between words; they also play a significant role in such language performances as speech perception and the memorization of sentences. In one series of experiments, Fodor and Bever (1965) played tape recordings of 30 different sentences. Superimposed on each sentence was a recorded "click." The subject's task was to write down each sentence and to indicate where the click had occurred. One of the sentences, for example, read: "That he was happy / was evident from the way he smiled." Different subjects listened to recordings of this sentence with clicks inserted around the major grammatical break (signified here by the /). The results indicated that when errors occurred, they were partially dependent on the surface structure, for the clicks that were mis-located were usually displaced *toward* the boundary that divided each sentence into its major constituents. A subsequent experiment by Garrett, Bever, and Fodor (1966) indicated that this effect could not be attributed to the *acoustic* events (for example, pauses or changes in intonation) that might have marked the major grammatical boundaries. These results suggest that the perception of spoken language may involve an implicit process of grammatical analysis rather than a passive "following" of acoustic cues.

Johnson (1965) has shown that phrase structures have a similar influence on the memorization process. In his research, subjects learned to repeat various sentences which were to be associated with different digits. For each word in a given sentence,

Johnson calculated the relative frequency of an error when the preceding word had been correctly recalled. He found that these *transitional errors*, going from a word that was successfully remembered to one that was not, were most common when the two words were located in different phrases. Thus, in the sentence "The tall boy/ saved the dying woman," transitional errors were most likely to occur on the word "saved," which starts the verb phrase. By contrast, transitional errors were less common within the boundaries of a *single* phrase; for example, if a subject had correctly recalled "saved," he was not very likely to forget the next word in the phrase ("the"). These results suggest that the memorization of sentences is, like perception, accomplished in phrase-like "chunks."

Deep structure

In Chomsky's analysis, the semantic interpretation of a sentence (what it means) is derived from an analysis of its deep structure; hence, we can recognize the commonality of sentences that may *sound* quite different, because they are similar in their deep structure. For example, the sentence "I told John to leave" has the same deep structure and the same semantic interpretation as the sentence "What I told John was to leave." On the other hand, sentences which seem similar on the surface may represent rather distinct deep structures. Ambiguous sentences provide classic examples. We cannot properly interpret a sentence like "The shooting of the hunters was terrible" unless we can uncover the deep structure from which it was derived, for surface structure alone does not indicate whether these words reflect (a) the hunters' inability to hit their targets or (b) the tragedy resulting from their failure to wear red jackets.

Chomsky's system involves a linkage of the deep structure and the surface structure by means of what he calls *grammatical transformations.* The base structure "I expected the doctor to examine John" may, for example, be transformed by appropriate grammatical operations into its passive form with no change of meaning, yielding "I expected John to be examined by the doctor."

Some sentences are closely related to their underlying deep structure; others are presumed to have a more complex origin, requiring one or more sequentially applied transformations to generate the surface form. Mehler (1964) hypothesized that in remembering sentences, the subject essentially stores the underlying base structure (rather than the word-by-word surface input) plus one or more "footnotes," which represent the transformational rules necessary to re-generate the surface form. According to this view, if a given sentence has a complex derivation requiring several transformational "footnotes," it should be more difficult to remember than a sentence more directly related to its underlying form. Mehler's results supported his hypothesis, for sentences that required multiple transformations were not recalled as well as those that were more simply derived from their underlying structures. Mehler (1963) also found evidence of a "shift" toward the underlying kernel, in that complex transformed sentences were often mis-recalled in kernel form.

If a grammatically complex sentence places greater demands on memory than a simple one, the memorization of a complex sentence should leave less "storage space" available for the recall of *other* materials. To test this notion, Savin and Perchonock (1965) presented a group of subjects with several sentences of varying transformational complexity; each sentence was followed by a series of eight unrelated words. After the presentation of each sentence and the words that followed it, the subjects were to repeat the sentence and as many of the succeeding words as they could. In accordance with theoretical expectations, the results indicated that when the surface form of a sentence required only *one* transformation, rather than *two*, the subjects were better able to remember the words at the end of the sentence. Although Savin and Perchonock's analysis has been questioned in more recent studies by Wright (1968) and Matthews (1968), there still appears to be some support for the view that our reaction to spoken sentences often involves an implicit interpretation at some underlying semantic level.

Language development

Biological factors in language development

American psychologists and anthropologists long held to the view that languages were intricate, largely arbitrary codes that were (somehow) mastered as a consequence of various learning processes. The arbitrariness of language seemed clear, in view of the wide range of semantic and grammatical patterns that had been observed in different linguistic communities; moreover, the fact that any normal man can master whatever linguistic code prevails in the home of his rearing (for example, an American Indian will speak flawless French if raised in a French atmosphere) made it seem only natural to explain language primarily as a learned phenomenon. Biological factors were considered of limited importance, except for the limitations they might impose on the vocal system or on the cognitive capacities of the organism.

Man's uniqueness as the only species with a highly developed system of communication was thus thought to result from two factors: (1) his intricate control over his vocal tract and (2) his general capacity for handling complex symbols (as opposed to any specialized capacity for language). The semantic aspects of language were handled most successfully through this approach; the arbitrary connection between specific objects and the vast array of sounds (words) with which they are associated in various languages seemed ample testimony to the plasticity of human behavior, under the guidance of a shaping environment.

More recently, the learning theory approach to language has been challenged on several grounds. The discovery of universal features in different languages (Greenberg, 1966) has been an important factor in the reaction against the learning theorist's position. Recent research on language development has had a similar impact, for many investigators believe that our grammatical skills develop too rapidly and too regularly to reflect a simple inductive learning process; they suggest, instead, that biological characteristics may play a much larger role than previous theorists had recognized.

Eric Lenneberg (1960), an ardent proponent of the biological viewpoint, notes several universal characteristics of language that appear to result from innate propensities rather than from learning. First, all spoken languages are composed of *phonemic elements*; that is, they can be segmented into a finite number of "meaningless" sounds, despite the fact that, *in principle*, one could imagine a language in which each word or morpheme would be a unique Gestalt, not reducible to more elementary units. (Written Chinese presumably follows such a system, for the individual words are often pictographic symbols that cannot be meaningfully decomposed.) A second universal feature of language is the fact of *concatenation*, for there are no known languages that customarily restrict the speaker to one-word utterances like "water" or "eat." Lastly, concatenation is universally accomplished by means of *syntactic structures*, for there are always "rules" that govern the way in which the constituent words of a language are combined to yield more extended utterances.

Greenberg (1962) has added to this list of linguistic universals. He notes that all languages appear to have grammatical classes analogous to our *subject, verb,* and *object*. A study of 30 widely varied languages revealed, in addition, that in constructing declarative sentences, these categories were arranged in accordance with only three of the six possible orderings; thus, in all 30 languages, declarative sentences exhibited one of the following patterns: verb-subject-object (VSO), subject-verb-object (SVO), or subject-object-verb (SOV). The existence of these universal linguistic patterns has led some investigators to conclude that the languages of the world may, to some extent, represent variations on a common biologically based pattern.

Recent research in language development has provided additional support for the biological theorists. For example, McNeill (1966) contends that a detailed study of the child's early utterances suggests that noun phrases (such as "my horsie") and predicate phrases ("want that coat") appear virtually from the start. He feels, moreover, that these structures could not be learned very easily, since they may not be clearly reflected in the surface features of adult speech, which frequently obscures basic structures through the operation of grammatical transformations (see above). McNeill thus theorizes that these basic grammatical relations (noun phrase and predicate phrase) probably reflect one aspect of the child's innate linguistic capacity; his argument gains additional force from the fact that these structures are among those that are believed to be universal (Greenberg, 1966). What role, then, does learning play in the acquisition of grammar? McNeill contends what while the innate capacity for speech is mainly reflected in the deep structure of our language, the transformational rules that vary from one language to another, and ultimately determine surface structure, are probably *learned*.

The biological approach to language seems particularly compatible with the fact that there is a fairly regular pattern of language acquisition. A normal child will usually begin to say single words when he is about one, and will be capable of two- and three-word sentences by the age of two. (See the discussion of "open" and "pivot" classes on p. 145.) By the age of four, he will have mastered most of the more abstract structures of his language. This sequence appears in a similar form in a great variety of linguistic communities, suggesting that it may have some biological basis. The "critical periods" concept also has a role here, since there is substantial evidence (Lenneberg, 1967) that language learning can most effectively be accomplished prior to puberty, presumably because the young are biologically "primed" for this type of development.[1]

Language development in young children

Several studies on the development of syntax have recently been undertaken through the simple procedure of recording the speech of very young children and then attempting to infer their implicit grammar. The procedures used in these investigations

[1] An important paper by Gardner and Gardner (1969) stands in interesting contrast to the biological theories of language, which typically place great emphasis on the innate characteristics of the human mind as an important factor in language development. The Gardners attempted to teach the sign language of the deaf to a young chimpanzee, in an effort to take advantage of the exceptional manual dexterity that this species displays. The apparent success of this enterprise (the chimp's final level of achievement has not yet been determined) suggests that the cognitive capacities necessary for language development may be found to a degree in some infra-human organisms, thus limiting somewhat the biological theorists' claims that the human mind is unique. Premack (1970) also offers evidence that chimps may be able to learn language.

are closely related to those of the linguist who unravels the syntactic structure of some primitive language with which he is unfamiliar; in both cases, the investigator tries to uncover the underlying grammar without imposing his *own* syntactic rules and assumptions.

A good example of this approach may be found in the work of Roger Brown and his associates (Brown and Fraser, 1963; Brown and Bellugi, 1964). These investigators intensively studied the linguistic development of a young boy and girl by visiting their homes every other week; tape recordings were made of everything that the children said and of everything that the mothers said to their children. At the start of the study, the boy (Adam) was 27 months old and the girl (Eve) was 18 months.

There are several interesting aspects to these recordings. For one thing, as noted by earlier investigators, the children's conversations were mainly concerned with things in the here and now, in contrast to adult speech, which often deals with matters drawn from other times and places. Secondly, the children's utterances were often imperfect imitations of things their mothers had just said. Consider Table 1:

*Table 1**

Model Utterance	Child's Imitation
Tank car	Tank car
Daddy's brief case	Daddy brief case
Fraser will be unhappy	Fraser unhappy
He's going out	He go out
That's an old time train	Old time train

*Adapted with permission of The Macmillan Company from *Social psychology* by Roger Brown. Copyright © 1965 by The Free Press.

There are several regular characteristics that are apparent in these imitations. For example, note that although there are often words omitted, the words that *do* appear are always in the same order as in the original. We have indicated earlier that word order is used to convey important information in English (see p. 136), and it is possible that the preservation of order partially reflects this fact; as Brown suggests, it would be interesting to know whether this aspect of the imitation would appear so regularly in children exposed to languages that do *not* use word order as an important linguistic indicator.

Careful study of the children's imitations further indicates that verbal omissions cannot be attributed to random forgetting, for the words that are left out follow a clear-cut pattern. In the main, there is a regular tendency to omit inflections, conjunctions, auxiliary verbs, articles, and prepositions; these words are often referred to as *functors,* since they mainly serve a grammatical function. In contrast, children usually retain words with a clearly defined semantic content, the so-called *contentives.* Thus, in the records obtained by Brown and his associates, the children's imitations usually included the verbs and nouns which appeared in the original (model) sentences, and to a lesser degree, the adjectives.

The resulting imitations were thus largely *telegraphic* in character, for they lacked the sorts of words that we normally omit (for economy's sake) in sending telegrams. How can we account for this selective imitation? There are several factors that seem to be operative. First, the words that are retained in children's imitations are generally quite *informative,* in the sense that this term is used by the information theorist; that is, since contentives come from syntactic classes that are extremely large, it is quite difficult to infer the precise word that is missing when a contentive is omitted from the flow of speech. In contrast, the functors come from rather small syntactic classes, and thus when a functor is missing it can often be guessed from the context. As a result, the omission of functors does not normally reduce the speaker's utterance to gibberish. These considerations suggest that the child, being incapable of repeating a complete sentence because of his limited memory span, in some way recognizes the higher information value of the contentives and thus retains them in his utterances. Another, possibly related consideration is the fact that in normal English speech, contentives tend to receive heavier stress than functors. Thus the child may retain those words that have been stressed in the model's utterance.

Despite the systematic omissions that characterize children's imitations, it is conceivable that imitations play a role in the development of a "socialized" grammatical system. We might expect, for example, that imitations may include grammatical features that are not yet manifest in the child's *spontaneous* utterances; presumably, these features would eventually be incorporated into his normal speech pattern. To test this chain of reasoning, Susan Ervin (1964) conducted an experiment in which, for each of her five subjects, she constructed a "grammar," based on their spontaneous utterances; she then compared these grammars with the children's imitations to see if the two samples of speech (the imitations and the free utterances) were based on the same or different grammatical systems. Her results indicated that the "rules" she had derived from spontaneous utterances were consistent with the children's imitations, suggesting that the speech of the model is not "played back" through rote memory, but is instead "reconstructed" in accordance with the child's customary linguistic patterns (see p. 35 for a related view of the memory process). This study leads to the further conclusion that the progression to a more adult-like grammatical system is probably *not* achieved through the imitative process, for as noted above, the child's imitations are no more mature (in a grammatical sense) than his spontaneously generated speech.

Apart from the child's imitations of adult speech, another important aspect of the verbal interaction between mother and child is the tendency of the mother to imitate and expand the utterances of her children. Table 2 presents some of the expansions that were obtained by Brown and his associates.

*Table 2**

Expansions of child speech produced by mothers.

Child	Mother
Baby highchair	Baby is in the highchair
Mommy eggnog	Mommy had her eggnog
Eve lunch	Eve is having lunch
Mommy sandwich	Mommy'll have a sandwich
Sat wall	He sat on the wall

How does a mother decide on the proper expansion for a given utterance? Most likely, she first attempts to guess what her child is trying to say and then expands his utterance as a means of verifying her interpretation. For example, the utterance "Eve lunch" could reasonably be expanded in several ways, depending upon the particular circumstances that prevailed. Thus, it might be a telegraphic version of "Eve is having lunch" or "Eve had lunch" or "Eve will have lunch." In expanding the child's utterance, the mother would obviously be guided not only by the child's verbal output but also by the surrounding circumstances of the utterance.

Some investigators (Cazden, 1965; McNeill, 1965) believe that expansions play a significant role in the acquisition of a mature linguistic system, since when they are correct (presumably a common occurrence), they provide the child with a grammatical rendering of his intended message at a time when his attention and motivation should provide favorable conditions for learning. To assess this hypothesis, Cazden compared the linguistic progress of three groups of 2½ year olds, all of whom came from deprived homes. In one group (the expansion group), the children met with an adult each day for a series of 40-minute sessions that continued for a period of three months; in these sessions, the adult would systematically expand everything that the children said. When these children were compared to a control group, in which linguistic progress was simply checked twice—at the beginning and end of the three-month period—the results indicated that the expansion group had shown speedier linguistic advancement. Unfortunately, however, this evidence is far from compelling, since the skeptic may maintain that the obtained difference between the groups was mainly attributable to the daily contact of the expansion group with a relatively well-educated adult. This interpretation is consistent with the view that the quality of the child's early linguistic environment is of critical importance as a determinant of language development (Carroll, 1960).

Perhaps the most surprising aspect of Cazden's results was the fact that the youngsters showing the greatest rate of improvement were those assigned to an *expiation condition,* in which the children met daily with an adult who would comment and enlarge (rather than simply expand) each of their verbalizations. For example, if the child said "Dog bite," the adult might respond "Yes, he seems angry," in contrast to the obvious expansion "The dog is biting." In discussing this unexpected result, McNeill (1965) suggests that the performance of the expansion group may have been adversely affected by the fact that in many cases, the overall context did not provide sufficient information to permit an *accurate* expansion of the child's utterance; however, the adult tutors were instructed to expand *all* comments (unlike the mothers in Brown's study, who spontaneously expanded only 30% of their children's verbalizations), and the resulting confusions due to "expansion errors" may have interfered with the children's progress.

Open and pivot classes

Several investigators (Braine, 1963; Brown and Fraser, 1963) have reported that in the early speech of the child, a rather typical construction is the two-word utterance. Here are several examples drawn from the data of Brown and Fraser (1963), some grammatical (by adult standards) and some ungrammatical: a coat, a celery, my Mommy, that knee, more coffee, more nut, dirty knee. Since these utterances (and the larger set from which they are drawn) seem to result from the application of some reasonably simple rules, they have occasionally been dignified by the honorific term "sentence."

Careful study of these "sentences" suggests that many of them may be produced through the systematic combination of two grammatical classes: the "pivot" class and the "open" class. For example, the sentences reproduced above (plus several others) could be generated from the formula, Sentence = Pivot (P) + Open (O). Here, the P class includes the words *a, my, that, more,* and *dirty,* and the O class includes *coat, celery, Mommy, knee, coffee, nut,* and *knee.* Typically, the pivot class includes fewer words than the open class, and as a result the various pivot words tend to be used more frequently; moreover, new members are less readily admitted to the pivot class.

Words in the pivot class represent a diverse lot when viewed from the adult's grammatical perspective; in the present example they include pronouns (*my* and *that*), adjectives (*more* and *dirty*), and articles (*the* and *a*). The open class also appears to be rather diverse in most studies, although this is less readily apparent from the sentences given above. Although for Brown's subjects most of the words in the open class qualify as nouns, the subjects apparently failed to distinguish between *mass* and *count* nouns, leading to the construction of such ungrammatical (to the adult) sentences as "more nut" and "a celery."

In considering the P + O rule, one should remember that words are placed in the same syntactic class according to their privileges of occurrence. If two words are classed together (for example, *my* and *that*), this is a reflection of the fact that these words have appeared in similar verbal contexts (as in *my celery* and *that celery; my milk* and *that milk; my stool* and *that stool,* and so on). Obviously, such a procedure will lead to different grammars for each child being studied, in the sense that different words may appear in the pivot and open classes; however, since the existence of these two grammatical classes (regardless of their specific contents) has been noted in several studies of American children, as well as in studies of Japanese and Russian youngsters, they may well represent a universal stage of language development.

The preceding discussion should not be taken as an indication that *all* of the child's two-word utterances are constructed according to the P + O paradigm, because psycholinguists have also recorded the presence of O + P sentences (although these are less common than P + O) as well as O + O constructions. The P + O construction, however, has excited unusual interest among psycholinguists because of its possible universality (to judge from the limited data currently available) and because of the way in which this simple rule later develops into a more finely differentiated grammatical system.

Other findings

The tendency to include an increasing number of morphemes in a single utterance was perhaps the most striking change that was observed by Brown and his associates as Adam and Eve, the children they were studying, matured. Figure 2 shows this trend clearly. Results of this sort have been obtained by many investigators, even though the details of these studies have varied widely. It is interesting to note that

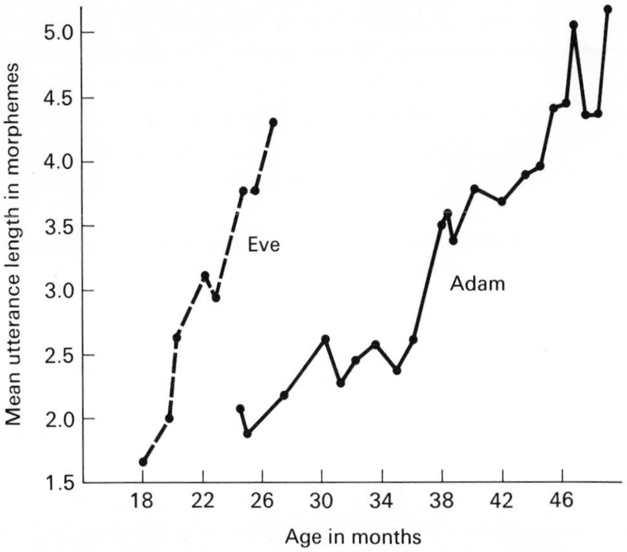

Figure 2

Relation between mean utterance length and age for two children. Adapted from Roger Brown, 1966.

this trend toward increasingly lengthy utterances may also be observed in written language, and the trend apparently continues into the college years. For example, Stormzand and O'Shea (1924) found a continuing increase in the number of words per sentence in the written compositions of students who ranged from the fourth grade of elementary school (11.1 words per sentence) through the later years of college (21.5 words).

Inspection of Figure 2 reveals the fact that Adam's speech is less advanced than Eve's, when appropriate consideration is given to their age differences. Thus, when Adam was 27 months old, his average utterance contained 2.00 phonemes; at the same age, Eve was able to produce utterances containing an average of 4.25 phonemes. Although a comparison of just two children is hardly compelling evidence for *any* broad conclusion, data from other studies point to the fact that linguistic development occurs somewhat more rapidly in girls than in boys. For example, girls tend to use longer and more complex sentences, are likely to have larger vocabularies, and are less likely to develop reading disabilities or speech defects such as stuttering or stammering. Despite the *consistency* of this sex difference, however, the magnitude of the observed effect is usually rather small; moreover, it is not clear whether these results reflect a modest female superiority in the linguistic domain, or whether, alternatively, they reflect a more general sex difference in the rate of overall intellectual development.

Summary

1. Despite the grammatical constraints that guide our verbal behavior, overt speech does not always follow the "ideal" patterns that are implied by the rules of syntax. It has therefore been customary to distinguish between linguistic *competence* (e.g., our implicit knowledge regarding the underlying rules of English) and linguistic *performance* (our imperfect expression of this competence in everyday speech).

2. Granting the distinction between competence and performance, several investigators have attempted to determine whether the syntactic patterns that constitute our linguistic competence are actually involved in the average person's everyday production and comprehension of speech. An alternative view suggests that these syntactic patterns should more properly be conceived as convenient idealized "fictions" that are only dimly reflected in the concrete actions of real speakers. The results of several recent studies suggest that language mastery includes an implicit familiarity with underlying grammatical rules, and that these stored patterns exert a reliable effect on our performance in various perceptual and associative tasks. Thus, the concept of linguistic competence seems to have a fair degree of psychological validity.

3. Adult mastery of a language enables the individual to speak and understand "original" sentences that he has neither heard nor used before. This *productive* characteristic of speech is presumably achieved through our ability to organize words into more complex structures (such as phrases and sentences) through the application of syntactic rules.

4. Chomsky has argued that the rules of syntax may be divided into two major classes: those that determine the *surface structure* of the various sentences in the language and those that determine the *deep structure* underlying the manifest content that we hear.

5. The deep structure of a sentence (what it means) is related to the surface structure by means of various grammatical *transformations.* Our implicit understanding of these transformations enables us to recognize the underlying commonality between sentences that sound quite different but derive from the same deep structure. There is also some evidence that mature speakers are sensitive to the complexity of the transformations that are presumed to underlie a given surface form. For example,

our ability to remember a meaningful sentence is partly dependent on its "transformational history" (whether the surface structure is *closely* related to the deep structure or is the result of *several* sequentially applied transformations).

6. Several investigators have suggested that biological predispositions may play a greater role in language acquisition than had previously been recognized. This view is partly based on the discovery of various features that characterize all languages. Moreover, our grammatical skills are thought to develop too rapidly and regularly to be the result of a purely inductive learning process; hence, language development is thought to be partly based on the maturation of innate structures.

7. Recent studies of language development have attempted to infer the implicit grammar that underlies the young child's speech. Studies in this tradition have often focused on (a) the child's frequent, but imperfect, imitations of parental speech and (b) the mother's attempts to expand her youngster's spontaneous utterances into more adult-like grammatical forms. There is also some evidence for the existence of a possibly universal stage in language development, during which spontaneous utterances are constructed through the combination of two grammatical categories that psychologists call "pivot" and "open" classes. Typically, the pivot class includes fewer words than the open class; as a result, pivot words tend to be used more frequently in generating utterances like "my coat," "my Mommy," "my knee," and so on. As a general rule, the pivot class is enlarged relatively slowly, in comparison with the open class.

8. As the child matures, one of the most striking characteristics of his speech is the increasing length of his utterances. This trend appears in both vocal and written output, and it apparently continues into the college years.

Supplementary reading

Carroll, J. B. *Language and thought.* Englewood Cliffs, N. J.: Prentice-Hall, 1964.
Deese, J. *Psycholinguistics.* Boston: Allyn and Bacon, Inc., 1970.
Miller, G. A. and McNeill, D. Psycholinguistics. In G. Lindzey and E. Aronson (Eds.), *The handbook of social psychology, Vol. III.* (2nd ed.) Reading, Mass.: Addison-Wesley, 1968.

3 Thought

7 Piaget's theory of cognitive development

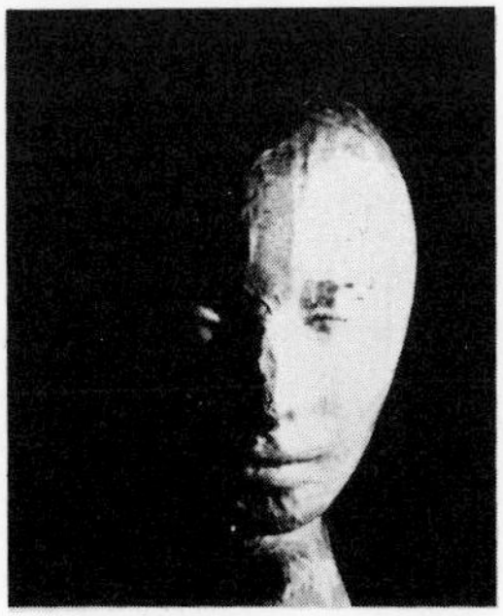

The extensive writings of Jean Piaget represent psychology's most ambitious and influential attempt to trace the development of human intelligence from infancy to adolescence. Piaget's theory assumes that there are qualitative differences between the intellectual structures of the child and the adult. It is not simply that the child lacks the adult's highly developed skills in matters of thought and logic; the child's cognitive processes are presumed to be distinctively different and thus must be understood in their own right, not simply as a dim and poorly executed version of the "adult model" that ultimately develops.

According to Piaget's theory, the course of intellectual development may be divided into four relatively distinct periods. While the precise boundaries that separate these periods are difficult to specify, the highest achievements within each period are, nonetheless, assumed to be qualitatively distinct—hence Piaget's choice of a developmental model that changes discontinuously rather than gradually. Despite Piaget's rejection of an incremental model, the stages of development that he proposes constitute a logical hierarchical arrangement; that is, the structures and capacities that characterize a given stage are presumably incorporated in the stages that follow. Perhaps the best example of this is the way in which the mental processes that are applied to the child's interaction with the here-and-now world during the period of *concrete* operations (about 7–11 years) are subsequently utilized in the solution of *symbolic* (verbal) problems in the succeeding period of *formal* operations. The *ordering* of the developmental period is thus most important in Piaget's scheme; indeed, the sequence in which the various stages appear is assumed to be constant in all Western cultures (and perhaps beyond). The particular *age* at which a given development is manifested may vary rather widely, however, depending on the child's learning experiences and rate of maturation.

Piaget hypothesizes that the changes in structure and content that occur during the course of development are attributable to certain *functional invariants* that operate continuously, serving as the primary "shapers" of intellectual growth. Two of the most important functional invariants are *assimilation* and *accommodation,* which together enable the organism to engage in successful *adaptation* to its environment. Piaget's choice of terms here is intended to suggest that there is a basic similarity between intellectual and biological functioning.

Biologically, *assimilation* takes place when the organism alters the structure of various elements in its environment in order to permit their incorporation into the ongoing system. For example, food is chewed and further broken down through the processes of digestion before it can be utilized for nutritional purposes. A similar process is operative within the domain of intelligence. Here, however, the concept of assimilation refers to the individual's tendency to perceive new objects and concepts in terms that maximize their similarity to familiar elements, so that they may be incorporated into existing cognitive structures. For example, through assimilation a young child may respond to a new spherical toy essentially as he has responded to other, more familiar spherical objects in the past (visual exploration, touching, holding, etc.).

The child's response to a new toy will not be identical to patterns enacted in the past, however, for enjoyment of the toy will normally require *some* modification of previously developed structures (or *schemas*); these modifications constitute the child's attempts at *accommodation.* (A biological example of accommodation would be the organism's adjustment to the specific physical and chemical properties of a newly ingested food, through variations in chewing and in the digestive processes.) Piaget theorizes that as the individual's experience broadens, his attempts at intellectual accommodation produce relatively permanent changes in cognitive structure, which make him capable of accommodating to still other objects and experiences in the future. But cognitive development is not solely attributable to the individual's encounters with novel aspects of his environment; Piaget also posits a continuing process of *internal* (self-induced) reorganization and integration.

The four periods of cognitive development

Piaget has proposed that there are four main periods of cognitive development in the years from infancy to early adolescence. Some of the more important characteristics and accomplishments of the child in these periods are given on the following pages.

I. The sensory-motor period (0–2 years)

The sensory-motor period is primarily a time in which the infant develops a variety of instrumental skills, after starting life with a limited repertoire of uncoordinated reflex responses. Initially, there are modest behavioral acquisitions; for example, scratching and grasping responses are repeated more-or-less automatically, without any sign of intentionality or any particular interest in their environmental effects. These repeated responses, which are termed *primary circular reactions,* become increasingly consolidated as they are repeated. With the infant's increasing maturation (4–8 months), the *secondary circular reactions* make their appearance; here, as the child attempts to prolong or reinstate interesting occurrences that his actions have produced, new response patterns are repeated because of their *consequences.* At the age of 3 months, for example, Piaget's daughter Lucienne repeatedly shook her bassinet, since this produced a swinging motion in the dolls that were hung above her.

Near the end of the sensory-motor period (12–18 months), the *tertiary circular reactions* come into play. In this stage the child is not content simply to *repeat* action patterns; rather, he *varies* his responses in an effort to explore the consequences of variation and to gain further information about the objects that surround him. In this sequence, from the primary to the tertiary circular reactions, we see a gradual change from a self-centered organism—an organism relatively unconcerned with external events—to an organism that actively *seeks knowledge* through deliberate variations in established response patterns.

The sensory-motor period is not simply characterized by the proliferation of new schema; important intercoordinations are also established *between* schema. For example, as the child begins to coordinate hand and mouth movements, he may develop the capacity to bring his thumb into a mouth that has previously been opened in anticipation. Similarly, coordinations are established between sight and hearing (looking in the direction of a sound) and between vision and grasping. All of these coordinations develop gradually. The infant's ability to grasp and manipulate objects follows a particularly complicated evolution: in one stage, for instance, manual activity is enhanced when he simply views his own hand; in another stage he can grasp a viewed object *only* if the object and his hand appear in a single visual field.

As the infant's development proceeds, the coordinations that have been established between diverse modalities are sometimes applied to new situations, with one schema providing the means whereby another schema can accomplish some desired goal. For example, the infant may remove an obstacle in order to reach an interesting object. The appearance of these coordinations is regarded by Piaget as a clear-cut indication of intentional behavior, for the child is apparently performing a preliminary act with the aim of attaining a more distant goal.

The development and coordination of new schemata during the sensory-motor period is accompanied by important changes in the infant's perception and understanding of the world around him. Piaget particularly emphasizes the development of such concepts as *space* and *causality*; but more striking, perhaps, are the child's evolving conceptions of external *objects.* Piaget theorizes that the infant perceives objects not as independent entities but as sensations that are inseparable from his attempts to see and hear. With further development, the child begins to look for hidden objects (suggesting some degree of objectification), but he often seems to assume that the object of his search will always be found in its own "special place" (that is, the place in which it was first found). To demonstrate this point, Piaget has described a revealing incident in which his daughter Jacqueline, at the age of 10 months, watched her father place her toy parrot under a mattress on her left. She immediately retrieved it from this "hiding place," and the episode was then repeated. On a third trial, *while Jacqueline watched,* Piaget again placed the toy parrot under the mattress—but this time on his daughter's *right.* Surprisingly, after watching him attentively, Jacqueline once again tried to find the parrot in its initial hiding place, on her *left.*

Piaget suggests that this behavioral pattern may derive from the infant's inability to identify the object apart from the total perceptual field in which it was first experienced. With the infant's further development, however, this limitation is overcome; the object is then conceived as an entity that exists permanently in space along with other objects (including the self) and is independent of the infant's changing perceptions and activities.

Piaget hypothesizes that the concept of *causality* derives, during these early years, from a sense of *efficacy*—from the infant's vague feeling that his efforts and desires are in some way effective in producing external occurrences. As the infant matures, efficacy is ultimately transformed into a more articulated sense of *psychological causality,* in which the infant may be aware that he wishes to perform various actions before engaging in the relevant behaviors. There is also a noticeable change in the infant's understanding of the *external* world. Initially, Piaget suggests, the infant is guided by a crude belief in *phenomenalism*: the assumption that events occurring one after another are probably causally related, even if they do not occur in the same place. With the passage of time, however, this naive phenomenalism gives way to a belief in *physical causality*: the assumption that causal events must have direct contact with the effects that they produce. It is interesting to note that Piaget describes an intermediate stage in this development in which the infant presumably believes that genuine causality can occur only if his own actions are somehow involved with the external events he observes.

The ultimate development in the concept of causality is reached when the child demonstrates his capacity to infer a probable cause after observing an effect, and to anticipate effects that have not yet become manifest.

II. The period of pre-operational thought (2–7 years)

The primary intellectual achievement of the pre-operational period is the child's developing capacity to represent the world *internally,* through the use of symbols. As a result of this development, he is no longer restricted to simple sensory-motor reactions to concrete, "here-and-now" instigators; he becomes capable of representing events which are *not* in his immediate surroundings. Piaget terms this representational ability the *symbolic function,* and he carefully distinguishes it from the infant's reaction to simple sensory cues, which indicate that some anticipated event will soon occur (e.g., the infant's anticipatory crying when his mother puts on her hat prior to leaving the house).

In contrasting the representational abilities of the older child with the infant's sensory-motor reactions, Piaget notes that the infant cannot clearly differentiate between the symbol and the thing it signifies; both may appear to be vaguely related aspects of a common whole. Moreover, unlike the older child, the infant is presumably incapable of evoking *internal* signifiers such as images and words; as a result, he is largely reliant on *external* cues to direct his cognitive activities.

In discussing the development of the symbolic function, Piaget theorizes that it is intimately related to the child's growing capacity for imitation, for the earliest symbols are thought to be interiorized re-enactments of things the child has done or seen before. These symbolic responses are initially quite overt, but they are gradually reduced in magnitude and visibility as maturation proceeds.

Throughout his writings, Piaget is most insistent on the role played by the motor components of thought in the process leading to symbolization. For example, during the sensory-motor period the infant is thought to recognize familiar objects through a process of *motor recognition;* that is, he enacts an *abbreviated version* of his customary reactions to the object (note the similarity of this conception to Osgood's emphasis on "lightweight" mediating responses, p. 116). An incident involving Piaget's daughter Lucienne provides a striking illustration of the special role that Piaget assigns to the phenomenon of imitation. Lucienne had been given a match box that contained a small chain, with which the young girl had previously been playing. Although the box was not fully closed, it was impossible for her to remove the chain without opening the box more completely. Faced with this perplexing dilemma, Lucienne *imitated* the state of affairs she desired by repeatedly opening and closing her mouth to represent the opening of the box. Following this period of overt symbolization, she unhesitatingly opened the match box until she was able to reach the chain with her hand. With the infant's further development, overt imitations of this type are thought to become more schematic and internalized, culminating in the appearance of full-fledged symbolization.

Many theorists have emphasized the importance of speech in the development of thought. Piaget, however, is strongly opposed to the view that representational thought *results* from the internalization of speech (Watson, 1914; see also p. 180 in this book). He notes, for example, that symbolic behaviors appear *before* the development of speech; also, many *animals* show evidence of representational capacity (see p. 189). Thus, rather than suggesting that thought is a derivative skill, based on the child's ability to speak, Piaget theorizes that speech may represent a later development, occurring only in organisms capable of symbolization. It is interesting to note the striking congruence between Piaget's view and that of Chomsky and his associates, who emphasize biologically given cognitive predispositions as the basis for later language development.

Piaget, along with many other observers, has noted that the child's first words are largely idiosyncratic and may represent a variety of meanings. He suggests that these first "semi-words" are incidental accompaniments to sensory-motor activities. Later on, however, they are assumed to develop into a means whereby objects may be represented and recognized; these more advanced verbalizations, which may *describe* things and actions, provide a greater objectivity to the surrounding world. In this transition from idiosyncratic to descriptive language, the child's frequent question "What's that?" is presumed to play a special role; the question implies that he has acquired the adult-like notion that objects and events have socially recognized names. Moreover, the answers he receives serve to correct his idiosyncratic associations between words and their referents.

Representational ability is characterized by several distinct advances over the level of functioning that is typical of the sensory-motor period. First, the symbolic capacity enables the child to conceptualize swiftly and to relate separate occurrences almost simultaneously; in contrast, the infant of the sensory-motor period proceeds more slowly and sequentially through his successive perceptions and actions (see p. 189 for a more behavioristic account of the advances made possible through representational techniques). Representational thought is also less oriented toward the achievement of immediate concrete goals. At a more sophisticated level, this relative independence from the concrete "here-and-now" may ultimately be manifested in such abstract activities as scientific and mathematical thinking.

Despite these significant gains, however, the pre-operational child is still severely limited. Most limiting, perhaps, is his *egocentrism*: the child's inability to recognize that his own point of view is but one of many, and his associated inability to see things from another's perspective. This egocentrism partly accounts for the difficulties in communication that are often noted among pre-operational children; for example, failing to take account of the listener's informational needs, they may make statements that are quite vague and incomprehensible.

This deficiency was clearly exposed in one of Piaget's experiments. The functioning of a simple water tap was explained to one child, who was then asked to explain what he had learned to a *second* child. The explanations that were "passed on" were often deficient—in failing to define terms that were used in idiosyncratic ways, and in failing to provide antecedents for various pronouns ("what was he referring to when he spoke of 'it'?"). Flavell (1963) has further developed this work, using an experimental task in which children were to explain the operation of a game to a blindfolded adult. The younger speakers often revealed their egocentricity by virtually ignoring the listener's temporary handicap and attempting to convey crucial information by *pointing*.

Apart from its egocentricity, pre-operational thought is limited because of its susceptibility to *transductive reasoning*. In transduction, the child does not proceed deductively from general propositions to the more particular, nor does he proceed inductively from the particular to the general. Instead, he moves from one particular to another, relying on "and-connections" rather than logical implication. J. McV. Hunt (1961, p. 191) has described transduction as "argument by simile." The child leaps from the fact that A resembles B, in *some* respect, to the conclusion that A and B are alike in *all respects*. The following incident, originally reported by Piaget (1951), is a good example of transductive reasoning:

> Shortly after her second birthday, Piaget's daughter Jacqueline asked her father why it was that one of the neighborhood boys was hunchbacked. Piaget's explanation stressed the fact that this condition was due to an illness. Several days later, Jacqueline was informed that this boy, who had for a time been bedridden with influenza, had now recovered, and was once again up and about. On hearing this news, Jacqueline spontaneously leaped to the conclusion that the child's recovery from influenza had probably resulted in the disappearance of his hump as well (which was, of course, the consequence of a *different* illness). Jacqueline had apparently concluded that since influenza was an illness, then it would follow (by transduction) that a recovery from this one illness would probably be accompanied by a recovery from the other illness (hunchback).

III. The period of concrete operations (7–11)

Piaget hypothesizes that between the ages of seven and eleven, the child evolves a cognitive *system* for organizing the world around him. He postulates, moreover, that the cognitive structures which underlie the thought and behavior of the concrete-operational child may be fruitfully represented by a series of rather complex mathematical-logical structures. While the child of eleven is obviously incapable of stating these structures in the verbal-logical form that Piaget employs, it is nevertheless assumed that his cognitive behavior parallels this formal system. We should note, however, that in the opinion of at least one investigator (Flavell, 1963), these hypothesized structures embody a more logical and orderly model than is warranted by the child's cognitive attainments. Moreover, some of the hypothesized structures seem to derive primarily from Piaget's interest in mathematics and logical systematization, rather than from any particular observations that have been (or might be) reported. With these considerations in mind, the present discussion will focus on the empirical manifestations of cognitive growth that appear during the period of concrete operations. The interested reader can find a thorough discussion of Piaget's formal models for the concrete operational period in Flavell (1963).

The conservation problems

One of the child's most surprising achievements during the period of concrete operations is the mastery of so-called conservation problems; the surprise here resides in the discovery that there is indeed something to be mastered. Consider, for example, a study dealing with the conservation of continuous quantities. In the typical experiment, a child is first presented with two identical glass tumblers (call them A_1 and A_2) that are filled with the same quantity of liquid. The contents of one tumbler (A_2) are emptied into a third container (A_3) with *different dimensions* than the other two. For example, A_3 may be much broader in diameter than the other tumblers. The child is then asked to indicate if the new container (A_3) contains the same amount of liquid as A_1. Surprisingly, even though the pouring operation has just been completed in full view, young children often believe that the new tumbler (A_3) contains less liquid than A_1, because the contents of A_3 do not reach as high a level as the contents of A_1. They may also state that if the liquid was poured from A_3 back into A_2,

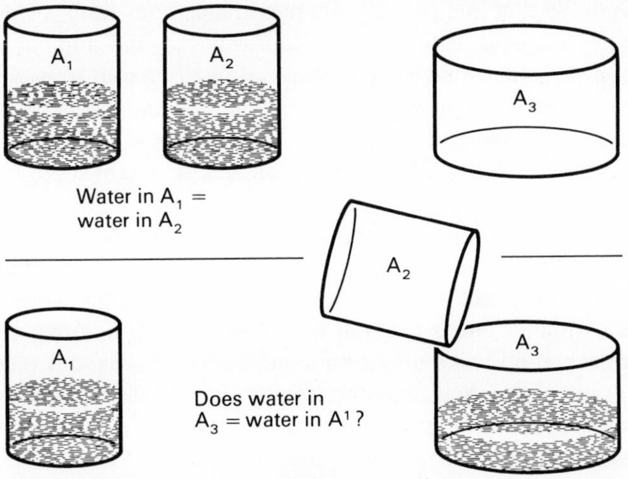

Figure 1

A procedure for assessing the conservation of liquids.

it would not rise to its former height—thus strengthening the assumption that their confusion is not simply due to a faulty understanding of the term "same amount." Not all children who "fail" this type of problem respond in the same way, however; there are many who will assert that in the above example, tumbler A_3 contains *more* liquid than A_1 because of its noticeably wider diameter. In both cases, the child's error results from his inability to consider *simultaneously* both the height and the diameter of the tumblers that are being compared. Piaget explains such errors as resulting from the child's chance *centering* (focusing) on one of the two relevant dimensions.

In contrast to the pre-operational child, a child of eight or more will usually recognize that the quantity of the liquid is unaffected by the shape or size of its container; more-

Piaget's theory of cognitive developmen

over, the older child will approach the problem in a *conceptual* (as opposed to a *perceptual*) manner, not spending as much time in the careful visual comparisons typical of younger children. Piaget contends that this more mature, more *cognitive* approach derives from the older child's certain knowledge that the pouring operation is *reversible*; that is, since he recognizes that the liquid in container A_3 (see Figure 1) could easily be restored to its former appearance by returning it to container A_2, a child who has entered the period of concrete operations presumably concludes that the pouring operation could not have affected the quantity of liquid which was involved. However, in a provocative discussion regarding the origins of conservation, Wallach (1969) notes that this reversibility hypothesis does not provide a conclusive explanation. After all, even if the child recognizes that the original state of affairs could readily be re-established simply by pouring the liquid from A_3 back into A_2, there is no clear reason for him to reject the possibility that the quantity of liquid may have been *temporarily* changed when it was poured into A_3 (even though it could be changed back again once the original situation was re-established).

Bruner (1966) has shown that the failure to achieve conservation in problems like this may often be due to the misleading perceptual disparity between the samples being compared—to the fact that a liquid will not rise to its initial level if it is poured from a narrow container into a broader one. Bruner reasoned that performance in the various conservation tasks might be significantly improved if these misleading perceptual cues were somehow shielded from the child's visual field, and he devised an experimental procedure to test this line of thought. The subjects in this study were children between the ages of four and seven. In one part of the experiment, after responding to a traditional conservation test, the children were shown a standard beaker which was half filled with colored water, together with an empty comparison beaker that was much broader in diameter; both beakers were then placed behind a screen, so that only their tops were visible. Next, the water was poured out of the standard and into the comparison beaker, at which point the children were asked if the amount of water was (or was not) the same as before. The screen, of course, prevented them from seeing the height that the water had reached. The results indicated that performance was generally improved when the conservation test was conducted in this manner. However, in a post-test which was administered with the screen removed, many of the children were unable to ignore the now-visible perceptual cues, and lapsed to their initial performance levels. Figure 2 shows the percentage of children at each age level who showed conservation (a) in the pretest, (b) in response to the "screening" condition, and (c) in the final post-test. Note, in particular, how the four-year-olds revert to their pretest performance level once they are forced to respond with the test beakers in full view.

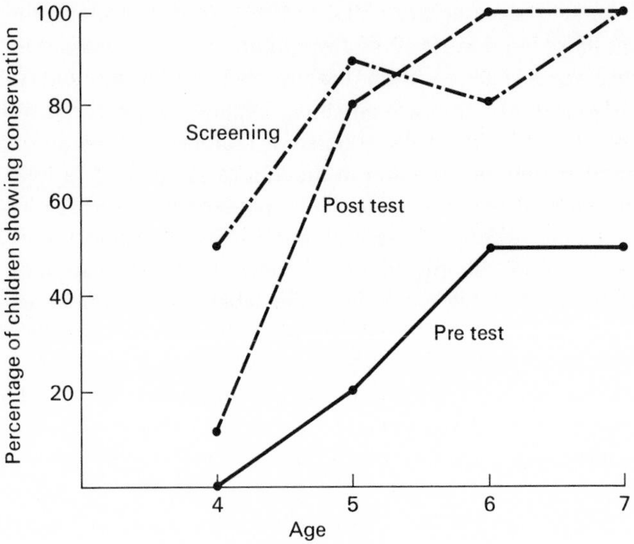

Figure 2

Percentage of children showing conservation at different points in screening procedure. (Adapted from Bruner, J. S. *Studies in cognitive growth.* New York: Wiley & Sons, Inc., 1966, p. 197.)

Conservation problems may take many forms. The child may, for example, be presented with two clay balls of identical size, shape, and weight. The experimenter may then transform the *shape* of one ball, perhaps by rolling it into a long "sausage," and ask the child whether the "sausage" or the "ball" weighs more. Pre-operational children are often unduly impressed by either the long length or the narrow diameter of the newly-formed sausage, and will accordingly state that it weighs either more or less than the ball. In either case, they fail to recognize that the weight has remained unchanged despite the transformation in shape. At a later age, on the other hand, most children will quickly recognize the irrelevance of the shape transformation as a determinant of weight.

How should we regard the young child's "non-conserving" performance in tasks like these? Might it simply be due to inadequate experience, which could perhaps be overcome through intensive training? Or is the deficiency more general—perhaps due to inadequate maturation? To answer this question, several researchers have tried to teach the conservation principle to pre-operational children (Wallach, 1963). In training for conservation of weight, for example, the child might be given many test trials; on each trial, after the child had made his judgment, the experimenter would give him immediate feedback by weighing the two shapes (the "ball" and the "sausage") on a scale balance, thus directly confronting him with the fact that the two shapes still weigh the same, despite their disparate appearance. While the results of these efforts do not yield a fully consistent picture, the overall pattern suggests that conservation is difficult to teach in the laboratory, particularly when training is applied to children who would not otherwise be expected to master these problems for some time. There are also some indications that the performance changes that *do* result from intensive training are not accompanied by the subjective confidence and logical certainty that are typically found when these capacities develop "naturally."

To test how resistant to extinction such specially induced skills might be, Smedslund (1961) compared two groups of children, aged 5–7, who had apparently mastered the conservation-of-weight problem (see above). One group had acquired the conservation principle naturally; the other group had been taught conservation during two intensive training periods. Both groups were subjected to a series of extinction trials in which the experimenter surreptitiously pinched off a piece of the experimental material (clay) while carrying out the shape transformation. The two samples were then weighed, and the children were asked to explain the observed discrepancy in weight. The specially trained conservers quickly reverted to their former pattern of behavior, giving nonconservation responses based on perceptual appearances. Among the natural conservers, however, nearly half of the children refused to accept the empirical results of the weighing, arguing either that the experimenter must have removed some of the clay or that perhaps some had fallen on the floor.

However, in reviewing this area of research, Miller (1970) reports that natural conservers do *not* typically show greater resistance to extinction than trained conservers. In several studies, more than 50% of the natural conservers failed to provide acceptable explanations for the apparent weight difference between the transformed and the untransformed samples of clay. These results are clearly contrary to Piaget's theory, which emphasizes *logical necessity* (rather than simple learning) as the basis for conservation. In theory, the belief in conservation should be highly resistant to extinction; if it were not, the entire logical network that supports the concept would presumably be threatened. In clarifying this issue, Miller discusses some of the theoretical and methodological problems encountered in extinction studies of this type.

There is also evidence that when conservation is achieved through special training, the underlying principle may be applied rather narrowly. For example, a child who has been taught that the quantity of a liquid is unchanged when it is transferred from one container to another of rather different dimensions may, nevertheless, revert to nonconservation when the liquid is poured into a large wash tub in which the liquid does not completely cover the bottom. The extreme perceptual disparity between the liquid in its original container and in the tub presumably disrupts the newly won cognitive gains.

Observations like these have led many of Piaget's followers to the conclusion that the achievement of conservation is significantly different from the sorts of short-term acquisitions typically studied in the learning laboratory. It may be, for example, that there is an important readiness factor involved, based partly on biological maturation and partly on the child's general experience with liquids, shapes, and so on. The necessary prior experience may thus develop much in the manner of a learning set, which builds cumulatively over diverse but related situations, to yield a fully developed operational skill.

Arithmetic and measurement

Piaget and his colleagues have performed several experiments concerning the development of number concepts. Some of these are similar to the conservation studies mentioned above. In one study, for example, children were presented with an equal number of eggs and egg cups. They were then asked to put one egg in each cup, thus insuring that they observed the one-to-one correspondence between the two sets. Following this, the eggs were removed from the cups and placed in a haphazard spatial arrangement; the children were then asked whether there were still as many eggs as egg cups. As in the previously cited conservation problems, pre-operational children seemed unduly impressed by the disparity between the regularly spaced row of egg cups and the disorderly array of eggs, and concluded that the two sets were no longer of equal size. Older children, on the other hand, recognized that the numerical equality of the two sets was independent of their spatial arrangement.

Some related research by Greco (Greco, Grize, Papert, and Piaget, 1960) revealed the interesting fact that while children may, by counting, recognize that the two sets of things may have the same *number* of constituent objects (e.g., seven), they may still maintain that the two sets are not necessarily equal in *numerosity*. That is, the number *seven* may simply be applied to certain collections of objects as a sort of "numerical title," without the accompanying recognition that two sets which merit the same "title" are, as a result, *equal* in the number of elements that they include.

While Piaget contends that the conservation of numbers is a cognitive attainment that first emerges at about the age of five or six years, there is some evidence that numerical conservation may be shown by children between the ages of $2^1/_2$ and 3 years, 2 months. In some experiments (Mehler and Bever, 1967; Bever, Mehler, and Epstein, 1968), children in this age range were able to choose which of two rows contained the greater number of objects, even when the objects were arranged so the length of each row provided a misleading cue as to its numerosity. On the other hand, slightly older children—between the ages of 3 years, 2 months and $4^1/_2$ years—acted as if the length of a row was a *good* way to judge its numerosity (even when faced with a long row that contained *fewer objects* than a short row). Later, this temporary incapacity vanished, and the child of $4^1/_2$ or older showed good evidence of numerical conservation. Because of its early appearance, Mehler and Bever imply that the capacity for numerical conservation may be part of the child's innate intellectual equipment; however, it may be temporarily "submerged," following its initial appearance, due to the child's overdependence on misleading perceptual cues (for example, the length of a row may bias the child's judgment as to the number of objects it includes). Mehler and Bever thus contend that numerical concepts may constitute one aspect of the innate cognitive structure that is posited by Chomsky and his associates (see p. 139). Piaget, however, remains unconvinced by these experiments (1968) and strenuously argues against the view that the young child has innate ideas regarding the concept of number.

Logical classes and their relationships

In studying the development of different logical operations, Piaget has focused on the child's understanding of the relationship between subclasses and their supraordinates. Mastery of this so-called *inclusion relationship* requires the ability to recognize the distinctiveness of *coordinate* subclasses (such as men and women) while simultaneously recognizing their relationship to the *supraordinate* class (all adults). In one experiment designed to explore the development of this skill (Piaget, 1952; Chapter 7), a group of children were presented with 20 wooden beads—17 of them brown, and 3 white. In algebraic terms, the set of beads could be described by the equation: brown beads + white beads = wooden beads. The children were asked if they could make a longer necklace using the *brown* beads or the *wooden* beads (which, you will recall, were equal to the brown *plus* the white beads). In essence, then, the experimenter's question may be restated in the form: "Which is larger: brown, or brown + white?"

Pre-operational children found this problem rather difficult and often responded incorrectly; sometimes they remarked that because there were only "three white beads," the brown would make a longer necklace. Although it had previously been shown that even the younger children recognized that *all* the beads were made of wood, this erroneous response suggests that when attention was focused on the *brown* beads, the children found it difficult to recognize that the beads were also (still) made of *wood*. The younger children thus concentrated on the part-part relationship (brown beads versus white beads), even though the experimenter's question required an understanding of the part-whole comparison (brown versus brown + white). In contrast, children who had reached the level of concrete operations found the problem relatively simple, presumably because the increased "reversibility" of their thought processes enabled them to consider the parts and the whole at the same time.

Conceptions of space

Piaget and his colleagues have studied the child's developing ability to conceptualize spatial arrangements through a variety of techniques. They have shown, for example, that young children have considerable difficulty in recognizing such familiar objects as a comb through their sense of touch (when the object cannot be seen). Children below the age of four appear to fail mainly because of their limited and unsystematic manual exploration of the objects; with added maturity, however, the manual exploration becomes more active and systematic, culminating in the careful, planful approach of the child who has entered the period of concrete operations.

The child's conception of space is also affected by his egocentrism. In one of their more famous experiments, Piaget and Inhelder (1948, p. 211) set each of their subjects at a table on which was placed a model of three mountains; the children were asked to represent the way in which the scene might appear to a doll, which was placed at one of the other three sides of the table. The children were to respond either by selecting the "correct" drawing from several with which they were presented, by drawing their own conceptions, or by indicating the doll's perspective by means of cardboard cut-outs. Below the age of 7 or 8, the children appeared quite incapable of "taking another's view" in this situation; sometimes they would simply reproduce their *own* perception of the scene. During the period of concrete operations, however, noticeable gains were manifested, as the children presumably overcame the egocentrism characteristic of earlier years.

IV. The period of formal operations (11 years and above)

Despite the marked advances displayed during the period of concrete operations, there is still a considerable gap between the cognitive structures of the 11 year old and those which he will achieve in succeeding years. A notable deficiency of the younger child is the fact that the operations he has mastered are typically limited to concrete, here-and-now situations and are not readily applied to more abstract verbal problems. Thus, during the period of concrete operations, a child may exhibit the capacity to make intelligent transitive inferences that enable him to go beyond the evidence that is immediately available to him when comparing concrete *objects* (dolls) that differ in height; he may, nevertheless, perform at a less adequate level when similar problems are presented *verbally* (e.g., If Allen is taller than John and John is taller than Frank, who is the tallest of the three?).

A related deficiency of the concrete operational period is the fact that the child's thought processes are still relatively dominated by his immediate perceptual field. In contrast, the attainment of formal operations is accompanied by an increased emphasis on things which are only hypothetically possible; these imagined entities may at times *dominate* the adolescent's thought and action. As a result, with the new realms that are opened in the domain of the hypothetical, the child may recognize the apparent arbitrariness of various present-day social customs—which represent only one of many conceivable social arrangements—and may passionately argue (on mainly logical grounds) for some drastic change in the ways of the world.

The adolescent's newly developed skill in dealing with hypothetical states of affairs enables him to consider rationally the *form* of an argument, as distinct from its *content*. He can thus ignore propositions that may be contrary to fact, and he can focus instead on the consistency and validity of a logical chain. Consider the following nonsense-sentence: "I am very glad I do not like onions, for if I liked them I would always be eating them, and I hate eating unpleasant things." In attempting to explain a contradictory statement of this sort, a pre-operational child may moralize ("It is *wrong* not to like onions") or refuse to accept the problem as stated ("Onions are really *pleasant*"); by contrast, an older child who has already mastered formal operations would more typically concentrate on the inconsistency of the assertions (e.g., between the hypothesized "liking" for onions and the assertion that they are "unpleasant").

The capacity to focus on hypothetical states which do not exist in the individual's immediate perceptual field is also manifested in the adolescent's approach to quasi-scientific problems. Inhelder and Piaget (1958) presented a group of children with a variety of objects (matches, a key, a metal cover, etc.) and several containers of water; the children's task was to determine which objects would float, to summarize their observations, and if possible, to formulate a workable "law." Children who were capable of concrete operations often noted that the sheer weight of an object did not necessarily predict whether it would float or not; thus, a heavy piece of wood might float, but a light metal key would not. During the period of concrete operations, a child would notice this difficulty and might make some effort to explain the contradiction between these observations and a simple "weight theory." A still higher level of performance was exhibited following the mastery of formal operations, when the children appeared capable of conceptually comparing the weight of a given object (a metal clamp, for example) with the weight of an *equal volume* of water. Note that this achievement requires the "intellectual construction" of a quantity of water that is nowhere directly visible in the experiment; moreover, it demonstrates a naive grasp of the traditional scientific practice of varying one factor at a time (metal versus water) while holding other factors (like volume) constant.

Apart from the not-surprising *substantive* advances that appear during the period of formal operations, Piaget and his collaborators have also noted a rather different *approach* to the basic processes of hypothesis-testing and verification. For example, in the "floating" experiment just cited, an analysis of the verbal protocols indicated that adolescents who were capable of formal operations often discarded hypotheses on the basis of their *logical implications* (e.g., the capacity to float cannot be simply a matter of lightness, as in the case of large, heavy pieces of wood); by contrast, youngsters in the period of concrete operations relied mainly on their *immediate observations* for rejecting earlier formulations. At preconceptual levels (before the age of about 4) children were often quite content to accept a variety of conflicting conceptions that occurred to them without considering the logical incompatibilities between these accounts; moreover, they were unconcerned with the validity of their explanations and were incapable of providing proof when questioned. The concrete operational child, on the other hand, was capable of verification, although he rarely manifested a spontaneous interest in such proof; if pressed to defend the validity of a given account, he typically proceeded through the accumulation of empirical facts. Lastly, during the period of formal operations, verification was more a *logical justification*, often involving "the rule of one variable" (i.e., the comparison of cases that are similar in all respects save for the hypothesized crucial factor).

In studying the child's understanding of various physical phenomena, Inhelder and Piaget (1958) noted that the period of formal operations is normally accompanied by a more differentiated and sophisticated grasp of the reversibility operation. For the child in the period of concrete operations, reversibility is typically understood as a simple "undoing," based on a literal process of *negation*. For example, consider a U-shaped tube, partly filled with liquid, and imagine that one arm of the tube is subjected to pressure from a weighted piston; the child of concrete intelligence can accurately predict that by increasing the weight on the piston, he can increase the height of the liquid in the opposite arm, and that this effect can also be reversed through a *negation* process (by subtracting the weight on the piston). In addition to simple negation, however, the adolescent who has passed through the period of formal operations may recognize that the effect produced by adding weight to the piston can also be reversed through a reciprocal operation, by increasing the density of the liquid. Moreover, he may also understand that if a negative operation is applied to this reciprocal (by *decreasing* the density of the liquid), the net effect on the height of the liquid is the same as that produced by the addition of weight. This combined operation involving both negation and reciprocity is referred to as a *correlative transformation*.

In analyzing the adolescent's comprehension of such systems, Inhelder and Piaget concluded that in the later stages of formal operations the child has typically learned to master a complex system of operations involving changes produced by negative, reciprocal, and correlative transformations. Moreover, these operations are presumed to be applicable to the child's comprehension of physical systems as well as logical propositions.

Critique

It is interesting to note that despite Piaget's rather unique theoretical approach, some of his basic assumptions have been closely parallelled by developments in other programs of research. For example, Piaget emphasizes the idea that cognitive developments are partly brought about by the individual's attempted accommodation of novel elements and experiences. This assumption concerning the beneficial consequence of novelty is well supported by a considerable body of experimental evidence gathered from a different theoretical perspective. For example, animals that are reared in a perceptually rich and varied environment subsequently exhibit a greater capacity to solve problems than those reared in less stimulating surroundings (Hunt, 1961, Chapter 4). Despite his emphasis on novel experiences, however, Piaget continually reminds us that the individual can respond adaptively only to those elements for which his past experience has prepared him. There must, in brief, be some continuity between past and present. Similarly, investigators interested in the development of programmed learning techniques have stressed the importance of proper sequencing of material.

Viewed from the perspective of American psychology, Piaget's work seems imaginative and stimulating, yet not wholly convincing. To some, this theorizing appears to be overelaborate, in that it is less directly and unambiguously linked to experimental observations than is the fashion in American laboratories. Moreover, Piaget's basic observations have not been obtained in tightly controlled experimental situations; instead, they represent the product of extensive observations and probing interviews, sometimes with relatively small samples (for example, his studies of infant development were mainly based on observations of his own three children). Piaget's writings have thus been criticized on several counts:

1. The size and representativeness of the sample (can we safely construct a *general* theory of infantile cognitive development by observing the growth of three children who were born and reared in a household headed by a remarkably brilliant and renowned father?).

2. Given the relatively unstructured situation in which Piaget gathered much of his data, the skeptical may fear that the investigator's scientific predilections might have inadvertently colored his results. Extensive data show that the researcher's theoretical expectations may have a significant impact on the results he obtains (Rosenthal, 1966). If such results can be clearly demonstrated in situations where the experimenter's role is relatively fixed and standardized (as it presumably is in the typical animal learning experiment, for example), it seems only reasonable to assume that such effects may appear even more powerfully when the experimenter is given greater freedom to "follow his head" while collecting essentially qualitative data.

Piaget, on the other hand, has consistently maintained that his experimental approach is the one that is best-suited to the study of intellectual development, given our present state of knowledge. While he is well aware of current practice and ideals with regard to experimental design, and has made use of these procedures in a variety of studies concerned with the perceptual process, he apparently believes that a looser approach is, at present, more likely to prove successful in the study of cognition. He thus contends that the researcher may lose potentially valuable information if he strictly follows an experimental procedure that has been predetermined (by *adult* investigators) without delving more freely and deeply into the child's spontaneous thought patterns. He believes, however, that as we learn more and more about cognitive development through the utilization of free and flexible procedures, we should move into a more rigorous program of experimentation, using tighter controls and more refined methods of analysis.

3. Piaget's early experiments tended to rely heavily on his subject's verbalizations as a means of uncovering his underlying thought processes. If we consider this type of approach skeptically, however, there is some possibility that the results Piaget

obtained may derive mainly from this particular methodology; for example, the child's apparently inadequate explanation of a natural phenomenon may be explicable in terms of his verbal habits and shortcomings rather than his lack of symbolic thought processes. More recently, Piaget has come to accept the validity of this last criticism and has revised his methods so that they now rely more upon nonverbal manipulations and responses than in the past.

Even if we grant the validity of these points, they seem of limited importance. Piaget's work stands as an ambitious and creative contribution in a complex field of investigation. His work as a theoretician and experimentalist has forcefully drawn attention to the scientific problems posed by the phenomena of intellectual development, and his efforts have stimulated much of the recent interest in this area.

Summary

1. Piaget's theory of cognitive development is based on the assumption that there are four reasonably distinct periods of intellectual functioning that determine the content and style of the child's thought as he develops into the years of early adolescence. While these stages of development do not follow a rigid chronological timetable, the sequence in which they appear is assumed to be virtually universal.

2. Despite the changes of cognitive structure and content that characterize the course of intellectual development, Piaget theorizes that there are certain *functional invariants* that are always operative, which serve as the continuing "shapers" of the child's intellectual development. The two most important functional invariants are termed *assimilation* and *accommodation;* by their joint operation, they enable the organism to engage in a successful adaptation to his environment. Briefly stated, assimilation is said to occur when new objects or concepts are perceived in such a manner as to maximize their similarity to more familiar elements, thus permitting the individual to utilize existing cognitive structures in his response to novel stimuli. Novel stimuli, however, will normally require some accommodation (or alteration) of previously developed schemas, and these accommodations produce reasonably permanent changes in the individual's cognitive structure; they thus enable him to successfully accommodate to a greater range of experiences than was previously possible.

3. Regardless of the rate at which he progresses, the child's cognitive capacities are presumed to reflect his passage through the following periods of cognitive development: (a) the *sensory-motor* period (until the age of about 2), during which a variety of simple instrumental skills are developed; (b) the period of *pre-operational thought* (roughly between 2 and 7), during which time the child's symbolic capacities are presumably developed; (c) the period of *concrete operations* (between the ages of 7 and 11), at which time the child develops a cognitive system that is applied in his

comprehension of the here-and-now world; and (d) the period of *formal operations* (sometime after the age of 11), when the child finally masters the ability to utilize his cognitive skills in the realm of abstract *verbal* problems, as contrasted with the concrete situations that he has mastered during the preceding periods of development.

Supplementary reading

Elkind, D. and Flavell, J. H. (Eds.) *Studies in cognitive development: Essays in honor of Jean Piaget.* New York: Oxford University Press, 1969.

Flavell, J. H. *The developmental psychology of Jean Piaget.* Princeton: Van Nostrand, 1963.

Hunt, J. McV. *Intelligence and experience.* New York: Ronald Press, 1961.

8 Thinking and problem solving

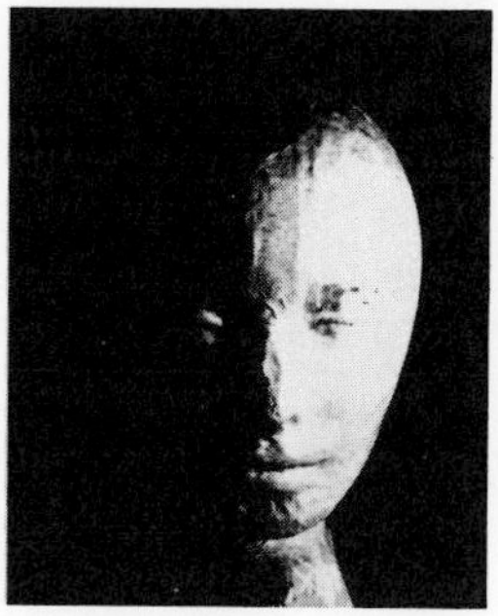

The phenomenon of thought involves internal mechanisms that are not directly observable. A student seated almost motionless in a study hall may be actively thinking about a problem in statistics, and yet from our vantage point we cannot examine his thought processes directly.

What are some of the characteristics of thought? As a rule, the *discovery* of a correct mode of response is of prime importance in thinking. Puzzles, riddles, and scientific problems—and other tasks generally regarded as involving thought—typically place maximum demands upon the individual's ability to discover the "right answer." Learning situations, on the other hand, often provide the correct answer in a rather direct form (as when the child learns the multiplication table). A second characteristic of thought is that it often takes place almost instantaneously. For example, after repeatedly failing to solve a mechanical puzzle, an individual may suddenly discover the correct solution; and having mastered the problem just once, he may have little difficulty with it when it is presented a second time. In contrast, the child who has correctly given the product of "2 × 2" for the first time (following a memorization period) may make subsequent errors before mastering the problem completely. These observations suggest that the successful thinker may rapidly achieve a state in which he knows the solution well, with no intermediate transitions such as we often encounter in learning situations. This rapid spurt in performance is the main characteristic of *insight*—an almost instantaneous reorganization of the elements in a problem, leading to successful solution. Comic strips generally depict insight with the time-worn symbol of the electric light bulb suddenly lighting inside the thinker's head.

One last feature of thought that we should consider is its *generality*. Some investigators have suggested that generality may be a prime feature distinguishing *repro-*

ductive thinking (simple learning of correct responses) from *productive* thinking. With productive thinking, when a person has succeeded in solving a given problem, he should be able immediately to generalize his solution to other problems of the same class. For example, suppose I present the following series of equations to an adolescent who has not yet learned about squaring: $2^2 = 4$, $3^2 = 9$, $4^2 = 16$. I then ask him to tell me what 5^2 equals. Through *reproductive thinking* (simple learning) he may succeed in remembering the numerical values equal to 2^2, 3^2, and 4^2, but be unable to give the value of 5^2. If, however, our adolescent has grasped the underlying principle of the problem through *productive thinking,* he will be able to generalize the information he has been given and be able to provide us with the correct answer to a great variety of squaring problems—for example, 5^2, 9^2, 10^2, etc.

Learning and thinking

The distinction between thinking and learning has troubled psychologists for many years. Historically, one of the most famous experiments concerning this distinction was Thorndike's (1898) study of cats in a problem box. Thorndike placed each of his cats in a cage-like apparatus from which they could escape if they would first perform some preselected response, such as pulling a string or turning a door latch. On observing the animals' resultant behavior, Thorndike was struck by the lack of any clearly identifiable evidence of thinking. In the main, the cats seemed to respond in an almost random fashion until, usually by "accident," they would hit upon the correct response and escape from their confinement. Significantly, when they were returned to the box after their first successful escape, the animals did not show evidence of insight; rather, acting as if they had not "caught on" to the solution to their dilemma, they returned to their seemingly unintelligent thrashing about before they repeated the correct response for the second time. With repeated trials, of course, the animals would perform appropriately almost immediately after being placed in the box, but this speed of response developed gradually.

Thus, in Thorndike's view, the animals' behavior was characterized by an initial period of almost random activity followed by the *accidental* performance of the correct response; after this accidental discovery, the law of effect (p. 90) led to a gradual strengthening of the appropriate solution until this response came to dominate consistently the other possible modes of action.

Note that Thorndike's account does not seem to require any assumption that the animal's escape resulted from thinking. For one thing, the original discovery of the correct response seemed to be an accident. Moreover, even after their first performance of the correct response, the cats seemed to require many repetitions before they would turn to the response without delay. Their need for repeated trials, even after a workable solution had been found, suggests that they were gradually *learning* how to behave, rather than discovering through insight that their accidental response was the route to escape.

Thinking and insight

In contrast to Thorndike's trial-and-error account of thinking, Wolfgang Köhler (1925), a famous Gestalt psychologist, placed considerable emphasis on the importance of planning and insight. He argued that Thorndike's experiment was inappropriate for studying problem solving, since the experimental conditions made it virtually impossible for the animal to arrive at a solution through foresightful planning. For example, the animal could not understand the workings of the trick doors Thorndike often used, since certain important aspects of the release mechanism were placed outside the animal's field of vision. Secondly, Köhler pointed out that Thorndike's problems typically required a response that was not natural for his animal subjects (turning a door latch, for example). The fact that these responses were somewhat foreign to the animal's normal repertoire meant that they could be discovered only by sheer chance.

In Köhler's own studies, which were conducted with apes and chimpanzees, all of the elements necessary for solution were placed in clear sight. One of his most famous experiments involved placing a chimp's food for the day out of his reach, suspended from the top of the cage. However, a box in the cage could be moved under the food and used as a platform, enabling the animal to obtain his meal easily. Several of Köhler's chimps seemed to show insight. Instead of responding in a random, unthinking manner until they accidentally "stumbled" onto the solution, they seemed suddenly to "discover" the correct response, which they then carried out speedily and directly. The main evidence for insight here was the fact that the solution seemed to follow from a foresightful plan. Moreover, when placed in the situation once again after the initial solution, the animal solved the problem immediately, and did not exhibit the slow trial-by-trial improvement that Thorndike had observed. In contrast to Thorndike's emphasis on learning, Köhler contended that successful problem solving was mostly a matter of insight and perceptual reorganization (seeing how the elements of the problem might be related), and could not readily be explained in terms of prior experience.

In one case, when an animal did not succeed in getting to the food after a full day of fruitless attempts, Köhler demonstrated the solution by placing the box in an appropriate position, standing on it, and then reaching up to the food. Although this animal had apparently been unable to discover the solution without aid, he immediately understood (perceived?) the significance of Köhler's demonstration, for he was subsequently able to solve the problem without requiring direct reinforcement for his *own* behavior.

How are we to reconcile the findings of Thorndike with those of Köhler? Is problem solving a trial-and-error affair, or does insight play an important role? One might, of course, be tempted to accept both these conflicting accounts as possible because Thorndike primarily studied cats, while Köhler worked with phylogenetically higher-level animals, chimpanzees. However, this proposed solution seems unsatisfactory, for several experiments have shown insightful behavior even in the lowly rat (Maier, 1929).

Some investigators have suggested that learning and insight may be more closely related than they seem at first glance. For example, Birch (1945) has demonstrated the importance of past experience in the development of insight. In Birch's experiment, chimpanzees were presented with a problem in which some food was placed beyond reach, outside their cage. They were, however, given a hoe with which they could reach the food and rake it into range. Of the six animals that Birch tested, four were unable to solve the problem. (Of the other two, one solved it "accidentally," using a trial-and-error method; the other seemed to show insight.) To demonstrate the role of experience, Birch next presented his animals with some short straight sticks that they played with for three days. During this time, they gradually learned through trial and error to use the sticks for prying, shoveling, and poling. When the chimpanzees were then re-tested with the hoe problem, they were able to solve it with relative ease. Studies like this suggest that insight may be built upon a network of simple habits learned in the past; without these earlier experiences, problems are more likely to be solved through trial-and-error methods—if they are solved at all.

A series of famous experiments by Harlow (1949) provided further evidence that insight depends upon previous trial-and-error learning. Perhaps the simplest experiment of this series involved a straightforward discrimination learning test. Monkeys were presented with a board on which were placed two objects that differed in size, shape, and color. On each presentation the monkey was to choose one of the objects; if the monkey's choice was correct it was rewarded, for under one object in each pair the experimenter had previously placed some raisins or peanuts. A given pair of objects would be presented over and over, in different positions on the board; the reward could always be found under the same object. When the monkey had finally learned which object of the pair he was to choose (that is, when he could choose the correct object on every trial), a *new* pair of objects was presented. With the new pair of objects, the monkey was given another series of trials in which he could earn a reward by choosing the correct object; as before, trials were continued until the problem was mastered. By presenting a long series of different discrimination problems, Harlow was able to observe dramatic changes in the animal's problem-solving behavior. In brief, while the early problems were learned through laborious trial and error, the animals gradually developed their learning capabilities until they eventually showed a type of insight; they could respond to a new problem with near-perfect accuracy after only one trial. The first response to each problem was, of course, a "guess," since the animals had no way of knowing in advance which of the two objects in a pair had been designated as correct. Figure 1 shows the results of this study

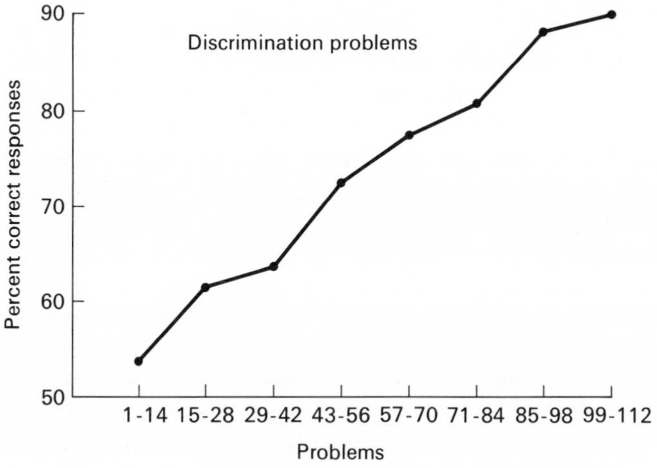

Figure 1

Development of learning set. Graph shows steady increase in percentage of correct responses on second trial of successive problems. (Adapted from Harlow, H. F. The formation of learning sets. *Psychological Review,* 1949, **56,** 51–65. Reprinted by permission of the author and the American Psychological Association.)

in graphic form. Note that the percentage of correct responses on the second trial of each problem showed a steady rise as the animals gained additional experience in problem solving. Thus, on the second trial of the *early* problems, the animals responded correctly somewhere between 50 and 55 percent of the time; by problems

99–112, on the other hand, their performance on the second trial had risen to a level of about 90 percent correct.

In discussing his results, Harlow contended that the ability to solve problems in an insightful manner is *not* an innate capacity, but is instead gradually developed through learning. He thus suggested that by solving problems we gradually learn how to learn—that is, we develop "learning sets" and gradually acquire problem-solving skills that may be applied to future problems. For example, when faced with a pair of objects from which to choose, Harlow's monkeys may have learned to follow an implicit strategy of "win-stay, lose-switch" (if a previous choice has been correct, stay with it on the next trial; if it was incorrect, the choice should be switched for the next trial). Such an approach might reasonably evolve during learning, for it would constitute an adaptive strategy that could be profitably applied regardless of the particular pair of objects presented.

Harlow further suggested that in previous investigations of insightful behavior in animals and humans the researchers knew very little of the early history of the experimental subjects. As a result, it was quite possible that the insight observed represented the result of a long learning period, during which problem-solving skills had been gradually acquired.

Thought and language

What are the building blocks of thought? This complex and difficult question cannot be answered with any certainty. However, many psychologists have suggested that there is an intimate connection between language and thought. John B. Watson, the founder of the behaviorist school of psychology, was one of the early advocates of this position. He objected to the use of such "subjective" terms as "thoughts," "ideas," and "images," for these concepts could not be readily employed in an approach that insisted upon *observable* stimuli and responses. (How can an experimenter see his subjects' ideas?) Watson's position led him to the view that thinking is a "materialistic" activity something like speaking, except the thinker restrains himself from overt expression. Thus, thinking was regarded as subvocal or implicit speech.

Max (1935, 1937), who investigated the thought processes of deaf-mutes, performed one of the most influential studies in support of the theory of implicit speech. Unlike people with normal hearing, deaf-mutes "talk" with their fingers, and Watson's theory would therefore suggest that thinking should be closely associated with finger movements among a group of deaf subjects, but not within a group of normal people. To assess his subjects' finger movements—which according to Watson's theory might occur on a very minute level—Max constructed an electrical recording device that enabled him to detect very small electrical changes in the muscles that control the fingers. By means of this apparatus it was possible to observe muscular changes too minute to produce observable movements. In one study, subjects were trained to fall asleep while recordings were being taken. Max noted that sleep was generally accompanied by a decrease in muscular activity. For the deaf subjects, muscular activity during sleep typically coincided with dream episodes. For the normal (nonmute) subjects, dreaming was *not* necessarily associated with bursts of activity. In another experiment, Max found that his deaf-mutes showed more activity in their fingers than did normals when both groups were asked to solve various problems "in their heads."

More recent work by Stoyva (1965), however, has resulted in a failure to replicate some of Max's observations. Thus, when Stoyva's subjects were awakened during periods when they showed electrical activity in the muscles controlling the fingers, they too (like Max's *deaf* subjects) reported that they had been dreaming. On the other hand, in contrast to Max's results, Stoyva found that this association between muscular activity and dreaming was characteristic both of subjects who were deaf and of those with normal hearing. Stoyva's results thus support the view that mental activity (dreaming) is often associated with muscular activity; however, they fail to substantiate the idea that the muscles involved in "speech" are of critical importance.

Even if we accept the available evidence concerning the association between mental effort and activity in the speech apparatus (McGuigan, 1966, 1970), we may still question the claim that implicit speech is basic to all thinking. It might be contended, for example, that the muscular changes noted by many investigators are not *necessary* for thought, but are of secondary importance and merely reflect a sort of "neural overflow" from the brain and down the motor pathways. In contrast to Watson's position, with its emphasis upon peripheral motor activity in the thought process, this interpretation emphasizes the role of *central neural mechanisms.*

These two theories, the peripheral versus the central, represent two classic approaches to the problem of thought. A definitive answer to their conflicting claims is not presently available, partly because of our limited ability to observe the complex interactions that occur in the brain. One interesting suggestion, however, amounts to a compromise between these approaches; this is the notion that during their early development, symbolic (thinking) processes may require the participation of observable peripheral systems, as suggested in Watson's theory among others. With further development, however, peripheral components tend to become less important and ultimately drop out, leaving central processes as the main mechanisms of thought. Two pieces of evidence seem pertinent here. One is the fact that Max's most intelligent subjects showed relatively little motor activity during thought, as compared to the activity levels of their duller colleagues. Secondly, children seem to place greater reliance on peripheral mechanisms than do adults; they may, for example, count on their fingers, or move their lips while reading silently.

In concluding this section on the relationship between speech and thought, we should take note of an important body of data which further challenges the view that verbal factors are central in the development of cognitive processes. It is a well-established fact that deaf children are grossly deficient in language development, and that only those few who are born to deaf parents are able to use the conventional sign language during their childhood years. Nevertheless, despite the fact that these children are generally quite limited with respect to linguistic skills, they do not appear to be especially handicapped in their *cognitive* capacities, as measured in a variety of experimental tasks (Furth, 1971). This implies that verbal processes may be of limited importance in guiding intellectual development—a view that is quite congruent with the theories espoused by Piaget and Chomsky.

The Whorfian hypothesis

The writings of Benjamin Lee Whorf (1956) provide us with a rather different hypothesis regarding the relationship between thought and language. In essence, Whorf took the position that language largely determines the way in which we perceive and think about the world in which we live. He opposed the common-sense notion that people brought up in different language communities perceive and think about external reality in similar terms, differing only in the code (language) they use to express their thoughts. Whorf suggested that language serves as more than the passive "interpreter" or "translator" of mental life; instead, it provides an all-pervasive framework that actively contributes to our thoughts and perceptions.

This is, of course, a strikingly relativistic doctrine. It does not merely assert that people of differing backgrounds are likely to evaluate the world according to different norms and ethical standards; according to Whorf, the world itself—the things that seem so palpably objective and "out there"—is partly "constructed" by the linguistic habits that we have learned. Reality is different for peoples who speak different languages.

Recent discussions of the Whorfian hypothesis have differentiated between *strong* and *weak* versions of his basic views. The strong interpretation of Whorf's theory suggests that cognitive processes are *inevitably* affected by language, whether or not there is an active involvement of verbal mechanisms; thus, even though the individual's thought at any given time may be nonverbal, his language is assumed to pervade the cognitive categories and mechanisms that he applies. By contrast, the weak version of the Whorfian hypothesis is more restricted; this version suggests that language will not affect thought unless the cognitive task engages the individual's linguistic processes. As we shall see, there are several experiments that support the weak version of Whorf's theory, but the strong version remains in doubt.

What types of language differences might we expect to affect our thoughts? Vocabulary differences have often been suggested as playing a crucial role. However, this is not to say that the particular sounds that a language employs are particularly important; the fact that the object from which you are now reading is called *un livre* in French, rather than *a book,* does not produce the cognitive differences Whorf had in mind. Whorf was, instead, impressed with those cases in which one language provides a rather detailed and differentiated set of labels for a given range of experience, while another language fails to differentiate these experiences (or events) and labels them all with the same word. Whorf notes, for example, that the Eskimos use three distinct words in labeling different varieties of snow, while in English these differences are glossed over. Thus, events that require three labels for the Eskimo are labeled with a single term in English: snow. This is not to suggest that English *generally* fails to make distinctions that are embedded in other languages. In the language of the Hopi, all flying things, with the exception of birds, are called by the same name; we regard this as an overly broad class of objects, and speak of planes, insects, kites, aviators, and so on. The languages of the world simply differ in the specificity with which they label various areas of experience; the Eskimo has a precise vocabulary for speaking about snows, while the American readily provides specific labels for the different varieties of flying objects.

How might these vocabulary differences affect our thoughts and perceptions? One possibility would be that the American is unable to distinguish between the varieties of snow that the Eskimo sees as being so very different from one another. This hardly seems likely; Whorf was apparently capable of seeing these differences, for he clearly describes the different types of snow. Similarly, it is difficult to believe that the Hopi is incapable of perceiving the difference between butterflies, airplanes, and kites. A milder version of this doctrine might assert that perceivable differences among similar objects or events are not *automatically* detected unless the perceiver's language alerts him to the relevant distinctions. Thus, while Whorf found it possible to describe the differences between the various types of snow, it is likely that he would not normally note or attend to these differences if he was, let us say, waiting for a bus in his native city of Hartford.

Further, the distinctions captured by a *single word* in some languages may require several words, or phrases, in others. While the Eskimo has a separate single word for the different varieties of snow, the American requires many; thus, Whorf describes "snow packed hard like ice," "falling snow," and "snow on the ground." Similarly, we may surmise that with proper modifying terms the Hopi can describe the difference between various flying objects—although this may require more effort and verbiage than in English.

It is interesting to consider how Zipf's law might be applied to these observations. Recall first that, according to Zipf, the words that are used most frequently in a given language tend to be shorter than those that are used infrequently. Thus, if a given event or category of experience is referred to frequently and named by a *single* word in one language (English, let us say), but is seldom referred to and requires a rather *lengthy phrase* in another language (Hopi, for instance), we may assume that for English-speaking people this event is probably of some importance. By contrast, the event is probably of lesser importance within the Hopi community. Some psychologists have gone one step further to propose that if the label for some particular event appears frequently within a given *language,* this event probably also appears quite frequently in the *thoughts* and *perceptions* of those who speak the language.

In an ingenious experiment by Brown and Lenneberg (1954), the names associated with various nonlinguistic events were shown to influence the ease with which these events could be remembered. This study, conducted with American college students, sought to demonstrate that color patches which are readily "coded" in English could be remembered more easily than those that English codes less effectively. The investigators first showed a series of colors to twenty-four students at Harvard and Radcliffe. The students were asked to name each color as quickly as they could. As you might expect, some colors, such as *red* or *blue,* could be named with little delay; others were not named so quickly. The experimenters noted that in general, the colors that were named quickly had *short names;* these colors also tended to elicit the *same* response when a given subject was tested twice, or when the responses of different subjects were compared. By way of contrast, the colors that could not be named immediately typically had *long* names and often failed to elicit consistent responses from one person to the next. These results suggested that one might quite meaningfully speak of the *codability* of the different colors—the relative ease with which they could be named. Colors that elicited short, consistent names with virtually no delay were regarded as highly codable in English.

Do these differences in codability affect the ease with which a given color might be remembered? If so, we might infer that people generally find it easier to recall events that are highly codable for them. Moreover, as we have discussed above, the events most codable in one language may not be very codable in another. If it could be demonstrated that codability affects memory, this would suggest that an event readily codable in English might be recalled easily by an American, but with greater difficulty by the speaker of some other language. In brief, the language of the memorizer would be a determinant of his cognitive behavior, as hypothesized by Whorf.

Having determined the codability of twenty-four different colors, Brown and Lenneberg next enlisted a new group of subjects who were shown four of these colors at a time. Following each presentation, the subjects were provided with a collection of 120 different colors and were asked to point to the four they had just seen. As anticipated, the colors with high codability were recognized more frequently than the others. Moreover, codability had a greater effect upon recognition when a 3-minute delay was introduced between the initial exposure to the colors and the presentation of the recognition test. These results suggest that as the experimenters placed increasing demands upon their subjects' memories, the codability of the various colors became more and more important in determining whether or not the subjects could recall what they had seen.

It is relatively easy to see how codability operated in this situation. When subjects were asked how they had remembered the various sets of color patches, they typically reported that they had tried to recall the *names* of the colors. We would expect, of course, that if a color was associated with a long descriptive name including several words, the subjects would be more likely to forget it. Moreover, since the low-codability colors were not consistently associated with any *single* name, they might be quite difficult to select from the larger set of colors—even if the subject succeeded in recalling the description he had initially "stored" in memory. In the language of general semantics (Korzybski, 1933), we might say that the extensional meaning (referent) for these color names was rather vague. Even if the subject could recall that he had been shown "a rather hazy combination of blue and dark green," he might have considerable difficulty in picking out the appropriate color patch in the recognition test. In contrast, the extensional referent for "red" would be quite clear.

Recent research by Lantz and Stefflre (1964) lends further credence to this interpretation. Using a memory-for-colors task similar to the one described above, these investigators found that the subjects' ability to *communicate* about a given color was an accurate predictor of the likelihood that it would be successfully recognized in the memory test. More specifically, Lantz and Stefflre devised a method for measuring communicability in which subjects were asked to name various test colors in such a way that someone else would be able to pick the color out from a large set. As you might expect, some colors were simpler to communicate about than others; that is, some colors could be readily identified from the subjects' names for them, and others could not. When the various colors were later presented to a new group of subjects in a memory task, these subjects were most successful in remembering the colors that could be accurately communicated; they were less successful in remembering the colors that had presented difficulties in the communication task.

The experiments by Brown and Lenneberg, along with the work of Lantz and Stefflre, demonstrate the influence of *labeling* (the association between words and things) on *memory,* an important form of cognitive behavior. Note, however, that the memory tasks employed in these experiments directly engaged the subjects' linguistic skills, for they normally attempted to store that which was to be remembered in *verbal terms,* and then used this stored information to guide their subsequent attempts at recall.

These results thus support the *weak* version of Whorf's theory. At present, Whorf's hypothesis receives its strongest support from these experiments, with their heavy reliance on verbal storage. The evidence for a *strong* version of the theory is less encouraging; for example, it has been difficult to obtain consistent results in experiments that involve classification and judgment, where performance is presumably guided by the subject's *present perceptions* rather than by *verbal memory* (Miller and McNeill, 1968).

Forced observations in language

Knowledge of a given language often requires the speaker to attend automatically to certain aspects of reality that may be largely ignored in other linguistic communities. For example, the speaker of English conjugates his verbs depending upon the *time* of the action in question. In order to speak grammatically about Jack's interest in swimming, it is necessary to indicate whether he *wishes* to swim now, *wished* to swim a few days ago, or *will want* to swim tomorrow. This characteristic of English requires that we continually take note of time as an important ingredient in any verbal utterance.

We should hasten to add that verbs are *not* conjugated by tense in all languages. The Wintu's language does not "force" him to distinguish past, present, and future. He must, however, choose verb forms that automatically indicate the sort of *evidence* that lies behind his statements. If the speaker is describing an event within his field of vision, the verb is conjugated in one manner. If the speaker's assertion is based on hearsay, a different verb form would be required. Still another form is used when the speaker comments on a predictable and recurrent event by asserting, for example, that "The chief is hunting" (based on knowledge that he regularly hunts at this time). These observations suggest that the speaker of Wintu may be continually forced to note the evidence that stands behind each of his statements. While it is quite clear that we too can pay close attention to this matter of evidence under appropriate conditions (when testifying at a trial, for example), the Wintu *must* do so continually and habitually in order to speak correctly. There is, however, little in the way of systematic evidence to sustain the view that the "forced observations" which are "built" into various languages continue to be operative in situations where the individual's language skills and habits are inoperative.

Social class, language, and cognition

In analyzing the speech patterns characteristic of middle- and lower-class England, Basil Bernstein (1959, 1961) has drawn a contrast between so-called "restricted" and "elaborated" codes. Bernstein contends that the lower-class Briton invariably speaks in a restricted linguistic code, which limits the variety of meanings that he can convey. The restricted code is well-suited, however, for the communication of concrete (as opposed to abstract) information, and it serves quite effectively to facilitate communication about the here-and-now and to maintain group solidarity. On the other hand, the restricted code is thought to be deficient as a means of conveying complicated conceptual matters.

Middle-class Britons are capable of using both the restricted and elaborated codes. While the restricted code tends to be used in standardized, routine situations—where the speaker's output may represent a ready-made pattern that has been used over and over in stereotypic fashion—the elaborated code is involved in the construction of novel, newly-created messages. Following the Whorfian principle, Bernstein suggests that the elaborated code produces a flexible and differentiated social outlook, since it is often used in situations where the listener does not proceed from the same cognitive and social premises as the speaker. By contrast, the restricted code is usually based on the assumption that the speaker and his listener have a *common* frame of reference, which enables them to communicate despite the simple and often unfinished messages that are actually emitted. At a cognitive level, the exclusive use of a restricted code by those in the working class is presumed to result in a focusing of attention on concrete facts (rather than on abstract underlying processes) and in a hampering of curiosity. At present, however, there is no clear evidence that these differences in linguistic code produce the hypothesized effects on cognitive functioning.

Conclusion

In examining the differences between various linguistic systems, it seems quite natural to inquire about why one culture (or subcultural group) develops a finely differentiated vocabulary for labeling certain events while these distinctions are largely ignored in other languages. Why *does* the Eskimo have a different name for the various types of snow, while we have but one? Why does our language contain such explicit information concerning the time that a given event takes place, while others do not? It seems reasonable to assume that, through evolutionary changes, a community's language will most accurately reflect those aspects of reality concerning which exact information and communication are required. For the Eskimo, the distinctions between different snows are of critical importance, and consequently his vocabulary enables him to convey these distinctions easily. Similarly, this line of reasoning suggests that the importance of time within our culture was perhaps a causal factor in determining the manner in which we conjugate verbs.

Following this line of thought, it is interesting to note that, within a given culture, specialized groups often develop their own vocabularies to enable members to speak more precisely about matters of particular concern to them. For example, clinical psychologists and psychiatrists have found it necessary to develop a specialized labeling system for referring to various forms of psychopathology. While the layman may find it quite satisfactory to use a broad term like "emotional disturbance," this label is too undifferentiated for the specialist; he develops a more precise vocabulary and speaks of manic-depressive psychosis, or passive-aggressive personality, or hebephrenic schizophrenia, to name but a few. A similar process seems to occur in informal interest groups. Note, for example, the detailed terminology of "jazz" (blues, Chicago style, bebop); many of us do not find it necessary to make these distinctions, and hence we have not learned this special vocabulary.

If we grant that differences in cultural and subcultural emphasis eventually have an impact upon our language, might this be interpreted as a challenge to the Whorfian position? Does language tend to develop *in response* to cultural and cognitive factors? Or, as Whorf suggests, does language *shape* culture and cognition? At present it seems plausible to synthesize these conflicting approaches by hypothesizing a circular process in which the language is shaped by cultural emphasis (such as the importance of time, or the need for precise communication concerning a given domain). In turn, however, successive generations, upon learning to speak, are thereby predisposed to pay particular attention to those aspects of reality that the language reflects most faithfully and easily. Thus, the American child may find it easier to adjust to our emphasis upon time, since the very language that he speaks has made this an important aspect of reality.

The representational nature of thought

Thinking often involves responding to *symbolic representations* of a problem. For example, to find the shortest route between my home and my office, I can consider the various alternatives (in my head) and then choose one without leaving my chair, for mechanisms of thought can represent the external environment. For some people this representational process is primarily visual—the problem situation is vividly "seen."

In addition to representing the *environment* in symbolic terms, the thought process often leads the individual to a symbolic representation of the various *action possibilities* available. Thus, in thinking about the various routes to my office, I may symbolically "try out" the available possibilities before rendering my judgment about the shortest way. In brief, then, thinking often involves the use of symbolic processes to represent *situations* and *responses,* and may in this way be contrasted with more rudimentary trial-and-error problem-solving methods that rely mainly upon the *overt* "trying out" of various behaviors in the "real world."

Evidence for representational thought in animals

The representational capacities discussed above are not restricted to man. Available evidence indicates that some animals are also capable of representational thought. For example, in the *delayed reaction experiment,* the animal is permitted to watch as the experimenter places a food reward under one of two cups. However, the animal is not permitted to approach either of the cups until a predetermined period has elapsed. When the animal is released, he can respond correctly only if he can somehow symbolically represent to himself (visualize?) the earlier situation in which the reward was placed in position. In this experiment, then, consistent success cannot be achieved by reliance on the external stimuli present during the test; instead, success depends upon the animal's ability to represent past occurrences symbolically. Using this experimental method, Hunter (1912) demonstrated wide species differences. Dogs, for example, could be delayed for 5 minutes and still respond correctly, while rats had a maximum delay of about 10 seconds. In general, the higher the phylogenetic level of the animal, the greater was its capacity for delay.

The *double alternation problem* provides another approach to the study of symbolic representation in animals. In this situation the animal is placed into a maze like the one diagrammed in Figure 2. The animal's task is to learn that, upon reaching the

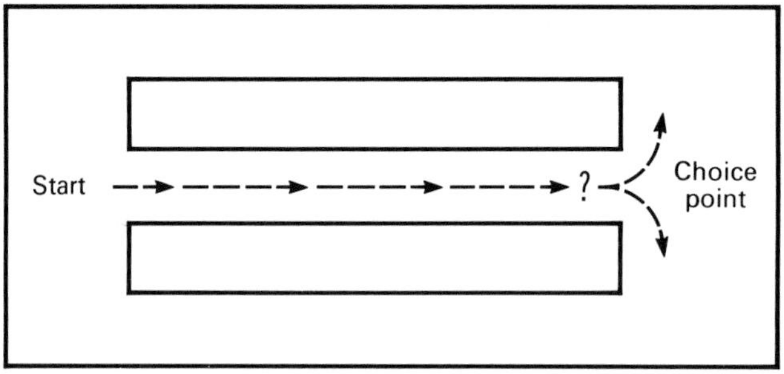

Figure 2
The double alternation problem.

choice point, the proper response depends upon his prior choices. Thus, upon approaching the choice point, the animal should first turn left; when he arrives at the choice point for the second time, he should turn left again. Having run twice around the left side of the maze, he should then shift and turn to the right on his next two choices. If he successfully executes this LLRR pattern, he is given a reward. Note that this is a somewhat complicated procedure, for in order to respond appropriately the animal must recall (symbolically represent) his performance on the two preceding choices. If he has turned in the same direction on both of these choices, it is time for him to switch—otherwise he must repeat his most recent turn.

Results of the double alternation problem again show a systematic relationship to phylogenetic level. While the lowly rat finds the problem impossible to solve, raccoons and cats do not. In the human realm, it is interesting to note that while children who have not yet learned to speak can solve the double alternation problem (although they find it quite difficult), the task is usually rather simple for older children who are able to verbalize (Hunter and Bartlett, 1948). These last observations remind us again of the important role that language plays in problem solving. It is clear from the results of animal studies, however, that language is not a necessary skill for the successful mastery of representational problems.

Representation of the future

Man's capacity to concern himself with situations beyond those that confront him in the immediate environment provides a valuable tool for everyday living. By thinking about the expenses involved in sending his children to college (even though this may be several years off), the young father may be motivated to set up a systematic savings plan. On the other hand, a person with poorly developed symbolic capacities may be primarily dependent upon the more tangible problems and rewards that immediately surround him, and may consequently find it difficult to engage in behaviors that do not yield a "pay-off" here and now. Such a person may, for example, find it difficult to complete his education, since, to continue in school, he must be willing to accept the discipline, hard work, and lack of income that go with being a student—all in the expectation that these difficulties will be more than counterbalanced by the educational, social, and financial benefits that an adequate education can provide.

Research by Mischel (1961) provides us with an interesting picture of the child who is mainly concerned with present rewards. In these studies, the children are first led through a series of experimental procedures (or questions), and are then thanked for their help. To reward them for their efforts, the experimenter offers them a choice between two candy bars—a *small* one available immediately, and a *larger* candy bar the experimenter has "just run out of," but which will be given to the child on the next day if he chooses it. Using this basic technique in a study conducted on the island of Trinidad, Mischel found that juvenile delinquents were less likely to choose the larger, delayed reward than were nondelinquent youngsters. Moreover, within the delinquent group, those who did prefer the delayed reward were more socially responsible and had higher aspirations for achievement. These data indicate the systematic manner in which foresight and the capacity to delay gratification may be related to personality variables.

Representation as an aid in problem solving

Man's capacity to react symbolically to his environment before engaging in *overt* behavior provides many advantages. At a very simple level, we should note the speed and minimum effort with which various solutions can be considered in thought and, if they are found wanting, discarded. In contrast, when solutions are attempted overtly, rather than symbolically, there may be considerable "costs" in time and effort before a given solution is proven to be inadequate. Consider, for example, the problem faced by someone driving home from a crowded football game. If he simply tries out the various possible routes in the order that they occur to him, he may expend considerable effort before he hits upon a satisfactory solution. He may encounter traffic jams, detoured roads, and the like in his initial attempts. By approaching this problem symbolically before putting his ideas into overt practice, he can often avoid these effortful, time-consuming, and possibly dangerous attempts at solution. Despite these potential advantages of the symbolic approach, we have all had experiences in which our carefully formulated plans have gone awry. In many instances this occurs when our symbolic representation of the environment is deficient in some regard. For example, in choosing a road home, we may fail to remember that the route we have selected is now being repaired. Consequently, while our choice may have seemed wise in symbolic anticipation, in actuality it may involve unexpected difficulties.

Apart from the speed, safety, and relative ease with which symbolic procedures may be applied in approaching a problem, this mode of response has still other virtues when compared with overt problem solving. Dollard and Miller (1950) point to the fact that, in the "real world," problems can be solved only by dealing *in sequence* with the various obstacles that lie between one's present position and the ultimate goal. In symbolic reasoning, on the other hand, it is possible to consider the more distant goal first, and then cast about for ways it may be reached. By reversing the normal sequence in this manner, it is sometimes possible to discover immediate solutions to problems that might otherwise prove difficult or impossible. Figure 3 provides us with a simple example.

> . . . In the heavy traffic leaving a football game, a driver was caught in a long line of cars all waiting to make a left turn on a four-lane highway. . . . Most of the cars leaving the game were all waiting to make the same left turn. There was just enough traffic coming from the other direction to make the left turn difficult so the line was advancing quite slowly. Once the cars negotiated the difficult left turn, they could drive ahead rapidly on the other highway.
>
> As the long line of cars crept slowly ahead, the man became increasingly impatient. He wished he could pull out of the line into the almost empty lane on the right and drive ahead.

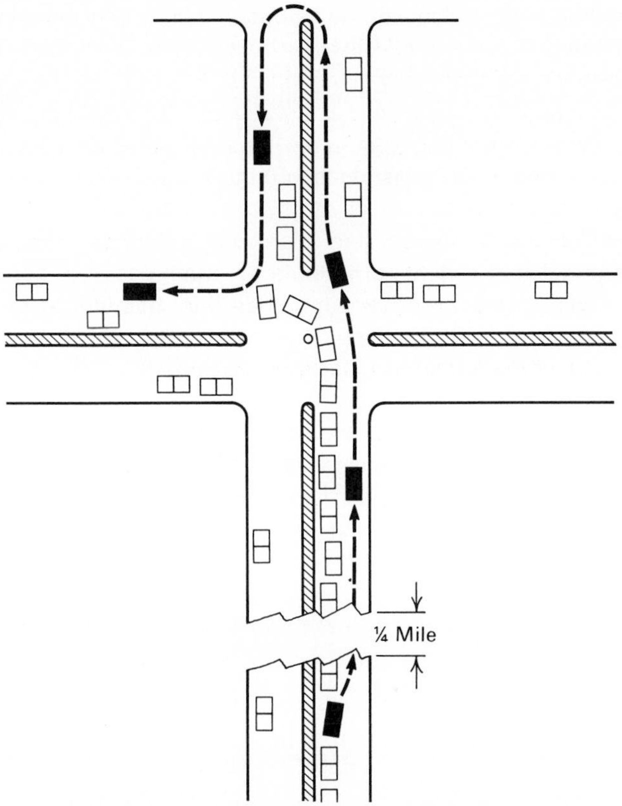

Figure 3

Example of symbolic problem solving. (Adapted from J. Dollard and N. E. Miller, *Personality and psychotherapy.* New York: McGraw-Hill Book Co., Inc., 1950.)

But this thought led to the one of being stopped by the other drivers when he tried to turn left in front of the long line so this solution was immediately rejected. The driver continued, however, to think of the road he would like to get onto. He noticed that the few cars coming in the opposite direction had no difficulty in making their right turns onto this road and driving rapidly on down it. He said to himself, "If I were only going the other way, it would be so easy." This led to the question, "How could I be going the other way?" From here on he was dealing with a problem that he had a great deal of practice in solving. He immediately thought of pulling out into the outside lane, driving up the highway, finding a place to turn around, coming back the other way, and making the right turn onto the other highway. While thinking of this, he felt a triumphant sense of relief from the frustration of waiting in line and immediately proceeded to carry his ideas through to successful action.[1]

Note how the driver was ultimately able to arrive at a solution to his problem by first considering the fact that a right turn would be much easier to accomplish than a left turn, and then taking appropriate action based on this realization.

Problem solving and the fixation of incorrect responses

In an earlier section we referred to the fact that successful thinking and problem solving typically involve the sudden discovery of appropriate solutions. This emphasis on discovery is important, since by definition problems usually prove to be troublesome for the simple reason that our initial and dominant reactions are likely to be incorrect—thus the solution must be discovered.

Figure 4 represents various solutions that occurred to one subject when he was faced

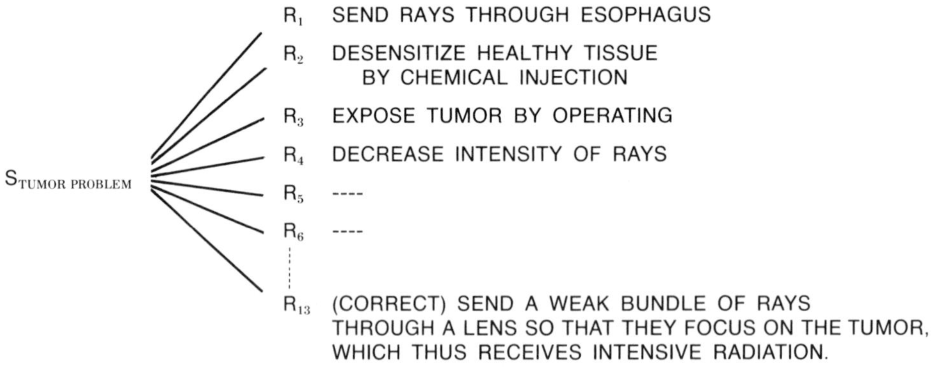

S TUMOR PROBLEM
R1 SEND RAYS THROUGH ESOPHAGUS
R2 DESENSITIZE HEALTHY TISSUE BY CHEMICAL INJECTION
R3 EXPOSE TUMOR BY OPERATING
R4 DECREASE INTENSITY OF RAYS
R5 ----
R6 ----
R13 (CORRECT) SEND A WEAK BUNDLE OF RAYS THROUGH A LENS SO THAT THEY FOCUS ON THE TUMOR, WHICH THUS RECEIVES INTENSIVE RADIATION.

Figure 4

Diagrammatic representation of subject's successive responses to problem, based on habit-family hierarchy model.

[1] From J. Dollard and N. E. Miller, *Personality and psychotherapy*. New York: McGraw-Hill Book Co., Inc., 1950. Quoted with permission of the publisher.

with the following problem: Assume that a person has an inoperable stomach tumor that can be destroyed by a ray. How can we rid our patient of the tumor without harming the healthy tissue that surrounds it, when the surrounding tissue is just as vulnerable to the ray as the tumor itself? Note that in Figure 4 which is modeled after Hull's habit-family hierarchy, our subject's early solutions (responses 1, 2, 3, etc.) are all inappropriate for one reason or another; in order for him to succeed, the correct solution (R_{13}) must rise to the position of dominance.

Unfortunately, people often find themselves "fixed" on an incorrect solution or approach and are unable to give it up in favor of a more appropriate response. Karl Duncker (1945), who has investigated this problem most thoroughly, suggests that this is often attributable to the individual's tendency to utilize the elements of the problem in a conventional manner that may be quite ineffective for the problem at hand. In one of his experiments, Duncker presented his subjects with the task of attaching three small candles to a door; they were given a variety of materials to help them, including some tacks, some matches, and several small match-boxes. Successful solution of the problem required that the subjects tack the boxes to the door and use them as "platforms" on which to stand the candles; to secure the candles to the boxes, they were to use the matches to melt the wax. Duncker's experiment compared the performance of two groups of subjects. For one group, the boxes were empty; for the second group, each box was filled with one of the other experimental materials (tacks, candles, or matches). The problem proved to be relatively simple when the boxes were empty—all the subjects in this group succeeded in finding the solution. In contrast, the subjects who were presented with the *filled* boxes showed much poorer performance. Duncker interprets this as indicating that the filled boxes were less likely to be perceived as miniature "platforms," as called for in the solution. The empty boxes, on the other hand, did not evoke the "container" association so strongly, which made the problem considerable easier. The main point here is that the various elements of a problem situation often have more than one use; conventional uses of an element may blind us to other possible uses.

An experiment by Adamson and Taylor (1954) provides further evidence that if we emphasize the *conventional* uses of an object, we may temporarily reduce the likelihood that it will subsequently be employed in a novel, creative fashion. In this study, electronic parts that had been used conventionally just prior to the introduction of a test problem were largely ignored in the search for a solution. This effect dissipated with the passage of time, however. That is, the inhibitory effect of the "fixating" experience was greatly reduced when the test problem was presented one day later, and the effect vanished completely after a week.

Fixation and drive level

We are all aware that our effectiveness as problem solvers may vary from one time to the next. Several investigations suggest that our level of motivation may play an important role here. In one of these studies, Glucksberg (1962) used the match-and-box problem that is discussed above (see p. 195). The investigator started from a premise extensively explored in both human and animal learning: strong motivation generally results in a strengthening of the dominant responses in a habit-family hierarchy.

In Figure 5 we have depicted two habit-family hierarchies. The left diagram represents the relative strength of various responses (solutions) under low motivational conditions, and the right diagram shows the strength of these same solutions under conditions of strong motivation. The fact that the left diagram depicts responses 1, 2, 3, and 4 as being relatively close together on the vertical dimension indicates that these responses have similar (but not equal) probabilities of occurring when motive strength is low. In contrast, high motivation strengthens all four response possibilities; and most importantly for our present concerns, a high level of motivation increases the *differences* between the various responses. In effect, a dominant response like R_1 is now more likely to occur than it was before, while relatively weak responses like R_3 and R_4 are less likely to occur, because they cannot compete as effectively with R_1.

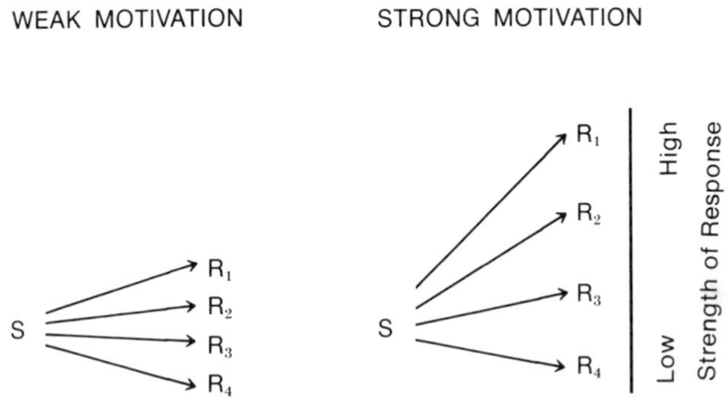

Figure 5

Effect of increased motivation on relative strengths of competing responses.

Let us now recall that in a situation like the match-and-box problem, the correct solution is not likely to be dominant initially; instead, it is rather weak relative to the other responses evoked. This means that the correct response (in this case, assume it is R_4), being relatively low in the hierarchy, should be even *less likely* to occur when motivation is high. That is, since increased motivation strengthens the stronger responses relative to the weaker ones, we should generally anticipate that high levels of motivation will further intensify the subject's fixation on the dominant (incorrect) response and thus impair performance. This is exactly what happened in the Glucksberg experiment. A "high drive" group of subjects who had been offered a financial reward if they could solve the problem turned out to be less successful in reaching the solution than was another group that had not been promised any money.

Fixation and past experience

In the examples discussed above, we have tried to show how the individual's perception of the problem and the solutions that he will consider may be significantly determined by the structure of the situation that now faces him and by his level of motivation. Of course, *previous experience* may also fixate incorrect solutions to a given problem; this phenomenon has been investigated most thoroughly by Luchins (1942, 1948; see also Luchins and Luchins, 1959).

Luchins' experiments involved the presentation of several rather simple computational problems, as shown in Table 1. The second problem in the table can be solved

Table 1
Problems used by Luchins (1942) in his studies of fixation.
(Used with permission of author.)

Problem	Given: The following empty jars as measures*			Obtain: The following amount of water*
1. (Sample)	29	3		20
2.	21	127	3	100
3.	14	163	25	99
4.	18	43	10	5
5.	9	42	6	21
6.	20	59	4	31
7.	23	49	3	20
8.	15	39	3	18
9.	28	76	3	25
10.	18	48	4	22
11.	14	36	8	6

*Figures represent capacity in quarts.

by (a) filling the large 127-quart jar, then (b) spilling off 21 quarts into the medium-sized jar, and finally (c) spilling off an additional 6 quarts by filling the smallest jar twice: $127 - 21 - (2 \times 3) = 100$. The experiments were constructed so that this approach could be applied to problems 2 through 6. All subsequent problems, however, could be solved in more than one way. One possibility was to follow the method that had been employed previously. Thus, in problem 7, we could obtain 20 quarts by first filling the 49-quart jar, removing 23 quarts, and then removing an additional 6 quarts by filling the 3-quart jar twice. Problem 7 and those following it could also be solved in a far simpler fashion, involving the use of only two jars; in problem 7, for example, we could get 20 quarts by simply filling the 23-quart jar and spilling off 3 quarts from it. Luchins' most important finding was that the presentation of the early problems led to a fixation on the method that had previously been successful. The subjects' earlier successes with this method apparently prevented them from seeing that a simpler approach was possible. However, it was possible to eliminate this type of fixation if, prior to the critical test series, the subjects were intermittently presented with problems that required *different* methods of solution. Other experiments by Luchins suggest that increases in motivation intensify the subject's fixation on the dominant responses in his hierarchy. In particular, Luchins found that if people were forced to solve the various water-jar problems while under time pressure, they showed increased fixation on the solution that was successful in the early problems. It seems plausible that the imposition of a short time limit elevated the level of motivation, which in turn strengthened the dominant responses in the individual's hierarchy.

Luchins' results seem to fit quite neatly into our earlier discussion of reinforcement, for the responses that were initially successful apparently gained in strength and prevented the occurrence of simpler solutions that were applicable to the later test problems. More recent work by Maltzman, Eisman, Brooks, and Smith (1956) suggests, however, that this effect can be largely overcome through the judicious use of instructions. In their experiment, the subjects first worked on a series of anagrams, each of which had an animal name as its solution. While repeated trials of this type significantly impaired performance on later anagrams which did *not* have animal solutions, this inhibitory effect was greatly reduced when the subjects were *verbally informed* of the change to "non-animal" problems.

Restructuring the problem situation

Problems are often insoluble because of our inability to discard approaches that have previously been successful. How, then, can we facilitate problem solving? One suggestion is to approach the problem from different perspectives, in the hope that the problem's elements will be perceived in a new and more fruitful light. Unfortunately, it is easier to talk about this procedure than to put it into practice. We may, however, point to some clear-cut examples to see how this suggestion might work.

One good example of restructuring has to do with the manner in which a problem is stated. Difficult problems often turn out to be quite simple if they are posed appropriately. For example, consider the following: How can a person build a house so that it has southern exposure on all four sides? As stated in this form, the problem is rather difficult, yet it may be made far simpler if restated with an emphasis on *where* one might build such a house (answer: at the North Pole).

Duncker (1945) provided another example of this rewording technique. He spoke of a mountain trip on which he planned to descend from a peak by the same path he had used for the ascent on the previous day. Assuming that the ascent and descent both took place at about the same time (from five to twelve o'clock), he posed the problem of whether there must be a point that he would pass at exactly the same time of day during the ascent and descent. Stating the problem in this form, Duncker could reach no conclusive answer. Rewording the problem, however, made the answer clear. Suppose there were *two* climbers—one at the top and one at the bottom of the mountain. If they used the same path and started at the same time, they must surely *meet* (that is, both be at the same place at the same time). Hence a single climber must pass some point at the same time of day during the course of his ascent and descent.

What are colloquially referred to as "hints" often provide another means for restructuring a problem situation. An experiment by Maier (1931) provides a good illustration. In this study, the subjects were individually led into a room that contained a variety of objects: tables, chairs, poles, pliers, and clamps. In addition, two cords hung from the ceiling to the floor—one in the center of the room and the other near a wall. Each subject's task was to tie the ends of the cords together. The problem was that the cords were well separated, and if the subject held one in his hand, he was unable to reach the other. One way of solving this problem was to tie a weight to the cord hanging from the center of the ceiling and then swing it like a pendulum. This would make it possible for the subject to catch the swinging cord while standing in a position near the center of the room and holding the other cord. In one experiment, subjects who were about to give up, after failing to discover this solution, were given the following hint: the experimenter merely walked about the room and, upon passing the cord hanging in the center, "accidentally" put it in motion.

This hint proved relatively successful in inducing the correct solution. In explaining his results, Maier reasoned that the cord, when swaying, was more like the needed pendulum than it was when stationary. Many of these subjects commented on the suddenness with which the problem situation became reorganized. It is particularly interesting to note that these people were rarely aware of the role played by the experimenter's hint; this illustrates that problem-solving attempts may often be influenced by factors that escape our conscious deliberations.

Problems can also be restructured by varying the *order* in which the elements of the problem are considered; in this way our approach to the problem may be modified. Judson and Cofer (1956) demonstrated this in a study in which subjects were given several problems, each consisting of four words. The subject's task was to pick out the one word that was unrelated to the other three. One group of words, for example, included the words "subtract," "increase," "multiply," and "add." This is an ambiguous item; from one point of view we might feel that "increase" is the unrelated word, since the others all refer to some arithmetic operation. Alternatively, perhaps "subtract" is the odd word, since each of the others implies increasing magnitude. Judson and Cofer found that responses to ambiguous items of this sort were affected by the order in which the words appeared. While "increase" was the most common response when the words were presented in the order given above, the sequence "multiply," "increase," "add," "subtract" tended to elicit "subtract" as the most common response—perhaps because of the expectations produced by the early words.

Judson and Cofer also found that their subjects' personal values and interests played a significant role in the way they structured the various test items. Given words like "prayer," "temple," "cathedral," and "skyscraper," religious subjects were likely to say that "skyscraper" did not belong with the other words. People without much religious interest, on the other hand, were less likely to accept the word "prayer"; to them the remaining words all appeared to have architectural referents.

Summary

1. Psychologists have long been concerned with the distinction between thinking and learning. Thorndike argued that he could see little evidence of insight in problem solving; rather, he emphasized the importance of trial-and-error behavior plus the law of effect. Köhler, on the other hand, felt that problem solving could not be reduced to these simple concepts. He contended that insight, based on the perceptual reorganization of problem elements, plays a crucial role in problem solving.

2. Harlow's research on learning sets provides evidence concerning the importance of trial-and-error experience for the development of insight. In his studies, he demonstrated that animals "learn to learn" and gradually progress from a stage in which their problem-solving efforts are characterized by *gradual* improvement, much as suggested by Thorndike's law-of-effect theory. With further problem-solving experience, animals become more skillful at such tasks until they are ultimately capable of showing insightful behavior in response to new problems.

3. Watson theorized that thinking is similar to speaking but without overt expression; thus, he regarded thought as implicit or subvocal speech.

4. According to Benjamin Whorf, language and thought are quite closely related in the sense that language provides the basic framework on which thought is constructed. This view assumes that people with different linguistic backgrounds are likely to think about and perceive the world in rather different ways.

Recent discussions of the Whorfian hypothesis have differentiated between *strong* and *weak* versions. The strong version of Whorf's theory suggests that cognitive processes are *inevitably* affected by language, whether or not there is an active involvement of verbal mechanisms. By contrast, the weak version of the theory suggests that language will not affect thought unless the cognitive task engages the individual's linguistic processes. There are several experiments that support the weak version of Whorf's theory; the evidence supporting the strong version of the theory is less conclusive.

5. In thinking, it is often necessary for us to represent symbolically the various elements of the problem with which we are dealing. However, this ability is not restricted to man; it can be demonstrated in animals as well.

6. Attempts at problem solving are often unsuccessful because of the individual's tendency to become fixated on some incorrect solution or approach. Karl Duncker theorized that this is usually attributable to the fact that various problem elements may be perceived in a conventional manner quite ineffective for the problem at hand. This type of fixation is most likely to occur when the individual is highly motivated.

Supplementary reading

Duncan, C. P. (Ed.) *Thinking: Current experimental studies.* New York: J. B. Lippincott Company, 1967.

Wason, P. C. and Johnson-Laird, P. N. (Eds.) *Thinking and reasoning.* Baltimore: Penguin Books, Inc., 1968.

9 Computer simulations of thought

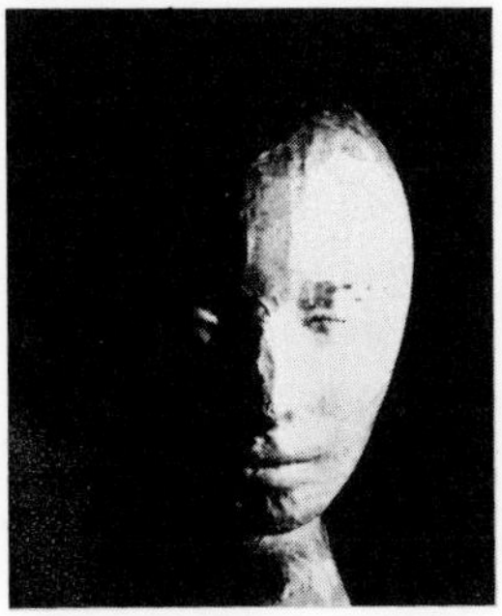

In recent years cognitive research has been enriched by a revolutionary new development: with the aid of high-speed computers, an imaginative group of researchers has set themselves the task of creating programs (that is, "instructions" for the computer) that enable the machine to simulate human problem-solving behavior.

An important aspect of most simulation research has been the attempt to recapitulate the *process* by which problems are solved. Simulation researchers have thus tried to trace the problem solver's component steps as he proceeds along the route to a final solution. By contrast, the more traditional approach of the behaviorist has focused primarily on the success or failure of the individual's efforts and has paid little attention to the intermediary processes that are involved. In tracing the problem-solving process, simulation researchers often make extensive use of "thinking-out-loud" procedures. Thus, an experimental subject might be instructed to verbalize the successive steps that he takes in attempting to solve a problem that has been set before him; his ensuing comments are referred to as a "protocol." The program that is finally developed is usually designed to simulate the final solutions that are proposed by human problem-solvers, as well as the intermediary processes and false starts that are verbalized in the protocol.

Some observers have expressed skepticism about this procedure because of the heavy reliance that is placed on the subject's introspective description of his thought processes. It has been suggested, for example, that the very act of verbalization may have a significant impact on the subject's approach to the task at hand. Moreover, it is difficult to dismiss the possibility that there may be significant cognitive events that for some reason fail to reach the level of conscious verbalization (see Chapter 4 for an extended discussion of this issue).

Dreyfuss (1965) suggests, for example, that in choosing their moves, skilled chess players *automatically* notice promising situations (that is, without conscious deliberation), and then proceed in a more rational and deliberate fashion to consider the various ways in which these openings can be exploited. While these latter deliberations are conscious and may be verbalized, Dreyfuss suggests that the initial (and very important) "zeroing in" represents a very different type of process. Despite criticisms of this sort, simulation researchers continue to rely on introspective reports. While granting the possibility that some processes may operate *silently* (without conscious awareness), simulation researchers typically assume that these processes are probably rather similar to those that *do* appear in their subjects' verbal descriptions.

Having written his program, just what does the investigator *do* in a simulation experiment? In an early study concerned with the simulation of proofs in symbolic logic (Newell, Shaw, and Simon, 1958), the following operations were employed. First, the computer was loaded with the program of instructions. The computer was next presented with a set of axioms and theorems which were to be treated as "givens" in the proofs which were sought. Finally, an expression which was to be proved was introduced into the system, and the computer was instructed to generate a proof. The results of this early experiment were encouraging, for proofs were, indeed, discovered for many theorems. Moreover, the ease with which the proofs were discovered was partially dependent upon the presence of previously proved theorems in the computer's "memory."

Simulation research may also involve the "line-by-line" comparison of machine output with the comments (or protocols) of human subjects who have been instructed to think aloud. In this procedure, the computer is programmed to print out the various steps (mechanisms) that were attempted during the solution of a problem, and the investigator searches for similarities and differences between the output of the machine and the problem-solving efforts that are verbalized by human subjects.

In contrast to the use of computers as a means for simulating human thought, some investigators have sought to create so-called *artificial intelligence systems* that are capable of solving complex problems by *any* workable programming techniques, even though the processing mechanisms might be quite distinct from those used by humans. An artificial intelligence system might have considerable practical value in solving business problems, for example, despite its inadequacies as a simulation of human thought. Note, moreover, that if a simulation attempt is judged unsuccessful because of its "unrealistic" processing devices, it may still prove valuable in the domain of artificial intelligence.

The necessity for explicitness

Many observers feel that the main virtue of the simulation approach is that it requires the investigator to specify his theory (program) in explicit detail so that it may successfully guide the behavior of his stupid and concrete-minded accomplice, the computer. In writing about this aspect of simulation research, Carl Hovland (1960) comments: "It is one thing to say, as earlier students have said, that problem-solving involves a number of different states, for example, those of preparation, incubation, illumination, and verification, and quite another thing for one to specify exactly what is involved in each stage."

Simulations also serve a useful function in explicitly showing us the implications of a given theoretical system. As Reitman (1965, p. 14) notes:

> "We may design a system to reflect particular psychological assumptions and then run it on the computer to observe the behavioral implications it generates. Actual runs also may point up other unexpected aspects of the system's behavior, and thus make us aware of consequences of our psychological assumptions we would not otherwise have anticipated."

By contrast,

> "With verbal models, it is practically impossible to be sure that conclusions follow only from explicit assumptions and that they in no way depend upon 'unprogrammed' elements entering informally into the argument. With laboratory experiments, we cannot get a test of the theory in and of itself. We must settle for a test of the theory taken together with all the assumptions about manipulations, measures, and conditions that couple the theory by means of operational definitions to the real world. If unexpected results occur, we are unable to say whether the difficulty is in the theory, ancillary assumptions, or both. In an information-processing (simulation) model, we can state, manipulate, and deduce implications from our theories in a way that is at once sure, unambiguous, and yet independent of operations relating the theory to data on human behavior."

In brief, simulation is felt to provide a unique method for explicitly determining the sort of behaviors that would be generated by the system we hypothesize in our model. Perhaps this claim is too boldly stated, however, for Reitman later notes that "The operation of a system depends both on the psychological assumptions and the *specific encoding by means of which the assumptions are made concrete* (Reitman, 1965, p. 25, italics added)." This suggests that the observed output of a system is not solely determined by the substantive psychological assumptions it contains, but also reflects what may be arbitrary programming details in the realization of these assumptions; the deductive consequences of the system may thus be more than a simple resultant of the theorist's substantive assumptions.

Simulations and the sufficiency test

Despite the reservations discussed above, simulation attempts are undoubtedly of value in providing a counterbalance to the analytic efforts of the experimentalist. Most experiments investigate the impact of a limited number of variables upon problem solving and result in the construction of relatively restricted theories, designed to account for those aspects of the behavioral universe that have been studied. However these miniature systems do not, as a rule, attempt to characterize the overall act of problem solving, and hence leave us with a series of isolated and possibly incomplete accounts of the relationship between input and output. By contrast, the simulation approach attempts to synthesize the *entire process,* from the statement of a problem, through a series of intermediary steps, and on to solution or failure.

If the computer can, in fact, be programmed to synthesize the problem-solving process, the underlying program (or theory) may be judged to have passed a *sufficiency test*. The investigator will have effectively demonstrated that his programmed system provides a model of sufficient power and complexity that it can successfully generate many of the achievements shown by human problem-solvers. Note that the sufficiency of a system does not necessarily establish its "correctness," for there may well be a family of diverse programs capable of passing a sufficiency test (just as it is often possible to explain a given experimental result in terms of several rather distinct theories). Despite this caution, however, it is clear that a successful demonstration of sufficiency is no small achievement, given the fact that most cognitive theories have not yet been shown to be adequate by this criterion.

The elementaristic assumption

The fact that successful simulations have already been devised in such complex domains as symbolic logic and concept formation provides an important demonstration of the extraordinary "power" that may be achieved through the skillful organization of *elementary* cognitive mechanisms, for computer simulations are typically based on relatively simple sub-processes, which perform such tasks as the searching, sorting, and storing of information. This accomplishment should not be underrated.

> "The achievements of the problem-solving process—the bridges it designs, the organizations it builds and maintains, the laws of nature it discovers, have an impressiveness all out of proportion to the groping, almost random, processes that we observe in the problem-solver at work. Little wonder that we invent terms like 'intuition,' 'insight,' and 'judgment,' and invest them with the mystery of the whole process (Simon, 1965, p. 78)."[1]

Nevertheless, in contrast to this widespread assumption of mystery and complexity, the present success of simulation research leads Simon to this conclusion:

> "The processes of problem solving are the familiar processes of noticing, searching, modifying the search direction on the basis of clues. The same symbol-manipulating processes that participate in these functions are also sufficient for such problem-solving techniques as abstracting and using imagery. The secret of problem-solving is that there is no secret. It is accomplished through complex structures of familiar simple elements. The proof is that we can simulate it, using no more than those simple elements as the building blocks of our programs (Simon, 1965, pp. 82–83)."

Algorithms, heuristics, and self-modification

One point which should be stressed in this discussion is the fact that simulation models do not achieve their effects by blindly trying all possible combinations of the methods with which they are endowed, until eventually an effective solution is found. There are, of course, many situations where "brute force" approaches of this sort (they are often called *exhaustive algorithms*) would ultimately be certain to achieve success, assuming that a virtually limitless amount of computer time was available. This method is not particularly elegant, however, and is in many ways reminiscent of the famous story about the monkeys who allegedly were seated at typewriters in the hope that if they typed long enough, the resulting mass of gibberish might include, among other things, the complete works of Shakespeare. Apart from this lack of elegance, moreover, it is clear that humans rarely solve problems through the system-

[1] From *The shape of automation for men and management* (1965) by Herbert A. Simon. Copyright © 1960 by School of Commerce, Accounts and Finance, New York University. Reprinted by permission of Harper & Row, publishers.

atic use of exhaustive algorithms. The human problem-solver is, instead, likely to have several alternative strategies or "rules of thumb" that he follows. These so-called *heuristic* methods may not guarantee success, but they are nevertheless useful ways of proceeding, and they have been widely adopted in computer simulations. Proceeding from appropriate rules of thumb, a program can often be arranged so that it recognizes which one (of several) solution strategies is most likely to prove successful, given the structure of a particular problem. For example, Gelernter and Rochester (1958) devised a system to prove various propositions in Euclidean geometry. When the proposition presented for proof was one involving parallel lines and equal angles, the machine was instructed to apply (if possible) the theorem: If two parallel lines are intersected by a third line, the opposite interior angles are equal. This instruction often served as an effective shortcut to solution, although there were some problems on which it proved useless.

In concluding this introduction to simulation research we should note that the programs currently available are not necessarily fixed and static; some of them are constructed so that they may be self-modifying, within limits. Samuel (1959), for example, has developed a checker-playing program that changes its behavior based on past experience. The program "remembers" previous board positions and the outcomes they produced; it also relies on previous experience in evaluating the desirability of a potential move. Similarly, the *logic theorist* (Newell, Shaw, and Simon, 1958), a program for the proof of logical theorems, was programmed to remember previously proven theorems and to use them in the solution of subsequent problems. One experiment showed that when previous proofs were removed from the computer's "memory," subsequent proofs required an increased number of steps, as compared with the relatively rapid solutions that were obtained when all earlier theorems were retained in memory.

Some examples of simulation research

Given this introduction to the simulation field, the reader may now be wondering about the specific ways in which this research is carried out. Unfortunately, a major communication problem is involved here, for the sheer volume of information required to describe a simulation program is considerable; a publication describing only the main details of one system ran to over 100 pages, and even so it assumed a sophisticated knowledge of related publications.

The General Problem Solver

Despite the communication problems that are noted above, perhaps we can succeed in conveying the general ideas involved in one program known as the General Problem Solver (Newell, Shaw, and Simon, 1958), by quoting the following simplified analogy (Simon, 1965, p. 83):

> "Supposing that we are camping in the woods and decide that we need a table. How do we solve the problem of providing ourselves with one? We state the problem: we *need* a flat horizontal wooden surface: we *have* all sorts of trees around us and some tools. We ask: What is the *difference* between what we need and what we have? Trees are large, vertical, cylinders of wood attached to the ground; a table top is a smaller, horizontal, movable slab of wood. Hence there are differences in detachability, size, flatness, and so on between what we have and what we need. We ask: What tools do we have to *reduce* these differences—for example, to detach the tree from its roots? We have axes. So we apply an ax to a tree and we have solved the first subproblem—to change an object rooted in the soil into an object detached from the soil."

As suggested in the preceding passage, the model devised by Newell, Shaw, and Simon goes about solving problems by "erecting goals, detecting differences between present situation and goal, finding in memory or by search tools or processes that are relevant to reducing differences of these particular kinds, and applying these tools or processes (Simon, 1965, p. 83)."

Each problem leads to associated subproblems until a subproblem is found for which the solution is available in the computer's "memory." Problem solving thus proceeds (when it is successful) through the solution of subproblems that have been identified as relevant to the eventual achievement of the original goal. When a subgoal presents difficulties, still another subgoal is erected as a means of overcoming the obstacle. Stated more abstractly, the General Problem Solver has three main types of goals:

> "1. *Transform goals:* Change *a* into *b.*
>
> 2. *Reduce difference goals:* Eliminate or reduce the difference between *a* and *b.*
>
> 3. *Apply operator goals:* Apply the program (or operator or method) *Q* to the situation *a.*
>
> With each of these types of goals is associated one or more methods for accomplishing it. When the goal is formulated . . . these methods are evoked from memory and tried. A method, for example, for changing *a* into *b* is to find a difference, *d,* between them and formulate the Reduce Difference Goal of eliminating this difference. A method for reducing a difference between *a* and *b* is to find an operator that is

> relevant for removing differences of the kind in question, and to apply that operator. A method for applying an operator is to compare the actual situation with the situation that would make it possible to apply the operator, and to formulate the goal of changing the actual situation into the required situation (Simon, 1965, p. 84)."

In creating a tree-like system of subgoals that are relevant to the solution of a given problem, the General Problem Solver employs several self-monitoring devices to regulate its activity. For example, the program is arranged so that a subgoal will not be attempted if it is more difficult to achieve than one of its supergoals; there is also a limit on the number of subgoals that will be tolerated as intermediary steps in the solution of a given supergoal.

While it is clear that the terminology adopted above can be fruitfully applied to a virtually infinite variety of problem settings, in fact, the General Problem Solver has thus far been employed in only one type of problem: the task of proving theorems in symbolic logic, a task that is somewhat similar to the problems encountered in high school geometry.

Simulating human performance in algebra word problems

A recent program developed by Bobrow (1964) reveals some of the mechanisms and problems that sometimes appear in simulation research. Bobrow's program is known as STUDENT; it can set up equations and solve them, when presented with "word problems" of the sort that appear in high school algebra courses. While this program was originally developed as a project in *artificial intelligence* (the system was simply designed to solve certain types of algebra problems, using *any* workable techniques), more recent research by Paige and Simon (1966) suggests that the system may also have merit as a simulation of human behavior, in that the program uses many of the same processes as human problem-solvers.

STUDENT can handle problems like this: "If the number of customers Tom gets is twice the square of 20 percent of the number of advertisements he runs, and the number of advertisements he runs is 45, what is the number of customers Tom gets?" The important thing about STUDENT is that it can translate a verbal problem of this sort into a set of equations, using a limited type of translation system (from English to algebraic equations). How is this accomplished? Stated generally, there are four main steps: (1) Through the use of a simple list of "synonyms," certain terms are translated into a standard form; in the present case, for example, the word "twice" becomes "2 times." (2) The computer next "tags" certain words to indicate their grammatical function; as an example, the word "what" is identified as a *question word.* (3) Using the word-tags as clues (see step (2)), the overall problem is next divided into a series of component sentences. For example, consider a generalized problem-to-be-solved that reads: "If . . . . . . , how many . . . . . . ?" Such a problem would be divided into two sentences, one starting with the word "if" and ending with the comma, and the second commencing with the question words "how many" and ending with the question mark. In the problem concerning Tom and his advertisements, the computer identified three simple sentences:

a) The number of customers Tom gets is 2 times the square of 20 percent of the number of advertisements he runs.

b) The number of advertisements he runs is 45.

c) What is the number of customers Tom gets?

(4) In the last step, the component sentences are converted into equations by treating question words (like "what") and noun phrases (like "the number of customers Tom gets") as variables. The three sentences identified in step (3) may thus be translated into the following algebraic expressions:

a) Number of customers Tom gets = 2 times $(.20[\text{number of advertisements he runs}])^2$.

b) Number of advertisements he runs = 45.

c) Number of customers Tom gets = X.

Once the problem has been reduced to this form, the solution may be readily obtained through substitutions. Thus the three equations may be combined into the statement: $X = 2$ times $(.20[45])^2$, which reduces to $X = 2(9)^2$, or 162, which is the answer to our problem.

It is interesting to note that in solving problems such as this, the program is mainly responsive to those terms in the text that have *mathematical significance* ("percent," "7 times," "square"), and terms that serve a primarily *syntactic role* (words like "if," "and" and so on). In contrast, the words and phrases that have *substantive meaning* are simply treated as variables (thus the phrase "the number of customers Tom gets" is equated with the unknown, X). Note, moreover, that in order to solve our sample problem, it is not at all necessary for the machine (or a human either, for that matter) to have any information concerning the meaning of words like "Tom," or "customers," or "advertisements." To demonstrate this, Paige and Simon (1966, p. 83) offer the following rewording of the original problem: "If the number of glubs *X* biks is twice the square of 20 percent of the number of quonks he dobs, and he dobs 45 quonks, how many glubs does he bik?" Despite the esoteric wording this is clearly a solvable problem with the same structure and solution as the formulation from which it was derived.

Although STUDENT is devoid of any mechanisms for processing ("understanding") most substantive terms, such mechanisms may prove a necessity if systems of this type are ultimately to serve as fully effective simulations. Consider the following problem: "The number of quarters a man has is seven times the number of dimes he has. The value of the dimes exceeds the value of the quarters by two dollars and fifty cents. How many has he of each coin?"

In responding to such a problem, human subjects will sometimes comment on the impossibility of the situation that is described (if the man has more quarters than dimes, how could the dimes be worth more than the quarters?); a program like STUDENT, however, will not recognize this fact, since it responds solely to the verbal statement with which it is presented and is completely insensitive to the contradiction that is described. By plodding straight ahead and processing the problem in the manner described earlier, STUDENT would conclude that our hypothetical man had −50/33 dimes and −350/33 quarters! While there is little doubt that the program could be modified to detect specific incongruities of this sort, the resulting system would lack the general adaptability of the human problem-solver, for it would be unable to handle problems in areas where substantive information had *not* been provided. Moreover, it is difficult to see, at the present time, how we can supply our computer with the endless volume of information that humans might call upon; algebra problems may, after all, be concerned with an infinite range of substantive topics.

Considerations of a similar sort have proven particularly troublesome in recent attempts to construct machine translation systems which would automatically convert input messages from one language (English, let us say) into another (Russian). Recent work on this problem has revealed that although a skilled human translator can interpret most well-constructed sentences in unambiguous terms, he will to a large extent rely upon substantive background information, for there are a surprising number of sentences whose meaning is ambiguous when analyzed from a *purely linguistic* point of view.

Consider the following example, originally suggested by Bar-Hillel (1960, p. 94): *"The box was in the pen."* Assume that this sentence was taken from a passage which read: "Little John was looking for his toy box. Finally he found it. The box was in the pen. John was very happy." The reader of this passage, if he is sufficiently skilled in English, will immediately recognize that the word "pen" must refer to a "play pen" rather than an implement for writing, for we all know that a pen which has a box in it cannot be a fountain pen (nor can it be a ball point). What seems most critical here is the human's rapid access to vast amounts of structured knowledge; information of this type enables us to infer automatically which one of several competing possibilities is the proper interpretation for a potentially ambiguous utterance.

Unfortunately, the available computer systems cannot rely on substantive cues of this type, for the amount of potentially relevant information seems without limit, and it is thus not clear how it can be "built into the system." The computer's limitations here are similar to those encountered in our discussion of STUDENT; in both cases, "human-like" performance seems to depend in part upon a virtually limitless pool of substantive background material which cannot readily be listed and incorporated into a computer program.

Computer simulations and ill-defined problems

Virtually all of the simulation work which has been completed to date has been concerned with *well-defined* problems. In general, such problems typically begin with a definite and clearly stated *input* (such as the axioms of Euclidean geometry), a specific, well-defined *goal to be attained* (such as a theorem which is to be proved), and a finite, well-specified set of *operations* which are to be applied in transforming the input situation into the desired goal. While the problem solver (or computer) may have difficulty in achieving the desired state of affairs, there is no question as to the desired goal or the methods that are permissible (although many of these may not apply in any particular problem). Lastly, there are established rules of procedure for determining whether or not a given proof has validly been established, and these rules may be built into our program to guide the operation of the computer.

By way of contrast, let us now consider an ill-defined problem: Suppose that our task is to devise an effective system for selecting candidates from among the applicants to a medical school. Note the vagueness of the problem as stated. For one thing, the goal we are seeking—"an effective system"—is not clearly specified, for many relevant considerations have not been made explicit. For instance, we are given no information as to the factors that our sponsor thinks of as important in medical education. Should our system be designed with the exclusive goal of training practicing physicians, or should we be willing to accept candidates who show great potential as researchers, despite a lack of interest and aptitude for clinical work? Unless we can get clear-cut answers to questions of this type, we run the risk of setting up a procedure that satisfies our *own* interpretation of the problem but fails to satisfy our sponsor. Even if we can get agreement regarding a concrete goal, we next face the problem of delimiting our procedures so that we can avoid methods that our sponsor may find objectionable, perhaps because of the heavy investment in time and money that they would require. In the geometry problem, by way of contrast, we have a perfectly explicit set of acceptable procedures from which we may choose those that seem useful.

Most of the problems that we face in everyday life are relatively ill-defined, in that we must first restructure the task (perhaps implicitly) into a more delimited version of the problem as originally stated; only then can we proceed with the task of finding a solution. It may be that many of the people we regard as creative and effective problem solvers are particularly gifted in their ability to redefine vaguely stated problems in ways that contribute to their eventual solution. It seems quite likely, moreover, that these attempts at providing the needed constraints for an ill-defined problem are guided in large part by the human adult's ready access to vast quantities of information that provide an implicit background for his thinking. Thus, in suggesting a procedure for medical school admissions (see above), the human problem-solver implicitly recognizes that his proposed solution must be relatively simple to apply and cannot require the candidates to expend unreasonable amounts of time and money. Unfortunately, we know relatively little about the way in which humans go about providing such constraints when they have not been made explicit in the original statement of a problem. Our present inability to construct programs that will solve ill-defined problems is doubtless related to the difficulties that have been encountered in trying to provide the computer with the *general* background knowledge that plays such a central role in human problem-solving. The development of computer programs that can solve ill-defined problems remains a task for the future. Reitman (1965) believes that such programs are possible; we shall simply have to wait and see.

The influence of "hardware" on cognitive theory

Despite the optimism of simulation researchers, some observers have expressed severe reservations about the entire enterprise. Many of these critics have been concerned that in attempting to create simulation programs for use on a computer, we may unavoidably base our efforts on a set of "hardware premises" that are drastically different from the machinery of the nervous system, and that the resulting models may suffer accordingly. For example, present-day computers are so constructed that they operate in a *serial* fashion and can only do one thing at a time; it is conceivable, however, that humans are capable of *parallel* processing—that is, of carrying out several operations simultaneously. In responding to criticisms of this type, Reitman (1965) has noted that animal studies are often regarded as quite useful, despite the unquestioned differences between animals and men; similarly, he contends, we need not assume that man is "nothing but" a computer in order to profit from the efforts of simulation researchers.

In some ways, this discussion regarding the impact of "hardware" upon simulation models reminds one of earlier debates regarding the necessity or desirability of reducing all psychological processes to an ultimate (?) neurophysiological base. By this time, most psychologists have come to recognize the value of theories that succeed in the prediction and explanation of behavioral events, even if the major concepts of the system bear no resemblance to underlying organic events; this position has long been upheld by such prominent theorists as Skinner, Hull, Tolman, and Spence. In a similar vein, simulation models may prove helpful in clarifying our conceptions of symbolic structures and processes, regardless of *how* these systems are ultimately realized at the neurophysiological level. Just as theorizing and experimentation on learning phenomena have profited from the development of behavior theories that are "silent" with respect to the underlying processes of neurophysiology, we may anticipate the possibility of similar gains through simulation attempts, despite the "neurological vacuum" that surrounds much of this work.

Summary

1. Cognitive processes have been simulated in recent years with the aid of high-speed computers. The goal of this research has been to create programs (that is, instructions for the computer) that will enable the machine to mimic the behaviors displayed by human problem-solvers.

2. The programs that have been developed in this tradition have often relied heavily on the verbalizations of human subjects who have attempted to solve problems "thinking aloud." While this method undoubtedly has weaknesses, it has been used extensively as a means of identifying the intermediary processes that intervene between the presentation of a problem and the various solutions (whether correct or otherwise) that are elicited.

3. Most observers feel that the greatest value of simulation research is the necessity for *explicitness* that it imposes on the theorist. Moreover, simulation models are thought to provide a valuable means of determining the deductive consequences of any clearly stated theoretical system.

4. The results of the simulations that have been conducted to date suggest that

through the skillful combination of various elementary processes, it is often possible to generate cognitive processes of surprising power and complexity.

5. Virtually all of the simulations that have been completed to date have dealt with well-defined problems—that is, with problems which begin with a clearly stated *input,* a well-defined *goal-to-be-attained,* and a well-specified set of *operations* that are to be used as "tools" in transforming the input into the desired goal. Unfortunately, however, we are often faced with ill-defined problems; it is unclear at present just how to go about simulating the efforts of the human who is faced with problems of this type.

Supplementary reading

Feigenbaum, E. A. and Feldman, J. (Eds.) *Computers and thought.* New York: McGraw-Hill, 1963.

Reitman, W. *Cognition and thought.* New York: Wiley, 1965.

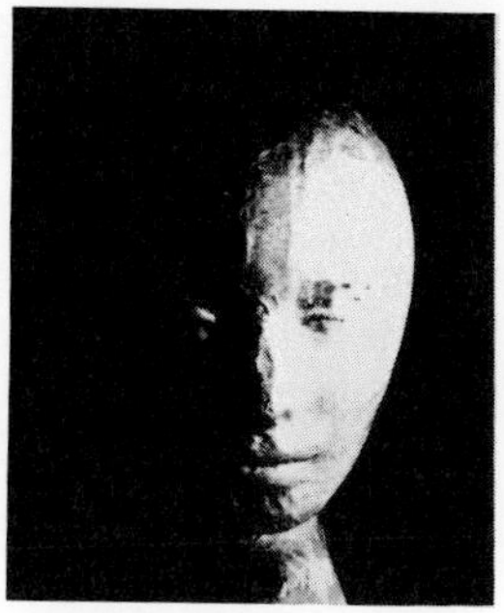

10 Creativity

How can we account for the genius of Leonardo Da Vinci? How can we increase the creativity of our children? Many people believe that creativity is simply one aspect of intelligence. This view has sometimes been questioned in recent years, however, for while it seems undeniable that outstanding creative accomplishments demand above-average intelligence, creativity may not be very important in the typical IQ test. For example, intelligence tests place considerable emphasis on the individual's ability to recall items he has learned in the past (such as the definitions of various words), but they do not give him an opportunity to demonstrate his originality or inventiveness. Some researchers have gone as far as to suggest that since traditional intelligence tests normally include questions with only one "correct" answer, they may penalize people who have novel patterns of thought. Nonetheless, despite these cautions regarding the difference between creativity and IQ, there seems to be fairly good evidence that highly intelligent persons are more likely to be creative than those who are relatively dull. It is also true, however, that extremely intelligent people do not *necessarily* excel in creative activities. Many researchers thus believe that while high creativity is rarely found among people who have limited intellectual ability, one can readily find both creative and uncreative individuals among the highly intelligent.

One of the important factors in creativity seems to be the ability to see things in an original way. People we honor for their contributions to art, literature, and science have generally approached their work in an inventive and novel manner. We should hasten to add, however, that originality is not the only ingredient in the makeup of the creative individual. After all, an original reaction to a problem situation may ultimately turn out to be worthless. For example, while I may be the first homeowner on my block to think of fertilizing the lawn with shaving cream, this original idea would not qualify as a creative act, since it would hardly prove to be a worthwhile plan in the long run. Similarly, while paranoid schizophrenics may sometimes give original and inventive accounts for various phenomena ("Congealed blood is an essential ingredient in the production of India ink"), we hesitate to classify these unique and eccentric utterances as evidence of creative ability because of their shortcomings when evaluated by the community at large. Creativity, then, demands more than just originality; a creative act also fits some worthwhile purpose.

One way to study the creative process is to find out all that we can about people who have shown unusual creativity. How might we select such a group? One technique is to have experts in various fields select the most creative members of their professions. When we have identified such a gifted group, we may then compare them with a less distinguished group drawn from the same occupation. We may, for example, compare creative scientists and their less creative scientific colleagues.

A series of studies following this general approach has been conducted at the University of California in Berkeley (Barron, 1965). The general plan was to invite selected individuals from such areas as mathematics, creative writing, and architecture to participate in an extensive three-day assessment procedure. During the assessment, the participants lived in a former fraternity house on the Berkeley campus and interacted with the assessment staff in a rather open social relationship. The participants also completed a variety of personality tests to elucidate further their individual characteristics.

The assessment staff found that the creative people were relatively unconventional and individualistic; they were also felt to be somewhat self-centered and moody. This emphasis on individuality and self-centeredness was also shown by the fact that creative people are likely to be particularly steadfast in maintaining their independence of judgment in situations where they find themselves at odds with those around them. The fact that creative people are often individualistic and independent should not surprise us; after all, truly creative work is characterized in part by its distinctiveness and originality. The scientist or writer who was unduly sensitive to the opinions of others would doubtless find it difficult to initiate successful innovations.

How about the psychological health of the creative person? Some people have felt that creative writers and scientists tend to be a bit disturbed (the stereotyped "mad scientist" is particularly pertinent here). The findings of the California studies are rather complex in this regard. One measure of psychopathology is the Minnesota Multiphasic Personality Inventory (MMPI), which enables us to compare the individual's test responses with those of people previously diagnosed as suffering from various psychological maladies, such as hypochondriasis, depression, hysteria, etc. On this test, outstanding creative writers showed consistently more evidence of psychopathology than did writers who were less eminent; similar findings were reported in a study of creative architects.

Despite the MMPI results, the creative person cannot simply be described as more disturbed than average, for his effective achievements are inconsistent with this view. Moreover, other test findings show the creative individual in a more favorable light than his less creative colleagues. For example, in the Berkeley studies, the more creative people tended to be high in self-acceptance, in flexibility, and in the ability to achieve through independence (rather than conformance). They were also significantly lower than the general population on a scale that assessed the individual's "effort to make a good impression." These findings point to the creative person's psychological strengths and his tendency to rely on his *own* resources.

One finding that may surprise you in these studies is the fact that, in certain respects, the creative scientist resembled the artist. This similarity was most strikingly revealed on a test measuring the individual's liking for complex and asymmetric forms, as opposed to forms that are simple, balanced, and regular. In this test, the individual was given a series of line drawings to separate into two groups: those that he liked and those that he disliked. Early research indicated that artists had a strong preference for complex and asymmetric figures, while the average person was likely to prefer designs that were more regular and balanced (see Figure 1). More recent work with this test indicates that a preference for complexity is also characteristic of creative scientists, writers, and architects. Frank Barron, a most active investigator in this area, theorizes that the creative person may be more at home with disorder and complexity, partly because of his ready acceptance of the unconscious aspects of himself, which also partake of turbulence and instability. Presumably these unconscious origins, rather than logic and rationality, are an important source of the creative impulse.

Age and creativity

For several decades psychologists have been interested in the effect of age upon various aspects of human behavior. Thus, studies have shown the relationship between age and reaction time, age and intellectual performance, and, more recently, between age and creative performance. In what is doubtless the most extensive study in this domain, Lehman (1953) has investigated the ages when men of various profes-

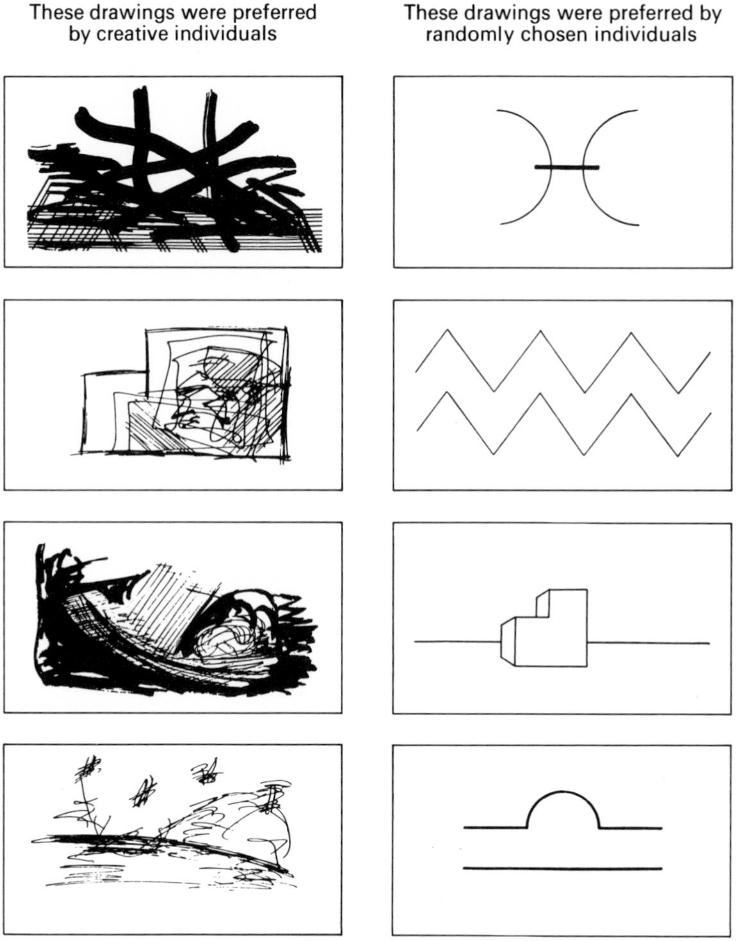
These drawings were preferred by creative individuals
These drawings were preferred by randomly chosen individuals

Figure 1

Drawings preferred by creative and randomly chosen individuals. (Adapted from Barron (1958) and reproduced by special permission from the Welsh Figure Preference Test by George Welsh © 1959. Published by Consulting Psychologists Press Inc.)

sions are most likely to make superior contributions to their fields. Table 1 summarizes his findings. As you can see, Lehman's results suggest that the most highly regarded creative contributions are usually produced by men between the ages of 30 and 40. This association between youth and creativity is particularly marked in the sciences. It is also interesting to note that in most fields the gifted contributor not only produces his *best work* at a relatively early age, but he is also *most productive* (in terms of the total number of works produced) during these early years.

Table 1

Ages at which Lehman found maximum rate of very superior contributions in different fields. (From *Introduction to psychology,* 3rd edition, by Ernest R. Hilgard, copyright © 1953, 1957, 1963 by Harcourt Brace Jovanovich, Inc., and reproduced with their permission. Data from Lehman, 1953.)

<table>
<tr><th rowspan="2">General Field of Creative Work</th><th colspan="4">Age at Time of Maximum Rate of Contribution</th></tr>
<tr><th>25–30</th><th>30–35</th><th>35–40</th><th>40–45</th></tr>
<tr><td>Physical sciences, mathematics, inventions</td><td>Chemistry</td><td>Mathematics
Physics
Electronics
Practical inventions
Surgical techniques</td><td>Geology
Astronomy</td><td></td></tr>
<tr><td rowspan="2">Biological sciences and medicine</td><td rowspan="2"></td><td>Botany
Classical descriptions of disease</td><td>Bacteriology
Physiology
Pathology
Medical discoveries</td><td rowspan="2"></td></tr>
<tr><td colspan="2">Genetics
Entomology
Psychology</td></tr>
<tr><td rowspan="3">Philosophy, education, and social sciences</td><td rowspan="3"></td><td colspan="2">Economics and political science</td><td rowspan="2">Metaphysics</td></tr>
<tr><td rowspan="2"></td><td>Logic
Ethics
Esthetics
"General philosophy"
Educational theory and practice</td></tr>
<tr><td colspan="2">Social philosophy</td></tr>
</table>

Table 1 continued

General Field of Creative Work	Age at Time of Maximum Rate of Contribution			
	25–30	30–35	35–40	40–45
Musical compositions	Instrumental selections	Vocal solos Symphonies	Chamber music Nonsymphonic orchestral music Grand opera	Cantatas Light opera and musical comedy
Literary compositions	Lyrics and ballads (German) Odes Elegies Pastoral poetry Narrative poetry Sonnets Lyric poetry	Satiric poetry Short stories Religious poetry (hymns) Comedies	Tragedies "Most influential books" Hymns by women	Novels "Best books" Best sellers Miscellaneous prose writings
Painting and sculpture		Oil paintings	American sculpture	Modern architecture Oil paintings (contemporary artists)

Despite the striking consistency of Lehman's results in a variety of creative areas, we can only speculate at the underlying factors that produced them. One possibility may simply have to do with the individual's acceptance of the prevalent views and approaches in his field; the older man may more likely be steeped in traditional methods and find it difficult to conceive of a truly original and creative approach.

Another way of interpreting these data emphasizes the fact that age differences are probably associated with differences in sheer energy output. Thus it seems possible that a young man's creativity may be related to his high energy level and his high resultant rate of production. The main point here is that the young person demonstrably produces *more* than his older colleagues (perhaps because of his more abundant energy level). Having created many works, the youthful contributor is thus more likely to produce an *outstanding* contribution than is his less productive older colleague. Note that this line of argument leads to the further expectation that, regardless of age, the more productive an individual is (in terms of number of contributions), the more likely he is to create a work of outstanding significance. This expectation is, indeed, borne out by the facts, for it is clear that in virtually all fields of intellectual endeavor, the eminent workers tend to produce more works than their less distinguished colleagues. While it is probably true that a man's sheer productivity (apart from the *quality* of his work) may be an important factor in establishing his eminence, this line of approach does not seem completely satisfactory. It seems more reasonable to hypothesize that the creative individual probably has more good ideas and more energy to carry them out than his less creative colleagues.

Stimulating creativity in groups

It is widely agreed that creativity is often limited by the individual's inability to divorce himself from the traditional approaches to the problem with which he is faced. In some instances, this inability may be attributed to the individual's fear that what he perceives as a fresh and possibly promising approach may be dismissed by others as silly and worthless. Under these circumstances, creative ideas will frequently be suppressed and not voiced publicly. Indeed, we may anticipate that after repeated suppressions of this sort, the individual may ultimately find it difficult to generate truly original proposals even in the privacy of his own thought.

To escape from this dilemma, some investigators (Osborn, 1953) have suggested the use of "brain-storming" sessions in which the members of a group are encouraged to offer possible solutions to a problem, with particular emphasis on the *production* of new ideas rather than on their *evaluation.* It is hoped that in this type of permissive atmosphere the group will benefit from the individual's freedom to explore "way-out" possibilities that might otherwise be quickly rejected as too hare-brained or never offered at all. Only after the conclusion of this idea-finding stage is the group encouraged to consider the "goodness" of the various proposals. This approach to problem solving, with its heavy emphasis upon *deferred judgment* (postponing the evaluation of ideas until a large number have been collected), has also been adapted to the *individual* thinker. In this case, the problem solver is instructed to reserve all judgments about the value of his tentative solutions until he has completed an initial period of idea finding.

Unfortunately, despite the wide publicity that these brain-storming methods have received, and despite the very reasonable theoretical basis on which they were formulated, there is at present only scant supporting evidence for the brain-storming approach to creative problem-solving. In one study, for example, the brain-storming method failed to produce any more original ideas than were generated by individuals working alone (Taylor et al., 1958); similar results have been reported by Dunnette, Campbell, and Jaastad (1963).

N. R. F. Maier (1962) suggests that problem-solving conferences can be made more effective if the group leader emphasizes problem-mindedness, rather than solution-mindedness. This suggestion derives from the fact that the average group member strives too quickly for a solution—often before agreement has been reached about the nature of the problem with which the group is faced. Maier also stresses the importance of having a group leader who will encourage diversity of opinion and protect minority views, since creative ideas often come from these origins. Laboratory studies indicate that when the personalities of group members are diverse, the group often solves problems more effectively (Hoffman and Maier, 1961)—probably because a group composed of diverse personalities is likely to consider many more possible solutions than is a group whose members are similar to one another.

Stimulating originality

Maltzman and his co-workers (1960) offer another approach to the problem of conformist, stereotyped thinking. These investigators attempted to increase the individual's capacity to respond in original ways to word-association tests and to a somewhat related task known as the Unusual Uses test, in which subjects are instructed to list unusual uses for such everyday objects as a newspaper or a brick. In both kinds of tests, originality of response was determined by comparing the individual's answers with those of others. People who gave unusual word associations, or who listed object uses that did not commonly appear, were regarded as original.

The experimenters took the position that originality in these test situations might be enhanced if the subjects were first reinforced for showing original behavior in some other context. The assumption was that the reinforcement of original responses in a preliminary *training session* would indirectly strengthen *other* original responses through response generalization (see p. 15), and this indirect strengthening would presumably be reflected in the word-association and Unusual Uses test. To investigate this hypothesis, Maltzman et al. developed a procedure in which subjects were first administered a word-association test in an unusual manner: the same stimulus words were presented six different times, and subjects were instructed to give a different response on each repetition. In this way, subjects were forced to go beyond the common associations to the various stimulus words and were induced to respond in a more original manner. Following this training procedure, they were presented with a final word-association test (just once, in the usual manner) and with the Unusual Uses test. The results indicated that the training procedure did in fact enhance the originality of subjects' responses on these last two tests (as compared with control subjects). While these results do not deal with creativity—since creativity is more than originality—they do suggest an interesting approach to the problem of stereotyped, conformist thinking.

Creativity as the formation of new associative linkages

Many students of creativity have commented upon the fact that creative productions often seem to result from a novel combination of previously disconnected elements. Creativity in scientific fields often takes this form and is perhaps best examplified by the scientist who formulates a new theory that encompasses several diverse phenomena. For example, Einstein's general field theory was able to account successfully for observations in widely scattered areas. Similarly, creative productions in art and literature often appear to result from an original combination of distinct elements that had not previously been brought together.

Starting with this essential notion, Mednick (1964) developed a procedure for assessing creativity called the Remote Associates Test (RAT). The test is composed of a series of items, each consisting of three unrelated words; the subject's task is to think of a response word that might serve as a connective link for the three. Table 2 presents several sample items; the correct answers appear in footnote 1. In principle, each item of the test provides the individual with an opportunity to respond creatively. That is, the respondent is given a set of elements (words) that are but dimly related to one another, and he is asked to find some underlying link (response word) that ties them together.

Table 2
Three items from the Remote Associates Test (Mednick, 1964).

				Response Word[1]
Sample item 1:	rat	blue	cottage	?
Sample item 2:	railroad	girl	class	?
Sample item 3:	surprise	line	birthday	?

[1] The "correct" answers to these items are: (1) cheese, (2) working, and (3) party.

The Remote Associates Test has been used in a variety of studies and has proven to be a promising instrument. Some studies have simply sought to determine the *validity* of the test—that is, to see if high scorers on the test manifest creativity in other aspects of their everyday lives. Perhaps the earliest of these studies (Mednick, 1962) showed that there was a substantial correlation ($r = .70$) between RAT scores and the creativity of a group of architecture students (as rated by their instructors in a design course). Another study of this type was conducted at the University of Michigan, where graduate students in psychology were rated for creativity by the professors who were supervising their research projects (Mednick, 1963). Once again, the students who were rated as most creative generally scored higher on the RAT than did those who were less highly regarded.

Additional studies of this sort have explored the relationship between creativity (as measured by the RAT) and on-the-job performance of professional scientific researchers. The results here have been more complex.

Thus, in a study by Gordon and Charanian (1964), there was essentially *no correlation* between RAT scores and the rated creativity of the scientists participating in the study. The scientists who scored high on the RAT did, however, submit more research proposals than their lower-scoring colleagues; moreover, the proposals of the high scorers were more likely to be *approved* for financial support, and generally received larger grants.

Andrews (1969) has suggested that the relationship between the individual scientist's creative ability and the quality of his work may depend on the setting in which he works. He reasons that a man's basic creativity may be directly reflected in his scientific performance if the work setting favors innovative thinking. In other circumstances, however, innovations may be inadvertently discouraged; in these situations there may be virtually no relationship between a man's creative capacity and his performance as a scientist. A man whose potentially creative suggestions are consistently blocked by his superiors may, for example, lose self-confidence and refrain from further innovative thinking. To explore this general hypothesis, Andrews studied the relationship between the RAT scores of over 100 scientists and the innovativeness that they displayed in their projects. He found that creative ability was positively related to innovativeness in settings where the scientists felt that they had a substantial opportunity and responsibility for innovation and for influencing various decisions concerning their work. Similarly, the scientists who were identified as high in creativity displayed more innovativeness than their less creative colleagues when they felt stable and secure in their jobs and when their administrative superiors stayed "out of the way." By contrast, when these facilitating conditions were *absent* (for example, when the scientists had relatively little capacity to influence decisions that affected their work), those who were identified as highly creative were no more innovative than their colleagues, and in some cases actually performed less effectively.

As an extreme example, Figure 2 shows the relationship between creative ability and scientific innovativeness in two contrasting work settings: (a) in laboratories that were characterized as offering very stable conditions of employment and (b) in those that offered little or no stability. Note that in the unstable situations, the more creative men do not perform as well as their less creative colleagues. In stable work settings, on the other hand, creativity is associated with a relatively high level of innovativeness.

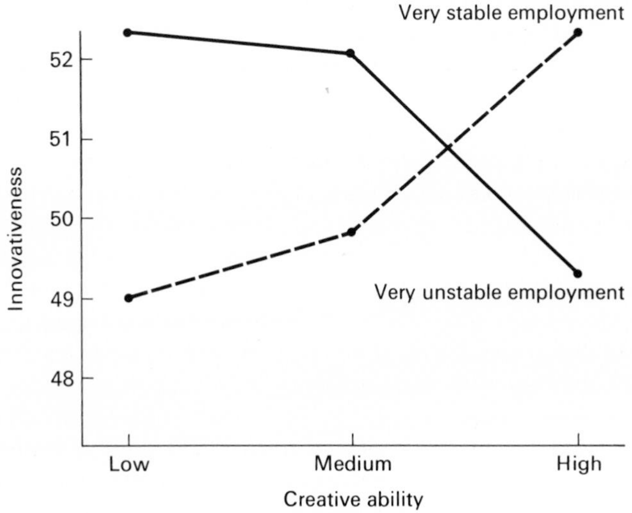

Figure 2

Innovativeness of project directors, as a function of creative ability and stability of employment. (Data from Andrews, 1969.)

In addition to validity studies like those cited above, the RAT has also been used in experiments designed to explore some of the personal characteristics that accompany creative ability. One study (Houston and Mednick, 1963) suggested that creative people may have an unusually strong need for novelty. In this experiment, the subjects were given 180 trials in which they were presented with two words, one a noun and one a non-noun; on each trial the subjects selected one of the two words. If, on a given trial, the subject selected the noun, the experimenter responded with an unrelated word; if the non-noun was selected, the experimenter responded with a common association. Thus, if the words "father" and "white" were presented, and the subject selected the noun ("father"), the experimenter might say "egg-beater"; when the word "white" (the non-noun) was selected, the experimenter would say "black." According to the hypothesis underlying the experiment, the creative person should have shown an increasing tendency to choose the nouns—since these choices would invariably be followed by novel associative stimuli, which would presumably satisfy his need for novelty and strengthen (through reinforcement) his preceding choice. By contrast, the less creative person would presumably gain little if any satisfaction from the experience of novelty and hence would be less strongly reinforced when he chose a noun and was presented with a novel association. The results supported this chain of reasoning. That is, as the trials progressed, the creative subjects showed an increasing tendency to choose the nouns—presumably because of the novel associations that were presented to them following such choices. The less creative subjects, on the other hand, showed a steady decline in their choice of nouns, suggesting that they may have preferred to *avoid* novelty. To test whether the novel associations had played a significant role in these differing performance patterns, the experimenters studied two additional groups of subjects; in this control condition, the experimenter always responded with a *common* association (for example: "father-mother," rather than "father-eggbeater")—even on those trials where the subject selected the noun. Under these conditions, the creative and the noncreative groups showed similar performance patterns, suggesting that the novel associative "rewards" had indeed played a critical role among previously described experimental groups.

Two studies by Mendelsohn and Griswold (1964, 1966) suggest that the creative individual may also be more sensitive to peripheral, incidental stimuli, which he may utilize (providing they are relevant) in subsequent attempts at problem solving. Nicely complementing Houston and Mednick's work on the creative person's need for novelty, the data in these studies suggest that creativity is normally accompanied by a wider deployment of attention and by a less rigid "screening out" of seemingly irrelevant past experiences. It is conceivable that these traits are an important factor in the creative person's capacity for original thought. What remains something of a mystery, however, is the mechanism whereby the creative individual is able to evaluate the various original (but ineffective) solutions that occur to him *prior* to his discovery of a truly creative and useful response. Thus, while the research cited above points to some of the factors that presumably enable the creative individual to generate original responses, relatively little is known concerning the way in which effective solutions are selected from the pool of original (but unevaluated) responses that may occur during problem solving.

Summary

1. Creativity should not be confused with high intelligence, for the typical IQ test does not assess originality or inventiveness. However, there is some association between intelligence and creativity, since people with but limited intelligence are rarely very creative.

2. We should also be careful to distinguish between creativity and originality. An idea that is original (in the sense that no one else may think of it) may ultimately prove to be worthless. Creativity is thus more than originality; a creative act must also serve some worthwhile purpose.

3. Creative people are often somewhat unconventional and individualistic. They also seem to prefer complex, asymmetric drawings, rather than more balanced and regular designs. This preference for complex designs is characteristic not only of creative artists but also of creative writers, scientists, and architects.

4. Outstanding creative works are usually produced by relatively young people; this finding appears in many fields and particularly in the sciences.

5. "Brain-storming" sessions represent an attempt to overcome traditional approaches to a problem by encouraging the members of a group to focus upon the *production* of new ideas before evaluating the various suggestions offered. Presumably, a permissive atmosphere encourages the exploration of original possibilities that might otherwise be rejected as silly or worthless. Unfortunately, at present there is no really good evidence to support the optimistic claims voiced in behalf of the brain-storming technique.

6. Creative productions often seem to result from a novel combination of elements previously not connected. This form of creativity is particularly pertinent in scientific fields, where a new theory may encompass several seemingly diverse phenomena. Mednick has developed a remote associates test (RAT) in which the individual attempts to provide a single verbal response associated with each of three unrelated stimulus words.

Subsequent research with this instrument suggests that under favorable working conditions, creative ability may be directly related to the innovativeness shown in scientific research; under unfavorable conditions, however, the researcher's creativity may be ineffectively expressed, and his work may resemble that of his less creative colleagues. Other studies suggest that creativity (as assessed by the RAT) is often associated with a strong need for novelty and with an enhanced readiness to utilize peripherally presented cues in the solution of subsequent problems.

Supplementary reading

Barron, F. The psychology of creativity. In T. M. Newcomb (Ed.), *New directions in psychology II*. New York: Holt, 1965.

Taylor, C. W. (Ed.) *Creativity: Progress and potential.* New York: McGraw-Hill, Inc., 1964.

4 Social cognition

11 Cognitive consistency

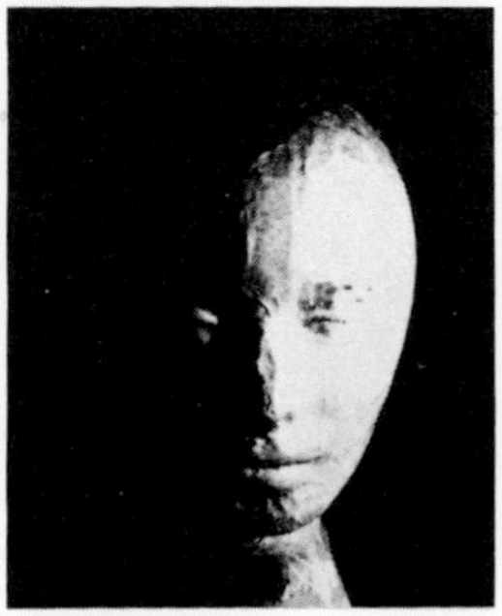

A great deal of theoretical and experimental effort in recent years has been devoted to the concept of cognitive consistency. Several theories have been proposed, all based on the general notion that men normally prefer to avoid illogical, or "nonfitting," patterns of thought. It is important to note that the inconsistencies which concern these theorists are not necessarily dealt with in treatises on formal logic, however, for man seems to be bound by a *psycho-logic* that is but dimly related to the rules of the philosopher or the mathematician. The consistency theorists are thus mainly concerned with the *subjective logic* that so often guides our beliefs and perceptions.

If, as these theorists assert, nonfitting cognitions result in a state of discomfort, we might ask why it is that the individual *ever* tolerates inconsistency. After all, a person who was truly dedicated to the goal of consonance would presumably readjust his thoughts and beliefs (when necessary) to avoid inconsistency. There are several factors, however, which seem to limit our success as consistent thinkers.

First, we may simply lack the cognitive ability to trace all the implications of our various beliefs. This problem is made even more acute by the fact that if we rearrange our opinions to adjust to a new input, we may inadvertently create an imbalance in other cognitive spheres, where consonance had previously reigned.

A second major factor that limits the consistency of thought is man's tendency to believe in things that gratify his wishes, whether or not these beliefs are consistent with one another. In a study by McGuire (1960), for example, a sample of high school students indicated the degree to which they endorsed a series of syllogistically related propositions. Among other issues, the students indicated their belief in statements concerning:

> (a) the probability that *any* city which could easily be reached by air from the European continent would be destroyed in an atomic attack if there were another world war;
>
> (b) the ease with which their *own* city could be reached by airplanes based in Europe; and
>
> (c) the likelihood that their city would be destroyed through bombing in the event of a world war.

As you might expect, the students' responses to an item like (c), which represents the conclusion of the syllogism, were significantly related to their beliefs regarding the premises, (a) and (b). There was thus evidence of cognitive consistency. However, the students also showed clear evidence of *wish fulfillment,* in that they tended to believe most fervently in statements that depicted desirable, rather than undesirable, states. There was also clear evidence that this tendency to believe in wish-fulfilling statements had impaired the internal consistency of the students' beliefs.

Despite the dampening effects of wish fulfillment, it is interesting to note that in McGuire's study, the simple arousal of related beliefs by means of the questionnaire resulted in a spontaneous reduction in the incongruities that had initially been displayed. That is, when the students' opinions were reassessed one week later, there was evidence of increased cognitive consistency. This effect was presumably due to the heightened salience of the beliefs that had been assessed, which ultimately motivated the students to reduce the existing discrepancies between "nonfitting" cognitions. In discussing these results, McGuire suggests that the individual's *awareness* of his initial inconsistency was relatively unimportant in the results that were obtained. More recent research by Brock (1968) points to a similar conclusion, although Brehm and Cohen (1962) have argued that the subject's awareness may play a critical role in motivating consistency reactions.

Balance theory

One of the most influential of the consistency theories was enunciated by Heider (1958), who focused attention on the concept of *structural balance*, emphasizing the systematic patterning of man's likes and dislikes. According to Heider's theory, we have a built-in "bias" to perceive balance; imbalanced structures, which Heider assumed to be unstable, presumably evolve (over time) into more balanced structures.

Perhaps the simplest illustration of structural balance is the widespread assumption that the people we like (or dislike) probably like (or dislike) us in return; that is, we normally expect people to have *symmetric* feelings about each other. There is considerable evidence to support this proposition. DeSoto and Kuethe (1958, 1959) found that when people are given information such as "Bill likes (or dislikes) Norman," they readily infer that Norman probably reciprocates Bill's feelings. Similarly, Taguiri, Bruner, and Blake (1958) have shown that we frequently assume that our own likes and dislikes will be reciprocated even in cases where reciprocation does not actually exist.

But balance theory is not restricted to the study of reciprocation; it has frequently been applied to *three-unit* systems in which two interacting persons have similar (or dissimilar) attitudes toward some third entity. For example, suppose we learn that Al and Bob like each other, and that both of them like modern jazz. According to Heider's theory, this would represent a stable, balanced structure; since the various "links" seem quite compatible with one another, there is no cognitive strain. In general, balance theory assumes that we expect people to like one another if they have similar attitudes. Thus, if we learn that Al and Bob are friends, and that only one of them likes modern jazz, the structure will be *imbalanced*; however, if *both* of them react negatively (or positively) to modern jazz, the system will again be balanced and stable, for the friends will then be in apparent agreement. If people *dislike* each other, balance theory suggests that we will expect them to have rather *different* attitudes. A balanced structure may thus result if Al appears to dislike Bob, as well as the modern jazz that Bob finds so appealing.

Heider formulated these requirements for a balanced structure: a system with three links will be balanced (a) if there are *no* negative bonds involved, or (b) if *two* of the constituent bonds are negative and one is positive. While Heider himself was uncertain whether triads involving *three* negative relations were balanced or imbalanced, subsequent researchers have typically assumed that this combination qualifies as an unbalanced structure.

Empirical studies based on the balance theory of cognitive consistency have utilized a variety of experimental procedures. Here are some examples.

Preference ratings

Several investigators have explored the hypothesis that people normally prefer balanced states to unbalanced states. Jordan (1953) presented his subjects with a series of hypothetical situations, each including information concerning (a) the subject's presumed attitude toward *o,* another person; (b) his attitude toward *x,* an undefined entity; and (c) the relationship between *o* and *x*. For example, one situation was described as follows: "I like *o*; I like *x*; *o* has no bond or relationship with *x*." The subjects were to imagine themselves in 64 such settings and were to rate the pleasantness which they might feel in each setting. Although there were some discrepancies between the detailed theoretical predictions and the data that were obtained, the balanced triads were generally rated as more pleasant than the unbalanced triads.

Predictions

Since balance theory is based on the notion that certain conceptual structures seem "more natural" than others, several investigators have tested the implications of this notion by having subjects attempt to predict missing items of information in various social settings. Feather (1967) gave his subjects a questionnaire that included items like this: "Joe knows that Jack is mildly in favor of the present immigration policy. Joe is strongly opposed to the present immigration policy. Does Joe like Jack?" The subjects' predictions were generally consistent with balance theory. For example, in response to the above item, most people concluded that Joe probably did *not* like Jack, whose opinion on immigration differed from his own. Studies like this support the hypothesis that there is a widespread strain toward cognitive consistency; the average person apparently assumes that social structures typically adhere to the formulas suggested by the balance theorists.

A closely related method of research focuses on the presumed instability of unbalanced structures. Burnstein (1967) conducted a study of this sort during the presidential campaign between Lyndon Johnson and Barry Goldwater. Each subject was presented with information of the following sort:

> When Joe and Bob first met as dorm roommates—
> a. Joe liked Bob
> b. Bob liked Joe
> c. Joe favored Barry Goldwater
> d. Bob was against Barry Goldwater

Each subject's task was to indicate which of these items, if any, were likely to *change* during the succeeding weeks. The results indicated that structures were changed relatively infrequently if they were initially balanced, or if they involved symmetric feelings between the roommates. Moreover, the changes that were anticipated usually served to produce balanced structures.

Imbalanced situations can be changed into balanced ones in a variety of ways, some of which require *several* changes in the original situation. Abelson and Rosenberg (1958) have suggested, however, that there is a normal tendency to achieve balance through the easiest route (the one involving the fewest changes). Burnstein's data were consistent with this formulation; there was an overwhelming tendency for subjects to achieve balance by anticipating minimal changes in the original situations.

Burnstein's results also revealed an interesting cognitive bias based on the respondents' *political attitudes.* As an illustration of this bias, consider a hypothetical pair of roommates who presumably like each other, but who differ in their presidential choices—one favoring Johnson, the other favoring Goldwater. This is an unbalanced structure, but it can be balanced in a variety of ways. For example, we might expect (a) that the roommates would come to disapprove of one another because of their conflicting views, or (b) that they would both eventually tend to favor Johnson, or (c) that they would both come to favor Goldwater. Burnstein hypothesized that the changes anticipated by each respondent would probably be those that would bolster the respondent's *own* attitudes. Thus, given initial disagreement, a pro-Johnson subject should foresee a situation in which *both* roommates eventually favor Johnson; a pro-Goldwater subject should anticipate eventual agreement in support of *his* preferred man, Goldwater. Burnstein's results were in general accord with these expectations.

Learning

Zajonc and Burnstein (1965a, 1965b) have conducted several experiments to assess the impact of cognitive balance on learning. In these studies, the subject's task was to memorize the interpersonal preferences of various pairs of individuals (e.g., Does Bill like or dislike Bob?), as well as the attitudes of these persons toward some social issue (Does Bill favor or oppose integration?). In some cases the structures which were to be learned were balanced, and in other cases they were not. A balanced structure, for example, might be one in which Bob and Bill liked one another and in which they both favored integration. The results indicated that balanced structures were memorized more quickly than unbalanced structures.

Other biases

It is interesting to note that the strain toward balance represents only one of several widely shared cognitive biases. For example, in Zajonc and Burnstein's learning experiments (1965a, 1965b), *positive* relationships (e.g., Bob likes Bill) were learned more quickly than negative relationships; there was also clear evidence that *reciprocal* choices were easier to learn than those which were not reciprocated.

In a thorough review of the literature on cognitive balance, Zajonc (1968) concluded that the evidence for one bias—the bias toward agreement—was at least as strong as the evidence favoring the balance postulate. Thus, a reanalysis of several experiments indicated that hypothetical social situations involving people with similar attitudes were typically rated as more pleasant than those involving people with dissimilar views. It is important to note here that a relationship which reflects agreement need *not* be in balance; if Jim and Joe hold similar views regarding civil rights, but nevertheless *dislike* each other, the resulting structure is unbalanced.

Concluding comments

Zajonc (1968) and Newcomb (1968) have noted that Heider's balance postulates seem most successful in predicting our reaction to social situations in which the interacting individuals respond positively to one another. Thus, if Jim and Joe are *friends,* people find it disconcerting to learn that the friends have contradictory views on civil rights. On the other hand, if Jim and Joe *dislike* each other, most observers seem to regard this relationship in rather neutral terms, and are unaffected by information concerning the similarity (or dissimilarity) of the opinions held by these two.

Observations like this led Newcomb (1968) to suggest that the theory of cognitive balance may be inapplicable unless there is a positive bond between the interacting individuals; he proposed that situations involving negative relationships should be termed *nonbalanced* (rather than balanced or unbalanced), since they tend to elicit an unusual number of "neutral" reactions. Newcomb reasoned that balance may be relatively unimportant when we learn of the preferences and aversions of someone we dislike, since we may be simply indifferent to this person's views. Negative relationships clearly have little appeal, and this seems to be the case even when such relationships appear to be justified (explainable) as resulting from a conflict of opinion.

As noted above, Heider's theory has proved to be an effective stimulant for empirical research. It has also been subjected to a good deal of critical scrutiny, and some critics have maintained that the balance theory is, at best, incomplete. Consider, for example, the following case: If John likes Mary, and Tom likes Mary, and John and Tom are friends, we would appear to have a balanced structure. But what if both John and Tom are so strongly attracted to Mary that each wishes to marry her? Is this still a harmonious, balanced situation? Clearly, Mary as "wife-for-John" is a different conception from Mary as "wife-for-Tom," and hence the two friends are not really in agreement; in fact, as we intuitively recognize, we have an unbalanced structure. Note that a further effect of recognizing the exact nature of the cognitions concerning Mary is that we then see John and Tom in different roles—not as friends, but as competitors. A satisfactory formulation of balance theory will have to take account of such factors; such revisions, however, add greatly to the complexity of the theory and hence may cloud its predictive power.

A second shortcoming of the balance theory is that it does not provide an adequate means of dealing with the *importance* or *relevance* of an issue. Balance theorists recognize that the tension (if any) resulting from a disagreement between friends depends largely on the particular issue involved; some disagreements may lead to the end of a friendship, while others are placidly endured. Nevertheless, it has been difficult to specify in *theoretical* terms what it is that makes a particular issue important (or relevant) for a given relationship; further work on this problem is clearly needed.

Cognitive dissonance

While Heider's work was the first of the modern consistency theories, Festinger's theory of cognitive dissonance has proven to be the most influential and has stimulated by far the most research. Festinger (1957) emphasizes the motivating effects of "nonfitting," or dissonant, cognitions. His main hypothesis is that the simultaneous belief in two or more dissonant cognitions normally results in a noxious drive state that motivates behavioral or cognitive changes designed to reduce dissonance.

How can we tell when dissonance exists? Along with most other consistency theorists, Festinger bases his approach on a subjective, informal logic; he contends that two ideas are in a dissonant relationship whenever the obverse of one idea seems to follow from the acceptance of the other.

For example, a registered Democrat who consistently votes for Republicans will presumably recognize the inconsistency between the cognitions: (1) I am a Democrat, and (2) I normally vote for Republicans. According to the theory, the resulting dissonance should motivate our hypothetical voter to find some means to resolve this inconsistency. There are several possible ways in which this could be accomplished. One simple technique would be to resign from the Democratic party and reregister as a Republican. Another possibility would be for our voter to convince himself that his "disloyal" voting behavior was justified, perhaps because the local Democratic organization had been "captured" by a self-serving group that had repeatedly nominated poor candidates. In a sense, this type of justification appeals to a higher form of consistency: "I consistently vote for the best man (even if he is not the nominee of my party)." Still another dissonance-reducing technique would be for our voter to *rationalize* his inconsistent behavior by emphasizing the social pressures from relatives and neighbors that led to his present Democratic affiliation; this solution "excuses" the inconsistent voting pattern by attributing it to external forces rather than to a spontaneous, freely chosen course of action.

Festinger's conception of dissonance, together with his striking and controversial style of research, have stimulated a profusion of experimental studies. Some examples are presented below:

Post-decision dissonance

Everyday life is a complicated matter, since we are often forced to make difficult decisions. If a person is faced with a decision between two courses of action (such as a choice between two automobiles), there will typically be positive and negative features associated with *both* alternatives. For example, one car may be quite comfortable, but too expensive; the other may lack visual appeal, despite its mechanical excellence. Normally, of course, there will be a good deal of thought and effort invested in making a decision of this type. Festinger has pointed out, however, that the buyer will still (*inevitably*) find himself in a state of dissonance once the decision has been made, because he knows that he has selected car A despite its negative features (inflated price, for example) and rejected car B despite its positive features (fine engineering). After all, if we recognize that a given car has an inflated sales price, it hardly seems logical to go ahead and purchase it, nevertheless. In order to reduce the dissonance that presumably exists *after* the purchase has been made, the buyer may justify his decision by reappraising the alternatives—that is, by emphasizing the positive aspects of the chosen alternative and derogating the rejected option.

Several experiments have yielded results in support of this prediction. In a study by Brehm (1956), several college students were asked to rate eight commercial products; then, as a "reward" for having participated in the experiment, the students were given a choice between two of the products that had received mid-range ratings. Following this choice, they were asked to assign a second set of ratings to the products. The results strongly supported the dissonance model; the chosen product typically was rated more favorably than it had been initially, and the rejected product was rated *less* favorably than it had been before. This post-decision effect was most pronounced when the subjects' choice was between two products that had originally received similar ratings (this would presumably generate a great deal of post-decision dissonance); the results were less clear-cut when the choice was between products that had received more disparate ratings.

Subsequent research (Brehm and Cohen, 1959) has shown that post-decision reevaluations emerge most clearly when the decision-maker must choose among many alternatives, rather than just a few. In such cases, the individual must reject *many* attractive possibilities in the process of choice, and thus post-decision dissonance should be high, leading to a relatively marked reappraisal process. Similarly, if the available alternatives are qualitatively distinct, there is more post-decision dissonance and reappraisal than there is when the alternatives are rather similar. When the various decision options are distinctive, the rejected alternative(s) are likely to contain attractive features that must unequivocally be "given up," since they are probably *not* included within the framework of the chosen option; on the other hand, it may be possible, in part, to "eat one's cake and have it too" when the competing options are similar.

Dissonance and the self-image

Malewski (1962) and Gerard, Blevans, and Malcolm (1964) have shown that post-decision reappraisals occur primarily among those who have high self-esteem. People who have a favorable view of their own decision-making abilities seem particularly upset when they recognize that a freely chosen course of action has forced them to "give up" something valuable. To reduce the discrepancy between his positive self-image and the negative consequences of his choice, a person with high self-esteem may attempt to "justify" his decision by enhancing the attractiveness of the chosen alternative, while derogating the rejected option(s). A person with low self-esteem, on the other hand, may be relatively unaffected by post-decision dissonance; for him, there is no great discrepancy between his negative self-evaluation and the knowledge that his chosen course has had certain undesirable consequences. He may, indeed, regard himself as a "born loser" who must learn to live with "foolish" decisions. Considerations of this sort suggest that an unstated variable in the research on post-decision effects may be the disparity (if any) between the decision maker's self-image and the negative aspect of his chosen course.

Malewski's analysis (see above) focuses on the discomfort that results when an individual with high self-esteem recognizes that there are certain negative consequences that follow from his freely chosen course of action. By contrast, a reinforcement theorist might contend that negative consequences are always disturbing, whether or not they conflict with the individual's self-image, and he might add that positive consequences are invariably welcomed (even by those who expect to do poorly). Although the literature in this area is far from clear, an experiment by Aronson and Carlsmith (1962) suggests that under certain (poorly specified) conditions, we may be disturbed when our performance at a task differs widely from what we had expected. This reaction is hardly surprising in the case where a person fails a task at which he had expected to do well; however, the Aronson-Carlsmith study suggests that we may also be disturbed to learn that we have *succeeded* at a task which we had expected to *fail,* and we may accordingly adjust our performance *downward* if given an opportunity to change what we have done. Similarly, Aronson, Carlsmith, and Darley (1963) have shown that a subject who expects to perform an unpleasant task is subsequently likely to select this task even if he is given a free opportunity to choose a less noxious alternative. These results suggest that it may be unpleasant to have our self-expectations disconfirmed, even when we are expecting to hear that we have done something badly, or expect that we will have to engage in some unpleasant activity. Unfortunately, however, this body of data has proven to be of uncertain reliability (Goldberg, 1963), and the results have sometimes been attributed to experimental artifacts (Ward and Sandvold, 1963). The frequent failures to achieve replications here (Silverman, 1968; Watts, 1968) suggest that while disconfirmed expectations may be unpleasant, the specific conditions that are essential in evoking this reaction are poorly understood at the present time.

Insufficient justification

Dissonance research has frequently focused on situations in which individuals engage in overt actions that are inconsistent with their beliefs. Festinger and his colleagues, for instance, hypothesize that dissonance should result when a person takes a public stand that is contrary to his private views. Since it may be difficult to change one's recollection of a recently completed public statement (or other public act), dissonance is often reduced in these situations through the mechanism of opinion change; that is, the individual may change his views to bring them more closely in line with his recent public behavior.

In further considering this paradigm, we should note that the degree of dissonance in these cases partly depends upon the amount of justification (broadly defined) that is available to support the actions that are performed. For example, if there appear to be good reasons for acting contrary to one's private beliefs (perhaps there is a large monetary reward involved), then there should be relatively *little* dissonance, for it is not illogical to espouse an opinion that we privately reject if there is a substantial reward to be gained. On the other hand, if the individual acts contrary to his beliefs even though he has *little* justification for doing so, he should feel more personally responsible for his action and more strongly committed to it. In this latter situation, the inconsistency between attitudes and actions should produce considerable cognitive dissonance, which should (according to the theory) be reduced through a change in attitude. This basic conception has been tested in a variety of experimental settings, some of which are outlined below.

Magnitude of reward

Perhaps the earliest experiment on insufficient justification and counter-attitudinal behavior was conducted by Festinger and Carlsmith (1959). The college students who served as subjects in this study were first assigned a series of dull and repetitive tasks, which they worked at for an hour in order to obtain individual "measures of performance." The students were then individually asked if they would serve as the experimenter's confederate in collecting similar data from the "next subject," since the person who normally served in this role was unavailable. The confederate's job was to tell the next subject that the experiment was interesting, enjoyable fun. Note that when someone agrees to serve in this capacity, he is engaging in behavior that is dissonant with his private views, for he is publicly telling another student that he enjoyed an experience which was actually dull and boring. The subjects were given varying amounts of money (financial "justification") before enacting the confederate's role, partly as payment for the assistance that they were to provide, and partly as a retainer for being available and "on call" should similar emergencies arise in the future. Some subjects were given $20 for agreeing to help while others were given just $1. In addition to these two experimental groups, there was a control group whose members were *not* called upon to serve as the experimenter's confederates.

Following the experimental session, all subjects were questioned by an independent interviewer, who simply appeared to be concerned with the students' evaluation of their experience as research subjects. Figure 1 presents the relation between (a) the amount of reward that subjects received for serving as the experimenter's confederate and (b) the subjects' ratings of how much they enjoyed their participation in the

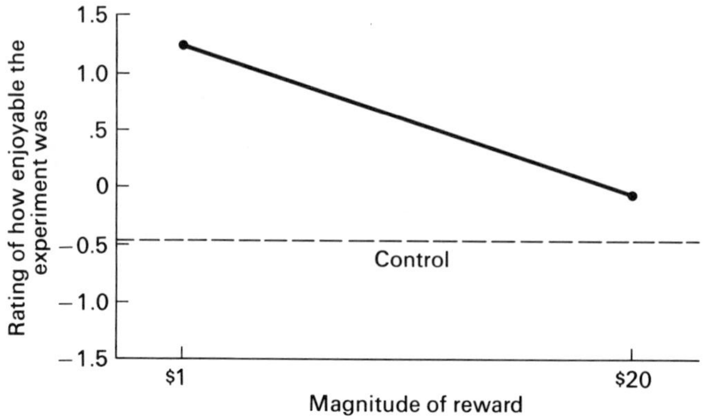

Figure 1

Relationship between magnitude of reward used to elicit compliance and subsequent rating of how enjoyable the experiment was. (Adapted from Festinger, L. The motivating effect of cognitive dissonance. In G. Lindzey (Ed.), *Assessment of human motives.* New York: Holt, Rinehart and Winston, 1958.)

experiment. Note that those who had received a $1 reward for acting as accomplices rated the experience as *more enjoyable* than did those who were given $20; control subjects (who had not engaged in deception) rated the experimental tasks as *less enjoyable* than did subjects in the other two groups.

Festinger and Carlsmith contend that for the subjects in the $20 condition, the relatively large reward provided adequate justification for their deceptive behavior, and hence there was little dissonance and relatively little change in their private opinions regarding the dull experimental tasks. For those in the $1 group, on the other hand, the relatively small reward did *not* justify the deception, and to reduce the resulting dissonance there were marked changes in the subjects' views; as a result, these subjects reappraised the dull experimental tasks and concluded that they were reasonably interesting.

In contrast to the dissonance interpretation of these effects, Bem (1968) has advanced a rather different explanation. Bem contends that the critical variables in the Festinger-Carlsmith experiment are rather similar to those that are involved when we attempt to infer the attitudes of others, based on their public statements. For example, if we hear someone speak in favor of a given brand of beer and we know that he has been paid a large sum for his efforts, we are likely to be cautious before concluding that his statement is a direct expression of his private views. However, we are less likely to question the sincerity of a statement if we believe that the speaker's comments are freely composed, in the absence of external incentives like money.

Starting from these premises, Bem suggests that insufficient-justification effects may derive from the subject's attempts to infer his *own* beliefs, based on his recent public behavior. For example, in the Festinger-Carlsmith experiment, the subjects who were paid $20 for making favorable statements about the boring experimental task probably recognized the fact that their stated opinions were largely determined by monetary incentives, and hence could not validly be taken as an indication of their private views. By contrast, a subject who had been paid only $1 would be less likely to attribute his statement about the "interesting" experiment to the small reward that he had received, and might, as a result, conclude that his stated opinions were perhaps a fairly accurate reflection of his underlying views. Note that this approach attempts to account for the Festinger-Carlsmith results (and others like them) without placing any special emphasis on the motivational forces that are so central to the dissonance theorists' formulation. There may be a beginning convergence of opinion, however, for some investigators (Berkowitz, 1968a, 1968b; Singer, 1968) have recently minimized the "drive-like" aspects of dissonance, suggesting instead that the various mechanisms of dissonance-reduction may simply reflect the respondent's attempts to "make sense" of the world that he experiences. If dissonance theorists accept this de-emphasis of the drive-like character of non-fitting cognitions, Bem's analysis will perhaps be seen as less and less dissonant with the views of the consistency school. On the other hand, there is a fair amount of evidence to support the view that dissonance involves many of the attributes of a heightened drive state (see p. 251), and hence the resolution of this controversy seems far from complete.

Dissonance versus reward

Perhaps the most striking aspect of the Festinger and Carlsmith experiment involving the $1 and $20 incentives was the fact that the results were diametrically opposed to those that might be anticipated from a classical reward theory. There are, indeed, several experiments which show that when students write essays that conflict with their private beliefs, the attitude change that results is sometimes *directly* related to the amount of incentive that is provided (Elms and Janis, 1965; Rosenberg, 1965).

In discussing these apparently contradictory results, Carlsmith, Collins, and Helmreich (1966) suggest that there may be a qualitative difference between (a) making a deceptive public statement to a fellow student who will presumably believe what he is told and (b) writing an essay for an experimenter who knows full well that the views which are expressed do *not* provide an accurate picture of the writer's beliefs. On the one hand, when a misleading statement is publicly addressed to someone who is unaware of the deception, there is probably considerable dissonance between the speaker's private beliefs and his public action. However, the deceptive behavior will appear to be "justified" (that is, there will be little dissonance) if there is a large reward involved, and hence we may find an inverse relationship between attitude change and amount of reward. On the other hand, dissonance may play a minor role when the writer of an essay recognizes that his *reader* (that is, the experimenter) is unlikely to regard his written statement as a valid reflection of personal beliefs. Under these conditions, the classical reward theory may be operative; large incentives may motivate the subjects to construct more effective arguments against their preferred views. As a result, large incentives may lead to more attitude change than would occur with smaller incentives.

This explanation is plausible, but it fails to account for two experiments reported by Scott (1957, 1959). In these studies several pairs of college students participated in classroom "debates" in which each speaker was required to take a public position that contradicted his own opinion. Following each debate, a "vote" was apparently taken, to determine the winner; in fact, however, the results of each debate were randomly determined ahead of time by the experimenter, who simply told one of the speakers that he had won in the class voting. A subsequent assessment of the speakers' views indicated that there was greater opinion change (toward the positions they had espoused) among those who thought they had "won." Scott interprets these results as a reflection of the "environmental support" that was provided by the reward of "winning"; subjects who believed that they had gained public approval after taking a position which contradicted their private views tended to adopt this new and apparently rewarding point of view. Note, however, that in contrast to the Festinger and Carlsmith experiment involving the $1 and $20 payments, Scott's subjects received their rewards *after* engaging in deceptive behavior, while Festinger's subjects received their payment *beforehand.*

From the dissonance point of view, an incentive that is not provided until after the completion of a misleading statement cannot be used to *justify* the deception, for such rewards do not adequately explain the subject's prior willingness to deceive others. In Scott's experiments we may therefore assume that the "winning" and "losing" debaters did *not* differ in dissonance, since they had been given similar reasons (beforehand) for making deceptive speeches. The greater amount of attitude change shown by the "winners," according to this interpretation, may reflect the classical efficacy of reward when other factors (such as degree of dissonance) are held constant. Scott's results may also reflect the information that was conveyed by the "voting audience" regarding *their* preferred views, for the speakers may have viewed the vote as a reflection of the opinions held by other students like themselves and changed their views toward the opinions of this "majority."

Severity of threat

In contrast to the studies cited above, some dissonance experiments have induced subjects to *refrain* from actions that might normally be associated with their private views. For example, children in a play situation have been forbidden to use certain attractive toys (Aronson and Carlsmith, 1963; Turner and Wright, 1965; Freedman, 1965). In these experiments, children who had followed the experimenter's "rules" in order to avoid *mild* punishments, subsequently showed a less favorable evaluation of the forbidden toys than did those who complied in order to avoid *severe* punishment. As before, these results are explained by noting that subjects who have been exposed to *mild* threats do not have adequate justification for their subsequent compliance with the experimenter's rule, and thus they feel dissonance between (a) the original attractiveness of a forbidden toy and (b) the fact that they have (almost "spontaneously") refrained from playing with it. This inconsistency may be resolved, however, if the child changes his mind about the toy in question and evaluates it more negatively. By contrast, if the child has been threatened with *severe* punishment, he has ample justification for having avoided the forbidden toy, despite its attractiveness; thus, his compliance should generate little dissonance and there should be a corresponding lack of motivation to reevaluate his initial (favorable) opinion. In an interesting variation on this line of research, Carlsmith, Abelson, and Aronson (cited in Abelson, 1968) demonstrated that this effect could be intensified if the child's attention was forcibly drawn to the fact that he was not playing with the desired object. In this study, following a mild threat against playing with a given toy, a "janitor" entered the experimental room and casually asked the child why it was that he was not playing with "that toy." This activation procedure apparently stimulated an increase in dissonance-relevant thinking and resulted in a more marked devaluation of the toy than was obtained in a control (no activation) condition.

Compliance, communicator prestige, and attitude change

Persuasive messages from prestigious sources are usually more successful in producing opinion change than are those that emanate from sources low in prestige (Hovland and Weiss, 1952; Kelman and Hovland, 1953; Aronson, Turner, and Carlsmith, 1963). Nevertheless, there is some evidence to suggest that if a low-prestige source can somehow induce behavior that conflicts with the individual's personal preferences, the respondent may have a greater tendency to "adjust" his private opinions than he would if the behavioral compliance had been secured by a source of high prestige. This curious effect is presumably due to the fact that a low-prestige source cannot provide adequate "justification" for actions that conflict with one's private beliefs; the dissonance resulting from discrepant acts may be reduced, however, if the subject revises his previously held opinions. Smith (1961), for example, found that when enlisted men were persuaded to eat grasshoppers by a leader that they *disliked,* they subsequently showed less aversion to grasshoppers than did men who had performed the discrepant act at the suggestion of a more popular leader. Similarly, Powell (1965) found that following a session in which subjects had signed up to participate in a Red Cross Blood Bank campaign, attitudes toward the Red Cross were most positive when the compliance had been induced by a communicator of *low* rather than *high* credibility.

Difficulties in goal attainment: Initiation and effort

Dissonance theory has inspired several studies concerning the impact of various initiation-like procedures on the individual's evaluation of a subsequently attained goal. The main prediction in these studies has been that if a chosen course of action requires the individual to *suffer* a certain amount before reaching his goal, the goal will thereby appear more attractive than it would in the absence of suffering. It is presumably dissonant to endure pain in order to achieve a worthless incentive; hence, given the irrevocable knowledge that one *has* suffered, dissonance may most readily be reduced by enhancing the attractiveness of the goal. The reasoning here perhaps provides us with a psychological basis for the folk-saying "the sweetest fruit grows on the highest bough."

The first experimental test of this proposition was conducted by Aronson and Mills (1959). In this study, college girls were recruited to participate in group discussions concerning the psychology of sex. The researchers were presumably interested in studying the dynamics of discussion as revealed in these sessions. Before entering into the groups, however, the girls were first interviewed individually, ostensibly to make certain that they all felt capable of discussing sex without inhibition or embarrassment. For those assigned to the control condition, the subject's personal assurance in this matter was accepted as sufficient proof that she met the experimenters' requirements. The girls assigned to the two experimental conditions, however, were required to *demonstrate* their capability by passing an "Embarrassment Test." The test for one experimental group constituted a *severe* initiation, and the girls were required to read aloud to the male experimenter from some erotic prose passages, as well as from a list of obscene words. The second experimental group was presented with a *milder* initiation, as their task was to read aloud from a series of sex-related words which were not obscene. After these "tests" all subjects were informed that the first group meeting had already started, but that since the other participants had previously prepared themselves for the discussion by reading from a book on the sexual behavior of animals, it would be best if they simply "listened in" so as to become more familiar with the operation of the group. Unknown to the subjects, the exceptionally dull discussion which they all then heard was a *tape recording* dealing with the sexual behavior of lower animals. After the recorded session the girls were asked for their opinions of the discussion and of the other participants. The results supported the dissonance point of view in that the girls who had been assigned to the *severe* initiation rated both the discussion and the other participants in more favorable terms than did those assigned to the other experimental conditions.

As is often the case with provocative experimental data, this study on initiation has been subjected to extensive reinterpretation. For example, it can be argued that if the severe initiation was sexually stimulating, the subsequent discussion of sex—despite its banality—may have seemed more interesting than it did to the girls in the other experimental groups; or perhaps this hypothesized arousal led the girls who had read the obscene passages to "interpret" the recorded session as dealing (indirectly) with more provocative matters than it actually did. Note that both these explanations are based on the assumption that the substantive similarity between the initiation and the later discussion (both of which dealt with sex) may have been a critical factor in producing the obtained results. To assess the validity of this assumption, Gerard and Mathewson (1967) repeated the original experiment, using a rather different initiation technique; subjects in their study were forced to accept several *severe* (versus *mild*) electric shocks before listening to the recorded discussion. Again, however, the results conformed to the dissonance interpretation, for the subjects who experienced the severe initiation rated the discussion more favorably than did those assigned to the mild initiation. The replication of this result, despite the qualitative change in the initiation procedure, strengthens our belief in the generality of these findings.

In a sense, the effort involved in reaching a goal may be regarded as functionally similar to an initiation, in that both represent obstacles that must be overcome in order to reach a goal. Moreover, just as it is dissonant to endure a severe initiation in order to achieve a goal of dubious value, it is also dissonant to expend a great deal of effort to attain an objectionable goal. Pursuing this line of thought, Zimbardo (1965) performed an experiment in which subjects improvised arguments for a position that contradicted their own preferred views. Subjects in a high-effort group produced their arguments under special acoustic conditions, in which a tape recorder was adapted to provide a .3-second delay between the production of speech and its "return" to the speaker through a set of earphones. Delayed feedback of this type requires a considerable expenditure of effort, for it drastically interferes with normal speech fluency. Zimbardo reasoned that a subject who had expended a good deal of effort in an attempt to produce an argument that contradicted his private views would probably experience more dissonance than would a subject who was not exposed to the delayed feedback (and hence had expended less effort). This dissonance could be reduced, however, through a change of attitude; after all, there is nothing dissonant about expending effort in support of one's personal convictions. Zimbardo's results supported this dissonance analysis, in that subjects in the high-effort group showed more attitude change (toward the position they had espoused in the tape recording) than did those in the low-effort condition.

Selective exposure

In his original exposition of dissonance theory (1957), Festinger hypothesized that people were normally motivated to avoid information that conflicted with their beliefs, since the exposure to such material might generate dissonance. In support of this prediction is the well-known fact that political audiences generally tend to agree with the views to which they expose themselves; for example, Democrats account for the majority of listeners to a Democratic campaign speech. However, such evidence is ambiguous for the dissonance hypothesis, for it may simply reflect the fact that those social influences (such as family, friends, and social position) that have led to Democratic affiliation may also operate to determine one's exposure to political propaganda. Because of this ambiguity, recent attempts to evaluate the selective-exposure hypothesis have been conducted in an experimental context.

In the typical experiment on selective exposure, people are asked to indicate their stand on some issue, and are then given an opportunity to choose between various persuasive messages that are labeled to indicate whether they *support* or *contradict* the subject's chosen position. This experimental design has been used in the study of such topics as attitudes toward television teaching (Mills and Ross, 1964), preferred verdicts in a mock jury trial (Sears, 1965; Sears and Freedman, 1965), and opinions regarding the relative importance of heredity versus environment in child development (Adams, 1961). In general, the results of such experiments have failed to provide clear-cut support for the dissonance point of view.

In discussing this literature, Zajonc (1967) suggests that many of the studies are weak because the subjects are presented with what seem to be trivial issues; thus, when indicating their opinions, subjects may not feel any significant degree of commitment. Consequently, given an unimportant, unfamiliar issue, there may be relatively little dissonance produced even if the subject *does* expose himself to a message that contradicts his preferred stand. On the other hand, studies dealing with the more important issue of smoking and lung cancer have also failed to support the selective-exposure hypothesis (Feather, 1962, 1963; Brock, 1965), for smokers and non-smokers exhibit similar reading preferences in choosing among articles dealing with the dangers (versus harmlessness) of smoking. It is possible, of course, that the negative evidence in the smoking studies is due to the presence of other mechanisms for dissonance reduction—mechanisms *previously* developed to cope with the vast quantity of information on smoking and cancer to which most people have unavoidably been exposed. Nevertheless, the net result of this research has thus far failed to demonstrate the original proposition concerning selective exposure; nor has it convincingly identified some more restricted set of conditions where selective exposure *does* prevail.

Dissonance as a drive state

Most investigators in the dissonance tradition have focused mainly on dissonance *reduction* and have shown little interest in the physiological arousal and other signs of stress that should presumably accompany dissonance if it is a drive state. However, in one study addressed to this issue, Brehm et al. (1964) found clear evidence of arousal when experimental subjects found themselves in a situation where their publicly announced perceptual judgments were in striking opposition to the judgments of other group members. In a situation like this, we may assume that the individual experiences dissonance when his perceptions appear to be at variance with the perceptions of others. Brehm and her associates found that the elicitation of dissonance through this technique was accompanied by an increase in the plasma-free fatty acid level of the blood, a condition which is normally regarded as an index of central nervous system arousal.

Similar results, relating dissonance to physiological arousal, have been reported by Gerard (1968). In this experiment the subjects were shown slides of famous paintings, two at a time, and were to indicate which member of each pair they wanted as a gift. Throughout the experimental session a measure of blood flow through the capillaries of the fingertip was continuously recorded; previous research had shown that this technique provides a reliable means for assessing stress. In accordance with dissonance theory, the results showed that among the subjects who had to choose between paintings of roughly equal value, there was clear evidence of stress *after* the choice had been made—presumably because of the postdecisional inconsistencies that were involved (see above). Gerard's data also provided evidence of predecisional stress; that is, before making their preferences known, the subjects who were to choose between paintings of similar value showed more evidence of arousal than did those who were faced with a simpler choice.

Apart from its physiological manifestations, if dissonance is indeed a drive similar to hunger, or thirst, or anxiety, it should produce a variety of *nonspecific* effects which need not involve dissonance reduction. The theories of Hull and Spence, for example, suggest that drives have *general* energizing properties, and there is a considerable body of research showing that increments in drive level will frequently strengthen *whatever* responses are dominant in the individual's habit family. For example, in a paired-associate learning situation where, *from the start,* the correct response is strongly associated with the stimulus to which it has been assigned (as in the response "vacant" to the stimulus word "empty"), anxiety may facilitate performance. By contrast, the energizing effects of high drive typically impede performance in problems that require the individual to replace his initially dominant response tendency with a response that was initially somewhat weaker in strength (as in learning a word-pair like "empty-nomad").

Starting with this theoretical framework, Waterman (1969) designed an experiment to assess the impact of cognitive dissonance on performance in two distinct learning tasks. At the start of the session, subjects were asked to write essays that were either consonant or dissonant with their views regarding proper dress for students in introductory psychology classes. After the subjects had committed themselves to writing the essays, or had actually completed their writing, they were assigned to either a *simple* paired-associate list (where the correct responses were clearly dominant from the start) or a *complex* list (where there was initially a great deal of competition between responses). In the *simple* task, subjects assigned to the dissonant condition made fewer errors than those in the consonant group. On the other hand, in the *complex* task, the dissonant subjects showed poorer performance. These results parallel other findings (Cottrell and Wack, 1967; Waterman and Katkin, 1967) which suggest that dissonance (like other drives) may function as a nonspecific energizer that strengthens dominant responses, whether or not they are correct.

Concluding comments

While the theory of cognitive dissonance has generated considerable interest and enthusiasm, the ingenuity and daring of the experimenters have often exceeded their dedication to rigorous theory-building and experimentation. Derivations from the theory have thus seemed to require an excessive degree of "intuitive feel" in many instances; moreover, many of the experiments have involved extensive theatrics and role-playing, leading to potential difficulties in replication, since the apparent sincerity and credibility of the experimenter's accomplice doubtless plays a major role in the results which are obtained. Another difficulty which has often been noted is the problem of specifying which *one*, of the many *potential* methods of dissonance reduction, will actually be employed in a given situation? While this problem has been discussed by several investigators, there is not, at present, a satisfactory convergence of evidence and opinion to resolve the question.

In closing this section on cognitive dissonance, we should note that this research tradition stands in interesting contrast to a body of literature that emphasizes the importance of curiosity or "information-seeking" in animals and men (Fowler, 1966). The dissonance theorists seem to suggest that men are normally uncomfortable in the presence of the unexpected and unpredictable. Those who emphasize information-seeking, on the other hand, have repeatedly demonstrated that people (and subhuman species, too) will often seek out that which is new and informative (Jones, 1966), as opposed to the boring, the familiar, and the redundant. In considering these contrasting positions, it is interesting to note that the dissonance theorists have thus far been *least* successful in demonstrating their thesis in studies that focus on the individual's hypothesized need to *avoid* information that might challenge his opinions and beliefs. It will be interesting, in the years to come, to see how these two schools of thought become accommodated to one another.

Summary

1. Consistency theorists believe that we automatically seek to avoid illogical or "non-fitting" patterns of thought.

2. Heider's balance theory emphasizes the systematic patterning of our likes and dislikes. The balance formulation has led to a number of studies concerned with the individual's reaction to balanced versus unbalanced social situations. The available data suggest that people typically *prefer* balanced structures and feel that they are more *common* than unbalanced structures. Despite these results, however, some investigators have suggested that balance theory may be primarily applicable in situations where the participants *like* one another, as contrasted with situations in which they *dislike* each other.

3. The theory of cognitive dissonance is based on the hypothesis that the simultaneous belief in two or more "non-fitting" elements normally results in a noxious

drive state that motivates behavioral or cognitive changes designed to *reduce* dissonance. Dissonance theory has stimulated research on such topics as: post-decision changes in evaluation, counter-attitudinal behavior, and selective exposure to persuasive messages.

4. The dissonance approach stands in interesting contrast to various theories that emphasize the importance of curiosity and "information-seeking" in animals and men. While dissonance theorists suggest that men are normally uncomfortable in the presence of the unexpected, curiosity theorists have frequently demonstrated that people often seek out the new, as opposed to the familiar. The accommodation of these contrasting views remains a task for the future.

Supplementary reading

Abelson, R. P., et al. (Eds.) *Theories of cognitive consistency: A sourcebook*. Chicago: Rand McNally, 1968.

Zajonc, R. B. Cognitive theories of social behavior. In G. Lindzey & E. Aronson (Eds.), *Handbook of social psychology*, Vol. I (2nd ed.) Reading, Mass.: Addison-Wesley, 1968.

12 Social judgment

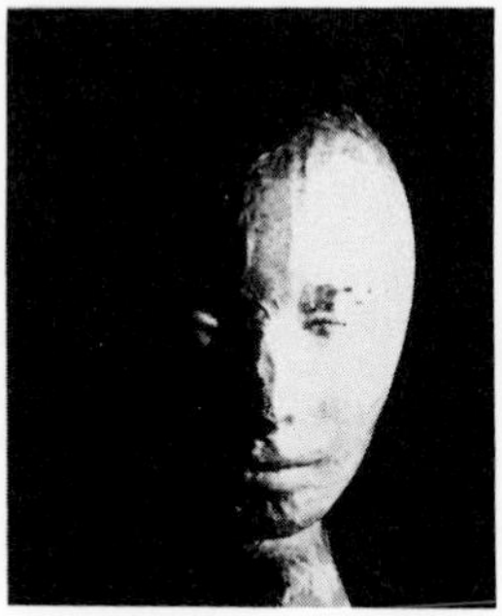

Social interaction requires a continuous interpretation of the events around us. We may, for example, attempt to evaluate the position advocated by a political speaker (How liberal *is* his position on civil rights?), or we may simply be concerned with "sizing up" the personal characteristics of a new acquaintance. A simplified way to look at such situations is to conceive of the person who is to be evaluated as occupying a position on one or more socially meaningful dimensions. For example, a political speaker may favor a certain degree of domestic liberalism (versus conservatism); and at the same time, he may espouse the cause of nationalism (versus internationalism) in his comments. There are a great variety of situations in which we are called upon to assess others; this chapter will review some of the cognitive factors that contribute to these assessments.

Context and judgment

One of the most replicable findings in psychology is the fact that our evaluation of virtually any event is partly determined by context in which the event appears. The effect of context usually takes the form of an apparent *contrast* between the overall context and the particular stimulus or event that is being judged. In one study, for example, Campbell, Hunt, and Lewis (1958) asked two groups of judges to rate the degree of disorganization and eccentricity of thought that was revealed in several vocabulary definitions. One group was presented with a predominance of "high-pathology" definitions (e.g., *fable* = the right thing when somebody else is equally right), while the other group evaluated "low-pathology" definitions. In addition to these extreme items, which served to establish distinctive judgmental contexts, both groups were asked to rate several "midscale" definitions. The results revealed clear-cut evidence of a *contrast effect*, for the subjects in the high-pathology group rated the "midscale" stimuli as implying *less* disorganization and eccentricity of thought than did those assigned to the low-pathology condition. Effects of this sort have been obtained in a great variety of studies (Helson, 1964), some dealing with linguistic stimuli (as above), and others focusing on such psychophysical continua as judgments of weight (Heintz, 1950) and the length of lines (Krantz and Campbell, 1961). Despite the generality of such contrast effects, however, the basic data that are obtained in these experiments lend themselves to two rather distinct and conflicting interpretations:

1. Some researchers favor a *perceptual* interpretation, based on the assumption that divergent contexts affect the *subjective impression* elicited by subsequent "test" stimuli. This would imply, for example, that in the study by Campbell et al. the judges who had been assigned to the pathological context would spontaneously "see" the midscale definitions as being relatively well organized, in comparison with those assigned to the low-pathology group. (See Figure 1A.)

2. A rather different view, emphasizing changes in the judge's *subjective scale* has been offered as an alternative explanation for the contrast phenomenon (Volkmann, 1951; Upshaw, 1968). According to this interpretation, contrast effects do not affect the judge's immediate subjective experience, but instead, influence the "language" that he uses to describe this experience. Contrast effects may thus reflect a *semantic*, rather than a *perceptual* phenomenon. Consider a judge who is instructed to rate the disorganization and eccentricity of various definitions that range from *extreme disorganization* to *average organization* (a point near the middle of the total continuum). Assume that our judge is to use a 9-category scale with "totally disorganized" and "well organized" as end-points. Note that the definitions that are to be evaluated cover a narrower range of experience than the available response categories; the semantic interpretation of the contrast phenomenon asserts that under these conditions the respondent will often reinterpret the term "well organized," to make the bounds of his subjective scale more congruent with the definitions that he *is* shown. (See Figure 1B.) Such a shift in the end-category of a subjective scale would, of course, result in a repositioning of *all* the category boundaries, since the instructions in these experiments normally require the judge to divide the total subjective continuum into categories of *equal breadth*.

Figure 1 depicts these alternative explanations for context-induced contrast effects. It is important to note that both accounts are completely consistent with the experimental observation that midscale stimuli usually elicit judgments that *contrast* with the bulk of the judge's prior experience.

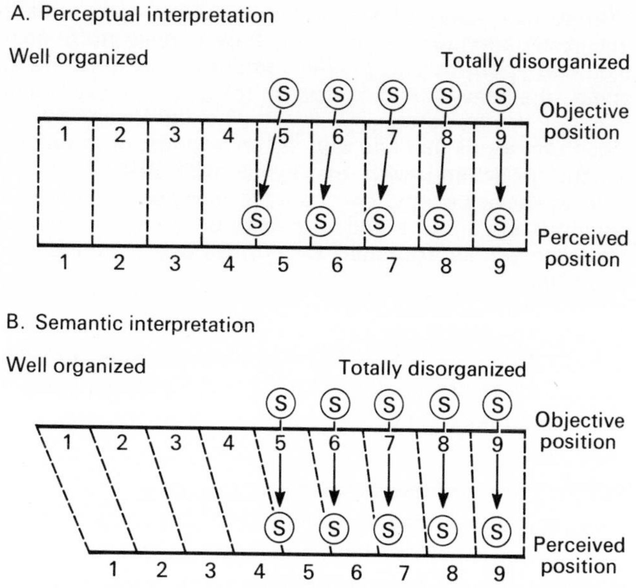

Figure 1

Two conflicting interpretations for the phenomenon of context-induced contrast effects. (The top part of the drawing is based on an assumed *perceptual* effect, while the bottom depicts a *semantic* effect—see text.) (Adapted from Manis, M. Context effects in communication. *Journal of Personality and Social Psychology*, 1967, **5**, p. 326.)

In discussing these divergent interpretations, Campbell, Lewis, and Hunt (1958) suggest that semantic shifts (as diagrammed in Figure 1B) may be particularly likely when the judge has been instructed to use a response scale created especially for the experiment. For example, our judge may have been instructed to construct a series of rating categories (in his head), to represent various degrees of thought disorganization; it is obvious, however, that these categories are both *novel* and *arbitrary*, for they do not represent conceptual divisions that are recognized in normal usage. The novelty of the response language implies that the judge must *learn* the significance of the various categories as he becomes familiar with the stimuli with which he is presented (how pathological must a definition be in order to qualify for a rating of 7?). Clearly, the results of this learning process might plausibly be affected by changes in the range of stimuli presented for judgment. The relativity of the typical response language produces similar problems. In the words of Campbell et al. (1958, pp. 220–221):

"Terms like *heavy* and *light* are in their proper semantic usage situationally relative, i.e., they convey no absolute meaning apart from a specific comparative setting. We can speak of a heavy truck, a heavy suitcase, or a heavy fishline. In such usage, terms like heavy and light contrast with 'absolute' terms like *one ounce, ten pounds,* or *three kilos,* which, in dealing with the same attributes of physical objects, have become extricated from specific immediate comparisons and are understood to be invariant attributes of the object, appropriately descriptive of it no matter what its setting."

In brief, given a brief and somewhat vague characterization for the various rating categories, there is little to prevent the judge from privately adjusting his understanding of the rating categories to "fit" the range of stimuli with which he is presented.

Upshaw (1962) has discussed this problem as it applies in studies of *attitude judgment*, where the judge's task may be to indicate the degree of favorability (toward the American Negro, for example) that is implied by various statements of opinion. He suggests that while rating responses may often be affected by truncations in the range of statements that are to be evaluated, the contrast effects that are thus generated may result from *semantic redefinitions* of the available response categories. Upshaw hypothesizes, however, that these semantic scale adjustments will *not* occur—despite the presentation of an "unbalanced" array of opinion statements—if the judge's *own opinion* is located outside the range of opinions that he is to evaluate. Under these conditions, he reasons, the meaning of the various response categories should be relatively unaffected, since the location of one end-category (*very favorable,* for example) might be fixed by the judge's own attitude toward Negroes, while the other end-category (*very unfavorable*) would be defined by the most extreme statement on the opposite side of the continuum. Figure 2A depicts the situation that faces an *out-of-range* judge, whose subjective scale is presumed to remain stable, despite the biased array of statements that he is to evaluate. Figure 2B, on the other hand, depicts a situation in which the judge's views are *within* the range of opinions that are presented for his evaluation. Upshaw's hypothesis suggests that the in-range judge may inadvertently adjust his subjective scale to make the endpoints congruent with the range of opinion statements with which he has been presented.

To assess this hypothesis, Upshaw conducted an experiment in which judges of varying opinion rated the favorability of several statements dealing with the social

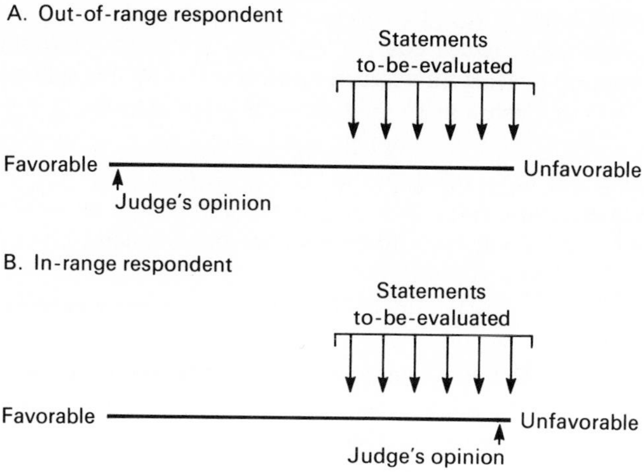

Figure 2

A graphic representation of the distinction between out-of-range and in-range judges. (Adapted from Upshaw, H. S. Own attitude as an anchor in equal-appearing intervals. *Journal of Abnormal and Social Psychology*, 1962, **64,** 85–96.)

position of the Negro. Some judges received a full range of statements, extending across the entire attitude continuum. Others were presented with truncated sets of opinion items. For some groups all *pro*-Negro statements were omitted, while others excluded all statements on the *anti*-Negro side of the scale. In accordance with Upshaw's hypothesis, the results indicated that the "out-of-range" judges were relatively unaffected when responding to truncated sets of opinions. For example, pro-Negro judges who were asked to rate statements that excluded all pro-Negro statements (as in Figure 2A), responded in the same manner as did pro-Negro judges who rated the *full range* of statements. On the other hand, restricting the range of opinions which were to be rated produced marked contrast effects among "in-range" judges. Thus, the omission of pro-Negro statements resulted in clear-cut contrast effects among those who opposed the Negro's right to social equality. (See Figure 2B.)

While Upshaw's results suggest that context-induced shifts in judgment partly result from semantic shifts in the judge's subjective scale, there are other experiments that clearly reveal the operation of *perceptual* factors. Campbell and his associates conducted two studies in which the judgmental shifts produced by truncations of the stimulus array were compared in two situations: (a) when the stimuli were rated in terms of response alternatives that were clearly anchored, and thus relatively resistant to semantic redefinition, and (b) when the response alternatives were less well defined. In one study (Campbell, Hunt, and Lewis, 1957), judges rated the amount of disorganization manifested in a series of vocabulary definitions. For some judges each of the nine points on the response scale was defined rather explicitly (for example, category 3 was to be used for definitions showing "very slight traces of disorganization and eccentricity"); other judges rated the same definitions, but used a response scale in which only the end-categories were explicitly defined.

In another study (Krantz and Campbell, 1961) the judge's task was to judge the length of various straight lines which were presented one at a time on a screen. Some judges used a familiar, absolute, and presumably stable response language, making their judgments in *inches;* other judges used an artificial, relativistic language, in which the response 100 was to represent lines of "average" length, 95 was reserved for "less than average" lines, and so on. In both of these experiments, biases in the stimulus array produced marked contrast effects when the response alternatives were unfamiliar and loosely defined. By comparison, contrast effects were reduced, *but not eliminated*, when the judges used a more firmly anchored set of responses. The presence of reliable contrast effects among judges who were provided with relatively unambiguous response alternatives argues against the claim that these effects are *solely* attributable to semantic relabeling.

Context effects in communication

Manis argued (1967) that results of this type have direct implications for the communication process. The receiver of a message is commonly faced with the task of inferring the referent that the communicator had "in mind" when he constructed his message; thus, as in the studies discussed above, each incoming stimulus (message) must be placed into one of several categories, each category representing a different referent. Manis reasoned that if extreme contexts lead to perceptual contrast, by biasing the receiver's prior experience, it should be possible to affect his choice from a set of *potential* referents, even if the various alternatives were reasonably familiar, unambiguous, and palpably present.

To test this hypothesis, three groups of receivers were presented with a series of 72 written messages, each message describing an actor's portrayal of some emotional state. All three groups were also given the eleven photographs that had been used to elicit the various descriptions. The subjects were simply instructed to indicate the picture (referent) that was being described in each passage. One group of respondents was presented with descriptions of emotional states that were predominantly pleasant; a second group was given mainly unpleasant descriptions; and a third group responded to an unbiased mixture of both pleasant and unpleasant descriptions. To assess the judgmental effects induced by these varied sets of descriptions, respondents in all three groups were also presented with 12 *test* descriptions that were essentially neutral with respect to pleasantness-unpleasantness.

Figure 3 shows, for successive pairs of test messages, the average pleasantness value for the photos that were chosen as matching the test descriptions. Note that the receivers assigned to the pleasant context selected less pleasant referents than did those assigned to the unpleasant context, while respondents in the unbiased group generally fell between these extremes. As in the studies by Campbell and his colleagues, the presence of such clear-cut contrast effects in a task involving relatively well-defined response alternatives suggests a *perceptual* basis for the obtained results. These data also suggest that, in everyday communication, the receiver's understanding of a message (that is, the referent which he assumes to have guided the communicator's output), may be significantly affected by the range of messages to which he has previously been exposed.

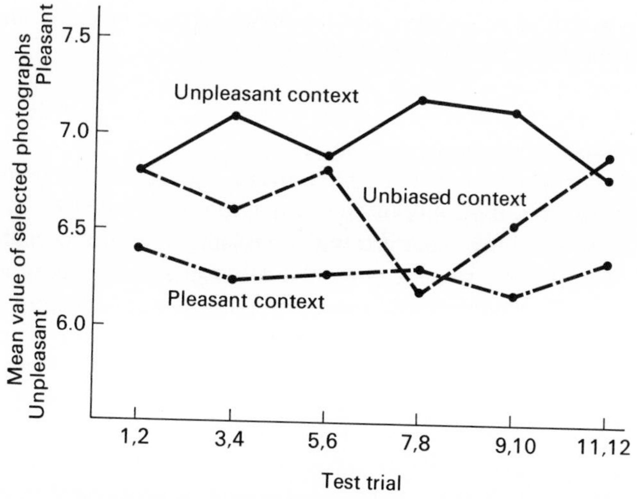

Figure 3

The effects of extreme contexts on the subject's response in the matching task. (Adapted from Manis, M. Context effects in communication. *Journal of Personality and Social Psychology*, 1967, **5,** p. 330.)

In a subsequent experiment (Manis and Armstrong, in press), contrast effects were produced in a situation where the subjects were simply required to describe a series of posed emotional expressions, using their own everyday language. All subjects described a common series of test photographs that were essentially neutral with respect to pleasantness-unpleasantness; all the test photographs appeared on a single sheet of paper, together with photographs of several *other* posed emotions. For some subjects, these accompanying (context) photographs depicted emotions that were predominantly pleasant, while for others the context photographs were predominantly unpleasant; a third group was presented with a balanced array of background poses. The descriptions that were produced in these varying contexts were then rated for *pleasantness* by an independent group of readers. The results were quite clear-cut in showing the anticipated contrast effects. That is, when embedded in an array of pleasant expressions, the neutral faces were described as being *less pleasant* than they were when presented within a group of unpleasant expressions; the neutral context yielded results which were intermediate in comparison with these extreme groups. This result seems particularly important as an example of contextually induced contrast effects since the respondents were given an opportunity to use a perfectly familiar response language (the language of normal speech), thus demonstrating again that contrast effects are not *solely* the consequence of the artificial (and perhaps semantically unstable) response medium that is more typical in studies of social judgment.

In a similar vein, Manis (1971) conducted a third study which yielded further evidence that the contrast phenomenon may play a significant role in communication. In this experiment, the subjects alternated between two tasks, one requiring them to read a series of written descriptions, the other requiring them to write their own descriptions. There were two main groups of subjects; one group read descriptions of *pleasant* emotional expressions, while the other group read descriptions of *unpleasant* emotions. In addition to this reading task, all subjects were intermittently asked to describe several photographs of an actor, depicting a variety of emotional expressions. These written descriptions were then rated for pleasantness. The results indicated that the subjects' descriptions were significantly affected by their reading experiences. As in the studies outlined above, a contrast effect was obtained, for the writers' descriptions were "displaced away" from the pool of descriptions that they had read. People who read about unpleasant emotions wrote descriptions that were judged to be relatively pleasant, as compared with those produced in the "pleasant" reading condition. This experiment is perhaps unique in demonstrating displacement effects in this kind of setting (that is, where the biased stimulus array providing the context consisted of verbal descriptions, and the test stimuli consisted of photographs).

Attitude and social judgment

Everyday speech abounds with statements of opinion. People are continually conversing about their views on a variety of topics, ranging from foreign policy to the current state of popular music. Some of these statements are intended to convince others of the validity of our views. In this way, the speaker may gain consensual validation for his beliefs; he may become more confident that his views are warranted if he can successfully convince others of their merit. Other statements of opinion may simply result from everyday inquiries: "What did you think of today's lecture?"

Consider a speaker who is bored by Dixieland jazz. When he tries to explain his position ("I find it difficult to get excited about Dixieland . . . It seems sort of out-of-date"), he is essentially providing the listener with information concerning his preferred location on an evaluative (favorable-unfavorable) continuum. The listener, on the other hand, must interpret the speaker's statement to determine just how favorable or unfavorable an attitude it reflects. Take the above statement about Dixieland, for example; if a rating of "1" represents an extremely *favorable* attitude and "7" represents an extremely *unfavorable* attitude, what numerical rating should we assign to the speaker in our example? Should we give him a 5 or a 6 or what?

If our language was completely unambiguous, such statements should enable us unhesitatingly to infer just how unfavorable are the speaker's underlying views. Moreover, in an ideal language, a given statement of opinion would be given the same interpretation by all listeners. As we shall see, however, although our language usually enables the listener to reach a general understanding of the speaker's views (pro or con), the listener's own attitudes often affect his interpretation of what has been said.

Let us therefore consider the influence of the listener's views on the interpretations that he places upon statements of opinion. Several studies have been completed on this question; one of the most famous (Hovland, Harvey, and Sherif, 1957) was conducted in Oklahoma during a campaign to repeal the prohibition laws in that state. The investigators first selected several groups of people who held quite divergent views concerning the dangers of alcohol. Some of these people opposed the use of all alcoholic beverages and were active members of the WCTU; others were active in the campaign to loosen the prohibition regulations; and still others were essentially neutral. People from these various groups were all presented with a persuasive message that took a mildly anti-prohibition stand, and they were asked to indicate the writer's preferred position along a pro-prohibition to anti-prohibition scale. The results indicated that there were systematic differences between the various groups

Social judgment

with respect to their understanding of the writer's views. People whose own beliefs were relatively similar to the views presented in the message generally minimized what little difference there was; that is, they interpreted the message as being even closer to their own beliefs than was actually the case. This type of distortion, in which the meaning of a message is displaced *toward* the receiver's preferred position, has been termed the *assimilation effect*. Not all subjects showed assimilation, however. Those whose views clearly conflicted with the contents of a message typically exaggerated the existing discrepancy by interpreting the message as being even more opposed to their own views than in fact it was. This type of distortion, in which the speaker's intended meaning is displaced *away* from the recipient's preferred views, has been termed the *contrast effect.*[1]

How might we explain the phenomena of assimilation and contrast? What are the underlying mechanisms? Unfortunately, there is no clear agreement on this question. Sherif and Hovland (1961) contend that the principles operating here are the same as those that determine judgmental responses in psychophysical experiments. In support of their proposition, they cite a study of weight-judgments in which, on every trial, subjects lifted an "anchoring stimulus" before being presented with each of the stimuli to be judged (Sherif, Taub, and Hovland, 1958). In different experimental conditions, this anchor was located at varying distances from the remaining stimuli, and the subjects were instructed that it represented the sixth category ("6") on a response scale ranging from 1 to 6. The results are shown in Figure 4. Note that when the anchor was located relatively close to the other stimuli, the judges' responses were displaced *toward* the anchor (assimilation). When the anchor was relatively distant from the other stimuli, the judgments were displaced in the opposite direction, the classic contrast effect.

How can these weightlifting results explain the assimilation and contrast effects that appear in studies of attitude judgment where there is *no* formal anchoring stimulus involved? Sherif and Hovland suggest that in these cases the judge's preferred position on the attitude continuum acts as an *implicit anchor*, producing assimilation effects when the statement to be judged approximates his own views, and contrast effects when the disparity becomes too great. How great must the disparity be in order to produce contrast effects? Sherif and Hovland suggest that the judge's *latitude of acceptance* is of critical importance here. That is, each judge presumably

[1] Note that when used in this sense, the term *contrast* has a somewhat different meaning than it does in studies of contextual phenomena. While the present usage focuses on the recipient's own opinion as a point of reference in analyzing his distortions, our previous discussion utilized the individual's prior *experience* (rather than his present *opinions*) as a reference point.

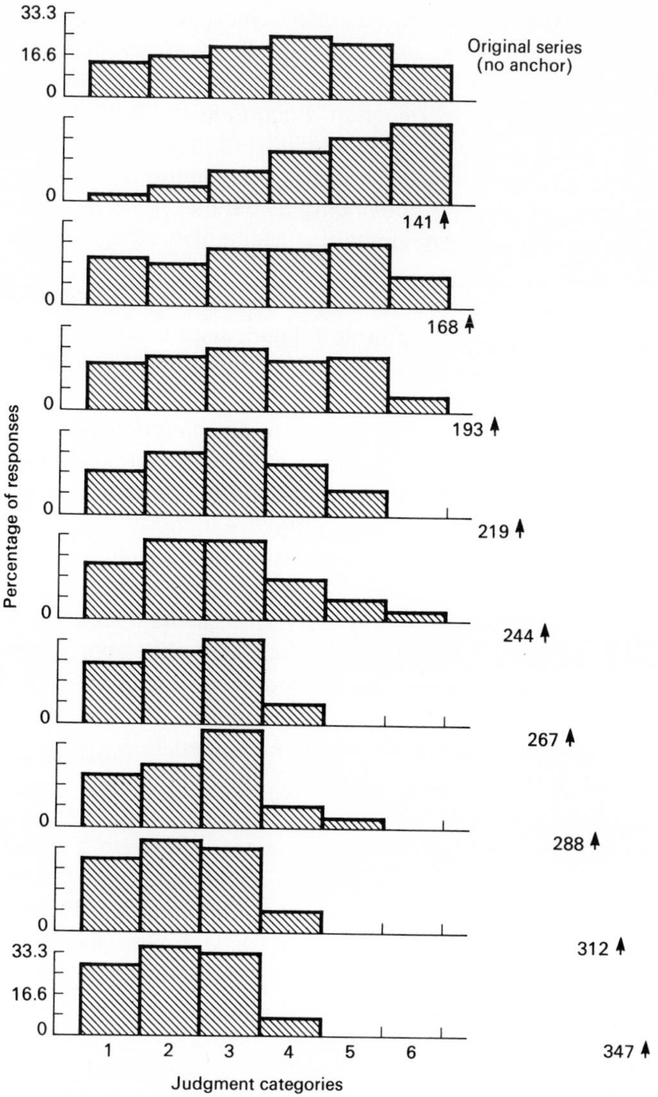

Figure 4

Distribution of judgments for weights without anchor (top) and with anchor at increasing distances above original series (bottom). Position of anchor indicated by arrows. (Adapted from Sherif, M., Taub, D., and Hovland, C. I. Assimilation and contrast effects of anchoring stimuli on judgments. *Journal of Experimental Psychology*, 1958, **55,** 150–155.)

finds a variety of opinions that are at least *acceptable* in the degree to which they approximate his preferred stand, and the latitude of acceptance represents the boundary that separates these acceptable viewpoints from those that elicit a reaction of indifference or outright *rejection*. According to the theory, opinions that fall within the latitude of acceptance are *assimilated*, and those outside this range tend to be displaced still farther away (*contrast*). Despite the clarity of this theoretical stance, there is, unfortunately, no convincing evidence for the assumption that the latitude of acceptance affects judgmental displacements in this manner.

In an alternative approach to the phenomena of assimilation and contrast, Manis has suggested (1961, 1961a) that attitude-related distortions may result from the judge's attempts to reduce the impact of incoming messages on his own beliefs. This approach is closely related to the theory of cognitive dissonance (see p. 239), for it assumes that a certain amount of subjective discomfort will be produced when the receiver of a message is presented with a statement that conflicts with his own views; thus, he may feel some pressure to change his opinions when they are attacked. Moreover, if we consider messages that are increasingly divergent with the judge's preferred stand, he should feel increasing pressure to change. Eventually, when the discrepancy between his own views and those embodied in the message becomes sufficiently large, the judge may feel *less* pressure to change. The available research suggests that this is most likely to occur when the source of the message is unknown to the recipient; under these conditions, if a statement of opinion is clearly at variance with the recipient's views, the unidentified speaker can be readily dismissed as a "crackpot" or some otherwise misguided individual whose divergent beliefs may be comfortably ignored.

What does all this have to do with message distortion? Figure 5 shows how these assumptions enable us to explain assimilation and contrast effects. In this graph, the horizontal axis represents various degrees of discrepancy between the views of the receiver and those of the speaker. The vertical axis shows the amount of pressure to change that the recipient would normally feel upon receiving persuasive messages that differ from his own views by these varying amounts. Assume, for example, that for the issue under consideration, the recipient favors an extremely "pro" position at the extreme left of the horizontal axis. The graph suggests that pressure to change will first rise and then fall, as the recipient receives incoming messages that diverge more and more from his preferred stand. Since an incoming message is almost always ambiguous (to a greater or lesser degree), the receiver must choose from a range of "possible" interpretations. Moreover, since he is generally motivated to maintain his existing views with little or no change, it is reasonable to predict that

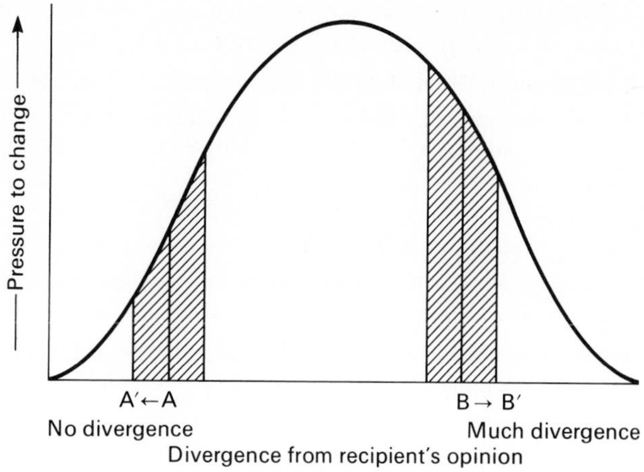

Figure 5

Pressure to change as affected by divergence of opinion between speaker and recipient. This diagram assumes that speaker's identity is unknown to recipient. Displacement effects from *A* to *A′* (assimilation) and from *B* to *B′* (contrast) result from attempt to minimize pressure to change. (Adapted from Manis, M. The interpretation of opinion statements as a function of message ambiguity and recipient attitude. *Journal of Abnormal and Social Psychology*, 1961, **63,** p. 80.)

each message will be interpreted in such a manner as to minimize the resulting pressure to change. Consider a message that, given a *proper interpretation*, might be moderately at variance with the listener's views; the "true meaning" of this message might be at position *A* in Figure 5. While a range of possible interpretations might be given to this message, as shown by the gray area of the graph, the model suggests that our hypothetical recipient will probably interpret the message as espousing position *A′*, rather than any of the other plausible alternatives in the gray, since messages at *A′* are associated with minimal pressure to change. Note also that the displacement from *A* to *A′* constitutes an assimilation effect, since it reduces the apparent discrepancy between the receiver's views and those that he attributes to the message source.

Figure 5 also shows how contrast might occur. Consider a message that deviates *markedly* from the receiver's views; assume that its actual location is *B*. As before, we assume that there is some ambiguity concerning the communicator's true position, as indicated by the gray area. Since, according to our model, the recipient should choose the interpretation that minimizes pressure to change, we are led to predict that the message will be interpreted as advocating position B', rather than one of the other "plausible" possibilities, thus resulting in a *contrast* effect. Note further that, as in our example of assimilation, this distorted interpretation helps the recipient to maintain his own views, for it effectively reduces the pressure to change that is associated with the message.

While assimilation and contrast have frequently been reported in studies of this sort, they do not always appear, nor should they, according to the theory proposed above. First, let us recall that in our previous examples we have always assumed that the author of the message is unknown to the receiver. Under this condition messages that the receiver sees as being highly discrepant with his views may be largely discounted, since they may be interpreted as "proof" that the source is not trustworthy. Obviously, however, in many instances the author's identity is well known. How might this affect our results? Consider, for example, a speaker who is well liked and respected by his audience. Under these conditions, regardless of the discrepancy between the message's content and the views of the listener, it is unlikely that the speaker's opinion will be discounted. Indeed, there is considerable evidence to show that under these "high-prestige" conditions, the recipient of a persuasive message may feel more and more pressure to change his views, as the incoming message shows increasing divergence from his preferred stand (Aronson, Turner, and Carlsmith, 1963).

Figure 6 graphically depicts this state of affairs. As in our previous examples, let us now assume that our recipient is presented with messages at positions A and B, remembering that in this case he knows that the communicator is a person worthy of his respect. As before, the messages are assumed to be somewhat ambiguous, thus permitting a variety of interpretations. Note that under these conditions, for both messages A and B, pressure to change can be most effectively minimized by a displacement *toward* the recipient's preferred stand (to A' and B')—in short, assimilation. Thus, regardless of how discrepant the speaker's message may be, the theory suggests that assimilation will effectively reduce the listener's felt need to change his views.

A study by Manis (1961b) reports results in good agreement with this prediction. In this experiment, several groups of college students who varied in their attitudes toward college fraternities were presented with a series of short essays, each of which described the author's views on the fraternity issue. Although the authors were not personally known to the subjects, they were described in rather glowing

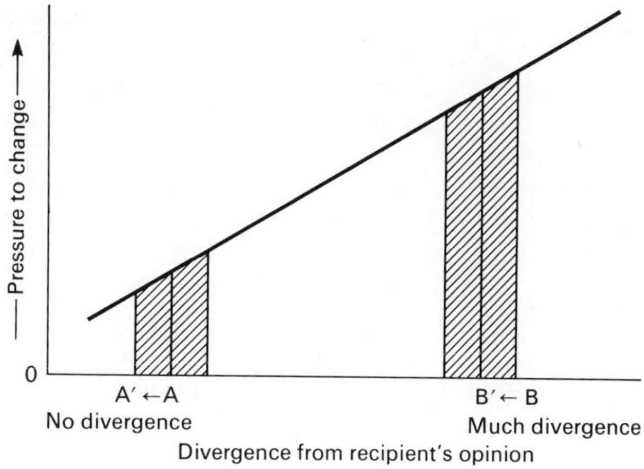

Figure 6

Pressure to change as affected by divergence of opinion between speaker and recipient. This diagram assumes that speaker is trusted and respected by recipient. Displacement effects from *A* to *A′* and from *B* to *B′* (both instances of assimilation) result from attempt to minimize pressure to change.

terms. Some were said to be excellent students, others were described as very popular, and still others were described as being exceptionally stable and personally mature. When the subjects attempted to infer the authors' attitudes toward fraternities after having read their messages, clear-cut assimilation effects were obtained regardless of the discrepancy between the readers' views and those of the authors. That is, there was a consistent tendency for the pro-fraternity subjects to interpret the messages as being more pro-fraternity than did those who opposed fraternities. It is interesting to note that when these same messages were presented as coming from less reliable sources, no consistent relationship was found between the subjects' own views and their interpretations of the messages. One might have expected that this would lead to consistent *contrast effects*, in that many people prefer to believe that their own views are rather different from the views of those they hold in low esteem. However, in a subsequent study of this sort (Berkowitz and Goranson, 1964), contrast effects *were* obtained when persuasive messages were attributed to a disliked source. Taken as a whole, these results testify to the importance of such "nonmessage" variables as the recipient's attitudes and the author's status as determinants of message interpretation. As suggested above, these factors should, in principle, be irrelevant to the communication process. As we have seen, however, human communication often falls short of this ideal.

At this point, the critical reader may raise a question that we have previously considered in our discussion of context effects. The question is this: How should we view these attitude-related judgmental distortions? Should we assume that a given statement of opinion elicits varying subjective interpretations among listeners who hold to different attitudes? Or, on the other hand, might it be that the various attitude groups do not differ in their *interpretations* of such statements, but do vary in the *rating responses* that are evoked by similar private reactions? (See p. 256 for a related discussion in the study of context effects.) Unfortunately, there is no clear answer to this problem, since relatively few of the studies in this area have used unambiguous response measures. What is required is a method for eliciting judgmental responses that permits us to assume (with confidence) that differences in judgmental response are *necessarily* reflective of underlying differences in subjective interpretation.

Perhaps the most sophisticated of the available studies on this issue was conducted by Ager and Dawes (1965). These investigators reasoned that much of the ambiguity that is associated with judgmental studies derives in large part from the widespread use of the rating-scale methodology. They sought, therefore, to investigate attitudinal effects on social judgment by means of a paired-comparison technique. The method they used was quite simple. Two groups of judges who varied in their attitudes toward science were given several pairs of opinion statements on this topic, and were asked in each case to indicate which statement of the two was more favorable to science. The constituent items for each of the pairs were relatively close together on the evaluative continuum, and thus there was often some uncertainty as to the correct response. Here is one of the pairs that they used:

> (1) A scientific analysis should always be preferred to any other.
>
> (2) Through science alone will man comprehend the universe.

Which statement would *you* select as most pro-science?

Since the correct answers to the various statement-pairs had previously been determined by obtaining the judgments of a large *unselected* group (including people of diverse attitudes), it was a simple matter to score the subjects' responses. In the pair presented above, for example, statement number 2 was considered to be more pro-science by most respondents. Not all subjects agreed with this choice, however. In general, when both members of a statement-pair came from the pro-science end of the attitude scale (as in the above example), people who were *themselves* pro-science rarely made an error, while those who opposed science made many errors. For pairs of statements that were mainly anti-science, however, most of the errors were made by subjects who favored science.

The Ager and Dawes study is of particular interest in demonstrating that the effects of attitude upon social judgment are *not* solely attributable to semantic differences in the use of rating scales, for, as described above, their experiment did not involve ratings. Note, however, that these results support previous findings in only the most general sense; they do not, for example, provide a detailed mapping of assimilation and contrast effects. Nevertheless, a start has been made in the important task of separating perceptual from semantic effects in the judgment of social attitudes.

The results of the Ager and Dawes study indicate that respondents with contrasting attitudes may at times reach divergent conclusions, when faced with the task of choosing the more extreme statement from a pair of closely related opinions. A subsequent study by Koslin and Pargament (1969) showed, moreover, that people with *extreme* opinions regarding the war in Vietnam were relatively *consistent* (in a logical sense) when responding to a task of this sort. For example, if an extremist felt that: (1) a certain statement (call it A) was more pro-war than statement B, and (2) that statement B was more pro-war than statement C, then he would quite commonly accept the logical inference (3) that statement A was *also* more pro-war than statement C. In contrast to the subjects with extreme views, a group of unselected moderates showed many more logical inconsistencies, presumably because of their limited interest and familiarity with the attitude issue.

Involvement and message interpretation

People differ not only in their *attitudes* toward various social institutions, but they may also differ in the degree to which a given issue *involves* them. That is, while some people may be highly favorable to the cause of civil rights, this may not be a particularly important issue for them; others with equally favorable attitudes may be more involved in civil rights, and may thus be more active in advancing their views.

An experiment conducted at the University of North Carolina (Ward, 1965) sought to determine the effect of differences in involvement on the individual's interpretation of various opinion statements. Three groups of subjects were presented with a series of statements concerning the social position of the Negro in the United States, and they were asked to rate each statement according to the favorability of its content.

While the three groups were all pro-Negro, they differed in involvement. Some of the students had actively participated in the picketing of local movie theaters in an attempt to eliminate segregated seating. Just prior to the experiment, half of these picketers were reminded of their membership in this group; hence it may be assumed that these people were maximally involved while participating in the study, both because of their voluntary picketing activity and because the experimenter had made their membership in this group a salient factor. The group next highest in involvement was comprised of people who had picketed the theaters, but who had been led to believe that their selection for the study occurred through chance; that is, their picketing membership was not made salient during the course of the experiment. The third, least involved group, was composed of pro-Negro students who had *not* participated in the movie picketing and whose attitudes on this issue were not salient at the time of the experiment. The results indicated that involvement led to a consistent contrast effect—a displacement of the statements away from the subject's own position. That is, among the three groups of subjects, all of whom were pro-Negro, those who were most involved in the topic at hand interpreted the statements of opinion as being *less favorable* to the Negro than did those who were relatively uninvolved. A subsequent study by Ward (1967) provides further support for the view that involvement often leads to judgmental contrast.

One interpretation of these studies holds that the involved person is very "choosy" before agreeing that a given statement actually supports the particular view that he favors; that is, he may have what has been referred to as an "elevated threshold" of acceptance, while the uninvolved individual may be *less critical* before accepting a statement as supporting his preferred point of view.

The contrast effects that result from personal involvement may also be interpreted as a reflection of the role played by the respondent's own views in establishing a context for his judgments (Ward, 1967). Recall that in our earlier discussion, we reviewed several studies documenting the fact that in a variety of judgmental tasks, respondents normally contrast any particular stimulus-object with other stimuli that have previously been presented for them to judge. (See p. 255.) An extension of this principle suggests that in interpreting opinion statements, the judge's *own* views may serve as one of the elements determining the effective contextual background. Moreover, if the issue in question is *important* (or involving), the judge's opinion may play a particularly salient role in establishing this context. Thus, in this view, which represents an elaboration of adaptation-level theory (Helson, 1964), context is regarded as the effective underlying variable in studies relating social judgment to (a) attitude and (b) involvement. Despite the attractive simplicity of this approach, it is not wholly satisfactory as an overall theory of social judgment—primarily because it seems invariably to predict contrast effects, whereas in fact attitude statements are sometimes displaced toward the judge's own opinion.

Evaluating complex stimuli

Social judgments are normally based on *multiple inputs*. A voter who believes that Candidate *X* is favorably disposed toward the United Nations has usually based his conclusion on a relatively large pool of statements and reactions that have been made by *X* or attributed to him during the course of the campaign. Moreover, since the statements made by *X* or attributed to him generally reflect a *range* of attitudes, they may include elements that are not wholly consistent with one another. Until recently, relatively little attention had been devoted to this matter of cognitive integration. In the past few years, however, this has become a rather active research domain.

One of the pioneering efforts in this area was conducted by Solomon Asch (1946). In Asch's *impression-formation* task, subjects were given a list of traits describing a hypothetical individual and were asked to form an overall impression of this person. They were then asked to select from a series of additional traits those that seemed consistent with the impression they had formed. In one of Asch's experiments, two groups of subjects read similar trait lists which were to be used in forming their impressions. One group read the following list: intelligent, skillful, industrious, *warm*, determined, practical, and cautious; the second group received a list that was identical with the one above, except the trait *warm* was replaced by its opposite, *cold*.

Asch's results indicated that the two groups developed rather distinct views of the person being described, for they responded quite differently when requested to check additional traits that were consistent with their impressions. For example, 91% of the subjects who had read the "warm" list believed that the trait of *generosity* would also be applicable; only 8% of the "cold" group held the same belief. Similarly, while 94% of the "warm" group checked the trait *good-natured*, only 17% of those in the "cold" group did so. There were other traits, however, such as *reliability* and *seriousness*, which were checked with equal frequency in the two groups. Nevertheless, the markedly different impressions that were produced by simply substituting the word *cold* for *warm* in the initial trait list led Asch to conclude that these were *central* traits in determining his subjects' final impressions. By contrast, when words such as *polite* and *blunt* were used in the initial list in place of *warm* and *cold*, there were only minor differences in the subjects' responses; Asch thus concluded that these traits had only a *peripheral* impact on the subjects' final impressions.

In attempting to clarify Asch's distinction between central and peripheral traits, Wishner (1960) focused on the relationship between the word-pair that was varied in the "given" list, and the individual traits in the "checklist." He found that the marked impact of the *warm-cold* variation was due to the close association between this particular pair of traits and the items that were included on the checklist. For example, a person who is *warm* is normally thought to be *sociable* as well, and a *cold* person is usually regarded as lacking sociability. There were apparently many terms on Asch's checklist which were, in this sense, closely related to the terms *warm* and *cold*, and on these items the group differences were large. The terms *polite* and *blunt*, on the other hand, which Asch had found to be of peripheral importance, were less closely related to the items that were fortuitously included on the checklist.

Averaging, primacy, and extremity

Recent work in impression formation has been designed mainly to develop a theory relating (a) the judge's *overall evaluation* of various compound (multi-element) inputs to (b) his evaluations of the *constituent parts*. Consider, for example, a modification of Asch's experimental task, where the judge is instructed to use a rating scale to indicate his *overall liking* for an otherwise unknown individual, who has been characterized by a series of descriptive adjectives ("kind, intelligent, impatient"). Some theorists suggest that the judge's response in such a situation will closely reflect the average favorability-value of the terms that are presented. Thus, in our present example, if the judge regarded kindness and intelligence as highly desirable (+3), and impatience as undesirable (−3)[2], a strict averaging model would predict an overall rating of 1.0 $\left[\frac{3+3-3}{3}=1\right]$.

Primacy

While there has been some experimental support for the simple averaging approach (Anderson, 1962), there are several studies which suggest that this model may have some serious deficiencies. One problem results from the fact that the component parts of a multi-element input are often given *unequal weight* in forming an overall

[2] The values included in parentheses represent the mean ratings elicited by these traits when they are evaluated one at a time on a −3 to +3 scale; these values are *not* normally included in the information that is provided to experimental subjects.

impression. It has been repeatedly demonstrated, for example, that the *order* in which the constituent elements are presented may have a sizeable impact on the judge's overall evaluation. Most typically, studies of impression formation show a *primacy effect*, in which the early elements in a series are given greater weight than those that appear later on. The replicability of the primacy phenomenon in a variety of studies, ranging from judgments of personality (Anderson, 1965b) to ratings of meals and news events (Anderson and Norman, 1964), suggests that primacy may reflect a basic characteristic of cognitive functioning.

In part, the primacy effect appears to derive from the fact that the judge pays progressively less attention to the incoming stream of information; as the series to be evaluated stretches on, interest seems to wane. This attentional interpretation is supported by evidence that primacy effects may be eliminated and may indeed be replaced by a *recency* effect (emphasis on the later items in the series), if the judge is forced to maintain a consistently high level of attention. In one study for example (Anderson and Hubert, 1963), primacy was disrupted when, in addition to giving an overall evaluative judgment, the judges were instructed to *remember* the personality traits that appeared in each description (and were subsequently tested for recall). Similarly, Stewart (1965) found no evidence for primacy when the task involved a series of *cumulative* judgments following the presentation of each successive adjective, rather than a single judgment at the end of the trait series.

Primacy effects may also derive from the judge's tendency to interpret the later items in a description so as to maximize their congruence with the material that preceded them. The marked impact of the early elements in a series may thus be due to their influence on the judge's evaluation of later elements (Asch, 1946; Wyer and Watson, 1969). For example, if we are asked to rate the likeability of a person who is described as "intelligent, honest, and talkative," our evaluative response to the adjective *talkative* (the way we interpret it) will probably be more positive than it would be if this word had appeared *first* in the set. If the more positive elements in a description are presented first, the later elements may be interpreted in a relatively favorable manner (to maintain consistency), thus producing a more favorable overall evaluation.

The extremity effect

In addition to the above-noted emphasis on the *early* items in a series of descriptive traits, judges typically weight the information that they receive in accordance with its *extremity* (deviation from neutrality). In a study by Manis, Gleason, and Dawes (1965), a group of college students read several pairs of opinion statements concerning college fraternities. Both statements in each pair had presumably been endorsed by a single individual. Using a semantic differential scale that ranged from favorable to unfavorable, the students attempted to indicate this unknown person's probable attitude toward fraternities. For example, they estimated the attitude of a person who had supposedly endorsed the statements:

> College fraternities are hopelessly out of date.
>
> The good and bad points of college fraternities balance each other.

The overall ratings were most clearly influenced by the more *extreme* component of each pair (the first statement in the above example), in contrast with the relatively weaker influence of the less extreme component.

Although the evidence here is not yet complete, it is possible that extreme attitude statements are given particular emphasis because the average person is confident that he knows how to interpret them correctly. For example, if a person endorses an *extreme* attitude statement we usually feel fairly certain that we understand his views and that we can accurately locate his preferred position on the attitude continuum; by contrast, the endorsement of a *neutral* statement may leave us with considerable uncertainty as to the other person's "true" opinions. Because of this difference in subjective confidence, a neutral statement may be given less weight than an extreme one in assessing someone else's overall views.

A somewhat different interpretation for the extremity effect is based on the suggestion that when we are assessing the views of others, neutral items may seem mainly reflective of a facade-like social role, while information that is more extreme appears to be relatively *personal* and *idiosyncratic*. Hence, in reaching an overall assessment, a greater emphasis may be placed upon extreme elements because of their apparent personal validity.

Summation and numerosity

The primacy effect and the extremity effect conflict with the uniform weighting of elements that is called for by a simple averaging model. Nevertheless, these phenomena do not constitute a challenge to the basic premises of the averaging approach, for we can easily accommodate them if we complicate matters slightly by introducing various *weighting* schemes to give particular emphasis to the early items in a series and to those items that are extreme. Unfortunately, however, a modified average approach is not completely satisfactory either, for there are many situations in which the component elements of a stimulus appear to combine in an *additive* fashion. For example, Hicks and Campbell (1965) found clear evidence for a *summative* model; in this study, compound stimuli were typically given more extreme ratings than any of their components, a result that is inconsistent with any type of averaging model. Similarly, Fishbein and Hunter (1964a, 1964b) have reported evidence for summation in several experiments on impression formation.

Results like this suggest that our overall reaction to a compound stimulus may simply reflect a crude summation of the evaluations that we associate with the constituent elements. Thus, according to the summation model, if a compound contains only positive terms, each additional element which is to be evaluated should enhance the value of our overall reaction; this enhanced evaluation should appear even if the "added" components are less positive than the elements with which they are combined. A similar pattern, showing continuing increases in *negativity* should be produced if we form compounds using exclusively negative terms. Fishbein and Hunter conducted several experiments based on this rationale (1964a, 1964b). Subjects in different treatment conditions received varying numbers of favorable traits and were asked for an overall evaluation of the "persons" who were described. The traits were grouped in such a manner that the judges who received the greatest *amount* of information were given items which were, on the *average*, less positive than those given to subjects who had received less information. For example, in one condition the subjects were to evaluate Mr. A, who was simply described as "*honest*" (+3). Other subjects heard Mr. A described as *honest* (+3) and loyal (+2). Note that the mean value of these traits is 2.5, which is less than the mean value for the preceding group (3.0), where the trait of honesty was the only item included in the description. A third group was told that Mr. A was *honest* (+3), *loyal* (+2), *successful* (+1), and determined (+0.5); note that for this last group—the group which received the greatest amount of information—the mean value for the trait list was the lowest of all: +1.6. Thus, if evaluation followed a simple averaging model, we would expect the evaluations of Mr. A to decrease in favorability, as the judges were given more and more information. On the other hand, according to the summation theory, since all of the component traits were favorable, the more information that a judge received, the greater the *sum* of the elements, and hence the more favorable should be his overall evaluation. Fishbein and Hunter's results favored the summation model; unfortunately, however, in a similar experiment, Anderson (1965) has obtained results that support an averaging approach.

In an effort to resolve the discrepancy between averaging and summative models, Lugg and Gollob (1970) suggest that the manner in which the trait information is presented may be critical. Their results imply that averaging is likely to occur when the judges in any given study are led to believe that the individual traits are somehow in conflict, perhaps because each of them has been presented as the *most accurate* characterization of the person being described (obviously, there can be only *one* trait that truly provides the *most* accurate characterization). Under these conditions, Lugg and Gollob hypothesize, the judge may resolve his conflict by taking an informal average of the evaluative impressions associated with the different constituent traits. Summation effects, on the other hand, are thought to be more likely if the instructions imply that each element in the trait list accurately conveys *some* aspect of the individual's personality, and thus encourages the judge to construct an overall view of the person being described; in this case, if we provide additional information that appears to confirm an initially positive (or negative) evaluation, the net result should be to intensify the judge's reaction.

In many instances, the occurrence of summative effects may reflect the fact that the sheer number of elements to be considered is a significant factor in the judge's evaluation (Brewer, 1968). In general, as we increase the number of elements in a compound (holding their mean value constant), the judge's impression becomes more and more extreme. Thus, a person who is described by two positive attributes will usually be rated less favorably than someone who has been described by four positive traits (Anderson, 1965a). This phenomenon may be due to the fact that in responding to a description, we consider not only the information that we *are* given, but may also make implicit assumptions concerning attributes that have *not* received explicit attention. As a consequence, if we receive a small amount of extremely positive information about someone, our overall evaluation may nevertheless be tempered by the possibility that this person may be quite average in other respects. If, however, we now receive additional favorable information concerning previously undiscussed domains (not only is he *honest*, but he is also *intelligent*), our overall assessment should rise—so long as the "new" material is more positive than our previous assumptions. Perhaps it is *this* which accounts for the surprising fact that our impression of another may sometimes be enhanced by learning something new about him that is favorable, even though this new information may be *less* positive than the things we had known before.

Redundancy

When evaluating others, the average judge is influenced not only by the specific items of information that are provided to him, but may also consider information that is "likely" to be true, even if it has not been explicitly mentioned (see above). For example, if John is said to be *friendly*, we will probably assume that he is also *generous* and may take account of both terms in our overall evaluation. Theoretically, this would suggest that the *explicit* addition of the term *generous* ("John is friendly *and* generous.") should have relatively little impact on the impression that we formed from the single trait of friendliness, for there is little new information that is conveyed. The two terms are highly *redundant.*

To test the validity of this reasoning, Dustin and Baldwin (1966) conducted a series of experiments in which their subjects evaluated several "others," each of whom was described by two "like-signed" adjectives (i.e., both positive or both negative). For most adjective-pairs, the evaluations which they obtained were more extreme than the average of the two components; that is, the data showed a rather consistent extremity effect (see above). The extremeness of the respondents' ratings was most marked, however, when the adjectives that comprised a given pair were independent (*not redundant*); indeed, the overall evaluations elicited by nonredundant compounds followed a roughly additive model. The final evaluations were less extreme, however, among adjective-pairs that were highly redundant. A subsequent study by Wyer (1968) yielded similar results. These experiments are fairly convincing in demonstrating that the internal structure of a compound stimulus (the redundancy or relatedness of its parts) plays a significant role in the overall impression that it evokes.

Linear and configural combination rules

A review of the impression formation literature suggests that in most studies the judges seem to follow a rather simple "linear" combinatorial rule, in which the implications of any given element remain *roughly constant*, despite variations in the other elements with which it is combined (Goldberg, 1968). Thus, in forming an impression of an unknown individual we are apt to regard him more favorably if he is *honest*, rather than *dishonest*, regardless of any other traits that he may possess. While Dustin and Baldwin's results indicate that this simple combination rule is not *completely* true (e.g., the gain in "positivity" that is normally associated with the trait of honesty may be attenuated, if the individual is known to have other characteristics that are redundant with this trait), the linear rule nevertheless seems to apply in a great variety of situations; it is, moreover, consistent with both averaging and additive models.

The linear combination rule seems applicable not only to the impression formation task but also to many diagnostic activities that are performed in the seemingly complex evaluation of psychiatric and medical syndromes. Even in cases where the judge believes himself to be following a more complicated rule, where the significance of a given sign is thought to be heavily dependent upon the context in which it appears, diagnostic inferences often follow the simple combinatorial pattern that is sketched above (Goldberg, 1968). For example, clinical lore suggests that an MMPI profile must be approached in a configural manner when attempting to determine the psychotic versus neurotic nature of a patient's condition; that is, the significance of any given test score as a sign of psychosis or neurosis is presumably dependent upon the *other* scores in the profile. Despite the widespread acceptance of this belief, however, an extensive study of 29 clinical psychologists indicated that in most cases, a linear combination rule provided a more accurate description of the clinician's diagnostic inferences than the more complex configural models with which it was compared (Wiggins and Hoffman, 1967). Similar results were obtained in a study of radiologists who attempted to make differential diagnoses between benign and malignant gastric ulcers, after being given various cues derived from X-ray examinations. Here, too, contrary to clinical lore, the clinicians appeared to be following a rather simple rule in which the significance of a given sign was largely independent of the other signs that accompanied it.

When we move from studies of clinical diagnosis and impression formation into the domain of natural language, however, there is better evidence for the operation of *configural* combination rules; the constituent elements of speech interact rather complexly and cannot be described in terms of simple summation or averaging. For example, several studies have focused on the manner in which adverbs and adjectives combine in producing a single unified impression. Consider an adjective like "disgusting" and the way in which it is successively modified when preceded by such adverbs as "slightly," "somewhat," "very," or "extremely." Some investigators (Cliff, 1959; Howe, 1963) have concluded that in such adverb-adjective pairs, the adverbs function as *multipliers*. That is, while an adverb like "slightly" is not associated with any particular quality (such as good or bad or active), it modifies the intensity of the adjectives with which it appears; thus, the strongly unfavorable connotations of a word like "disgusting" are reduced by about half in the phrase "slightly disgusting." Similarly, the favorable connotations of "charming" are reduced by half in the phrase "slightly charming." In general, we may predict that the favorability (or unfavorability) of the words "slightly *x*" (whatever adjective *x* may be—cruel or gifted or evil, etc.) will be about .5 times the favorability or unfavorability associated with *x*, when *x* appears in unmodified form. Other adverbs *intensify* the adjectives that follow them. The word "extremely," for example, generally increases the favorability (or unfavorability) of its associated adjective by about 50 percent, and may therefore be assigned a value of 1.5. Thus, the phrase "extremely *x*" (whatever *x* may be) will generally be rated as 1.5 times as favorable or unfavorable as the unmodified adjective *x*.

A study by Lilly and Rajecki (1969) explored a related phenomenon, by having college students rate a series of adjectives that were presented in basic form (e.g., *good*), comparative form (*better*), and superlative form (*best*). The superlatives were awarded ratings that were, on the average, about 1.4 times the rated values of these same adjectives in basic form. Surprisingly, however, the comparative and basic forms received rather similar ratings. These results suggest that if John is described as *better*, he will not necessarily be evaluated more favorably than someone who is simply *good*. This may perhaps be because we do not know what John is *better than;* he may, for example, be better than he used to be, which in some cases may not be much of a compliment.

A careful study by Gollob (1968) provides yet another example of a complex judgmental model within the realm of natural language. In this study, subjects were presented with a series of sentences of the general form: The *adjective* man *verbs noun*. Some representative sentences might thus read: "The vicious man dislikes beggars," or "The kind man befriends criminals," or "The cruel man praises physicians." Gollob collected evaluative ratings of "the man" who was described in each sentence and attempted to determine the manner in which these evaluations were related to the ratings elicited by the constituent sentence parts (adjectives, verbs, and nouns) when these parts were rated as isolated words and phrases. To some extent, the evaluation of the various "men" reflected a simple linear model, in which the modifying adjective (vicious, or kind, or whatever) combined additively with the sentence predicate (befriends criminals, or praises physicians). Thus, the most positive ratings were obtained when "the man" was described by a favorable adjective (e.g., kind) and performed a laudatory action (helps neighbors).

The ratings of the *predicates* (verb-object combinations) followed a more complex pattern. In part, they reflected a *multiplicative relationship* between the evaluative significance of the verb and its associated object. Thus the predicate *helps neighbors* was favorably evaluated, since a positive action was associated with a positively evaluated "other" (positive *x* positive = positive); predicates composed of a negative verb and a negative object ("hates criminals") also tended to receive favorable evaluations (negative *x* negative = positive). Negative evaluations, on the other hand, were produced by "good-bad mixtures," as in such predicates as "helps criminals," or "hates physicians."

Conservatism and the optimal revision of opinion

In the research that has been reviewed in the preceding pages, an attempt was made to characterize the individual's integration of diverse information in a *descriptive sense*; the investigators for the most part sought to develop models that would enable them to describe overall judgments, derived from diverse items of information. Some investigators, however, have not been content with these descriptive models; rather, they have sought to compare their subjects' behavior with that of an "ideal subject," one who might process the information that he was given in an optimal fashion. Workers in this tradition have typically focused on situations in which statistical techniques can be used to reach an *optimal* integration of diverse inputs; the subjects' *actual* behavior may then be compared with this optimal (or normative) response.

For example, imagine that you were the subject in one of these experiments and were faced with the following problem. (See Figure 7.) There are two large jars, each filled with poker chips. Suppose that one jar is red, and contains 700 red chips and 300 blue chips, while the second jar is blue, and contains 700 blue chips and 300 red. The experimenter plans to blindfold himself and select a series of 12 chips from one of these two jars; your job is to indicate the jar from which he is choosing. Before making his selections, the experimenter first tosses a coin, to determine the jar from which he will choose—there is thus a 50-50 chance that he will choose from the red jar or the blue one. Having tossed his coin and selected one of the two jars, suppose he then draws a set of eight red chips and four blue chips. Which jar did the sample come from, the red or the blue? Most of us would infer that in this situation, a predominantly red sample is most likely to have come from the red jar; and this conclusion is not only intuitively reasonable, but it is also consistent with the conclusion that would be drawn by a statistician, using a mathematical formulation known as *Bayes' Theorem.*

How *certain* would you be that the sample had come from the red jar? Most subjects report that they are about 75–80% certain. By contrast, however, our statistician tells us we should be 97% certain that the sample in question (8 reds and 4 blues) came from the red jar. This difference between the final judgment of a typical subject, and the optimal judgment that he "should" have reached has been labeled a *conservatism* effect. That is, as a general rule, most subjects express less certainty in their conclusions than they would if their judgments were guided by strictly statistical considerations. This form of conservatism has been observed in many studies that require the individual to reach probabilistic conclusions based on relevant, but fallible, information (Edwards, Lindman, and Phillips, 1965).

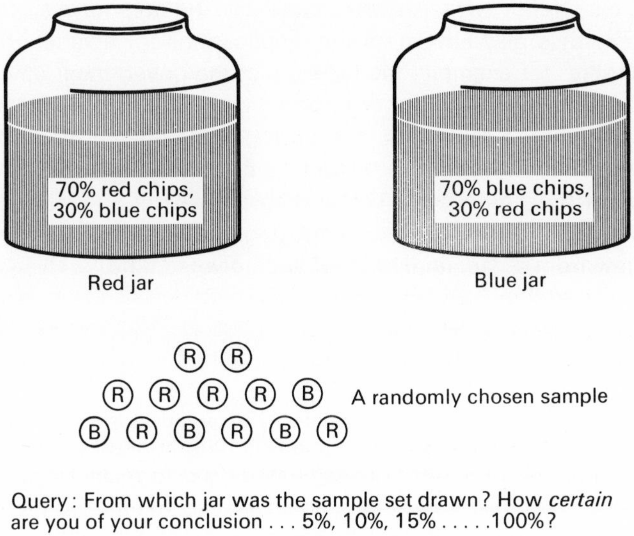

Figure 7

A schematic representation of a task that commonly produces a conservatism effect (see text). (Adapted from Edwards, W., Lindman, H., and Phillips, L. D. Emerging technologies for making decisions. In Newcomb, T. M. (Ed.), *New directions in psychology II*. New York: Holt, Rinehart & Winston, Inc., 1965.)

There seem to be two main factors at work here. For one thing, in a test situation like the one described above, most people will *overestimate* the likelihood that a predominantly red sample of chips could have been drawn from the blue jar. As a consequence, when shown a sample that is mainly red, they are unduly persistent in believing that it could nevertheless have been drawn from the blue jar. A second factor that contributes to the conservatism effect is the subject's "sluggishness" in *combining* the various inputs with which he is provided. That is, apart from an inability to evaluate properly the significance of particular samples of information when these are considered singly, most subjects fail to revise their opinions in an optimal fashion as they receive more and more information, and generally err on the side of conservatism (they fail to respond effectively to the *cumulative* impact of the information they receive).

The experimental procedure described above may strike you as a bit removed from the sort of judgments you are accustomed to, and it may thus seem largely irrelevant to your daily experience. Nevertheless, some investigators have argued that the results of such studies may have profound implications for a variety of practical decisions—including, for example, the problem of the government official whose task it is to combine various samples of information (derived from spies, radar, troop movements, intercepted messages, and so on) to determine the probable goals of some other nation (Are they really interested in cooperation, or should we continue to be suspicious of their motives?). The available research suggests that the human judge may often err in failing to develop the degree of subjective certainty that might rationally follow from an accumulation of such diverse data.

Summary

1. Studies of social judgment have repeatedly shown that the individual's evaluation (or other response) to a given stimulus is partly determined by the context in which that stimulus appears. This effect usually takes the form of an apparent contrast between the overall context and the particular stimulus or event that is being judged. Some theorists have proposed that this so-called contrast effect is primarily *perceptual,* and that it reflects the impact of the context on the *subjective impression* that is elicited by the stimulus which is to be judged. Others have suggested that the effect is largely *semantic,* and is mainly due to the way in which the judge labels his subjective experience. Several studies designed to clarify this issue have yielded results consistent with the perceptual point of view. It is clear, however, that semantic effects also play a role in the judgmental process.

2. Persuasive messages are often given diverse interpretations, depending upon the attitude and degree of involvement of the recipient. Two important trends noted in this research are *assimilation* (the tendency to displace the communicator's apparent meaning toward one's own preferred position) and *contrast* (the tendency to exaggerate the discrepancy between one's own views and those of the communicator).

3. Many of our social judgments are based on multiple inputs which we somehow integrate to reach a final, overall impression. There is some evidence that complex stimuli of this sort are often evaluated by essentially averaging the impressions elicited by the component parts. On the other hand, there are several facts which are inconsistent with this approach: (a) items that are presented early in a sequence generally affect our impressions to a greater extent than do later items; (b) extreme items tend to affect our judgments more than neutral ones; (c) the sheer number of items that are included in the compound to be judged often plays a significant role, as does (d) the redundancy of the component elements.

4. In many judgmental situations, the respondents seem to follow a simple "linear" combinatorial rule, in that the implications of any given element remain roughly constant, despite variations in the other elements with which it is combined. Within the domain of natural language, however, there are several studies in which the con-

stituent elements interact according to more complex (nonlinear) rules. For example, adverbs like "somewhat," or "very" seem to operate like multipliers to either attenuate or intensify the adjectives with which they are paired.

5. In combining informative but fallible data, most subjects show evidence of excessive *conservatism.* That is, in reaching an overall conclusion based on probabilistic information, they typically show *less certainty* than they would if they followed an optimal strategy for integrating the available information.

Supplementary reading

Abelson, R. P. et al. (Eds.) *Theories of cognitive consistency: A sourcebook.* Chicago: Rand McNally, 1968, 721–768.

Edwards, W., Lindman, H., & Phillips, L. D. Emerging technologies for making decisions. In T. M. Newcomb (Ed.), *New directions in psychology* II. New York: Holt, 1965.

Manis, M. Some recent trends in the study of social judgment. In J. Hellmuth (Ed.), *Cognitive studies,* Vol. I. New York: Brunner/Mazel, Inc., 1970.

Upshaw, H. S. The personal reference scale: An approach to social judgment. In L. Berkowitz (Ed.), *Advances in experimental social psychology,* Vol. 4. New York: Academic Press, 1967.

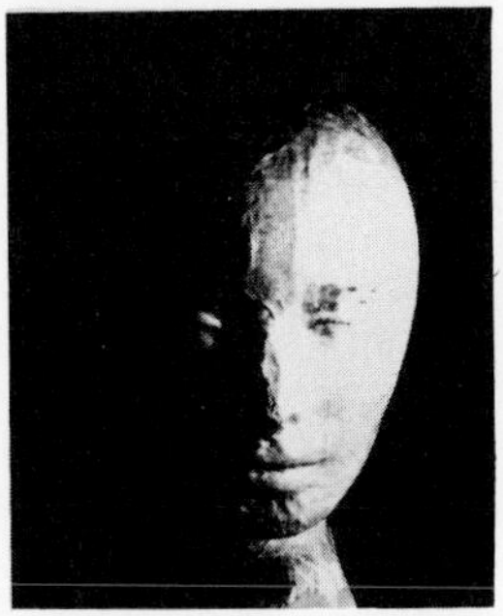

References

Abelson, R. P., & Rosenberg, M. J. Symbolic psycho-logic: A model of attitudinal cognition. *Behavioral Science,* 1958, **3,** 1–13.

Abelson, R. P. Psychological implication. In R. P. Abelson et al. (Eds.), *Theories of cognitive consistency: A sourcebook.* Chicago: Rand McNally and Company, 1968.

Adams, J. A. *Human memory.* New York: McGraw-Hill, 1967.

Adams, J. K. Laboratory studies of behavior without awareness. *Psychological Bulletin,* 1957, **54,** 383–405.

Adams, J. S. Reduction of cognitive dissonance by seeking consonant information. *Journal of Abnormal and Social Psychology,* 1961, **62,** 74–78.

Adamson, R. E., & Taylor, D. W. Functional fixedness as related to elapsed time and to set. *Journal of Experimental Psychology,* 1954, **47,** 122–126.

Ager, J. W., & Dawes, R. M. The effect of judges' attitudes on judgment. *Journal of Abnormal and Social Psychology,* 1965, **1,** 533–538.

Alter, M., & Silverman, R. E. The response in programmed instruction. *Journal of Programmed Instruction,* 1962, **1**, 55–78.

Ammons, R. B. Effects of knowledge on performance: A survey and tentative theoretical formulation. *Journal of General Psychology,* 1956, **54,** 279–299.

Amster, H. Semantic satiation and generation: Learning? Adaptation? *Psychological Bulletin,* 1964, **62,** 273–286.

Anderson, N. H. Application of an additive model to impression formation. *Science,* 1962, **138,** 817–818.

Anderson, N. H. Primary effects in personality impression formation using a generalized order effect paradigm. *Journal of Personality and Social Psychology,* 1965, **2,** 1–9. (a)

Anderson, N. H. Averaging versus adding as a stimulus-combination rule in impression formation. *Journal of Experimental Psychology,* 1965, **70,** 394–400. (b)

Anderson, N. H., & Hubert, S. Effects of concomitant verbal recall on effects in personality impression formation. *Journal of Verbal Learning and Verbal Behavior,* 1963, **2,** 379–391.

Anderson, N. H., & Norman, A. Order effects in impression formation in four classes of stimuli. *Journal of Abnormal and Social Psychology,* 1964, **69,** 467–471.

Andrews, F. M. Social and organizational factors affecting innovation in research. Unpublished manuscript, 1969.
Anisfeld, M. Disjunctive concepts? Paper presented at a symposium on the concept of structure in language and thinking. Eastern Psychological Association, 1961.
Archer, E. J. Re-evaluation of the meaningfulness of all possible CVC trigrams. *Psychological Monographs,* 1960, **74**(10).
Aronson, E., & Carlsmith, J. M. Performance expectancy as a determinant of actual performance. *Journal of Abnormal and Social Psychology,* 1962, **65,** 178–182.
Aronson, E., & Carlsmith, J. M. Effect of severity of threat on the valuation of forbidden behavior. *Journal of Abnormal and Social Psychology,* 1963, **66,** 684–588.
Aronson, E., Carlsmith, J. M., & Darley, J. M. The effects of expectancy on volunteering for an unpleasant experience. *Journal of Abnormal and Social Psychology,* 1963, **66,** 220–224.
Aronson, E., & Mills, J. The effect of severity of initiation on liking for a group. *Journal of Abnormal and Social Psychology,* 1959, **59,** 177–181.
Aronson, E., Turner, J., & Carlsmith, J. Communicator credibility and communication discrepancy as determinants of opinion change. *Journal of Abnormal and Social Psychology,* 1963, **67,** 31–36.
Asch, S. E. Forming impressions of personality. *Journal of Abnormal and Social Psychology,* 1946, **41,** 258–290.
Atkinson, J. W. The achievement motive and recall of interrupted and completed tasks. *Journal of Experimental Psychology,* 1953, **46,** 381–390.
Bandura, A. Influence of models' reinforcement on the acquisition of imitative responses. *Journal of Personality and Social Psychology,* 1965, **1,** 589–595.
Bar-Hillel, Y. The present status of automatic translation of languages. In F. L. Alt (Ed.), *Advances in computers,* Vol. 1. New York: Academic Press, 1960.
Barron, F. The psychology of creativity. In T. M. Newcomb (Ed.), *New directions in psychology II.* New York: Holt, 1965.
Bartlett, F. C. *Remembering: A study in experimental and social psychology.* Cambridge, England: Cambridge University Press, 1932.
Bastian, J. R. Associative factors in verbal transfer. *Journal of Experimental Psychology,* 1961, **62,** 70.
Bem, D. J. Dissonance reduction in the behaviorist. In R. P. Abelson et al. (Eds.), *Theories of cognitive consistency: A sourcebook.* Chicago: Rand McNally and Company, 1968.
Berko, J. The child's learning of English morphology. *Word,* 1958, **14,** 150–177.
Berkowitz, L. The motivational status of cognitive consistency theorizing. In R. P. Abelson et al. (Eds.), *Theories of cognitive consistency: A sourcebook.* Chicago: Rand McNally and Company, 1968. (a)
Berkowitz, L. On the discomfort of cognitive inconsistency. In R. P. Abelson et al. (Eds.), *Theories of cognitive consistency: A sourcebook.* Chicago: Rand McNally and Company, 1968. (b)
Berkowitz, L., & Goranson, R. E. Motivational and judgmental determinants of social judgment. *Journal of Abnormal and Social Psychology,* 1964, **69,** 296–302.
Berlyne, D. E. *Structure and direction in thinking.* New York: Wiley, 1965.
Bernstein, B. A public language: Some sociological implications of a linguistic form. *British Journal of Sociology,* 1959, **10,** 311–326.
Bernstein, B. Social class and linguistic development: A theory of social learning. In

A. H. Halsey, J. Floud, & A. Anderson (Eds.), *Education, economy, and society.* New York: Free Press, 1961.
Bever, T. G., Mehler, J., & Epstein, J. What children do in spite of what they know. *Science,* 1968, **162,** 921–924.
Birch, H. G. The relation of previous experience to insightful problem-solving. *Journal of Comparative Psychology,* 1945, **38,** 367–383.
Bjork, R. A. Positive forgetting: The non-interference of items intentionally forgotten. *Journal of Verbal Learning and Verbal Behavior,* 1970, in press.
Bjork, R. A., LaBerge, D., & LeGrand, R. The modification of short-term memory through instructions to forget. *Psychonomic Science,* 1968, **10**(2), 55–56.
Blodgett, H. C. The effect of the introduction of reward upon the maze performance of rats. *University of California Publication in Psychology,* 1929, **4,** 113–134.
Bobrow, D. A question answering system for high school algebra word problems. *Proceedings of the Fall Joint Computer Conference,* AFIPS, 1964, **26,** 591–614.
Boucher, J., & Osgood, C. E. The Pollyanna hypothesis. *Journal of Verbal Learning and Verbal Behavior,* 1969, **8,** 1–8.
Bourne, L. E., Jr. Hypotheses and hypothesis shifts in classification learning. *Journal of General Psychology,* 1965, **72,** 251–261.
Bourne, L. E., Jr. *Human conceptual behavior.* Boston: Allyn and Bacon, Inc., 1966.
Bourne, L. E., Jr., & Bunderson, C. V. Effects of delay of informative feedback and length of postfeedback interval on concept identification. *Journal of Experimental Psychology,* 1963, **65,** 1–5.
Bousfield, W. A. The occurrence of clustering in the recall of randomly arranged associates. *Journal of General Psychology,* 1953, **49,** 229–240.
Bousfield, W. A., & Barclay, W. D. The relationship between order and frequency of occurrence of restricted associative responses. *Journal of Experimental Psychology,* 1950, **40,** 643–647.
Bower, G., & Trabasso, T. Reversals prior to solution in concept identification. *Journal of Experimental Psychology,* 1963, **66,** 409–418.
Braine, M. D. S. On learning the grammatical order of words. *Psychological Review,* 1963, **70,** 323–348.
Brehm, J. W. Post-decision changes in the desirability of alternatives. *Journal of Abnormal and Social Psychology,* 1956, **52,** 384–389.
Brehm, M. L., Back, K. W., & Bogdonoff, M. D. A physiological effect of cognitive dissonance under stress and deprivation. *Journal of Abnormal and Social Psychology,* 1964, **69,** 303–310.
Brehm, J. W., & Cohen, A. R. Re-evaluation of choice alternatives as a function of their number and qualitative similarity. *Journal of Abnormal and Social Psychology,* 1959, **58,** 373–378.
Brehm, J. W., & Cohen, A. R. *Explorations in cognitive dissonance.* New York: Wiley, 1962.
Brewer, M. B. Averaging versus summation in composite ratings of complex social stimuli. *Journal of Personality and Social Psychology,* 1968, **8,** 20–26.
Bridger, W. H., & Mandel, I. J. Abolition of the PRE by instruction in GSR conditioning. *Journal of Experimental Psychology,* 1965, **69,** 476–482.
Broadbent, D. E. *Perception and communication.* New York: Pergamon Press, 1958.
Brock, T. C. Commitment to exposure as a determinant of information receptivity. *Journal of Personality and Social Psychology,* 1965, **2,** 10–19.

Brock, T. C. Dissonance without awareness. In R. P. Abelson et al. (Eds.), *Theories of cognitive consistency: A sourcebook.* Chicago: Rand McNally and Company, 1968.

Brookshire, K. H., Warren, J. M., & Ball, G. G. Reversal and transfer learning following overtraining in rat and chicken. *Journal of Comparative Psychology,* 1961, **54,** 48–102.

Brown, R. *Social psychology.* New York: Free Press, 1965.

Brown, R., & Bellugi, U. Three processes in the child's acquisition of syntax. *Harvard Educational Review,* 1964, **34,** 133–151.

Brown, R., & Berko, J. Word-association and the acquisition of grammar. *Child Development,* 1960, **31,** 8–14.

Brown, R., & Fraser, C. The acquisition of syntax. In C. N. Cofer & B. Musgrave (Eds.), *Verbal behavior and learning.* New York: McGraw-Hill, 1963. Pp. 158–197.

Brown, R., & Hildum, D. C. Expectancy and the perception of syllables. *Language,* 1956, **32,** 411–419.

Brown, R. W., & Lenneberg, E. H. A study in language and cognition. *Journal of Abnormal and Social Psychology,* 1954, **49,** 454–462.

Bruner, J. S. On the conservation of liquids. In J. S. Bruner, R. R. Olver, & P. M. Greenfield (Eds.), *Studies in cognitive growth.* New York: Wiley, 1966.

Bruner, J. S., Goodnow, J. J., & Austin, G. A. *A study of thinking.* New York: Science Editions, 1962.

Bruner, J. S., Olver, R. R., & Greenfield, P. M. (Eds.), *Studies in cognitive growth.* New York: Wiley, 1966.

Burnstein, E. Sources of cognitive bias in the representation of simple social structures: Balance, minimal change, positivity, reciprocity, and the respondent's own attitude. *Journal of Personality and Social Psychology,* 1967, **7,** 36–48.

Burtt, H. E. An experimental study of early childhood memory. *Journal of General Psychology,* 1941, **58,** 435–439.

Buss, A. H. Rigidity as a function of reversal and nonreversal shifts in the learning of successive discriminations. *Journal of Experimental Psychology,* 1953, **45,** 75–81.

Butterfield, E. C. The interruption of tasks: Methodological, factual, and theoretical issues. *Psychological Bulletin,* 1964, **62,** 309–322.

Campbell, D. T., Hunt, W. A., & Lewis, N. A. The effect of assimilation and contrast in judgment of clinical materials. *American Journal of Psychology,* 1957, **70,** 297–312.

Campbell, D. T., Lewis, N. A., & Hunt, W. A. Context effects with judgmental language that is absolute, extensive, and extra-experimentally anchored. *Journal of Experimental Psychology,* 1958, **55,** 220–228.

Carlsmith, J. M., Collins, B. E., & Helmreich, R. L. Studies in forced compliance: I. The effect of pressure for compliance on attitude change produced by face-to-face role playing and anonymous essay writing. *Journal of Personality and Social Psychology,* 1966, **4,** 1–13.

Carmichael, L., Hogan, H. P., & Walter, A. A. An experimental study of the effect of language on the reproduction of visually perceived forms. *Journal of Experimental Psychology,* 1932, **15,** 73–86.

Carroll, J. B. Review of the measurement of meaning. *Language,* 1959, **35,** 58–77.
Carroll, J. B. *Language and thought.* Englewood Cliffs, N. J.: Prentice-Hall, 1964.
Cazden, C. B. Environmental assistance to the child's acquisition of grammar. Unpublished doctoral dissertation. Graduate School of Education, Harvard University, 1965.
Chatterjee, B. B., & Eriksen, C. W. Conditioning and generalization of GSR as a function of awareness. *Journal of Abnormal and Social Psychology,* 1960, **60,** 396–403.
Chomsky, N. A review of B. F. Skinner's "Verbal Behavior." *Language,* 1959, **35,** 26–58.
Chomsky, N. *Aspects of the theory of syntax.* Cambridge, Mass.: MIT Press, 1965.
Chomsky, N. *Cartesian linguistics.* New York: Harper & Row, 1966.
Chomsky, N. Language and the mind. *Psychology Today,* 1968, **1,** No. 9, 48.
Cliff, N. Adverbs as multipliers. *Psychological Review,* 1959, **66,** 27–44.
Cofer, C. N., & Shevitz, R. Word-association as a function of word-frequency. *American Journal of Psychology,* 1952, **65,** 75–79.
Cohen, B. D., Kalish, H. I., Thruston, J. R., & Cohen, E. Experimental manipulation of verbal behavior. *Journal of Experimental Psychology,* 1954, **47,** 106–110.
Cohen, I. Programed learning and the Socratic dialogue. *American Psychologist,* 1962, **17,** 772–775.
Conrad, R. Errors of immediate memory. *British Journal of Psychology,* 1959, **50,** 349.
Conrad, R. On association between memory errors and errors due to acoustic masking of speech. *Nature,* 1962, **196,** 1314–1315.
Conrad, R. Acoustic confusions in immediate memory. *British Journal of Psychology,* 1964, **55,** 75–83.
Cottrell, N. B., & Wack, D. L. Energizing effects of cognitive dissonance upon dominant and subordinate responses. *Journal of Personality and Social Psychology,* 1967, **6,** 132–138.
Cramer, P. *Word association.* New York: Academic Press, 1968.
Crowne, D. P., & Strickland, B. R. The conditioning of verbal behavior as a function of the need for social approval. *Journal of Abnormal and Social Psychology,* 1961, **63,** 395–401.
DeBurger, R. A., & Donahue, J. W. Relationship between the meanings of verbal stimuli and their associative responses. *Journal of Verbal Learning and Verbal Behavior,* 1965, **4,** 25–31.
Deese, J. *The psychology of learning.* New York: McGraw-Hill, 1958.
Deese, J. Influence of inter-item associative strength upon immediate recall. *Psychological Reports,* 1959, **5,** 305–312.
Deese, J. *Principles of psychology.* Boston: Allyn and Bacon, 1964.
Deese, J. *The structure of associations in language and thought.* Baltimore: Johns Hopkins Press, 1965.
Deese, J. *Psycholinguistics.* Boston: Allyn and Bacon, Inc., 1970.
DeSoto, C. B., & Kuethe, J. L. Perception of mathematical properties of interpersonal relations. *Perceptual and Motor Skills,* 1958, **8,** 279–286.
DeSoto, C. B., & Kuethe, J. L. Subjective probabilities of interpersonal relationships. *Journal of Abnormal and Social Psychology,* 1959, **59,** 290–294.

Dinoff, M. Subject awareness of examiner influence in a testing situation. *Journal of Consulting Psychology,* 1960, **24,** 465.
Diven, K. Certain determinants in the conditioning of anxiety reactions. *Journal of Psychology,* 1937, **3,** 291–308.
Dixon, P. W., & Oakes, W. F. Effects of intertrial activity on the relationship between awareness and verbal operant conditioning. *Journal of Experimental Psychology,* 1965, **69,** 152–157.
Dollard, J., & Miller, N. E. *Personality and psychotherapy.* New York: McGraw-Hill, 1950.
Dreyfuss, H. L. *Alchemy and artificial intelligence. Rand Corporation Technical Report P3244.* Santa Monica, Calif.: RAND Corporation, 1965.
Dulany, D. E. Hypotheses and habits in verbal "operant conditioning." *Journal of Abnormal and Social Psychology,* 1961, **63,** 251–263.
Dulany, D. E. The place of hypotheses and intentions: An analysis of verbal control in verbal conditioning. In C. W. Eriksen (Ed.), *Behavior and awareness.* Durham, N. C.: Duke University Press, 1962.
Duncan, C. P. *Thinking: Current experimental studies.* New York: Lippincott, 1967.
Duncker, K. On problem solving. (Trans. from 1935 original.) *Psychological Monographs,* 1945, **58**(270).
Dunnette, M. D., Campbell, J., & Jaastad, K. The effect of group participation on brainstorming effectiveness for two industrial samples. *Journal of Applied Psychology,* 1963, **47,** 30–37.
Dustin, D. S., & Baldwin, P. M. Redundancy in impression formation. *Journal of Personality and Social Psychology,* 1966, **3,** 500–506.
Ebbinghaus, H. *Memory.* Trans. by H. A. Ruges, & C. E. Bussenius. New York: Columbia University Press, 1913.
Edwards, W., Lindman, H., & Phillips, L. D. Emerging technologies for making decisions. In T. M. Newcomb (Ed.), *New directions in psychology* II. New York: Holt, 1965.
Einhorn, H. J. The use of nonlinear, noncompensatory models in decision making. *Psychological Bulletin,* 1970, **73,** 221–230.
Elkind, D., & Flavell, J. H. (Eds.) *Studies in cognitive development: Essays in honor of Jean Piaget.* New York: Oxford University Press, 1969.
Elms, A. C., & Janis, I. L. Counter-norm attitude induced by consonant versus dissonant conditions of role-playing. *Journal of Experimental Research in Personality,* 1965, **1,** 50–60.
Eriksen, C. W. Unconscious processes. In M. R. Jones (Ed.), *Nebraska symposium on motivation.* Lincoln: University of Nebraska Press, 1958. Pp. 169–227.
Eriksen, C. W. (Ed.) *Behavior and awareness.* Durham, N. C.: Duke University Press, 1962.
Ervin, S. Imitation and structural change in children's language. In E. H. Lenneberg (Ed.), *New directions in the study of language.* Cambridge, Mass.: MIT Press, 1964. Pp. 163–190.
Feather, N. T. Cigarette smoking and lung cancer: A study of cognitive dissonance. *Australian Journal of Psychology,* 1962, **14,** 55–64.
Feather, N. T. Cognitive dissonance, sensitivity, and evaluation. *Journal of Abnormal and Social Psychology,* 1963, **66,** 157–163.
Feather, N. T. A structural balance approach to the analysis of communication effects.

In L. Berkowitz (Ed.), *Advances in experimental social psychology,* Vol. 3. New York: Academic Press, 1967.
Feigenbaum, E. A., & Feldman, J. (Eds.) *Computers and thought.* New York: McGraw-Hill, 1963.
Feldman, R. E. On the influence of value upon free recall. Master's thesis. Cited in J. Deese, *The structure of associations in language and thought.* Baltimore: Johns Hopkins Press, 1965.
Ferster, C. B., & Skinner, B. F. *Schedules of reinforcement.* New York: Appleton-Century-Crofts, 1957.
Festinger, L. *A theory of cognitive dissonance.* Stanford, Calif.: Stanford University Press, 1957.
Festinger, L., & Carlsmith, J. M. Cognitive consequences of forced compliance. *Journal of Abnormal and Social Psychology,* 1959, **58,** 203–210.
Fishbein, M., & Hunter, R. Summation versus balance in attitude organization and change. *Journal of Abnormal and Social Psychology,* 1964, **69,** 505–510. (a)
Fishbein, M., & Hunter, R. Summation vs. balance: A replication and extension. Paper read at a meeting of the Western Psychological Association, 1964. (b)
Flanders, J. P. A review of research on imitative behavior. *Psychological Bulletin,* 1968, **69,** 316–337.
Flavell, J. H. *The developmental psychology of Jean Piaget.* Princeton, N. J.: Van Nostrand, 1963.
Flesch, R. A new readability yardstick. *Journal of Applied Psychology,* 1948, **32,** 221–233.
Fodor, J., & Bever, T. The psychological reality of linguistic segments. *Journal of Verbal Learning and Verbal Behavior,* 1965, **4,** 414–420.
Fowler, H. *Curiosity and exploratory behavior.* New York: Macmillan, 1965.
Freedman, J. L. Long-term behavioral effects of cognitive dissonance. *Journal of Experimental and Social Psychology,* 1965, **1,** 145–155.
Freedman, J. L., & Sears, D. O. Selective exposure. In L. Berkowitz (Ed.), *Advances in experimental social psychology,* Vol. 2. New York: Academic Press, 1965.
Freibergs, V., & Tulving, E. The effect of practice on utilization of information from positive and negative instances in concept identification. *Canadian Journal of Psychology,* 1961, **15,** 101–106.
Freud, S. Collected papers, Vol. IV. London: Hogarth, 1946 (Original publication, 1915).
Furth, H. G. Linguistic deficiency and thinking: Research with deaf subjects 1964–1969. *Psychological Bulletin,* 1971, **74,** in press.
Gardner, R. A., & Gardner, B. T. Teaching sign language to a chimpanzee. *Science,* 1969, **165,** 664–672.
Garrett, M., Bever, T., & Fodor, J. The active use of grammar in speech perception. *Perception and Psychophysics,* 1966, **1,** 30–32.
Gelernter, H. L., & Rochester, N. Intelligent behavior in problem-solving machines. *IBM Journal of Research Development,* 1958, **2,** 336–345.
Gerard, H. B. Choice difficulty, dissonance, and the decision sequence. *Journal of Personality,* 1967, **35,** 91–108.
Gerard, H. B., Blevans, S. A., & Malcolm, T. Self-evaluation and the evaluation of choice alternatives. *Journal of Personality,* 1964, **32,** 395–410.
Gerard, H. B., & Mathewson, G. C. The effects of severity of initiation on liking for a

group: A replication. *Journal of Experimental Social Psychology,* 1966, **2,** 278–287.
Glaze, J. A. The association value of nonsense syllables. *Journal of Genetic Psychology,* 1928, **35,** 255–267.
Glanzer, M., & Clark, W. H. Accuracy of perceptual recall: An analysis of organization. *Journal of Verbal Learning and Verbal Behavior*, 1963, **1,** 289–299.
Glucksberg, S. The influence of strength of drive on functional fixedness and perceptual recognition. *Journal of Experimental Psychology*, 1962, **63,** 36–41.
Goldberg, L. R. Simple models or simple processes? Some research on clinical judgments. *American Psychologist*, 1968, **23,** 483–496.
Goldberg, P. A. Expectancy, choice and the other person. *Journal of Personality and Social Psychology,* 1965, **2,** 685–691.
Goldstein, L. S., & Gotkin, G. A review of research: Teaching machines vs. programed textbooks as presentation models. *Journal of Programed Instruction,* 1962, **1,** 29–42.
Gollob, H. F. Impression formation and word combination in sentences. *Journal of Personality and Social Psychology*, 1968, **10,** 341–353.
Gordon, G., & Charanian, T. Measuring the creativity of research scientists and engineers. (Working paper) Project on Research Administration, University of Chicago, 1964.
Gormezano, I., & Grant, D. A. Progressive ambiguity in the attainment of concepts on the Wisconsin card sorting test. *Journal of Experimental Psychology*, 1958, **55,** 621–627.
Greco, P., Grize, J. B., Papert, S., & Piaget, J. *Problems d' épistémologie génétique.* Vol. II. Paris: Presses Univer. France, 1960.
Greenberg, J. H. Some universals of grammar with particular reference to the order of meaningful elements. In J. H. Greenberg (Ed.), *Universals of language*. Cambridge, Mass.: MIT Press, 1962. Pp. 58–90.
Greenberg, J. H., & Jenkins, J. J. Studies in the psychological correlates of the sound system of American English, *Word,* 1964, **20**(2), 157–177.
Greenspoon, J. The reinforcing effect of two spoken sounds on the frequency of two responses. *American Journal of Psychology,* 1955, **68,** 409–416.
Grice, G. R. The relation of secondary reinforcement to delayed reward in visual discrimination learning. *Journal of Experimental Psychology*, 1948, **38,** 1–16.
Guthrie, E. R. *The psychology of learning*. New York: Harper, 1935.
Guthrie, E. R., & Horton, G. P. *Cats in a puzzle box.* New York: Rinehart, 1946.
Guy, D. E., Van Fleet, F. M., & Bourne, L. E., Jr. Effects of adding a stimulus dimension prior to a nonreversal shift. *Journal of Experimental Psychology,* 1966, **72,** 161–168.
Hall, J. F. *The psychology of learning*. New York: Lippincott, 1966.
Harlow, H. F. The formation of learning sets. *Psychological Review,* 1949, **56,** 51–65.
Harrow, M., & Friedman, G. B. Comparing reversal and nonreversal shifts in concept formation with partial reinforcement controlled. *Journal of Experimental Psychology,* 1958, **55,** 592–598.
Heider, F. *The psychology of interpersonal relations*. New York: Wiley, 1958.
Heintz, R. K. The effect of remote anchoring points upon the judgment of lifted weights. *Journal of Experimental Psychology*, 1950, **40,** 584–591.

Helson, H. *Adaptation-level theory: An experimental and systematic approach to behavior.* New York: Harper and Row, 1964.

Herman, D. T., Lawless, R. H., & Marshall, R. W. Variables in the effect of language on the reproduction of visually perceived forms. *Perceptual Motor Skills,* 1957, **7,** 171–186.

Hicks, J. M., & Campbell, D. T. Zero-point scaling as affected by social object, scaling method, and context. *Journal of Personality and Social Psychology,* 1965, **2,** 793–808.

Hilgard, E. R. *Introduction to psychology* (3rd ed.) New York: Harcourt, 1962.

Hoffman, L. R., & Maier, N. R. F. Quality and acceptance of problem solutions by members of homogeneous and heterogeneous groups. *Journal of Abnormal and Social Psychology,* 1961, **62,** 401–407.

Holmes, D. S. Search for "closure" in a visually perceived pattern. *Psychological Bulletin,* 1968, **70,** 296–312.

Houston, J. P., & Mednick, S. A. Creativity and the need for novelty. *Journal of Abnormal and Social Psychology,* 1963, **66,** 137–141.

Hovland, C. I. A "communication analysis" of concept learning. *Psychological Bulletin,* 1952, **59,** 461–472.

Hovland, C. I. Computer simulation of thinking. *American Psychologist,* 1960, **15,** 687–693.

Hovland, C. I., Harvey, O. J., & Sherif, M. Assimilation and contrast effects in reaction to communication and attitude change. *Journal of Abnormal and Social Psychology,* 1957, **55,** 244–252.

Hovland, C. I., & Weiss, W. The influence of source credibility on communicator effectiveness. *Public Opinion Quarterly*, 1952, **15,** 635–650.

Hovland, C. I., & Weiss, W. Transmission of information concerning concepts through positive and negative instances. *Journal of Experimental Psychology,* 1953, **45,** 165–182.

Howe, E. S. Probabilistic adverbial qualifications of adjectives. *Journal of Verbal Learning and Verbal Behavior,* 1963, **1,** 225–242.

Howes, D. On the relation between the probability of a word as an association and in general linguistic usage. *Journal of Abnormal and Social Psychology,* 1957, **54,** 75–85.

Hull, C. L. Quantitative aspects of the evolution of concepts. *Psychological Monographs,* 1920 (123).

Hunt, E. B., & Hovland, C. I. Order of consideration of different types of concepts. *Journal of Experimental Psychology,* 1960, **59,** 220–225.

Hunt, J. McV. *Intelligence and experience.* New York: Ronald Press, 1961.

Hunter, W. S. The delayed reaction in animals and children. *Animal Behavior Monograph,* 1912, **2**(1).

Hunter, W. S., & Bartlett, S. C. Double alternation behavior in young children. *Journal of Experimental Psychology,* 1948, **38,** 558–567.

Inhelder, B., & Piaget, J. *The growth of logical thinking from childhood to adolescence: An essay on the construction of formal operational structures.* (Trans. by A. Parsons & S. Milgram.) New York: Basic Books, 1958.

Jakobovits, L. A. Effects of mere exposure: A comment. *Journal of Personality and Social Psychology, Monograph Supplement,* 1968, **9,** Part 2, 30–32.

Jakobovits, L. A., & Miron, M. S. (Eds.) *Readings in the psychology of language.* Englewood Cliffs, N. J.: Prentice-Hall, 1967.
Jenkins, J. G., & Dallenbach, K. M. Obliviscence during sleep and waking. *American Journal of Psychology,* 1924, **35,** 605–612.
Jenkins, J. J., & Palermo, D. S. Mediation processes and the acquisition of linguistic structure. In U. Bellugi & R. Brown (Eds.), *The acquisition of language.* Monograph for the Society for Research in Child Development, 1964.
Johnson, N. The psychological reality of phrase structure rules. *Journal of Verbal Learning and Verbal Behavior,* 1965, **4,** 469–475.
Jones, A. Information deprivation in humans. In B. Maher (Ed.), *Progress in experimental personality research,* 1966, **3,** 241–307.
Jones, A., Manis, M., & Weiner, B. Learning as a function of subliminal reinforcements. *Psychological Reports,* 1963, **12,** 387–398.
Jordan, N. Behavioral forces that are a function of attitudes and of cognitive organization. *Human Relations,* 1953, **6,** 273–287.
Judson, A. I., & Cofer, C. N. Reasoning as an associative process: I. "Direction" in a simple verbal problem. *Psychological Reports,* 1956, **2,** 469–476.
Jung, C. G. *Studies in word-association.* London: Heinemann, 1918.
Kamin, L. Conditioning to the elements of a compound stimulus, *18th International Congress of Psychology, Symposium 4,* pp. 80–84.
Katona, G. *Organizing and memorizing.* New York: Columbia University Press, 1940.
Kelley, H. H., Thibaut, J. W., Radloff, R., & Mundy, D. The development of cooperation in the "minimal social situation." *Psychological Monographs,* 1962, **76** (19, Whole No. 538).
Kelman, H. C., & Hovland, C. I. "Reinstatement" of the communicator in delayed measurement of opinion change. *Journal of Abnormal and Social Psychology,* 1953, **48,** 327–335.
Kendler, H. H. *Basic psychology.* New York: Appleton-Century-Crofts, 1963.
Kendler, H. H., & D'Amato, M. F. A comparison of reversal and nonreversal shifts in human concept formation behavior. *Journal of Experimental Psychology,* 1955, **49,** 165–174.
Kendler, H. H., & Kendler, T. S. Vertical and horizontal processes in problem solving. *Psychological Review,* 1962, **69,** 1–16.
Kendler, H. H., Kendler, T. S., & Sanders, J. Reversal and partial reversal shifts with verbal material. *Journal of Verbal Learning and Verbal Behavior,* 1967, **6,** 117–127.
Kendler, T. S. Verbalization and optional reversal shifts among kindergarten children. *Journal of Verbal Learning and Verbal Behavior,* 1964, **3,** 428–436.
Kent, G. H., & Rosanoff, A. J. A study of association in insanity. *American Journal of Insanity,* 1910, **67,** 37–96.
Kimble, G. A. Classical conditioning and awareness. In C. W. Eriksen (Ed.), *Behavior and awareness.* Durham, N. C.: Duke University Press, 1962.
Kohler, W. *The mentality of apes.* New York: Harcourt, 1925.
Korzybski, A. *Science and sanity.* Lancaster, Pa.: Science Press, 1933.
Koslin, B. L., & Pargament, R. Effects of attitude on discrimination of opinion statements. *Journal of Experimental Social Psychology,* 1969, **5,** 245–264.

Krantz, D. L., & Campbell, D. T. Separating perceptual and linguistic effects of context

shifts upon absolute judgments. *Journal of Experimental Psychology,* 1961, **62,** 35–42.
Krasner, L. Verbal operant conditioning and awareness. In K. Salzinger & S. Salzinger (Eds.), *Research in verbal behavior and some neurophysiological implications.* New York: Academic Press, 1967.
Krauss, R. M., & Weinheimer, S. Changes in reference phrases as a function of frequency of usage in social interaction: A preliminary study. *Psychonomic Science,* 1964, **1,** 113–114. (a)
Krauss, R. M., & Weinheimer, S. The effect of feedback on changes in reference phrases. Paper read at a meeting of the Psychonomic Society, Niagara Falls, 1964. (b)
Lacey, J. I., & Smith, R. L. Conditioning and generalization of unconscious anxiety. *Science,* 1954, **120,** 1045–1052.
Lambert, W. E., & Jakobovits, L. A. Verbal satiation and changes in the intensity of meaning. *Journal of Experimental Psychology,* 1960, **60,** 376–383.
Lane, H., & Bem, D. A. *Laboratory manual for the control and analysis of behavior.* Belmont, Calif.: Wadsworth, 1965.
Lantz, D., & Stefflre, V. Language and cognition revisited. *Journal of Abnormal and Social Psychology,* 1964, **69,** 472–481.
Lanyon, R. I. Reports of awareness in verbal operant conditioning. *Psychological Reports,* 1967, **20,** (3, Pt. 2), 1051–1057.
Lanyon, R. I., & Drotar, D. Verbal conditioning: Intelligence and reported awareness. Paper read at meeting of the Eastern Psychological Association, 1966.
Lashley, K. S. The problem of serial order in behavior. In L. A. Jeffress (Ed.), *Cerebral mechanisms in behavior,* New York: Wiley, 1951. Pp. 112–136.
Lazarus, R., & McCleary, R. Autonomic discrimination without awareness. *Psychological Review,* 1951, **58,** 113–122.
Lehman, H. C. *Age and achievement.* Princeton, N. J.: Princeton University Press, 1953.
Lenneberg, E. H. Language evolution and purposive behavior. In S. Diamond (Ed.), *Culture in history: Essays in honor of Paul Radin.* New York: Columbia University Press, 1960. Pp. 869–893.
Lenneberg, E. H. *Biological foundations of language.* New York: Wiley, 1967.
Levin, G., & Shapiro, D. The operant conditioning of conversation. *Journal of the Experimental Analysis of Behavior,* 1962, **5,** 309–316.
Levine, M. Hypotheses behavior by humans during discrimination learning. *Journal of Experimental Psychology,* 1966, **71,** 331–338.
Lewis, D. J. Partial reinforcement: A selective review of the literature since 1950. *Psychological Bulletin,* 1960, **57,** 1–28.
Lewis, H. B., & Franklin, M. An experimental study of the role of the ego in work: II. The significance of task orientation in work. *Journal of Experimental Psychology,* 1944, **34,** 195–215.
Lilly, R. S., & Rajecki, D. W. Scale value of comparative and superlative forms of adjectives as a function of the basic form scale values. *Psychological Reports,* 1969, **24,** 399–403.
Lorge, I., & Thorndike, E. L. The influence of delay in the aftereffect of a connection. *Journal of Experimental Psychology,* 1935, **18,** 186–194.

Luchins, A. S. Mechanization in problem solving: The effect of Einstellung. *Psychological Monographs,* 1942, **54**(248).
Luchins, A. S. *Examination of rigidity of behavior.* New York: Regional Office of the Veterans Administration, 1948.
Luchins, A. S., & Luchins, E. S. *Rigidity of behavior: A variational approach to the effect of Einstellung.* Eugene, Ore.: University of Oregon Books, 1959.
Lugg, A. M., & Gollob, H. F. Conditions which affect whether trait words sum or average. Unpublished manuscript, 1970.
Mackintosh, N. J. Incidental cue learning in rats. *Quarterly Journal of Experimental Psychology,* 1965, **17,** 292–300.
Maddi, S. R. Meaning, novelty, and affect: Comments on Zajonc's paper. *Journal of Personality and Social Psychology, Monograph Supplement,* 1968, **9,** Part 2, 28–29.
Maier, N. R. F. Reasoning in white rats. *Comparative Psychological Monographs,* 1929, **6**(29).
Maier, N. R. F. Reasoning in humans: II. The solution of a problem and its appearance in consciousness. *Journal of Comparative Psychology,* 1931, **12,** 181–194.
Maier, N. R. F. Leadership principle for problem solving conferences. *Michigan Business Review,* 1962, **14**(3), 8–15.
Malewski, A. The influence of positive and negative self-evaluation on post-decisional dissonance. *Polish Sociological Bulletin,* 1962, **3–4,** 39–49.
Maltzman, I. On the training of originality. *Psychological Review,* 1960, **67,** 229–242.
Maltzman, I., Eisman, E., Brook, L. O., & Smith, W. M. Task instructions for anagrams following different task instructions and training. *Journal of Experimental Psychology,* 1956, **51,** 418–420.
Mandler, G. Organization and memory. In K. W. Spence & J. T. Spence (Eds.), *Psychology of learning and motivation,* Vol. 1. New York: Academic Press, 1967. (a)
Mandler, G. Verbal learning. In T. M. Newcomb (Ed.), *New directions in psychology III.* New York: Holt, 1967. (b)
Mandler, J. M., & Mandler, G. *Thinking: From association to Gestalt.* New York: Wiley, 1964.
Manis, M. The interpretation of opinion statements as a function of message ambiguity and recipient attitude. *Journal of Abnormal and Social Psychology,* 1961, **63,** 76–81. (a)
Manis, M. The interpretation of opinion statements as a function of recipient attitude and source prestige. *Journal of Abnormal and Social Psychology,* 1961, **63,** 82–86. (b)
Manis, M. Context effects in communication. *Journal of Personality and Social Psychology,* 1967, **5,** 326–334.
Manis, M. Some recent trends in the study of social judgment. In J. Hellmuth (Ed.), *Cognitive studies,* Vol. I. New York: Brunner/Mazel, Inc., 1970.
Manis, M. Context effects in communication: Determinants of verbal output and referential decoding. In M. H. Appley (Ed.), *Adaptation-level theory: A symposium.* New York: Academic Press, 1971, in press.
Manis, M., & Armstrong, G. W. More context effects in communication. *Journal of Experimental Social Psychology,* in press.
Manis, M., & Barnes, E. J. Learning without awareness and mediated generalization. *The American Journal of Psychology,* 1961, **74,** 425–432.

Manis, M., Gleason, T. G., & Dawes, R. M. The evaluation of complex social stimuli. *Journal of Personality and Social Psychology,* 1966, **3,** 404–419.
Manis, M., & Ruppe, J. The carryover phenomenon: The persistence of a reinforced behavior despite the absence of a conscious behavioral intention. *Journal of Personality and Social Psychology,* 1969, **11,** 397–407.
Matthews, W. A. Transformational complexity and short-term recall. *Language and Speech,* 1968, **11,** 120–128.
Max, L. W. An experimental study of the motor theory of consciousness: III. Action-current responses in deaf-mutes during sleep, sensory stimulation, and dreams. *Journal of Comparative and Physiological Psychology,* 1935, **19,** 469–486.
Max, L. W. An experimental study of the motor theory of consciousness: IV. Action-current responses in the deaf during awakening, kinesthetic imagery, and abstract thinking. *Journal of Comparative and Physiological Psychology,* 1937, **24,** 301–344.
McCullough, K. P. The influence of experimenter status upon verbal conditioning. Unpublished master's thesis, University of Iowa, 1962.
McGinnies, E. Emotionality and perceptual defense. *Psychological Review,* 1949, **56,** 244–251.
McGuigan, F. J. (Ed.) *Thinking: Studies of covert behavior.* New York: Appleton-Century-Crofts, 1966.
McGuigan, F. J. Covert oral behavior during the silent performance of language tasks. *Psychological Bulletin,* 1970, **73,** in press.
McGuire, W. J. Cognitive consistency and attitude change. *Journal of Abnormal and Social Psychology,* 1960, **60,** 354–358.
McNeil, D. Developmental psycholinguistics. In F. Smith & G. A. Miller (Eds.), *The genesis of language: A psycholinguistic approach.* Cambridge, Mass.: MIT Press, 1968. Pp. 15–84.
Mechanic, A. The responses involved in the rote learning of verbal materials. *Journal of Verbal Learning and Verbal Behavior,* 1964, **3,** 30–36.
Mednick, M. T. Research creativity in psychology graduate students. *Journal of Consulting Psychology,* 1963, **27,** 265–266.
Mednick, S. A. The associative basis of the creative process. *Psychological Review,* 1962, **69,** 220–228.
Mehler, J. How some sentences are remembered. Unpublished doctoral dissertation, Harvard University, 1964.
Mehler, J., & Bever, T. G. Cognitive capacity of very young children. *Science,* 1967, **158,** 141–142.
Melton, A. W. Implications of short-term memory for a general theory of memory. *Journal of Verbal Learning and Verbal Behavior,* 1963, **2,** 1–21.
Mendelsohn, G. A., & Griswold, B. B. Differential use of incidental stimuli in problem-solving as a function of creativity. *Journal of Abnormal and Social Psychology,* 1964, **68,** 431–436.
Mendelsohn, G. A., & Griswold, B. B. Assessed creative potential, vocabulary level, and sex, as predictors of the use of incidental cues in verbal problem solving. *Journal of Personality and Social Psychology,* 1966, **4,** 423–431.
Miller, G. A. *Language and communication.* New York: McGraw-Hill, 1951.
Miller, G. A. The magical number seven; plus or minus two: Some limits on our

capacity for processing information. *Psychological Review,* 1956, **63,** 81–97.

Miller, G. A., Heise, G. A., & Lichter, W. The intelligibility of speech as a function of the context of the test materials. *Journal of Experimental Psychology,* 1951, **41,** 329–335.

Miller, G. A. The psycholinguists. *Encounter,* 1964, **18**(1), 29–40.

Miller, G. A. & McNeill, D. Psycholinguistics. In G. Lindzey & E. Aronson (Eds.), *The handbook of social psychology,* Vol. III, (2nd ed.) Reading, Mass.: Addison-Wesley, 1968.

Miller, G. A., & Selfridge, J. A. Verbal context and recall of meaningful material. *American Journal of Psychology,* 1950, **63,** 176–185.

Miller, J. W., & Rowe, P. M. Influence of favorable and unfavorable information upon assessment decisions. *Journal of Applied Psychology,* 1967, **51,** 432–435.

Miller, N. E., & Dollard, J. *Social learning and imitation.* New Haven, Conn.: Yale University Press, 1941.

Miller, S. A. Extinction of conservation: A methodological and theoretical analysis. *Merrill-Palmer Quarterly,* 1971, in press.

Mills, J., & Ross, A. Effects of commitment and certainty upon interest in supporting information. *Journal of Abnormal and Social Psychology,* 1964, **68,** 552–555.

Mischel, W. Preference for delayed reward and social responsibility. *Journal of Abnormal and Social Psychology,* 1961, **62,** 1–7.

Mosher, F. A., & Hornsby, J. R. On asking questions. In J. S. Bruner, R. R. Olver, & P. M. Greenfield (Eds.), *Studies in cognitive growth.* New York: Wiley, 1966.

Neisser, U. *Cognitive psychology.* New York: Appleton-Century-Crofts, 1967.

Newcomb, T. M. Interpersonal balance. In R. P. Abelson et al. (Eds.), *Theories of cognitive consistency: A sourcebook.* Chicago: Rand McNally, 1968.

Newell, A., Shaw, J. C., & Simon, H. A. Elements of a theory of human problem-solving. *Psychological Review,* 1958, **65,** 151–166.

Newhall, S. M., & Sears, R. R. Conditioning finger retraction to visual stimuli near the absolute threshold. *Comparative Psychology Monographs,* 1933, **9**(43).

Noble, C. E. The meaning-familiarity relationship. *Psychological Review,* 1953, **60,** 89–98.

Norman, D. A. *Memory and attention.* New York: Wiley, 1969.

O'Neil, W. M. The effect of verbal association on tachistoscopic recognition. *Australian Journal of Psychology,* 1953, **49,** 333–338.

Osborn, A. F. *Applied imagination.* New York: Scribners, 1953.

Osgood, C. E. *Method and theory in experimental psychology.* New York: Oxford University Press, 1953.

Osgood, C. E., Suci, G., & Tannenbaum, P. *The measurement of meaning.* Urbana: University of Illinois Press, 1957.

Osler, S. F., & Fivel, M. W. Concept attainment: I. The role of age and intelligence in concept attainment by induction. *Journal of Experimental Psychology,* 1961, **62,** 1–8.

Osler, S. F., & Trautman, G. E. Concept attainment: II. Effect of stimulus complexity upon concept attainment at two levels of intelligence. *Journal of Experimental Psychology,* 1961, **62,** 9–13.

Page, M. M. Social psychology of a classical conditioning of attitudes experiment. Journal of Personality and Social Psychology, 1969, **11,** 177–186.
Paige, G., & Simon, H. Cognitive processes in solving algebra word problems. In B. Kleinmuntz (Ed.), *Problem solving: Research, method, and theory.* New York: Wiley, 1966.
Palermo, D. S., & Jenkins, J. J. Changes in the word associations of fourth- and fifth-grade children from 1916 to 1961. *Journal of Verbal Learning and Verbal Behavior,* 1965, **72,** 77–84.
Pelz, D. C., & Andrews, F. M. *Scientists in organizations.* New York: Wiley, 1966.
Piaget, J. *Classes, relations et nombres: Essai sur les "groupements" de la logistique et la reversibilité de la pensée.* Paris: Vrin, 1942.
Piaget, J. *Play, dreams, and imitation in childhood.* (Trans. by C. Gattagno & F. M. Hodgson.) New York: Norton, 1951.
Piaget, J. *The child's conception of number.* New York: Humanities, 1952.
Piaget, J. Quantification, conservation, and nativism. *Science,* 1968, **162,** 976–981.
Piaget, J., & Inhelder, B. *The child's conception of space.* London: Routledge and Kegen Paul, 1956.
Postman, L. The acquisition and retention of consistent associative responses. *Journal of Experimental Psychology,* 1964, **67,** 183–190.
Postman, L., & Adams, P. A. Performance variables in the experimental analysis of the law of effect. *American Journal of Psychology,* 1954, **67,** 612–631.
Powell, F. Source credibility and behavioral compliance as determinants of attitude change. *Journal of Personality and Social Psychology,* 1965, **2,** 669–676.
Premack, D. A chimp learns the language. *Psychology Today,* 1970, **4,** No. 4, 54–58.
Rees, H. J., & Israel, H. E. An investigation of the establishment and operation of mental sets. *Psychological Monographs,* 1935, **46** (6, Whole No. 210).
Reitman, W. *Cognition and thought.* New York: Wiley, 1965.
Renner, K. E. Delay of reinforcement: A historical review. *Psychological Bulletin,* 1964, **61,** 341–361.
Restle, F. The selection of strategies in cue learning. *Psychological Review,* 1962, **69,** 11–19.
Rheingold, H. L., Gewirtz, J. L., Ross, H. W. Social conditioning of vocalizations in the infant. *Journal of Comparative and Physiological Psychology,* 1959, **52,** 68–73.
Rosenberg, M. J. When dissonance fails: On eliminating evaluation apprehension from attitude measurement. *Journal of Personality and Social Psychology,* 1965, **1,** 28–42.
Rosenfeld, H. M., & Baer, D. M. Unnoticed verbal conditioning of an aware experimenter by a more aware subject: The double-agent effect. *Psychological Review,* 1969, **76,** 425–432.
Rosenstein, J. Cognitive abilities of deaf children. *Journal of Speech and Hearing Research,* 1960, **3,** 108–119.
Rosenthal, R. *Experimenter effects in behavioral research.* New York: Appleton-Century-Crofts, 1966.
Rosenzweig, S. An experimental study of "repression" with special reference to need-persistive and ego-defensive reactions to frustration. *Journal of Experimental Psychology,* 1943, **32,** 64–74.

Rouse, R. O., & Verinis, J. S. The effect of associative connections on the recognition of flashed words. *Journal of Verbal Learning and Verbal Behavior,* 1963, **1,** 300–303.

Russell, J. Reversal and nonreversal shifts in deaf and hearing kindergarten children. Unpublished master's thesis, Catholic University of America, 1964. Cited by H. G. Furth, Research with the deaf: Implications for language and cognition. *Psychological Bulletin,* 1964, **62,** 152.

Russell, W. A., & Jenkins, J. J. The complete Minnesota norms for responses to 100 words from the Kent-Rosanoff word association test. *Technical Report No. 11.* The Office of Naval Research and The University of Minnesota, 1954.

Ryan, J. J. III. Comparison of verbal response transfer mediated by meaningfully similar and associated stimuli. *Journal of Experimental Psychology,* 1960, **60,** 408–415.

Samuel, A. L. Some studies in machine learning using the game of checkers. *IBM Journal of Research Development,* 1959, **3,** 211–229.

Samuels, S. J. The effect of word associations on reading speed, recall, and guessing behavior on tests. *Journal of Educational Psychology,* 1968, **59,** 12–15.

Sapir, E. Time perspective in aboriginal American culture: A study in method. *Geological Survey, Department of Mines,* Canada, Memoir 90, No. 13, Anthropological series, 1916, **62,** 54–57.

Savin, H., & Perchonock, E. Grammatical structure and the immediate recall of English sentences. *Journal of Verbal Learning and Verbal Behavior,* 1965, **4,** 348–353.

Scott, W. A. Attitude change through reward of verbal behavior. *Journal of Abnormal and Social Psychology,* 1957, **55,** 72–75.

Scott, W. A. Attitude change by response reinforcement: Replication and extension. *Sociometry,* 1959, **22,** 328–335.

Sears, D. O. Biased indoctrination and selectivity of exposure to new information. *Sociometry,* 1965, **28,** 363–376.

Sherif M., & Hovland, C. I. *Social judgment: Assimilation and contrast effects in communication and attitude change.* New Haven, Conn.: Yale University Press, 1961.

Sherif, M., Taub, D., & Hovland, C. I. Assimilation and contrast effects of anchoring stimuli on judgments. *Journal of Experimental Psychology,* 1958, **55,** 150–155.

Shirley, M. *The first two years: III. Personality manifestations.* Minneapolis: University of Minnesota Press, 1933.

Sidis, B. *The psychology of suggestion.* New York: Appleton, 1898.

Simon, H. A. *The shape of automation for men and management.* New York: Harper & Row, Inc., 1965.

Singer, J. E. The bothersomeness of inconsistency. In R. P. Abelson et al. (Eds.), *Theories of cognitive consistency: A sourcebook.* Chicago: Rand McNally and Company, 1968.

Skinner, B. F. *Verbal behavior.* New York: Appleton-Century-Crofts, 1957.

Skinner, B. F. *The technology of teaching.* New York: Appleton-Century-Crofts, 1968.

Smedslund, J. The acquisition of conservation of substance and weight in children:

III. Extinction of conservation of weight acquired "normally" and by means of empirical controls on a balance scale. *Scandinavian Journal of Psychology,* 1961, **2,** 85–87.

Smith, E. E. The power of dissonance techniques to change attitudes. *Public Opinion Quarterly,* 1961, **25,** 629–639.

Smoke, K. L. Negative instances in concept learning. *Journal of Experimental Psychology,* 1933, **16,** 583–588.

Snider, J. G., & Osgood, C. E. (Eds.) *Semantic differential technique.* Chicago: Aldine, 1969.

Spear, N. E., Ekstrand, B. R., & Underwood, B. J. Association by contiguity. *Journal of Experimental Psychology,* 1964, **67,** 151–161.

Spielberger, C. D. The role of awareness in verbal conditioning. *Journal of Personality,* 1962, **30,** 73–101.

Spielberger, C. D., & DeNike, L. D. Descriptive behaviorism versus cognitive theory in verbal operant conditioning. *Psychological Review,* 1966, **73,** 306–326.

Staats, A. W., & Staats, C. K. *Complex human behavior.* New York: Holt, 1963.

Staats, C. K., & Staats, A. W. Meaning established by classical conditioning. *Journal* of *Experimental Psychology,* 1957, **54,** 74–80.

Stagner, R. The redintegration of pleasant and unpleasant experience. *American Journal of Psychology,* 1931, **43,** 463–468.

Stewart, R. H. Effect of continuous responding on the order effect in personality impression formation. *Journal of Abnormal and Social Psychology,* 1965, **1,** 161–165.

Stoyva, J. M. Finger electromyographic activity during sleep: Its relation to dreaming in deaf and normal subjects. *Journal of Abnormal Psychology,* 1965, **70,** 343–349.

Suppes, P., & Schlag-Rey, M. Observable changes of hypotheses under positive reinforcement. *Science,* 1965, **148,** 661–662.

Taguiri, R., Bruner, J. S. & Blake, R. B. On the relation between feelings and perception of feelings among members of small groups. In E. E. Maccoby, T. M. Newcomb, & E. L. Hartley (Eds.), *Readings in social psychology.* New York: Holt, 1958.

Taylor, D. W., Berry, P. C., & Block, C. H. Does group participation when using brainstorming facilitate or inhibit creative thinking? *Administrative Science Quarterly,* 1958, **3,** 23–47.

Taylor, W. L. "Cloze procedure": A new tool for measuring readability. *Journalism Quarterly,* 1953, **30,** 415–433.

Terrace, H. S. Discrimination learning with and without errors. *Journal of the Experimental Analysis of Behavior,* 1963, **6,** 1–27.

Thorndike, E. L. Animal intelligence. *Psychological Monographs,* 1898, **2**(8).

Thorndike, E. L. *The fundamentals of learning.* New York: Columbia University Press, 1932.

Thorndike, E. L., & Lorge, I. *The teacher's word-book of 30,000 words.* New York: Columbia University Press, 1944.

Thumb, A., & Marbe, K. *Experimentelle untersuchungen über die psychologischen grundlagen der sprachlichen analogiebildung.* Leipzig: W. Engelmann, 1901.

Trabasso, T., & Bower, G. H. *Attention in learning: Theory and research.* New York: Wiley, 1968.
Tulving, E. Subjective organization in the free recall of "unrelated" words. *Psychological Review,* 1962, **69,** 344–354.
Turner, E. A., & Wright, J. Effects of severity of threat and perceived availability on the attractiveness of objects. *Journal of Personality and Social Psychology,* 1965, **2,** 128–132.
Underwood, B. J. Interference and forgetting. *Psychological Review,* 1957, **64,** 49–60.
Underwood, B. J., & Hughes, R. H. Gradients of generalized verbal responses. *American Journal of Psychology,* 1950, **63,** 422–430.
Underwood, B. J., & Schulz, R. W. *Meaningfulness and verbal learning.* Philadelphia: Lippincott, 1960.
Upshaw, H. S. Own attitude as an anchor in equal-appearing intervals. *Journal of Abnormal and Social Psychology,* 1962, **64,** 85–96.
Upshaw, H. S. The personal reference scale: An approach to social judgment. In L. Berkowitz (Ed.), *Advances in experimental social psychology,* Vol. 4. New York: Academic Press, 1969.
Volkmann, J. Scales of judgment and their implications for social psychology. In J. H. Rohrer & M. Sherif (Eds.), *Social psychology at the crossroads.* New York: Harper, 1951. Pp. 273–294.
Walker, E. L. *Conditioning and instrumental learning.* Belmont, Calif.: Wadsworth, 1966.
Walker, E. L., & Weintraub, D. J. *Perception.* Belmont, Calif.: Wadsworth, 1966.
Wallach, L. On the bases of conservation. In D. Elkind & J. H. Flavell (Eds.), *Studies in cognitive development: Essays in honor of Jean Piaget.* New York: Oxford University Press, 1969.
Wallach, M. A. Research on children's thinking. In National Society for the Study of Education, 62nd Yearbook, *Child Psychology.* Chicago: University of Chicago Press, 1963.
Ward, C. D. Ego involvement and the absolute judgment of attitude statements. *Journal of Personality and Social Psychology,* 1965, **2,** 202–208.
Ward, W. D., & Sandvold, K. D. Performance expectancy as a determinant of actual performance: Dissonance reduction or differential recall? *Journal of Personality and Social Psychology,* 1963, **67,** 293–295.
Wason, P. C., & Johnson-Laird, P. N. (Eds.) *Thinking and reasoning.* Baltimore: Penguin Books, Inc., 1968.
Waterman, C. K. The facilitating and interfering effects of cognitive dissonance on simple and complex paired associates learning tasks. *Journal of Experimental Social Psychology,* 1969, **5,** 31–42.
Waterman, C. K., & Katkin, E. S. The energizing (dynamogenic) effect of cognitive dissonance on task performance. *Journal of Personality and Social Psychology,* 1967, **6,** 126–131.
Watson, J. B. *Behavior, an introduction to comparative psychology.* New York: Holt, 1914.
Weiner, B. Motivation and memory. *Psychological Monographs,* 1966, **80**(18, Whole No. 626).

Weiner, B. Motivated forgetting and the study of repression. *Journal of Personality,* 1968, **36,** 213–234.
Weiner, B. Motivational factors in short-term retention: II. Rehearsal or arousal? *Psychological Reports,* 1969, **20,** 1208.
Weiner, B., & Reed, H. Effects of the instructional sets to remember and to forget on short-term retention: Studies of rehearsal control and retrieval inhibition (repression). *Journal of Experimental Psychology,* 1969, **79,** 226–232.
Wells, H. Effects of transfer and problem structure in disjunctive concept formation. *Journal of Experimental Psychology,* 1963, **65,** 63–69.
Whorf, B. L. *Language, thought, and reality.* (J. B. Carroll, Ed.) Cambridge, Mass.: MIT Press, 1956.
Wickelgren, W. Acoustic similarity and retroactive interference in short-term memory. *Journal of Verbal Learning and Verbal Behavior,* 1965, **4,** 53–62.
Wickelgren, W. Phonemic similarity and interference in short-term memory for single letters. *Journal of Experimental Psychology,* 1966, **71,** 396–404.
Wiggins, N., & Hoffman, P. J. Three models of clinical judgment. *Journal of Abnormal Psychology,* 1968, **73,** 70–77.
Wishner, J. Reanalysis of "Impressions of personality." *Psychological Review,* 1960, **67,** 96–112.
Wolff, J. L. Concept-shift and discrimination-reversal learning in humans. *Psychological Bulletin,* 1967, **68,** 369–408.
Woodworth, R. S. *Experimental psychology.* New York: Holt, 1938.
Woodworth, R. S., & Schlosberg, H. *Experimental psychology.* New York: Holt, 1954.
Wouk, H. *The Caine Mutiny.* New York: Doubleday and Co., Inc., 1951.
Wright, P. Sentence retention and transformation theory. *Quarterly Journal of Experimental Psychology,* 1968, **20,** 265–272.
Wyer, R. S. The effects of information redundancy on evaluations of social stimuli. *Psychonomic Science,* 1968, **13,** 245–246.
Wyer, R. S. A quantitative comparison of three models of impression formation. *Journal of Experimental Research in Personality,* 1969, **4,** 29–41.
Wyer, R. S., & Watson, S. F. Context effects in impression formation. *Journal of Personality and Social Psychology,* 1969, **12,** 22–23.
Zajonc, R. B. Attitudinal effects of mere exposure. *Journal of Personality and Social Psychology, Monograph Supplement,* 1968, **9,** Part 2, 1–27. (a)
Zajonc, R. B. Cognitive theories of social behavior. In G. Lindzey & E. Aronson (Eds.), *Handbook of social psychology,* Vol. I (2nd ed.) Reading, Mass.: Addison-Wesley, 1968. (b)
Zajonc, R. B., & Burnstein, E. The learning of balanced and unbalanced social structures. *Journal of Personality,* 1965, **33,** 153–163. (a)
Zajonc, R. B., & Burnstein, E. Structural balance, reciprocity, positivity as sources of cognitive bias. *Journal of Personality,* 1965, **33,** 570–583. (b)
Zeaman, D., & House, B. J. The role of attention in retardate discrimination learning. In N. R. Ellis (Ed.), *Handbook of mental deficiency.* New York: McGraw-Hill, 1963. Pp. 159–223.
Zeigarnik, B. III. Das Behalten erledigter und unerledigter Handlungen. In K. Lewin (Ed.), Untersuchungen zur Handlungs und Affecktpsychologie. *Psychologische Forschung,* 1927, **9,** 1–85.

Zeller, A. F. An experimental analogue of repression: II. The effect of individual failure and success on memory measured by relearning. *Journal of Experimental Psychology,* 1950, **40,** 411–422.

Zimbardo, P. G. The effect of effort and improvisation on self-persuasion produced by role-playing. *Journal of Experimental Social Psychology,* 1965, **1,** 217–219.

Zipf, G. K. *Human behavior and the principle of least effort.* Cambridge, Massachusetts: Addison-Wesley, 1949.

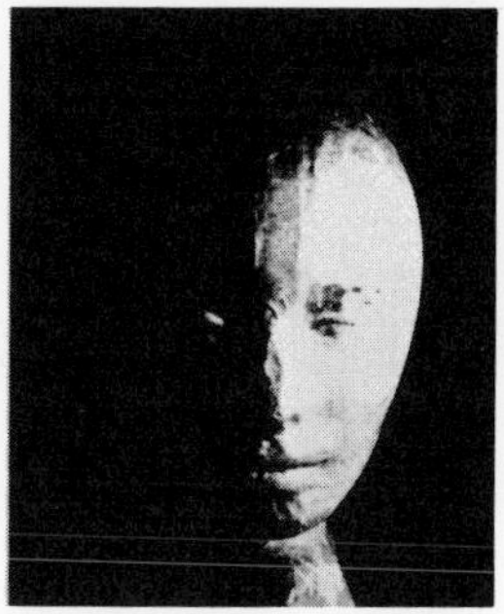

Author index

Subject index

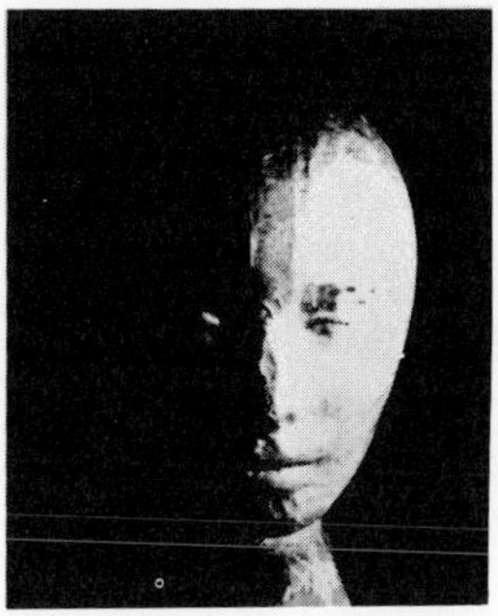